A STUDY GUIDE TO STEINBECK:

A Handbook to his Major Works

edited by
Tetsumaro Hayashi
Ball State University

The Scarecrow Press, Inc.
Metuchen, N. J.   1974

Library of Congress Cataloging in Publication Data

Hayashi, Tetsumaro.
Study guide to Steinbeck.

1. Steinbeck, John, 1902-1968--Study--Outlines,
syllabi, etc. I. Title.
PS3537.T3234Z7142   813'.5'2   74-735
ISBN 0-8108-0706-8

Dedicated to
Elizabeth R. Otis,
Eric Moon,
and
William L. Moore
as a token of my gratitude and friendship

TABLE OF CONTENTS

Page

Preface, by Tetsumaro Hayashi   vii

Acknowledgments   x

Foreword, by Warren French   xiii

1. Teaching Steinbeck, by Peter Lisca   1

2. America and Americans, by Richard Peterson   5

3. Cannery Row, by Charles R. Metzger   19

4. The Grapes of Wrath, by Warren French   29

5. In Dubious Battle, by Betty L. Perez   47

6. The Long Valley, by Robert M. Benton   69

7. The Pastures of Heaven, by Richard Peterson   87

8. The Pearl, by Martha Heasley Cox   107

9. Of Mice and Men (novel), by John F. Slater   129

10. Of Mice and Men (play), by Franklin Court   155

11. Sea of Cortez, by Richard Astro   168

12. To a God Unknown, by Robert DeMott   187

13. Tortilla Flat, by Arthur L. Simpson, Jr.   214

14. The Winter of Our Discontent, by Reloy Garcia   244

15. Steinbeck on Screen, by Robert E. Morsberger   258

Contributors   299

Index, by Donald L. Siefker   303

PREFACE

by Tetsumaro Hayashi

Since the inception of the Steinbeck Quarterly in 1968
and the Steinbeck Monograph Series in 1971, the central desire of the officers and contributors of these publications has
been to set Steinbeck in a clearer light, to make his canon
more easily accessible to students and critics alike. That
desire has now justifiably adjusted itself to the increased demand for assistance in the actual teaching of Steinbeck.
Thus, the specific purpose of this book is to enlighten students on Steinbeck's major works, to stimulate interest and
curiosity, and to encourage independent study and research
by providing a solid foundation. To build this foundation,
we have prepared extensive materials on topics worthy of
discussion and exploration, avenues to these topics, and
sources and resources to facilitate the study and research.
Our primary concern, then, has been to assist both English
majors and non-majors in such courses as American Literature Survey, American Fiction (on both the lower and upper
divisions), Introduction to Fiction, and even World Literature
courses, for we choose not to restrict so great a teacher to
the narrow confines of a strictly interpreted course division.

The secondary purpose of this book is to offer assistance to classroom teachers and reference librarians by providing up-to-date critical and background materials, which
they can use selectively in their courses and reference service. This book, therefore, should be used as a guide, not
as a package of final answers or definitive interpretations.
It is geared to offer advice, suggestions, methods, and
sources so that both teachers and students can further explore on their own the untouched regions of Steinbeck's literature.

The selection of works for inclusion is a delicate
and controversial problem. Undoubtedly, some readers will
be disappointed to find their favorite works missing from
this book. Others may be upset at the inclusion of books
which they do not regard as Steinbeck's major works. For

this volume I have selected chiefly those works of Steinbeck which are frequently taught at colleges and universities today.

A cursory review of the Table of Contents and Index will reveal both fiction and non-fiction, novels, plays, and films, largely because this book was written not only for English majors but also for non-English majors, reference librarians, sociologists, philosophers, political scientists, and all those who recognize that Steinbeck was not writing literature for literature's sake alone and that he was champion of the 1930s, a prophetic voice for America, a popular philosopher, an involved journalist, and a detached artist.

All the contributors are dedicated teacher-scholars. Nor only are they up-to-date and conversant in the subject, but they are enthusiastic about teaching Steinbeck's works and seriously interested in enlightening our college students and teachers about Steinbeck. Most of them are active contributors to the Steinbeck Quarterly. Some of them, such as Peter Lisca (author of The Wide World of John Steinbeck, 1958, and editor of "The Grapes of Wrath": Text and Criticism, 1972) and Warren French (author of John Steinbeck, 1961, and editor of A Companion to The Grapes of Wrath, 1963), are eminent senior scholars.

Others, such as Reloy Garcia (author of Steinbeck and D.H. Lawrence, 1972), Richard Astro (editor of Steinbeck: The Man and His Work with Tetsumaro Hayashi, 1971, and author of the forthcoming book, Steinbeck and Ricketts), and Robert DeMott (senior member of the Editorial Board of the Steinbeck Quarterly), are leading younger Steinbeck scholars. The combination of seasoned experience and youthful vigor, hopefully, will provide the necessary balance for a useful text.

The remaining members of the team, all of whom are active members of the Steinbeck Society of America, are also active Steinbeck teacher-scholars who have won my respect and confidence in recent years.

As we worked hard in this project, my esteem for my contributors continually grew; they proved to be not only first-rate teacher-scholars, but cooperative educators who know the value of team work. One of the by-products of a disciplined and cooperative project such as this is the strengthened sense of fraternity as teachers. I do hope this book will bring many students and teachers of Steinbeck together as we continue to teach, to study, to write about Steinbeck, and to encourage Steinbeck studies. After all, as Steinbeck puts it, one is related to all and each student and teacher is important as a co-worker in the field.

In order to give students a solid background to the respective works, each contributor begins his discussion with the "Background" of the work, thus placing the work into a proper, meaningful context as a novel, a play, or a work of non-fiction. Then the contributor provides a critique and plot synopsis. The student may or may not agree with the contributor, but the former will no doubt be enlightened or challenged by a unique essay and a pertinent plot summary. Finally, the contributor provides the work with "Suggestions for Classroom Discussions" and "Suggested Topics for Term Papers," together with a "Selected Bibliography." Thus, the contributor provides the reader with the kind of topic the latter may explore and sources for further studies. In other words, the book attempts first to enlighten the beginning student, then to challenge him with a unique criticism, and finally, to prepare him for his own research and independent study. One thing this book does not do is to give the student ready-made answers on each major work. Instead, it attempts to help him discover on his own the relevant meanings and new values in Steinbeck literature which help the student discover his universe, his mission in society, and the complex image of man as Steinbeck sees it.

Tetsumaro Hayashi

Muncie, Indiana
June 19, 1973

ACKNOWLEDGMENTS

Miss Elizabeth R. Otis, McIntosh and Otis, Inc. (18 East 41st Street, New York, N. Y. 10017), was generous enough to give us permissions to quote Steinbeck in this book.

The Viking Press (625 Madison Avenue, New York, N. Y. 10022), through Miss Nancy Schafer of the Permissions Department, graciously gave us permissions to quote Steinbeck from the Viking editions of Steinbeck's works.

America and Americans - (c) 1966 by John Steinbeck

Cannery Row - Copyright 1945 by John Steinbeck, (c) 1973 by Elaine Steinbeck, John Steinbeck IV, and Thomas Steinbeck

The Grapes of Wrath - Copyright 1939, (c) 1967 by John Steinbeck

In Dubious Battle - Copyright 1936, (c) 1964 by John Steinbeck

The Long Valley - Copyright 1934, 1935, 1936, 1937, 1938, (c) 1962, 1963, 1964, 1965, 1966 by John Steinbeck

The Pastures of Heaven - Copyright 1932, (c) 1960 by John Steinbeck

The Pearl - Copyright 1945 by John Steinbeck, (c) 1973 by Elaine Steinbeck, John Steinbeck IV, and Thomas Steinbeck

Of Mice and Men - Copyright 1937, (c) 1965 by John Steinbeck

Sea of Cortez - Copyright 1941 by John Steinbeck and Edward F. Ricketts, 1951 by John Steinbeck, (c) 1969 by John Steinbeck and Edward F. Ricketts, Jr.

To a God Unknown - Copyright 1933, (c) 1961 by John Steinbeck

Tortilla Flat - Copyright 1935, (c) 1963 by John Steinbeck

The Winter of Our Discontent - (c) 1961 by John Steinbeck

All reprinted by permission of The Viking Press, Inc.

Dr. John Ditsky, editor of the University of Windsor Review (Special Steinbeck Issue, Spring 1973), gave us permissions to reprint with minor revisions Robert DeMott's article on To a God Unknown, which was originally written for the said journal.

All the contributors and I should like to express our grateful thanks to these individuals and institutions for their generosity and kindness.

T. H.

FOREWORD

THE ARTIST AS MAGICIAN

by Warren French

John Steinbeck now seems unquestionably to occupy
the position in relationship to twentieth-century American
writing that Edgar Allan Poe does in relationship to nine-
teenth-century American writing. The evidence of text-
books and teachers' testimony indicates that Steinbeck's
works--especially The Red Pony and The Pearl, but often,
too, The Grapes of Wrath and other novels--are more
widely taught in secondary schools than the writings of any
of Steinbeck's contemporaries. He is the writer who
bridges the gap between the unsophisticated public and the
serious artist. Like Poe, he interests people in reading;
but the interest he creates is not--like that of many other
"best-selling" authors--simply a dead end. Steinbeck does
not simply entertain the reader; while entertaining, the
novelist raises questions in the reader's mind that may lead
him to go on to seek in creative literature things that he had
not expected to find there.

What these mysterious "things" are should be the
principal concern of the teacher of literature, but it rarely
is. There are few wider chasms in the United States than
that between the practice of literary criticism and the teaching of literature--especially in the secondary schools, where
readers are likely to have to be won if they are to be won
at all.

Criticism in this country has always been a mandarin
calling, based apparently on the assumption that only the
finest, most cultivated minds can possibly respond to the
arts and that the vast potential reading public can be ignored.
At the height of a vogue that probably bears heavy responsibility for a recent decline in interest in reading creative literature, presiding mandarins pronounced that criticism must
avoid scrupulously the "intentional fallacy" and the "affective

fallacy"--that, in short, one must treat works of art as artifacts existing in hermetic isolation and avoid any consideration of the author's intentions or the audience's responses.

Mandarin critics have little use for popular artists like Steinbeck--or Poe, for that matter--and the few that have contemplated his writings are responsible for those negative interpretations that have been the principal roadblocks to an understanding and enjoyment of his work. Edmund Wilson's The Boys in the Back Room and Arthur Mizener's condescending "Does a Moral Vision of the Thirties Deserve a Nobel Prize?" have planted in people's minds the notions that Steinbeck's works are, on the one hand, "animalistic"--insufficiently humanistic in their values--and, on the other, sentimental and dated.

Of course, we are only beginning, after a hundred years, through work like Stuart Levine's, to understand how we may effectively teach Poe's works. Curiously, critics have chosen to distrust the very clues which this most self-conscious writer provided for an understanding of his own work. "The Philosophy of Composition"--along with Poe's remarks on Hawthorne's stories--provides about the most useful insights available anywhere into the operation of the creative mind. Yet the response to this remarkable document has typically been that Poe really couldn't have written the poem this way; the notion that art is created in some kind of mad frenzy dies hard in the minds and hearts of emotion-and-experience-starved school teachers. Whether Poe proceeded exactly as he specifies in his essay is beside the point; the important thing is that "The Philosophy of Composition" shows us that the artist is a "maker," a fabricator, a conscious manipulator of stubbornly inert materials into something that gives the illusion of life--in short, a magician.

American teachers have traditionally been reluctant to come to terms with artists as magicians--principally because of the widespread American suspicion of magicians, who are looked upon as confidence men. Of course, all confidence men have to be magicians, and many magicians are confidence men; but not all are. The extremely difficult role of the literary critic--and all teachers of literature should be critics--is to separate the life-and-health-giving magicians from the confidence men trying to exploit and diminish us. Since making this division is a stupendously difficult task, most teachers have abdicated their critical responsibilities and become simply cultural torch-bearers.

As a result, we have no critical writing that helps us lead students into creative works. On the one hand, however, we have highly specialized analyses that treat literary works most often merely as embodiments of philosophical and political positions; on the other hand, we have "study guides" that replace the works themselves with uninspired summaries of them as if the users were afraid to experience the works directly.

This book intends to take a step in a new direction-- not a giant step, because the effort before us, if we are truly to reinvigorate interest in literature, is staggering to contemplate. The essays are directed, however, towards leading teachers and students into the works--to try to experience their magic--instead of avoiding or dismissing them. The one guiding principle that motivates the diversely minded contributors to this book is that students--especially in high schools and junior colleges--who are just beginning to discover the significance of the conscious operations of their mind, should talk about literature, not be told about it. In my essay on The Grapes of Wrath, for example, what I am concerned to do is to try to excite teachers and students to discover that significant literature does indeed operate in a variety of ways, on a variety of levels, and to begin consciously to participate with the artist in the discovery of these levels.

John Steinbeck left us far fewer clues than Poe to his magical techniques. In my essay, however, I stress the importance of one recently published letter in understanding his creative drive. The publication of The "East of Eden" Letters also provides us with unique insights into the artist's state of mind as he was working. Whatever we think of his particular achievement in this novel, serious study of Steinbeck should probably begin with his remarks about his relationship to the characters that he was creating for his novel. It is clear that he looked upon his characters as people, on himself as creating and populating a world, as a magician--in short--not soberly reflecting back the world around him with mirrors, but conjuring up a different world. The task of literary criticism is to probe the nature of these newly created worlds, to consider the artists' reasons for struggling to create them rather than being satisfied with the world they find already available to them, the readers' reasons for turning to these magical creations of alternate realities. Enthusiasm for literary study has unmistakably diminished over the last decade. Should it have? What responsibilities must we as critic-teachers bear for this decline? Can the trend be reversed?

Surely we should strive to work especially with those uncommon authors of widely popular novels who attempt to deal with serious problems of the human condition. John Steinbeck is one of these. It is important to try to discover why he has succeeded where he has and why he has failed where he has. During the 1930s when Steinbeck especially flourished, one tobacco company ran a series of advertisements explaining various magic tricks under the general title, "It's Fun to Be Fooled, But It's More Fun to Know." Teachers might well take this slogan to heart: as long as literature is simply something to enchant us it remains but an amiable way to pass the time. "Knowing" what lies behind an artist's magic is likely to be far more difficult than exposing a stage-magician's gimmicks; but we hope that we have provided in this book a storehouse of useful tools that may both encourage and assist you in the effort. Especially, I hope this book may interest teachers in using a wider range of Steinbeck's works in the classroom. The early books like The Pastures of Heaven and To a God Unknown, for example, though apparently rarely used, offer unusually rich reading experiences. I hope more students will get to know them.

Chapter 1

TEACHING STEINBECK

by Peter Lisca

The increasing frequency with which the work of John
Steinbeck has been appearing on the reading lists of college
and secondary school courses is an interesting phenomenon.
That he is not only being taught, but read by students, and
with enthusiasm, is even more interesting. To some extent,
no doubt, Steinbeck's popularity in the classroom is abetted
by the steady exposure which he has been receiving on television. This exposure includes not only the usual re-runs
of motion pictures made from his work (now totaling over
a dozen) but also specials made explicitly for the medium--
dramatizations of "The Harness, " Travels with Charley,
America and Americans. Television has even re-made
some Steinbeck films for its own use--The Red Pony and
Of Mice and Men. The availability of so much Steinbeck
in the visual media serves to stimulate the reading of his
works not only for their inherent interest, but, with increasing frequency, for purposes of precise comparison as a way
of teaching and understanding the differences between the
language of fiction and the language of film. A new critical
literature has evolved on these differences; film scripts
(including The Grapes of Wrath) are increasingly available,
and there is hardly an English department without its course
in cinema. Teachers of modern literature (and of Steinbeck) increasingly find themselves talking to audiences who
blink uncomfortably at the unaccustomed light in the audi-
torium. Those who wish to pursue multi-media comparisons
further can find in Steinbeck such works as Sweet Thursday,
which was made into a musical, or The Moon Is Down, which
is available in play form as well as on the screen, or ultimately Of Mice and Men--novel, play, film, videotape, and
opera!

Remarkable as the stimulus of visual media has been,
however, Steinbeck's increasing popularity in the classroom

1

also has its more traditionally literary reasons. One of
these reasons, perhaps working most obviously in the secondary schools and sophomore introductory courses, is the
over-view of modern American experience which Steinbeck's
works provide: homesteading in California at the turn of
the century (To a God Unknown, East of Eden); the stable
rural community of pre-depression days (The Pastures of
Heaven, The Red Pony); the violence and epic experience
of the 1930s (In Dubious Battle, The Grapes of Wrath); the
second world war (The Moon Is Down, Once There Was a
War); and subsequent moral lassitude (The Winter of Our
Discontent, Travels with Charley). And all along, in the
thirties, forties and fifties, there were such books as
Tortilla Flat, Cannery Row, and Sweet Thursday, using
American subcultures as a mirror to make us laugh a little
at ourselves and our pretensions. No other author embodies
such a range of our national experience, including even the
idealism, hypocrisy, shame and guilt of our involvement in
Indo-China as reflected in Steinbeck's widely read syndicated
letters from Vietnam. Compared to Steinbeck, for this purpose, Hemingway seems foreign; Faulkner grotesque and
exotic; Fitzgerald narrow and exclusive; Wolfe peculiar and
subjective.

Another reason for Steinbeck's appeal to young students is his anticipation of many of their concerns today.
In the narrative from Sea of Cortez (1941), especially, he
wrote eloquently of man's physical (ecology) and spiritual
(mysticism) necessity to relate to "the whole thing," from
the tidepool to the stars. And these interests are never
far from the center of his fiction. It is the violation of
ecological principles that leads to The Grapes of Wrath;
from Joseph Wayne's belief (To a God Unknown, 1933) in
the spiritual dimensions of Nature to Ethan Hawley's faith
in his stone talisman (The Winter of Our Discontent, 1961),
contemporary youth recognize their own more than casual
interest in the efficacy of rituals and the possibilities of
astrology. Their rejection of commercialized values and
their tendency toward drop-out and commune social structures
is found from Tortilla Flat to Sweet Thursday in surprising
detail. Modern youth's paradoxical social involvement--
from the SDS and SNCC efficient organization of violent
demonstrations against power (In Dubious Battle) to the
Peace Corps and VISTA belief in the one family of man
(The Grapes of Wrath, Burning Bright); their disillusion-
ment with government reforms is in The Short Reign of
Pippin IV. Modern interest in folk culture finds reflection

in The Grapes of Wrath, which in "The Ballad of Tom Joad"
has itself contributed to that culture. Steinbeck's interest in
such minority groups as the Mexican Americans (The Pastures of Heaven, Tortilla Flat) finds an audience in middle-
class youths who picket supermarkets for Chavez's lettuce
and grape pickers; in a single character, Crooks in Of Mice
and Men, Steinbeck has better expressed the plight of the
Black in American life than some who have written at length.
Finally, in Steinbeck's Travels with Charley today's youth
recognizes its own urge to just pick up (preferably in a
camper) and travel through this country to see it and understand it at first hand.

But beyond all these reasons for the popularity of
Steinbeck in the classroom, and more important, is the
work's literary quality, without which, of course, he would
not be the major writer that he is. One mark of that quality,
more particular to Steinbeck than any other American writer
of his time, is its variety of content and technique. Among
more than twenty-four volumes available in cheap paperback
editions, the teacher can choose widely to suit his purpose
and his students. The Pearl offers a parable-like short
novelette, set in Mexico, of surface simplicity but great
symbolic power; East of Eden offers a saga of six hundred
long pages covering three generations, a sizeable amount of
American history, and a re-interpretation of the Old Testament. Between these two poles lies a great variety: satires
of politics (The Short Reign of Pippin IV) and social conven-
tions (Tortilla Flat), an epic of social protest (The Grapes
of Wrath), a document of sociology and anthropology (The
Forgotten Village), a naturalistic strike novel (In Dubious
Battle), a journal of philosophy (Sea of Cortez), a tragic
pastoral (Of Mice and Men), a fable of universal brother-
hood (Burning Bright), and others besides. These variations in form and content are further enriched by a range
of reference embracing the Bible and Alice's Adventures,
and serving functions from the merely decorative to the
structurally and thematically essential, from the obvious to
the abstruse. And all along, the prose style of each work
is forged for its particular purpose and is so unique in each
case that it is impossible to identify a Steinbeck novel by
prose style alone. This variety makes it possible for the
teacher and students to explore widely in content and form
and style while retaining the common base of comparison
provided by their source in the mind and heart of a single
man.

In conclusion, as all of the above suggests, Steinbeck is a rewarding classroom experience because much of his work exists on several related and interpenetrating levels. Always there is an easily available surface to carry the interest of the most literal minded reader, while for the sophisticated reader (student or teacher) there is in addition the symbolic structure, the mythic or literary or philosophical or religious or historical or anthropological plane of reference. In his best work several of these are skillfully woven together. As Steinbeck himself once said, how far the reader can go in his pursuit of these levels is limited only by his particular abilities and his fund of knowledge.

Chapter 2

THE MYTHOLOGY OF AMERICAN LIFE:
AMERICA AND AMERICANS (1966)

by Richard F. Peterson

I. BACKGROUND

Steinbeck describes America and Americans as a
book, in text and pictures, of opinions unashamed and individual. The text is an informal commentary upon the emergence of something unique in the world: "America--compli-
cated, paradoxical, bullheaded, shy, cruel, boisterous, un-
speakably clear, and very beautiful" (p. 9).[1] The pictures,
taken by forty of the best photographers in America, supplement the opinions of the text and brilliantly support
Steinbeck's faith in the uniqueness of American life. Many
of them capture the special freshness of youth and the vital
restlessness of adulthood that Steinbeck sees in the American. Others reveal the group phenomenon in America of
shared feeling or purpose whether the group is united by
joy or sorrow. America and Americans, then, is a picture-
book commentary on American life which has its own individuality and purpose in Steinbeck's special understanding of
America and the graphic illustrations which enrich those insights.

Two other Steinbeck works of non-fiction, Sea of
Cortez (1941) and Travels with Charley in Search of America
(1962), offer important insights into Steinbeck's opinions and
sense of direction in America and Americans. In Sea of
Cortez, Steinbeck openly states his biological theory of man
and society which informs his fiction and lies at the heart
of America and Americans. His belief that the human
group, as in the animal world, functions as a single organism provides the basis for his view that Americans, despite
their vast differences, are a unified and individual body.
Each American functions individually, but his primary

5

purpose for existence is the renewal and perpetuation of the
whole.   Only when the group or body loses its sense of purpose or its capacity to adapt to change is its existence
placed in jeopardy.   In this sense, America and Americans
represents Steinbeck's examination of American life for evidence of the movement and adaptability which are necessary
for survival even if that search may uncover the stagnation
and entropy that means certain death for the organism.

Steinbeck's fear of the latter condition, compounded
by his own sense of having lost contact with America,
prompted a tour of the country with Charley, a French
poodle that was to be his sole companion.   The result of
the trip, Travels with Charley, is a rambling series of im-
pressions of American life.   The book tends to deal mainly
with Steinbeck's contact with the people and the land, but
his occasional reflections on what he finds anticipate the
much more profound attempt to understand America, past,
present, and future, which appears in America and Americans.   In Travels with Charley, he establishes the idea that
no matter where you travel in America, you see a likeness
in Americans which is far more significant than the more
obvious diversity.   Steinbeck is also, however, aware of a
change in American life which he fears is for the worse.
His visit to Monterey affirms only Thomas Wolfe's sad conclusion that you can't go home again.   As he travels across
the country, he is often stricken by the mechanization and
sterility of contemporary American life.

Steinbeck suspects that the possibilities Emerson
found in America are closing down, and this idea is behind
much of his writing in America and Americans.   It is balanced, however, by Steinbeck's effort to capture the essence
of the American character.   The end result is an examination of America that traces the history of the country, its
present condition, and its prospects for the future.   The
basic source for his study is, once again, the American
people and the land; but, an equally important source is the
collection of myths and traditions which shape the beliefs,
good or bad, which exist at the heart of American life.   In
these myths lies the renewed promise of America or the end
of the dream: "The path must have direction, it must have
purpose and the journey must be filled with a joy of anticipation, for the boy today hating the world, creates a hateful
world and then tries to destroy it and sometimes himself.
We have succeeded in what our fathers prayed for and it is
our success that is destroying us" (p. 177).

II.   PLOT SYNOPSIS

In his foreword to America and Americans, Steinbeck
adds an important dimension to the title of his book.   He
addresses his reader on the same subject approached by
19th century writers as diverse in interest and ambition as
Washington Irving and Herman Melville: Americans have
too often been content to accept and endure the opinions of
this country, most of them harsh and distorted, made by
visitors.   America has failed to produce a "blowed-in-the-
glass" American to counter these opinions by writing of his
own inspection of the country.   Steinbeck's work, accordingly, is to be the product of a totally committed American
writing about his own country: "It is informed by America,
and inspired by curiosity, impatience, some anger, and a
passionate love of America and Americans" (p. 8).   This
American, however, has a distinct view of America, based
upon the conviction that something uniquely American exists
among all the diversity and self-interest which is also a
part of American life.   At the same time, Steinbeck wants
to expose the paradox of the American experience, its
shame and pride, and, finally, to understand the essence of
America: "Our passionate devotion to it--to all of it, the
land, the idea, and the mystique" (p. 9).

America and Americans is divided into nine sections
or chapters, each of which deals with some distinct part of
American life.   "E Pluribus Unum" recounts the early settlement of America and it reiterates the book's central idea
of the paradoxical unity of the American people.   Steinbeck's
brief personal interpretation of the first settlers stresses
the development of a country by people who wanted to exclude other religious groups.   He tells the story of a minority that became a majority through restlessness, hard work,
and ferocity, yet that feared and struggled against the inclusion of the "strangeness, weakness, and poverty" of other
minority groups.   The eventual emergence of the American
out of the selfishness, bigotry, and bullying that marked the
settlement of America came about, according to Steinbeck,
through the natural and inevitable process of change and
adaptability: "What happened is one of the strange quirks of
human nature--but perhaps it is a perfectly natural direction
that was taken, since no child can long endure his parents.
It seemed to happen by instinct.   In spite of all the pressure the old people could bring to bear, the children of each
ethnic group denied their background and their ancestral
language" (p. 16).

"Paradox and Dream" extends the idea of paradox in
the American experience to include what Steinbeck feels is
the most paradoxical pattern of all: "Our passionate belief
in our own myths" (p. 33).   Self-reliant but strangely dependent on mechanical gadgets, publicly puritanical but sometimes privately profligate, the American continually exhibits
the gap between illusion and reality evident in a comparison
of the American dream and the American way of life.   The
dream, itself, drives the American as if he is caught by a
collective unconscious which stirs him to see his home as a
symbol of personal safety and comfort and allows him to
accept weapons and violence as an essential part of life.
At the same time, however, the dream embodies all hopes
for peace.   Steinbeck interprets our folk tales, though
rooted in violence, as essentially moral: "I wonder whether
this folk wisdom is the story of our capability.   Are these
stories permanent because we know within ourselves that
only the threat of violence makes it possible for us to live
together in peace?" (p. 40).

The next chapters, "Government of the People" and
"Created Equal," offer a paradox within themselves and between each other.   Steinbeck, on the one hand, points to the
fear and hatred Americans have for any form of religious,
political, or bureaucratic power.   He notes, however, that
regardless of the tendency of mediocre and corrupt individuals to control politics, the excellent architecture of our government has insured individual rights and political stability.
The individuals who have sought their rights as Americans
and endured the worst that Americans have done to other
Americans are the Blacks.   Steinbeck's history of the Black
in America focuses on the issue of slavery, and, after
slavery, the tactics whereby constitutional rights are denied
by local customs, law, and law-enforcement officers.   The
paradox he sees lies in the practice of Americans, who hate
power and oppression, preventing a minority group of Americans from assuming rights guaranteed by the finest governmental structure in the history of man.

In "Genus Americanus" and "The Pursuit of Happiness" Steinbeck focuses on other ominous paradoxes of
American life.   He observes the obsession with wealth and
position which exists in a society that in name is classless,
and the fascination that Americans, living in a democratic
society, have for rituals, titles, and secret organizations.
He also points out that the worst manifestations of this cul-
tism in America are the "screwball" groups which interfere

with the rights of others: the "Haywire Mother" who keeps
certain books from her children, the super patriots who
want to preserve the country by using techniques which will
destroy it, and the secret organizations which thrive on the
fear and hatred of minority groups. Even more ominous
for Steinbeck is the complete failure of many Americans to
find fulfillment in a society of abundance. The crisis between children and parents, the fear of growing old, the
male fascination with women's breasts, are all symptomatic
of the sickness of a society which combines mass production
with the obsession that each generation must be better, know
more, and have more than the previous one. The end result is the acquisition of a leisure which leads many into
destructive trouble, and leaves others with the persistence
of a vague desire to "go back to the country and try with
puzzled failure to re-create a self-sufficient island against
the creeping, groping assembly-line conformity which trou-
bles and fascinates them at the same time" (p. 119).

The final chapters in America and Americans examine
Americans and the land, the world, and the future. Steinbeck's discussion of the land contains a warning to Americans to cease the abuses committed against what once
seemed a limitless continent. His view of Americans and
the world stresses the importance of American literature in
establishing the image of America, and the struggle of
American writers to create literature totally independent of
outside influences: "They learned from our people and wrote
like themselves, and they created a new thing and a grand
thing in the world--an American literature about Americans"
(p. 162).

Steinbeck's final consideration is the one he regards
as the most serious. He feels that the darkest problem,
more threatening than all the others he has touched upon,
is the American's loss of principle and purpose: "Ethics,
morals, codes of conduct, are the stern rules which in the
past we needed to survive--as individuals, as groups, as
nations" (p. 175). Steinbeck has identified the destroyers
of nations: comfort, plenty, and security. He now wants
to reaffirm his faith in the people. His hope for renewal
lies in his feeling that Americans have not lost their energy;
they only waste it. The restlessness of the people remains
and the world and the sky are still as open as ever before.
The basic problem, which he states in his afterword, is,
once again, to find the right direction: "We have failed
sometimes, taken wrong paths, paused for renewal, filled

our bellies and licked our wounds; but we have never slipped
back--never" (p. 221).

III.   CRITICAL EXPLICATION

     The meaning of America and Americans lies in Stein-
beck's selection and interpretation of the myths of American
life. As the priest-exorcist, he celebrates the myths and
rituals of American life which he holds in reverence as he
summons forth the evils that have perverted the myths and
have driven Americans to commit crimes against their
neighbors and the land. In some respects, he is also the
old man, the leader of the people, who draws upon all his
wisdom and experience to examine the beliefs of America
and warn the people against an approaching disaster by lay-
ing out before them the essential values which shaped the
country and are now being abused. He can turn a stern
Calvinistic eye on Americans and see the behavior which
paves the way to an inevitable doom, but he can also be
completely Emersonian in his own belief in the eternal possibilities which still exist in America.

     Steinbeck establishes the relevancy of myth on both
an organic and historic level. Steinbeck's organic view of
man and society suggests the sort of primitive animism from
which spring the beginnings of mythology. J. G. Frazer's
The Golden Bough and Jessie Weston's From Ritual to Romance, books known by Steinbeck, trace many of the beliefs
and rituals still celebrated in modern times to ancient vegetation myths vitally connected with the cyclical patterns of
nature. Steinbeck also supports his interest in myth with
an idea that resembles C. G. Jung's collective unconscious.
He believes that the American dream, like all dreams, is
formed from powerful memories of real events which may
be part of an individual's life or part of his merger in the
historical pattern: "The national dream of Americans is a
whole pattern of thinking and feeling and may well be a historic memory surprisingly little distorted. Furthermore,
the participators in the dream need not have descended
physically from the people to whom the reality happened.
This pattern of thought and conduct which is the national
character is absorbed even by the children of immigrants
themselves, no matter how they may wish it; birth on American soil seems to be required" (p. 38).

     Steinbeck locates one of the central myths of American

life in our belief that all men are created equal. He offers
his version of American history, shaped by individual effort
and group unity, as support for the validity of the myth.
The settlement of the country, according to Steinbeck, came
about through an individual determination to overcome a
strange and hostile wilderness. Yet, despite the reality
that every single man was out for himself, that individual
groups sought only self-preservation, a unity was achieved.
Steinbeck strongly suggests that the process, contrary to
the original purpose behind the exploration and settlement
of America, was nevertheless an organic one, formed by
the strong individual and group instinct for survival and the
natural adaptability of one part of an environment or body
to another.

        The perversion of the myth of equality had already
begun before the myth, itself, was formalized into an accepted belief. The instinct for survival banded groups together, but once a minority merged with the majority, it
hastened to add its particular ferocity to the drive to exclude other groups from the main body. Other myths were
often formed to preserve the sanctity and separateness of
the group from outsiders. The central mythic pattern of
arrival, prejudice, acceptance, and absorption failed in
meaning particularly for two racial groups: the Indian and
the Black. The substitute myths created to deal with them
were destructive rather than hopeful in nature. After a
brief attempt to bargain with the American Indian for what
was rightfully his possession, it became convenient for the
early settlers who wanted the land to convince themselves
that the Indian was sub-human. If viewed from within the
traditional beliefs that many settlers brought with them from
Europe, the Indian was regarded as the devil's agent. The
less orthodox regarded him as a savage, dangerous animal.
Once it became obvious that the Indian, even though defeated,
would survive the attempts to destroy his race, the new
owners of the land shifted the ostensible purpose of the
myth and treated the Indian as a child, "incapable of learning and of taking care of himself" (p. 19). The perverse
myth of the dangerous animal was replaced by the equally
perverse myth of the dumb animal.

        Steinbeck finds a dual myth behind the exclusion of
the Black from American society. The Southerner, who
needed the labor of the black man and feared his physical
strength, found security in the belief that his slave "was a
lazy, stupid animal, who was also dangerous, clever, tricky,

thievish, and lecherous" (p. 73). The Northerner, who knew about the conditions of slavery primarily through self-righteous sermons, travelers' stories, and emotionally sensational novels, found it morally comfortable to believe that the Black "was a mistreated, brutalized, overworked, and starved creature, sometimes a hero, sometimes a saint, but never, by any chance, a man like other men" (p. 73). After the Civil War, the dual myth altered on the surface, but it remained the same in essence. The Southerner turned for protection to local laws and tactics of terror to control the Black, who was now more dangerous than lazy or stupid. The Northerner, now forced to accept his black brother, discovered that he, too, could only accept him on the same level as the Southerner had. Unable to use questionable legal means or secret terror because of his moral position, the Northerner found that he could exclude the Black by forcing him into a new form of slavery: "The servitudes of debt, of need, of ignorance, and the constant reminders of inferiority" (p. 75).

The unwillingness to merge the Black into the American experience reveals another paradox of the American character. On one level, the act is a perversion of the myth of equality which lies at the foundation of American beliefs and aspirations. Self-interest and self-preservation are as much behind the idea of separate-but-equal as they were behind the idea of slavery. On another level, the myths that have been created to deny equality to certain racial groups offer a perverse recognition of their individuality. What is twisted in that recognition is the failure to accept the Black other than as he fits the stereotype of racist myths. Steinbeck's point is that Americans "will not have overcome the trauma that slavery has left on our society, North and South, until we cannot remember whether the man we just spoke to in the street was Negro or white" (p. 77).

The attempt to deny individuality except on the basis of racial identity involves exclusion from another myth which Steinbeck feels is as critical to the American character as the myth of equality. He regards the American's belief in his self-reliance as the other critical factor in the formation of the American character. The myth of equality was primarily a creation of the 18th century and the writings of Thomas Paine, Thomas Jefferson, and Benjamin Franklin; the idea of self-reliance, however, was formed in the 19th century by the pioneer movement, and given mythic

significance in the writings of Ralph Waldo Emerson, Henry
David Thoreau, and other transcendental philosophers. This
belief allows the American to think of himself as uniquely
independent and restlessly mobile. He sees his home as a
symbol of security and comfort rather than a symbol of
wealth and social position. He envisions himself as a great
hunter or an adventuresome traveler, and, no matter what
his personal circumstances, still holds to the belief that
America is the best of all possible worlds and that all possibilities remain open to each individual.

          The perversion of the self-reliance myth began with
the advent of the machine age. As America prospered as a
nation, Americans were stifled by the deluge of commodity.
Gradually, the desire for gadgetry took precedence over the
basic need for independence and solitude. The way to seek
uniqueness was to own the latest automobile, the latest television set, and the latest mouth wash. The spirit of self-
reliance slowly gave way to the demon of modern mechanization. The instincts and restless imaginations which set-
tled and developed the country faded from the American
character which now accepted the blaring assault of modern
life and worshipped an image carved in the likeness of a
Ford assembly line: "Invention and improvisation were, for
a long time, almost national traits, destroyed only when
mass production made cheaper but not necessarily better
things people could afford to buy" (p. 119).

          The myth of equality, once perverted, divides Amer-
ica and disturbs its natural unity. Steinbeck, however, feels
that the perversion and potential loss of the myth of self-
reliance is even more destructive to the American character.
Any danger to the American's belief in self-reliance threatens the vital spirit of the people. Spiritual maladies, such
as what Steinbeck calls paedosis, the desire of parents to
see their frustrated dreams fulfilled in the lives of their
children, corrupt the American character and insure a life-
less future dominated by feelings of fear and guilt. Advertising groups, calculating the situation, exploit the parents'
fears, using the children as a market for food, clothes, and
various cosmetics, and further insure a future of alienation
and spiritual emptiness. The new leader of the people is
the Corporation Man. He represents all the negative characteristics which define the age in which he lives. His
whole being, his work, his family, and his future, is shaped
by his fear and admiration of the corporation. His life
style, revered by so many factions of American life, is a

tribute to the corporate status. The single driving force in
his life is to conform to those patterns and ideas which will
insure success for the corporation, and to convince others
to conform by their simple allegiance to the corporation's
products. The values of freedom and self-reliance are
shunned and replaced by one definite goal--to make money
for the corporate god.

Steinbeck feels that mechanization in American life is
so severe that only pockets of resistance remain. Too often,
however, the individual who senses the monotony and spiritual barrenness of an "assembly-line conformity" has only a
vague, groping desire to go back to the land. This feeling
has the greatest potential for assuming mythic value, but
the first Americans' love for the beauty and abundance of
the land, once critical to the American character, has long
since been perverted into lust and madness: "it is little
wonder that they went land-mad, because there was so much
of it. They cut and burned the forests to make room for
crops; they abandoned their knowledge of kindness to the
land in order to maintain its usefulness. When they had
cropped out a piece they moved on, raping the country like
invaders.... There has always been more than enough
desert in America; the new settlers, like overindulged children, created even more" (p. 146).

By the time Americans began to realize that the land
had its limit, the use and effectiveness of the machines had
already set in motion a destructive rape beyond the capability of the early settlers' wildest rage. At the present
moment, a new awareness of the vital need to preserve our
remaining resources exists, but whether this sense of the
necessity to conserve the land can overcome the greed and
destructiveness which still continues is a matter frightfully
open to question. Steinbeck feels that Americans are an
exuberant people, but they act as carelessly and harmfully
as active children. The only time they seemed to have consciously sensed that they had moved beyond moral boundaries
was after America dropped the atomic bomb on two Japanese
cities. In Steinbeck's personal reaction to the after-shock
of that terrible and tragic act lies his own feeling of the
moral and spiritual crisis in America: 'I did not know
about the bomb, and certainly I had nothing to do with its
use, but I am horrified and ashamed; and nearly everyone I
know feels the same thing. And those who loudly and angrily
justify Hiroshima and Nagasaki--why, they must be the most
ashamed of all" (p. 149).

There is a great deal in America and Americans to
suggest that it is a doomsday book. Though Steinbeck believes deeply in the value of myth, he finds that the myths
of equality and self-reliance which moulded the pattern of
life in America have been debased or forgotten. The tragic
result is a life style devoid of meaning and direction:
"Americans, very many of them, are obsessed with tensions.
Nerves are drawn tense and twanging. Emotions boil up
and spill over into violence largely in meaningless or unnatural directions" (p. 171). Steinbeck strongly suspects
that America's moral and spiritual disintegration comes
about from our inexperience with abundance. What makes
the condition so overwhelming and threatening, however, is
that the land which has been a constant source of spiritual
renewal as well as a source of wealth has now been abused
to the extent that the condition of waste may be irreversible.

Steinbeck concludes that the prospect of an America
with "no new path to take, no duty to carry out, no purpose
to fulfill" (p. 174) is contrary to the primary purpose of
mankind which is to survive in a world not always friendly
to man. In turn, his final statement in America and Americans is in response to that which he loves and that which
he believes exists in the natural order of things. He offers
a final word of faith in the midst of a ruined and chaotic
land. From Cup of Gold to East of Eden, Steinbeck has observed and studied human nature within the framework of
myth. In America and Americans he reiterates his faith in
the value of myth, even if the people have lost their visionary powers. He is not, however, a Tiresias wandering
about the waste land, admonishing himself to find order in
his own soul. Steinbeck's concern and love is for America.
As an observer of America, he has witnessed the terrible
things Americans do to each other and has faithfully and
sorrowfully recorded them. As an American, however, he
still expresses a belief in those myths and dreams which
comprise the spirit of America, and he insists that the
energy remains for America to re-discover its principles
and purpose. Steinbeck the novelist observes the fundamental realities of America, but Steinbeck the artist expresses
the hopes and dreams of Americans. This has been the
pattern of Steinbeck's writing and it continues as his own
creative myth in his final major work.

Notes

1. <u>America and Americans</u> (New York: Viking, 1968). All
    quotations which appear in this study are taken from
    this edition.

IV. APPARATUS FOR RESEARCH PAPERS

A. Ten Questions for Discussion

1. What value do the pictures have in illustrating each
    major point in <u>America and Americans</u>?
2. What pictures seem to illustrate most effectively Stein-
    beck's idea of the paradoxical unity of the American
    people?
3. How valid are Steinbeck's general summaries of critical
    phases in American history such as the history of the
    early settlement of the country and the history of slav-
    ery?
4. Have Steinbeck's fears about the loss of direction in
    American life proven more or less valid in the years
    since the publication of <u>America and Americans</u>?
5. Do you agree with Steinbeck's belief that Americans
    have lost their purpose but have not lost their energy?
6. How sound is Steinbeck as a child psychologist? Is his
    approach to the generation gap a valid one?
7. How universal are the values or truths which form the
    mythology of Steinbeck's America?
8. Is there such a phenomenon as the American experience
    or the American character or the American dream?
9. Of what value are the stories which appear from time
    to time during the course of Steinbeck's observations of
    America?
10. Is it possible to interpret Steinbeck's view of American
    life as a liberal or conservative philosophy? Is there
    a political paradox in his stress on individualism and
    his interest in social reform?

B. Suggested Topics for Research Papers

1. Steinbeck's Emersonian optimism.
2. Steinbeck's interest in American folklore.
3. The efficacy of Steinbeck's <u>Moma Americana</u>.
4. The myth of the individual in <u>America and Americans</u>
    and in Franklin's <u>Autobiography</u>.

5. Steinbeck and the American corporation.
6. Steinbeck's interest in the role of violence in American
    life.
7. America and Americans and Steinbeck's biological theo-
    ry of man and society.
8. Steinbeck's portrait of the American "Waste Land."
9. Naturalism in America and Americans.
10. The theme of mechanization in Travels with Charley
    and America and Americans.
11. Steinbeck's belief in the mythology of the land.
12. Steinbeck's interest in the Black and the American In-
    dian.
13. Steinbeck's theory of Group Organisms and his view of
    Screwball Groups in America.
14. Steinbeck's interest in social reform.
15. Steinbeck's role as prophet of American life.

C.   Selected Bibliography

        The following sources represent the various critical
reactions to the publication of America and Americans in
1966.

1. "Review of America and Americans," Times Literary
    Supplement, 1 Dec. 1966, p. 1128.
        The real strength of America and Americans lies in
the commentaries of Steinbeck. The pictures are brilliant
reflections of American life, but they are not representative.
The Middle West is nearly neglected, and there are few pictures of university life.

2. Richter, Conrad. "Review of America and Americans,"
    Harper's, 223 (Nov. 1966), 134.
        Conrad Richter also finds Steinbeck's writing to be
the essential value of America and Americans. He does
feel, however, that the individual and independent nature of
Steinbeck's observations are enhanced by some of the pictures. He laments the fact that there are not more individual stories in America and Americans, for he believes
that Steinbeck's strength lies in his story-telling ability.

3. Scherman, David E. "Review of America and Ameri-
    cans," New York Times Book Review, 4 Dec. 1966, p.
    46.
        Scherman feels that the pictures in America and
Americans are too obviously an attempt to boil down the

entire photographic output of America into "one big smash-
ing book that spells Yankeeland." His reactions to Steinbeck's writings are mixed. Steinbeck, at his best, offers
the intelligent ramblings of a first rate reporter. At his
worst, he writes what Scherman describes as "the opinion-
ated musings of a liberal Westbrook Pegler."

Chapter 3

STEINBECK'S CANNERY ROW (1945)

by Charles R. Metzger

I. BACKGROUND OF THE WORK

As Peter Lisca mentions in The Wide World of John
Steinbeck, Steinbeck wrote Cannery Row during six weeks,
finishing it in March 1944; it was published December 1944.
During the time of writing and at the time of publication
World War II was still very much going on. Steinbeck had
just returned from an overseas assignment with the military,
writing dispatches for the New York Herald Tribune. Steinbeck's motives for writing Cannery Row were probably
mixed. The two principal versions of these motives, both
attributable directly to Steinbeck, are not by any means incompatible. He might have wanted, as he later reported in
1953, to write for a change about something other than war-
fare, in order to amuse the homefront, in order to cheer
up service men who had time to read. Such motives are
not inconsistent with Steinbeck's dedication of the book to
Ed Ricketts. The book was, he said, "For Ed Ricketts
who knows why or should. " Cannery Row is clearly fo-
cussed around the character of Doc, for whom Ed Ricketts
is the model, and it concerns the non-military problems of
a highly intelligent and admirable man who is at one and
the same time friendly and yet lonely and set-apart.

Now that World War II has become history, Steinbeck's second motive for writing Cannery Row survives in
latter day perspective as the more significant of the two.
Cannery Row is, among many other things, a literary tribute
dedicated by Steinbeck to his admirable friend Ed Ricketts.

II. PLOT SYNOPSIS

Cannery Row is composed of thirty-two short chapters
preceded by an introductory prose poem. The prose poem
introduces Cannery Row as "a poem, a stink, a grating

19

noise, a quality of light, a tone, a habit, a nostalgia, a
dream" (p. 1). * It introduces Cannery Row as a physical
place and condition: "the gathered and scattered tin and
iron and rust and splintered wood, chipped pavement and
weedy lots and junk heaps, sardine canneries of corrugated
iron, honkey tonks, restaurants and whore houses, and little
crowded groceries, and laboratories and flophouses" (p. 1).
It introduces Cannery Row as the habitat of "whores, pimps,
gamblers, and sons of bitches" which "means everybody,"
who, when looked at "through another peephole," are also
"Saints and angels and martyrs and holy men,..." (p. 1).
It introduces Cannery Row's inhabitants in general, including
"Wops and Chinamen and Polaks" (p. 1) and bums. It introduces as well several of Cannery Row's citizens in par-
ticular--Dora Flood, Doc, Lee Chong, Henri the painter,
and Mack and the boys.

    The first six chapters of Cannery Row set things up
pretty much for the action which develops during the rest of
the novel. In general the first six chapters introduce important characters in their habitat: Lee Chong in his store,
Mack and the boys in the Palace Flophouse, Dora Flood in
the Bear Flag, Doc at Western Biologicals and out collecting, along with lesser characters such as the enigmatic old
Chinaman, Gay, who moves to the Palace Flophouse because
his wife hits him, Henri the painter and his never-to-be-
finished boat, Alfred the "watchman" at the Bear Flag who
"has triumphed over his environment" (p. 14). The first
six chapters also introduce two of the four suicides mentioned in the book: Horace Abbeville, who shoots himself
on a pile of fishmeal, and William, the dark and lonesome
looking "watchman" at the Bear Flag, who sticks an icepick
in his own heart.

    Chapters seven to thirty-two are concerned largely
with the two parties planned for Doc: the abortive one
which gets out of control before Doc gets a chance to attend
it, and the climactic one, superbly planned and executed, at
which Doc reads from the Sanskrit poem "Black Marigolds."
These chapters also include the frog-collecting episode and
the party with the Captain, as well as incidents involving
Frankie, the Malloys, las tripas de Josh Billings, Blaisdell
the poet, Henri the painter, the two soldiers from the
Presidio, Darling, the boys' bitch, Mary and Tom Talbot,

*All quotations are from Steinbeck, Cannery Row (Compass
paperback) (New York: Viking Press, 1972).

Richard Frost and the flagpole skater, as well as the influ-
enza epidemic at Cannery Row. These chapters also include reference to the remaining two suicides: that of the
beautiful girl who has drowned herself near La Jolla, and
that of Joey's father, who took rat poison. The novel ends
with Doc, the morning after the party, depressed, re-read-
ing "Black Marigolds. "

III. CRITICAL EXPLICATION:
      "PARTIES IN STEINBECK'S CANNERY ROW"

    Steinbeck's Cannery Row is about a lot of things. It
is about the place, Cannery Row, which is the habitat of
Doc, of Mack and the boys, of Dora and her girls, of Henri
the painter, Blaisdell the poet, Mr. and Mrs. Malloy, Lee
Chong, Frankie, Richard Frost, an anonymous Chinaman,
Tom and Mary Talbot, Joey, a gopher, and various dogs
and cats.

    During the first six chapters of the book Steinbeck
introduces in their natural habitat Lee Chong, Mack and the
boys, Dora Flood, Doc, and Henri the painter. The point
of view by which these and all other characters are seen is
that of what I would call the undetached observer--of the
warm and sentient human being as scientist, of the man who
can observe that "No one has studied the psychology of a
dying party" (p. 114).

    Starting with chapter seven and continuing to the end
of the book, all or nearly all action is related either to
Doc's collecting trips or to parties. During the last twenty-
six chapters of the book ten parties or their equivalent are
either mentioned or described in partial or in elaborate detail. Of these ten parties two are instigated by Mack and
the boys, and are given for Doc.

    The first of the two parties given for Doc is actually
the third of a cluster of three spontaneous parties. That
the first of this cluster of three parties actually is a party
at all only gradually dawns upon Mack. He and the boys
are out on the banks of the Carmel River, camped there
waiting for nightfall in order to collect frogs to sell to Doc
so that they can earn enough money to give him a surprise
party. Having brought with them bread, coffee, salt and
pepper, and their wining jug nearly half full, and having run
down a big red chicken and retrieved a sack of carrots

fallen from a vegetable truck, they are having what nowa-
days we would call an informal cookout. Having fed on
stewed chicken and carrots, and having drunk from the wining jug and finished off with coffee, Mack says suddenly,
"God damn it. I hate a liar" (p. 72)--referring to himself
and, by extension, to the boys. He says, "We worked it
out that we wanted to give Doc a party. So we come out
here and have a hell of a lot of fun" (p. 72). What Mack
recognizes is that he and the boys are having a party themselves, an unplanned, a spontaneous one, that has developed
without their realizing it.

      The second party of this cluster of three develops al-
most as spontaneously as the first, out of Mack and the
boys' confrontation by the Captain. The Captain is lonesome, therefore angry. His wife, having been elected to
the state Assembly, is off in Sacramento writing bills.
Starved for congenial company, the Captain brings out a
five-gallon keg of corn whiskey laid away during prohibition.
The party develops finally into what the Captain's wife could
only consider a disaster, except that, from their point of
view, Mack and the boys retire discreetly after the party
with a full gallon of well-aged corn whiskey, given to them
by the Captain, along with the bitch pup subsequently to be
named Darling.

      The final party of this cluster, the party originally
envisioned for Doc, develops from a casually planned party
into a spontaneous debacle. The unaccustomed wealth, a
whole gallon of corn whiskey and the liquid supplement
bought with frog currency, is too much for Mack and the
boys. Long before Doc returns from La Jolla they have
consumed everything and done $300 worth of damage to the
lab.

      Of the party, says Mack, after Doc hits him, "She
got out of hand, ..." (p. 119). He adds, "It don't do no
good to say I'm sorry. I been sorry all my life. This
ain't no new thing. It's always like this." Mack goes on
to describe his marriage by way of explaining analogically
why the party went wrong. "I had a wife," Mack said.
"Same thing. Ever' thing I done turned sour.... If I done
a good thing it got poisoned up some way. If I give her a
present they was something wrong with it. She only got
hurt from me. She couldn't stand it no more. Same thing
ever' place 'til I just got to clowning. I don't do nothin'
but clown no more. Try to make the boys laugh" (p. 119).

Returning to the party, Mack says, "The way I seen it, we was all happy and havin' a good time. You was glad because we was givin' you a party. And we was glad. The way I seen it, it was a good party. " He waves his hand at the wreckage on the floor. "Same thing when I was married. I'd think her out and then--but it never come off that way" (p. 120). Later on, while the second surprise party for Doc is developing, Mack says in retrospect of the first party, "Last time we forced her,... You can't never give a good party that way. You got to let her creep up on you" (p. 145). This second party for Doc and its preparations occupy the major portions of chapters fifteen to the end of the book. The party turns out to be a howling success, having at its climax "all the best qualities of a riot and a night on the barricades" (p. 174).

Unlike the first party for Doc, this second party given for him is not forced. "The knowledge or conviction about the party for Doc was no sudden thing. It did not burst out full blown. People knew about it but let it grow gradually like a pupa in the cocoons of their imaginations" (p. 145). Mack and the boys have the aid and counsel not only of Dora Flood and her girls but of the entire citizenry of Cannery Row. "People didn't get the news of the party-- the knowledge of it just slowly grew up in them. And no one was invited. Everyone was going" (p. 152). Even Doc participates in the preparations. Having got wind of the party, he secures the lab. , locking up everything breakable, and buys steaks, tomatoes and bread. "Doc hoped to make this party as non-lethal as possible without making it dull" (p. 162).

Steinbeck philosophizes regarding the nature of parties in chapter thirty. "The nature of parties, " he wrote, "has been imperfectly studied" (p. 168). It so happens that the nature of parties in Cannery Row is very well studied indeed. Steinbeck continues, "It is... generally understood that a party has a pathology, that it is a kind of an individual and that it is likely to be a very perverse individual. And it is also generally understood that a party hardly ever goes the way it is planned or intended" (p. 168). One might add that a good party is a cross between a natural organism (human) and a work of art, and that it is both planned and spontaneous in the ways that organisms and art forms are.

Steinbeck quite naturally excludes from his philosophical consideration the over-formal, over-structured activity

which sometimes masquerades as a party. This consideration regarding the nature of parties, Steinbeck concludes,
"excludes those dismal slave parties, whipped and controlled
and dominated, given by ogreish professional hostesses.
These are not parties at all but acts and demonstrations,
about as spontaneous as peristalsis and as interesting as
its end product" (p. 168).

In one sense Cannery Row is a poetic essay on how
to give a good party, particularly in this instance of the
second party for Doc, how to give a good party for a decent
person who needs one. For although Doc is the friendliest
of men, waving even to dogs who smile back at him, he is
also a lonesome man. "In spite of his friendliness and his
friends, Doc was a lonely and set-apart man. Even in a
group Doc seemed always alone" (p. 91). Doc is isolated
in part by his work. He "had to keep up his collecting"
(p. 91). He is isolated also by his unusual intelligence.
The number of people he can talk to, no intellectual holds
barred, is singularly limited. He is as isolated, in his
own particular way, as is Frankie, the mentally defective
boy who hangs around the lab., not being permitted, because of his deficiency, to go to school.

The two parties which Doc himself gives both involve
Frankie. At the first of these, Frankie, whom Doc says
generously is a great help to him, successfully gives a
glass of beer to an attractive and gentle girl guest. At
the second party, Frankie, overcome by a spastic seizure,
spills a whole tray of full beer glasses all over the same
girl guest. Frankie flees, sobbing, to a crate in the base-
ment of the lab. Like the wounded animal-human being that
he is, he flees with his deficiency into further isolation.
Frankie loves Doc. He steals the clock with Saint George
slaying the dragon on it to give to Doc for his birthday.
Frankie, as Doc knows, in his own different isolation, is
doomed upon puberty to institutional isolation. Frankie too
is lonely and set-apart.

Of the four remaining parties, one involves two soldiers from the Presidio and their girls. This party is described in chapter fourteen, occurring just before the chapter
in which occurs the party of Mack and the boys with the
Captain, whose wife is in Sacramento writing bills. As any
one who has been in the army knows, soldiers, for all their
company, are lonesome. The two soldiers with their girls
are strolling "softly in the pearly light" (p. 78) of dawn.

"They smiled like weary children remembering a party" (p.
78).   For indeed they had been having the only kind of party
which is readily available to soldiers, who are without
facilities for parties, yet need them.

The remaining three parties all revolve about Mary
Talbot, who is a very important character in the book.   She
is the beautiful and courageous wife of Tom Talbot, a de-
pressive young man struggling with the despondency that goes
with not being able to earn enough money to make both ends
meet, that goes with being unable to pay the rent, with having "a manuscript ... come back from Colliers and ... car-
toons ... come back from The New Yorker" (p. 139).

More than "anything in the world Mary Talbot loved
parties.   She loved giving parties and she loved to go to
parties" (p. 138). · Because "Tom Talbot didn't make much
money Mary couldn't give parties all the time so she tricked
people into giving them.   Sometimes she telephoned a friend
and said bluntly, 'Isn't it about time you gave a party?'"
(p. 138).   "Regularly," writes Steinbeck, "Mary had six
birthdays a year, and she organized costume parties, surprise parties, birthday parties.   Christmas eve at her
house was a very exciting thing.   For Mary glowed with
parties.   She carried her husband Tom along on the wave
of her excitement" (p. 138).   Often, "in the afternoon when
Tom was at work Mary ... gave tea parties for the neigh-
borhood cats" (p. 138), carrying on elaborate conversations
with them over doll china cups of simulated tea.   At one
such party, spoiled by one of her guests, Kitty Casini, who
had been torturing a mouse, Mary gave the party for Tom,
just home from work, and herself.

What Steinbeck has to say about Mary's attitude
toward parties has some bearing on the very "nature of
parties" which Steinbeck says "has been imperfectly studied"
(p. 168).   Of Mary's cat tea party, says Steinbeck, "it was
a kind of play she enjoyed very much--a kind of satiric
game and it covered and concealed from Mary the fact that
she didn't have very nice clothes and the Talbot's didn't
have any money" (p. 139).   Mary, Steinbeck adds, "could
infect a whole house with gaiety and she used her gift as a
weapon against the despondence that lurked always around
outside the house waiting to get in at Tom" (p. 139).

I should like to suggest that Steinbeck is indicating
that one of the principal functions of a genuine party is, as

Mary knew, to provide a defense against despondency.   It
so functions for Doc, the lonely and set-apart man.   I
should like to suggest further that Mary's parties are akin
to Mack's clowning, both intended to cheer people up.

Come to think of it, people are the only animals in
God's nature who give parties, or need, presumably, to do
so--to fight despondency, the feeling of hopeless isolation,
that goes with being human.   Parties have for human beings,
I think Steinbeck is suggesting, a measure of survival value.
I suspect that it has to do also with the presence in this
most amusing and apparently lighthearted book of four suicides, committed by lonely and/or despondent people who
need cheering up.

These suicides include Horace Abbéville, mentioned
in chapter one, the former owner of the Abbeville building,
become subsequently the Palace Flophouse.   Horace, with
"two wives and six children, " with "a sensitive and tired
face" (p. 5) and a monumental grocery bill, "shot himself
on a heap of fish meal" (p. 6) in what had been his building.
These suicides include "William ... a dark and lonesome
looking man" (p. 15), former watchman at the Bear Flag,
mentioned in chapter three, who stuck an icepick into his
heart.   They include the peacefully drowned corpse, mentioned in chapter eighteen, which Doc discovers at the edge
of the reef at La Jolla.   They include Joey's father, mentioned in chapter twenty-six, who took rat poison in despair
at not being able to get a job.

What I suggest, finally, is that Steinbeck is arguing
indirectly that parties or their equivalent help to keep us,
to keep Doc, to keep Ed Ricketts, as lonely, set-apart,
despondent human beings, going.

IV.   APPARATUS FOR RESEARCH PAPERS

A.   Ten Questions for Discussion

1.   Why is Doc lonesome and set-apart?   (For further an-
     swer, see also Sweet Thursday.)
2.   What do Mary Talbot and Mack have in common?
3.   How many of the characters mentioned in Cannery Row
     are, or have been, married?   Why is this information
     important?
4.   What skill do Mack and the boys have in common,

particularly as exemplified by Gay? In what way does
their special skill make them akin to Doc?

5. Why does Doc have to keep up with his collecting?
6. How many, and specifically which, kinds of marine animals are mentioned in Cannery Row? (Look these up
in Edward F. Ricketts and John Calvin's Between Pacific
Tides.)
7. Why does Steinbeck describe two watchmen at the Bear
Flag: Alfred, who has triumphed over his environment,
and William, who commits suicide?
8. How many different kinds of artists appear as characters
in Cannery Row? (Be sure to define what you mean by
artist.)
9. Chapter thirty-one is about a gopher. What is he doing
in the book?
10. The death of the great American humorist Josh Billings
is mentioned in chapter twelve of the book. Why?

B. Suggested Research Paper Topics

1. Women in Cannery Row.
2. Art and artists in Cannery Row.
3. Business enterprise in Cannery Row.
4. Mack, the boys, and others versus "the system" in
Cannery Row.
5. Techniques of wit and humor in Cannery Row.
6. Steinbeck on marriage in Cannery Row.
7. Survival and adjustment in Cannery Row.
8. Techniques of character revelation in Cannery Row.
9. Steinbeck's use of dialogue in Cannery Row.
10. Doc in Cannery Row and the real Ed Ricketts.
11. Cannery Row as an informal introduction to marine biology.

C. Selected Bibliography for Research

1. Steinbeck. Cannery Row. New York: Viking (Compass),
1972.
This is a paper back edition of the official text of
Cannery Row. It is readily available and inexpensive.

2. Steinbeck. The Log from the Sea of Cortez. New
York: Viking Press, 1951.
This is the narrative part of Steinbeck and Ricketts'
report on their collecting trip to the Gulf of California in

1940. It is of particular interest to students of Cannery
Row because of the prefatory section, "About Ed Ricketts"
(pp. vii-lxvii), inasmuch as Ed Ricketts is the model of
Doc in Cannery Row. Regarding speculations, biological
and philosophical, made by Steinbeck, Ricketts and the crew
of the Western Flyer that have bearing upon Cannery Row,
see especially chapters 10-16 in The Log.

3.   Lisca, Peter.   "Cannery Row," in The Wide World of
     John Steinbeck.   New Brunswick, N. J.:   Rutgers Uni-
     versity Press, 1958.   pp. 197-217.
     This is a chapter on Cannery Row in Peter Lisca's
invaluable book on Steinbeck's works. It gives information
regarding the dates and circumstances of composition and
publication, as well as reviewers' and critics' responses to
the work, also Steinbeck's own statements in letters regarding his novel. Lisca deals as well with the structural and
thematic features of the work. Lisca's is the most complete assessment of the work extant.

4.   Hayashi, Tetsumaro.   A New Steinbeck Bibliography,
     1929-1971.   Metuchen, New Jersey: Scarecrow Press,
     1973.
     This is the most complete collection of bibliographi-
cal information about Steinbeck and his works. For criticism and reviews of Cannery Row see especially pp. 219-
20.

5.   Ricketts, Edward F. and Jack Calvin.   Between Pacific
     Tides, 4th edition, revised by Joel W. Hedgpeth. Stan-
     ford, California: Stanford University Press, 1969.
     This is the best-selling textbook of marine biology
that Ed Ricketts and Jack Calvin published initially in 1939.
It is readily available in its present revised form. Anyone,
who wants to learn something about what Doc was up to in
the tide pools, ought to read, or at least examine, this
best-selling textbook.

Chapter 4

STEINBECK'S THE GRAPES OF WRATH (1939)

by Warren French

I. BACKGROUND OF THE NOVEL

The Grapes of Wrath scarcely needs introduction.
Since its publication in 1939 it has attracted millions of
readers around the world and it has been used in thousands
of classrooms--not only in literature courses, but in history, economics, sociology, political science, philosophy,
and popular culture classes. Has another American novel
since Harriet Beecher Stowe's Uncle Tom's Cabin--to which
Steinbeck's work is often compared--had a more universal
appeal and been so useful in the study of so many aspects
of American life and culture?

There is no shortage of teaching aids. Twentieth-
Century-Fox transformed the novel into a prize-winning film
in 1940. Warren French's A Companion to "The Grapes of
Wrath" (1963) brings together background material and critical accounts with Steinbeck's own newspaper articles about
the migrants. Agnes McNeill Donohue's A Casebook on "The
Grapes of Wrath" (1968) contains excerpts from nearly every
major criticism of the novel; and Peter Lisca's edition of
the novel for the Viking Critical Library, The Grapes of
Wrath: Text and Criticism (1972), includes material about
the "social context" of the novel and eleven critical essays,
written at different times and from different points of view,
along with some hitherto unpublished statements by Steinbeck
himself about the novel. The problem thus is not--as with
some other worthy works of Steinbeck's--getting The Grapes
of Wrath into the classroom, but providing a framework that
may show how all the various approaches to the novel can
be interrelated.

First, the novel itself--Steinbeck had been working

towards The Grapes of Wrath since the beginning of the Depression, when his second published novel, The Pastures of
Heaven (1932), established as the subject in which he is yet
to have a peer, farm life in the central valleys of California. The Pastures of Heaven is the kind of work that Forrest L. Ingram calls "a short story cycle,"[1] a group of
separate but closely related tales that make the ironic point
that long intrigued Steinbeck about the difference between
the natural beauty of a valley perceived from a distance and
the tortured lives of people who it seems should be happy
in this paradise.

    Even more closely related to The Grapes of Wrath
are Of Mice and Men (1937), also the story of migrant
workers with a dream of a happy life that eludes them, and
In Dubious Battle (1936), a harsh tale of the fearful encounter between the entrenched farmers and militant labor-
organizers during a migrant workers' strike in the apple
orchards of the Torgas Valley. Both of these works take
blackly pessimistic, almost nihilistic, views of situations
that Steinbeck would perceive quite differently as he shaped
The Grapes of Wrath.

    Specific preparations for the novel began with a trip
in September, 1936, to observe the migrant squatters'
camps near Salinas and Bakersfield, California. This expedition led to "Dubious Battle in California" (The Nation,
Sept. 12, 1936, pp. 302-304) and a series of articles, "The
Harvest Gypsies," which appeared in the San Francisco News
between October 5 and 12, 1936, and which were subsequently collected and expanded in Their Blood Is Strong
(1938, reprinted in Warren French, ed., A Companion to
"The Grapes of Wrath," pp. 53-92).

    Peter Lisca reports in The Wide World of John
Steinbeck that these expeditions led, by June, 1938, to a
sixty-thousand-word novel called "L'Affaire Lettuceberg,"
which Steinbeck told his publishers was a bad book that he
would not submit to them. As the title suggests, the book
was satirical; and Steinbeck complained in a letter, "My
whole work drive has been aimed at making people understand each other and then I deliberately write this book, the
aim of which is to cause hatred through partial understanding."[2] The tenor of his remarks suggests that he was still
in the despairing frame of mind that he was when working
on In Dubious Battle and Of Mice and Men. The manuscript
has never been made public, if indeed Steinbeck preserved

it; but the arch title and his own remarks leave the impression that while it might have been a very popular protest
novel (like some of the works of Upton Sinclair), it would
have lacked the breadth and depth of The Grapes of Wrath.

He went back to work in the summer of 1938. By
September he reported that the rewritten work would be
titled "The Grapes of Wrath," a phrase borrowed from
Julia Ward Howe's popular "Battle Hymn of the Republic."
Although the effort of writing this huge book exhausted
Steinbeck, he saw the work through the press. It was an
enormous success even before its publication on March 14,
1939. There were three advance printings. Fifty thousand
copies were ordered before publication, and it was necessary to halve all orders to supply every dealer with copies.
There were 19, 804 copies of the first printing. By April
29, Publishers' Weekly reported that The Grapes of Wrath
was selling 2, 500 copies a week; by May it was at the top
of the best-seller list, with 10,000 copies being sold weekly. By May 17, Viking Press had shipped 430,000 copies.
The novel remained at the top of the best-seller list through
1939 and became also one of the ten best sellers of 1940. 3
Despite the controversial nature of the work, Twentieth
Century-Fox rushed into production a motion picture version, directed by John Ford, which reached theatres in
January, 1940.

The first reviewers, confused by the structure of the
book and sometimes offended by the language and the vehe-
mence of Steinbeck's attack on the landowners, were divided
in their opinions; but as the novel grew more familiar,
critical appreciation grew steadily. No major book clubs
originally selected The Grapes of Wrath, but it won the 1939
Pulitzer Prize for fiction, the first annual fiction award of
Social Work Today, and was chosen by the American Book-
sellers Association as their favorite novel of 1939 (these
awards have been replaced by the National Book Awards).

Not everyone was impressed, however. In Oklahoma
and California the novel was widely attacked. Congressman
Lyle Boren of Oklahoma read a bitter attack upon the book
as "a lie, a black, infernal creation of a twisted, distorted
mind" into the Congressional Record, 4 and Commonweal collected unfavorable reviews from small town California newspapers. 5 The book was banned for "obscenity" by the Kan-
sas City, Missouri, Board of Education; and it was ordered
burned by the Library Board of East St. Louis, Illinois.

But one influential person called reading it "an unforgettable
experience"--Mrs. Eleanor Roosevelt in her syndicated
column, "My Day. "[6] Most subsequent readers have sided
with Mrs. Roosevelt rather than Mrs. W. H. Matlack of
East St. Louis, who found the novel "vile all the way
through. "

II. PLOT SYNOPSIS

        This epic of the dust bowl must indeed have puzzled
and outraged many early readers, for the major narrative--
the story of the Joad family's pilgrimage from a farm near
Sallisaw, Oklahoma, to California, after they are tractored
off the land that they have been share-cropping, does not
even begin until the second chapter.   The first chapter--
like more than half of those in the book--is what Peter
Lisca has called an "intercalary chapter, " in which Steinbeck makes--often angrily--a general point about the migration that he then illustrates specifically through the history of the Joads.   Because of the alternation of "inter-
calary chapters" with the Joad story, it is easiest to summarize the novel in three parts, dividing it at those two
points at which there are two successive intercalary chapters. [7]

Section One: Oklahoma

        Chapter One describes a dust storm and its effects
upon people.   In Chapter Two, Tom Joad gets a ride with
a talkative truck driver and admits to being paroled from
prison after serving four years for homicide.   Chapter
Three describes a box turtle--symbolic of the migrants--
crossing a highway with great difficulty.   In Chapter Four,
Tom Joad meets an ex-preacher, Casy, who has lost "the
sperit. " They discuss his loss of faith and the problems
that have reduced homesteaders to share-croppers.   Chapter Five describes the taking over of the share-croppers'
land by the tractors of the big owners.   In Chapter Six,
Casy and Tom reach the deserted Joad farm and learn from
neighbor Muley Graves that the family has been evicted and
gone to Uncle John's to prepare to move to California.
Chapter Seven reproduces the monologue of a dealer who
sells used cars to the migrants.   In Chapter Eight, Tom is
reunited with the family at Uncle John's and learns of plans
for the move.   Chapter Nine describes the migrants' selling

and destroying possessions in preparation for the move.   In
Chapter Ten, the Joads slaughter and salt down pigs and
make other preparations for the move.   After putting down
a rebellion by Grampa, who is determined to stay in Oklahoma, the family accepts Casy as a member and says good-
bye to Muley Graves.   Chapter Eleven describes the deserted
farms going back to nature.

Section Two: Route 66

Chapter Twelve is a montage of the movement of the
migrants westward on U.S. Highway 66, through Oklahoma.
In Chapter Thirteen, the Joads travel across Oklahoma to
Bethany and camp with the Wilson family.   Grampa dies of
a stroke and is buried by the roadside.   Chapter Fourteen
contains Steinbeck's central philosophical statement about
mankind constantly growing despite obstacles, "unlike any
other thing organic or inorganic in the universe."

Section Three: Into California

Chapter Fifteen opens the major portion of the book
with the sentimental account of truck stop attendants making
small gifts to a migrant family and being more than repaid
by two truck drivers who watch the incident.   In Chapter
Sixteen, the highway becomes the Joads' home.   The car
breaks down and the family is about to split up until Ma
threatens the others with a jack-handle.   Tom repairs the
car by talking a one-eyed junkyard attendant out of some
parts and tools.   At a campground, the family is disturbed
by a man who tells of coming back from California after
watching his wife and two sons starve to death there.
Chapter Seventeen describes the development of new com-
munal rules in the migrant camps.   In Chapter Eighteen,
the Joads cross Arizona; and the oldest son, Noah, decides
to stay by the Colorado River.   Ma Joad first hears the
term "Okie" from an arrogant California policeman.   The
Wilsons decide that they can go no further, so that the
Joads set off across the fearful Mojave Desert alone.   During the night crossing, Granma dies.   Chapter Nineteen contains Steinbeck's reflections about the struggle between the
California landowners and the migrants.

In Chapter Twenty, the Joads enter a Hooverville, a
ramshackle migrants' community, where hungry children

watch Ma Joad make stew. During a quarrel with a labor
contractor, Tom slugs a deputy sheriff; and Casy takes the
blame and goes to jail. Uncle John gets drunk and Rosasharn's husband, Connie Rivers, runs away. The family
moves quickly when Tom learns that an irate mob will burn
the camp that night. Chapter Twenty-One frames this sub-
section with Steinbeck's speculations on the possibility of
revolution.

In Chapter Twenty-Two, the Joad family arrives at
the neatly kept Weedpatch government camp and learns that
it is self-governing and that they will have to take part of
the responsibility for maintaining the camp. Tom has
breakfast with the Wallace family and goes to work with
them. The small farmer who employs them warns them
of the sheriff's plans to raid the camp during the next Saturday night dance. Chapter Twenty-Three describes the
migrants' search for entertainment. In Chapter Twenty-
Four, the committee of migrants that governs the camp
frustrates an attempt to start a riot that will enable deputies
to make the raid.

Chapter Twenty-Five is Steinbeck's denunciation of
the waste and destruction of food crops in California while
people are starving. In Chapter Twenty-Six, the Joads have
to leave the government camp for lack of work. They get
work picking peaches at the Hooper Ranch; but Tom meets
Casy, who has become a labor organizer, and learns that
the family is helping to break a strike that Casy is leading.
Deputies break up the meeting and club Casy to death.
Tom kills one of the deputies; but since he is recognizably
wounded, the family hides him under mattresses in the
truck and leaves the camp. Chapter Twenty-Seven is a
montage of cotton-picking scenes. In Chapter Twenty-Eight
the family at last finds familiar work picking cotton, but
Ruthie--the youngest daughter--spills the beans about Tom,
who is hiding out nearby. Tom decides that he must go
away and has a long conversation with Ma about Casy's
ideas. Chapter Twenty-Nine describes the migrants' despair during the long wet season when there is no work.
In Chapter Thirty, the rains come to the boxcar camp
where the Joads have been living while picking cotton. The
family and the other migrants fight to keep the camp from
flooding; meanwhile Rosasharn's baby is stillborn. Ma
leads the family to a barn on high ground, where Rosasharn
nourishes an old man with the milk intended for her dead
baby.

III.   CRITICAL EXPLICATION

Although Steinbeck has dismissed criticism as "tax-
onomy" and has claimed that he is not interested in the
"classification and pickling" of The Grapes of Wrath, [8] he
himself has provided the most useful clue to a suitable
framework for analyzing the novel.   In a letter to his editor, Pascal Covici, he observes that there are "five layers"
in the novel and that "a reader will find as many as he can
and he won't find more than he has in himself."[9]

Although I know of no elaboration of this remark
about "five layers," the author's phrase poses the strongest
possible challenge to the critical reader--How many "layers"
can he find?   Is the book his critic as well as he the
book's?

I don't know what "five layers" Steinbeck had in
mind; and I don't intend to set forth an interpretation of the
book in terms of "five layers" that I perceive, for that
would spoil the excitement and challenge of reading.   After
all, students should be encouraged to find out things for
themselves.   But I am going to provide some information
here that may help those who may not realize that the perception of several "layers of meaning" in a literary work is
not a new idea.

The most famous explanation of "levels of meaning"
in literature comes to us from St. Thomas Aquinas, but is
most usefully presented in some of the writings of Dante,
author of The Divine Comedy, who drew upon Aquinas.

In the Convivio, Dante explains:

> Exposition must be literal and allegorical.   And
> for the understanding of this you should know that
> writings can be understood and must be explained,
> for the most part, in four senses.   One is called
> literal; and this is the one which extends not be-
> yond the letter itself.   The next is called allegori-
> cal; and this is the one which is hidden beneath the
> cloak of these fables, being a truth concealed un-
> der pretty [not petty] fiction....   The third sense
> is called moral; and this is the one which readers
> must ever diligently observe in writings, for their
> own profit and for that of their pupils....   The
> fourth sense is called anagogical, or supersensual;

and this is when we expound spiritually a writing
which, even in the letter, through the very things
expressed, expresses things concerning eternal
glory. [10]

In a famous letter to his friend Can Grande della
Scala, Dante, explaining his own great work, applied these
four concepts to the Biblical story of the exodus from Isra-
el, which many critics find reflected in The Grapes of
Wrath:

For if we look to the letter alone, we are told of
the going forth of the children from Egypt in the
time of Moses; if we look at the allegory, we are
told of our future redemption through Christ; if we
consider the moral sense, we are told of the conversion of the soul from the grief and misery of
sin to the state of grace; if we consider the anagogical, we are told of the going forth of the
blessed soul from the servitude of this corruption
to the freedom of eternal glory.

Steinbeck probably knew the theories of either St.
Thomas or Dante, for he was an enthusiastic reader of
works about the Middle Ages, like Thomas Malory's Morte
d'Arthur. Possibly, however, his own concept of "layers"
of meaning may have come from a source much closer to
him, because his good friend Ed Ricketts--presumably the
model for Doc Burton in In Dubious Battle and Doc in Cannery Row--in an unpublished essay, "A Spiritual Morphology
of Poetry" (which I am able to quote through the assistance
of Richard Astro), [11] also sets forth what he calls four
"successive growth stages" of the poet.

On the first and lowest of these, poetry (we use the
word here not to mean formal verse, but any great work of
the imagination) "involves a simple and fresh statement of
the joy of existence, in the love of landscape, God, home,
wife, country, friend. " On the second level, the poets are
confused by problems of right and wrong and bewail worldly
conditions and seek an escape from them. On the third
plane, a few poets "catch glimpses of a new promised land, "
while in the highest category, the poet is in and speaks out
from "the heaven glimpsed by his predecessors. "

Now even though Ricketts is talking about poets and
not poems--as Dante is--and though the second and third

levels are reversed in the two systems, they have so much in common that it is possible to reconcile them and draw up a kind of table that will apply to classical or modern works.

First, both agree that the work has a literal, historical level. It tells a story of certain characters doing certain things at a certain time and in a certain place. Though the Joads are fictional, they had many prototypes among the migrants with whom Steinbeck traveled, so that on this level The Grapes of Wrath is the tale--a rather sad tale--of dispossession of the Oklahoma share-croppers and their migration to California in search of a new home.

Second, to allow St. Thomas the precedence of age-- his placing second what Ricketts places third shows something about a difference in priorities--allegorically, the Joads are not just Americans on the move; they symbolize all the dispossessed persons everywhere--from the ancient Israelites that Dante discusses to the modern Vietnamese and Bangla Deshians--who have suffered and yet have set out, against enormous odds, in pursuit of a dream.

Third, continuing to follow St. Thomas's priorities, these stories have a "moral" as well. The author writes from an ethically informed point of view. He is concerned with right and wrong, with the turning of the soul from sin to a state of grace. Dante found this hope in a particular religious promise; but as Steinbeck shows through his portrayal of Casy, traditional religion no longer commands such faith. Casy expresses not a hope of "pie in the sky," but outrage at "man's inhumanity to man."

Fourth--and at last again the levels converge--there is the hope of a land of "eternal glory," of a radiant security beyond the chaotic flux of man's material experience. Do the Joads achieve a vision of this land when Tom tells Ma that he'll "be all aroun' in the dark," "ever'where" (p. 572), and Rosasharn demurely offers the milk of life to a dying man? Here the controversy over the novel is likely to rage strongest.

So far, however, using both the classical and modern systems, we have been discussing only four levels of meaning. What of the "fifth" that Steinbeck mentions in his letter? Can there be a "layer" that transcends even the prospect of paradise and demands a different response?

I spoke in my description of the possible fourth level
of the work about the controversies that have arisen and
will continue to arise about the vision that inspires the final
action of the Joads as each reader belligerently contends for
his private paradise.   Even this vision as Aquinas and Dante
speak of it must be interpreted in terms of a specifically
Western Christian tradition; and not even Ed Ricketts could
escape in his categorization of the artist a cosmic version
of a little white house in an orange grove of which the Joads
dream.   Beyond this contention is there some level of ultimate harmony?

Perhaps we should look at a speech that almost all
critics have acknowledged is one of the most important in
the novel.   Early in the action, Casy explains to Tom Joad
that he is no longer a preacher and speculates that perhaps,
"There ain't no sin and there ain't no virtue.   There's just
stuff people do.   It's all part of the same thing.   And some
of the things folks do is nice, and some ain't nice, but
that's as far as any man got a right to say" (p. 32).   The
echo of the American transcendentalist philosopher Ralph
Waldo Emerson is evident here to anyone who has read his
essays on "Nature" and "Self-Reliance. "   His concept also
of the "Oversoul" can be explained by Casy's subsequent
remark, "'Maybe, ' I figgered, 'maybe it's all men an' all
women we love; maybe that's the Holy Sperit--the human
sperit--the whole shebang.   Maybe all men got one big soul
ever'body's a part of. '"   Tom Joad drops his eyes and replies, "You can't hold no church with idears like that" (pp.
32-33).

As frequently in this novel--returning to the allegorical level--one of the Joads is saying as a representative
human being far more than he understands as an individual,
because if Casy has such ideas he not only cannot "hold" a
church in being literally an acceptable pastor of a congregation, but he cannot "hold" in the universal sense to any
particular denomination or system of belief.   He has
transcended the traditions that provided the framework for
both Dante's and Ricketts' thought.

The aim of many "meditation" movements has been
such transcendence.   I speak not of just the recent "transcendental meditation" movement, though it is particularly
to the point here because of the adjective that links it to
Emerson's quest and because of the Maharishi Mahesh
Yogi's emphasis upon the achievement of "pure

consciousness" that allows man to transcend individual systems of belief without rejecting them. When we speak of
"pure consciousness, " we are speaking not of the immure-
ment of the individual in some private paradise, but of the
embodiment of all individual men in what Steinbeck in Chapter Fourteen calls "Manself" (p. 204), humanity as a continuing, struggling, evolving phenomenon. At this level of
"pure consciousness, " individual distinctions are obliterated
and men are perceived only in terms of what characterizes
life.

Contemplated in this light, The Grapes of Wrath is
not a story of the Okies' migration to California, of man's
perpetual pursuit of the elusive dream, of man's injustices
to man, or even of the eventual reward of the deserving.
It is rather the endless story of the strivings of the "life-
force" to manifest itself. Steinbeck perceives the pure
forces of assertion and negation contending within that which
strives to live.

It may offend many to find The Grapes of Wrath considered in terms appropriate to Thomas Mann's The Magic
Mountain, Walt Whitman's "Passage to India, " Shaw's Don
Juan in Hell; and I realize that some may not have been
able or willing to follow this compressed argument. But,
if I can trust my own intuitions about this fifth layer of
meaning, I am not concerned about being "right" or "wrong. "
I am concerned with having this novel explored and tested
against each individual's concept of these levels. I am
much concerned that those who find this concept of five
levels difficult, stretch their imaginations, expand their
consciousnesses in an effort to base their acceptance or rejection on a contemplation of the artist's labor, not a knee-
jerk reflex reaction to a new and threatening stimulus.

To plummet back to the first level of meaning, the
deplorable conditions that The Grapes of Wrath depicts re-
sulted in part from man's preferring easy, expedient solu-
tions for problems to facing the challenge of demanding
thought. Comparable repression often exists in our class-
rooms. I would hope that those teaching The Grapes of
Wrath would pay the artist and his concerns the tribute of
using the book to encourage students to think and grow rather than subjecting them to the dehumanization of instantly-
graded computer tests. I have never understood what con-
ceivable value to anyone--author, teacher, student--could
come from "teaching" a student to memorize and repeat

"facts" about a work of art.   Since art is possibly the only
way in which minds may meet, we do a great disservice to
artist and audience if we set up roadblocks to the union of
their consciousnesses.

Without spoiling the confrontation between reader and
artist that is essential to this union by explaining so much
that someone might "study" rather than respond to these remarks, I can perhaps summarize and clarify my remarks
about "five layers" of meaning by discerning a possible response on each level to the famous "turtle" episode--the
third chapter of the book (pp. 20-22).

On the literal level, this chapter describes a land
turtle's making his way with great difficulty across a highway, carrying along with him a head of wild oats--a com-
monplace sight wherever man has laid his concrete tracks
across the natural landscape.   On the allegorical level, the
hard-shelled turtle, with his "horny beak" and "old humor-
ous eyes," is obviously a symbol of all tough and weathered
migrants--like the Joads and the other Okies--who are
determined to battle their way to their destination against
all odds.

The moral level is introduced when two cars approach
the turtle.   One driver responds by endangering herself to
avoid hitting the turtle; the other deliberately goes out of
his way to hit the turtle, but, ironically, instead of destroying the animal, he speeds its journey across the road.
These actions are examples of what Casy calls "stuff people do"--even those things that aren't nice sometimes have
surprising consequences.

As usual, the greatest controversy will occur in a
consideration of the anagogical level.   Most men can come
to accept--though only with great difficulty--others' facts,
generalizations, and judgments, but not to believe that anyone who thinks differently can really be saved.   Some readers who have protested that Steinbeck is too obsessed with
biology will argue that the fable of the turtle can have no
anagogical significance unless the turtle is regarded in
purely anthropomorphic terms like the animals in classical
bestiaries.   Is man justified, however, in egotistically sup-
posing that he alone of God's creatures is capable of the
vision of paradise that motivates and sanctifies his quest-
ing?   Alone conscious of what he is doing--on those infre-
quent occasions that he is?

These questions are resolved on the level of pure consciousness, for the turtle and the oat seed can be seen to be the same thing, manifestations of the same spirit that Casy speaks of, a tough, protective outer covering for the vital life-force throbbing within. The turtle and the oat seed both contain the creative principle that exists not just within time, but beyond time. Beyond the consciousness that stresses the differences between turtle, oat seed, artist, man, a consciousness perceives the similarity between all forms of embodied life.

The "turtle" episode thus leads us from a report of individual behavior to an inference about universal behavior, to a moral judgment and to a vision of what may be permanent beyond all this temporal activity, to, at last, a perception of the struggle between a dynamic creative force seeking to exert itself and the inert obstacles to its self-realization.

Notes

1. See Representative Short Story Cycles of the Twentieth Century (The Hague and Paris: Mouton, 1971), especially page 19, for a definition of this interesting literary form. Steinbeck's The Red Pony is another example.

2. The Wide World of John Steinbeck (New Brunswick: Rutgers University Press, 1958), p. 147. Much of this and the next paragraph is summarized from Lisca's account of the genesis of the novel, based on Steinbeck's letters to his agents and publishers.

3. Details in this paragraph are selected from a longer account of the publishing history of the novel in A Companion to "The Grapes of Wrath" (New York: Viking Press, 1963), pp. 105-11.

4. Martin Staples Shockley, "The Reception of The Grapes of Wrath in Oklahoma," American Literature, 15 (May 1944), 351-61. This essay has been reprinted in most collections of writings about Steinbeck and The Grapes of Wrath.

5. "Red Meat and Red Herrings," Commonweal, 30 (October 13, 1939), 562-63.

6. Quoted from her column of June 28, 1939 in A Com-
    panion to "The Grapes of Wrath," p. 131. Other
    details in this paragraph are drawn from the same
    source book.

7. The plot synopsis reproduces one that appears also in
    Warren French, A Filmguide to "The Grapes of
    Wrath" (Bloomington: Indiana University Press,
    1973), along with a synopsis of the film version, so
    that it may be used to facilitate comparison between
    the two works.

8. "A Letter on Criticism," Colorado Quarterly, 4 (Autumn
    1955), 218-19, reprinted in Tedlock and Wicker, eds.,
    Steinbeck and His Critics (Albuquerque: University
    of New Mexico Press, 1956), pp. 52-53.

9. Peter Lisca, ed., John Steinbeck "The Grapes of
    Wrath": Text and Criticism, The Viking Critical
    Library (New York: Viking Press, 1972), p. 258.
    Parenthetical page references in subsequent portions
    of this essay are to the text of the novel in this
    edition.

10. Translation follows the text in C. H. Grandgent, Dante
    (New York: Duffield, 1916), pp. 273-75, in this and
    the next quotation.

11. This manuscript is the property of Ed Ricketts, Jr.,
    who has made it available to Professor Astro, who
    has graciously shared the material with me and per-
    mitted me to employ some extracts in this study.

IV. APPARATUS FOR RESEARCH PAPERS

A. Ten Questions for Discussion

A group of other "topics for discussion and papers"
may be found at the end of Peter Lisca's "Viking Critical
Edition" of The Grapes of Wrath (pp. 863-67). I have tried
to avoid repeating Lisca's suggestions except where the organization of my own critical explication has suggested that
certain important matters might be given a different slant.

1. Is Steinbeck's picture "fair" to all parties concerned or
    does he indeed champion the animal nature of man

through his emphasis upon the migrants at the expense
of respectable land-owning citizens whose views may
also merit consideration? Does the novel suggest that
the migrants are truly more "alive" than their oppon-
ents?

2. Is the novel "dated"--that is, do we read it principally
to learn about the dreadful conditions during the 1930s
or does the story have immediate applications to our
own lives and conditions around us?· How may it be
related to the current interest in ecology?

3. Much has been written about Steinbeck's use of Biblical
parallels, yet Steinbeck is often harsh in his criticism
of traditional religious bodies. How can his use of the
Bible be reconciled with the attitudes toward religion
expressed in the book? (Consider especially the conversation on pp. 437-38, as well as Casy's remarks on
page 32.)

4. Can you determine anything about Steinbeck's "politics"
from reading the book? Is he arguing for some specifically partisan point of view? Is he advocating certain
specific reforms through legislation? If not, what point
of view is he adopting toward his readers? Consider
Chapters 21 and 25 especially carefully.

5. What do you think of Casy's viewpoint that "There ain't
no sin and there ain't no virtue. There's just stuff
people do. " Would you feel comfortable explaining his
views to your grandmother, or boy friend, or minister?
In another of Steinbeck's novels, In Dubious Battle, a
character observes, when asked if he doesn't think that
the cause of the strikers is good, "I don't want to put
on the blinders of 'good' and 'bad' and limit my vision.
If I used the term 'good' on a thing I'd lose my license
to inspect it, because there might be bad in it. " What
are the problems about using words like "sin" and
"virtue"?

6. Steinbeck observes that there is a crime which "goes
beyond denunciation" (p. 477) in destroying food while
people are starving. If there is a crime, whose business is it to punish the criminals and to correct the
conditions? What does Steinbeck think of the success
of our traditional governmental and philanthropic institutions in dealing with such crime?

7. In John Steinbeck (New York, Twayne Publishers, 1961),
I describe the process through which the Joads pass
during the narrative as "the education of the heart. "
What does actually happen to the Joads? Although the
family has not achieved security or realized its dreams

at the end of the novel, has it changed as a result of
its experiences?

8. Why do certain members drop out of the party during
the narrative--Grampa, Granma, Noah, Connie, Tom?
What do you think will become of the surviving members of the family? Who is responsible for their future? Is it the business of novelists to tell us "what
came afterwards" as they often did in the nineteenth
century?

9. Stripped down to a basic pattern of movement against
obstacles, where else may we observe the history of
the Joads paralleled, besides in the travels of a land
turtle and the exodus of the Israelites from Egypt?
Would "consciousness" actually be possible if we were
not involved in some such process? A reading of
Steinbeck's short story, "The Leader of the People,"
may help you think about this question. Also if you
have not read Charles A. Reich's The Greening of
America, you may wish to become acquainted with his
characterizations of Consciousnesses One, Two, and
Three and work out their applications to The Grapes
of Wrath.

10. In J. D. Salinger's short story, "Teddy," the title
character--a young boy--tells of watching his sister
drinking milk. "All of a sudden I saw she was God
and the milk was God," he says. "I mean all she was
doing was pouring God into God, if you know what I
mean." How do Teddy's views relate to Casy's in
The Grapes of Wrath? Do you see what he means?
Does it help in an understanding of a "fifth layer" of
meaning in literature that I have talked about earlier?

B. Topics for Research Papers

1. What was the response of your community or region
to the novel and film versions of The Grapes of Wrath
when they appeared in 1939 and 1940? Consult the
local files of old newspapers at local newspaper offices
or libraries. Use this project to become familiar with
other aspects of the life of your community at the time
the novel and film appeared.

2. Has the condition of migrant farm workers improved
substantially since The Grapes of Wrath was published?
Learn to use indices like The Readers' Guide to Periodical Literature to find out about efforts like that of
Cesar Chavez to organize the grape and lettuce pickers

in California.

3. Study the many articles that have been written about
    Biblical parallels to The Grapes of Wrath to determine
    whether you think they are soundly and convincingly
    argued. Have other parallels been overlooked? Evalu-
    ate the critics' reasons for dwelling on these parallels.

4. Look up the newspaper and magazine features that Stein-
    beck wrote about the migrants and determine what ma-
    terial from these he did and did not incorporate into the
    novel. Then, from the differences between Steinbeck's
    handling of the subject in the two media, develop some
    hypotheses about the differences between journalism and
    fiction-writing.

5. What have writers other than literary critics had to say
    about The Grapes of Wrath? Look for references to it
    in the writings of historians, sociologists, economists,
    theologians, labor leaders, minority spokesmen, and
    others. This material may be difficult to locate, since
    it may not be separately indexed, but look for discus-
    sions of American fiction and conditions during the 1930s
    by such writers and see if they mention The Grapes of
    Wrath.

6. Did the novel have any direct influence in bringing about
    improvements in the conditions it describes? How was
    the novel received by politicians outside Oklahoma and
    California?

7. The Grapes of Wrath poses large questions about the
    general relationship between literature, politics, and
    religion. Study the literary criticisms of the work to
    see what basic assumptions about these relationships
    may underlie the criticism. See if you can classify the
    way some of the critics respond to the novel on the
    basis of the point of view from which they approach lit-
    erature. Books on the various forms of literary criti-
    cism like Austin Warren and René Wellek's Theory of
    Literature may be helpful.

8. Warwick Wadlington in "Pathos and Dreiser" (Southern
    Review, 7:411-29, 1971), a discussion of another promi-
    nent American novelist, explains the difference between
    "pathos" and "tragedy"--"In tragedy, our attention is
    focused upon a man who suffers disjunction within him-
    self; in pathos, more upon a man who suffers disjunc-
    tion with his world. " Find out whether other critics
    agree with this distinction; then apply your findings to
    a consideration of whether the story of the Joads should
    be called "tragic" or "pathetic. "

9. Isolate instances of those places in the "inter-calary"

chapters in which Steinbeck appears to be speaking for himself. Then compare what he says with the speeches he creates for some of the characters, like Tom and Casy, to determine the extent to which the fictional characters repeat the author's view or differ from it.

10. Acquire information about "Transcendental Meditation" as practiced by the Maharishi Mahesh Yogi and other forms of meditation, seeking especially information about possible relationships between literature and the practice of meditation. Then discuss the ways in which literature may prove an aid to meditation or in which meditation may be useful to an understanding of literature.

C. Selected Bibliography

Almost all of the useful criticism of The Grapes of Wrath is collected in three volumes described in the opening pages of this article:

Donohue, Agnes McNeill (ed.), A Casebook on "The Grapes of Wrath," New York: Crowell, 1968.

French, Warren (ed.), A Companion to "The Grapes of Wrath," New York: Viking Press, 1963. (Contains Steinbeck's Their Blood Is Strong.)

Lisca, Peter (ed.), John Steinbeck, "The Grapes of Wrath": Text and Criticism. (The Viking Critical Library) New York: Viking Press, 1972.

Chapter 5

STEINBECK'S IN DUBIOUS BATTLE (1936)

by Betty L. Perez

I. BACKGROUND

When Tortilla Flat appeared in 1935, Steinbeck had
already completed his next novel, In Dubious Battle, which
would be published in 1936. The latter work made a sharp
break with the appealing humorist tradition of Tortilla Flat
and other earlier works which had made Steinbeck a popular
American author. In Dubious Battle dealt not with mystical
romance or exotic people in faraway places, but with pressing contemporary problems in American life. Together with
Of Mice and Men (1937) and The Grapes of Wrath (1939)
which followed it, In Dubious Battle indicated Steinbeck's
bitter awareness of the social conflicts and individual trage-
dies and disappointments born of the turmoil and deprivation
of the Depression years. Devoid of the frivolity and lighthearted warmth of Tortilla Flat, In Dubious Battle seemed
a raw, harsh work, a book so violent that Steinbeck himself
called it "a brutal book. "

Not surprisingly, critical reaction to a novel which
explored the biased motivations, ruthless methods, and savage battles behind the newspaper headlines of strikes and
labor disputes was not entirely laudatory. Some readers
and reviewers judged In Dubious Battle a propaganda piece
and condemned or admired it for its ideological content
alone. Even Steinbeck's publishers at Covici-Friede had
reservations about the political nature of the material. [1]
Steinbeck, however, emphatically declared that he had written a novel and "not a tract" or "a treatise on social reform. "[2] Although he felt that In Dubious Battle should be
accepted as "just a story, " Steinbeck predicted that the book
would take a critical panning, with both sides jumping on it.
"The Communists will hate it, " he wrote, "and the other

47

side will too. "[3] As a novelist, however, Steinbeck was less
interested in political theory or ideological dogma than he
was in human behavior.   Thus, even though In Dubious Battle attempted to articulate the beliefs, feelings, desires, and
fears of striking men and their radical leaders, Steinbeck
tried to write the work without looking through "the narrow
glass of political or economic preconception. "[4]

Critics of more recent times, perhaps benefiting from
the objective distancing of the intervening years, have
viewed the novel more dispassionately. "Steinbeck wrote
neither to inspire, nor to provoke, nor to condemn, " wrote
one, "but to understand and portray honestly an aspect of
life he found fascinating and perhaps bewildering. "[5] Another
called it "a masterpiece of realistic and naturalistic fiction:
realistic in its completely objective narrative and accurately
reported dialogue, and naturalistic in its content. "[6]

A second type of critical reaction to In Dubious Battle
focused on the "brutality" of the work. The nature of the
strike situation and the exacting detail of Steinbeck's writing
almost guaranteed an abundance of "objectionable" material--
bloody acts of violence, realistically rough language, and
sharp pictures of ignorance, hostility, deprivation, cruelty,
and greed. Some found a surfeit of such material. "It
seems, " wrote Maxwell Geismar of In Dubious Battle in his
Writers in Crisis, "that violence in itself has an inherent
fascination for Steinbeck, that its appeal lies merely in the
glitter of the knife, the tearing of the flesh, the hangings,
shootings, mutilations with which his work is filled; and this
violence is used for effect more often than edification. "[7]
Citing a "rather debonaire delight in bloodshed, " Geismar
maintained that "the struggle for a better life simply affords
Steinbeck a better chance for his own familiar violence. "[8]

On the other hand, W. M. Frohock in his study entitled The Novel of Violence in America also notes that
"there is violence to spare in In Dubious Battle, " but he asserts that a strike is acceptable material for literature because "it involves suffering and violence. " As a source of
violence and suffering, however, the strike situation contains
at least two built-in pitfalls, namely that "the individual
participant sees very little of what is going on, so that
panoramic treatments are likely to ring false, " and that
"where there is so much violence the writer may litter his
stage with too many insignificant corpses, like the less successful Elizabethans. " "To exploit the natural tensions of a

strike, " warns Frohock, "without losing the reader in details or numbing him with brutality takes doing. " In In
Dubious Battle, however, states Frohock succinctly, Steinbeck "brings it off. "9

Even the critics who censured the violence in In Dubious Battle on aesthetic grounds could not really fault the
realism of the novel. Steinbeck apparently felt the credibility of his descriptions was so great as to necessitate a
statement that the persons and places in In Dubious Battle
are fictitious. That he did not need to exaggerate the violence of actual contemporary conflicts is pointed up by the
following description of a California strike in the Salinas
Valley which occurred the same year in which Steinbeck's
novel was published.

In 1936 a strike by lettuce packing shed workers
was crushed at a cost of around a quarter of a
million dollars. Civil liberties, local government,
and normal judicial processes were all suspended
during the strike and Salinas was governed by a
general staff directed by the Associated Farmers
and the big lettuce growers and shippers. The
local police were bossed by a reserve army officer
imported for the job and at the height of the
strike all male residents between 18 and 45 were
mobilized under penalty of arrest, were deputized
and armed. Beatings, tear gas attacks, wholesale
arrests, threats to lynch San Francisco newspapermen if they didn't leave town, and machine guns
and barbed wire all figured in the month-long
struggle which finally broke the strike and destroyed the union. 10

In Dubious Battle is, of course, built around the action of a similarly bitter confrontation, and the events of
the strike structure the narrative in the same manner as
the Joads' journey in The Grapes of Wrath provides the
framework for that later work. However, the book is more
than a story of the conflict between a certain group of apple
pickers striking for a reasonable wage and an organization
of orchard owners who adamantly refuse their demands.
Nor can it be characterized as "a conflict between the communist organizer who is dominated by an idea so completely
that he has lost his sense of the value of the individual and
the simple, pathetic goodness of the fruit pickers who he
'organizes' into strikes, starvation, bloodshed, and defeat. "11

The strike situation in In Dubious Battle, while real
enough in itself, is also emblematic of man's hopes for a
better life and illustrative of his need for cooperative effort
and unity with his fellow man.   Despite the fact that blood
is shed, deceptive methods are used, and the book ends in-
conclusively, the total picture is not as bleak as some
critics have painted.   Geismar, for example, has deplored
not only the violence but the sensibilities of those involved.
"Human life is ... wasted for the sake of dogma, and the
strike--portrayed on the surface of 'In Dubious Battle' as so
glamorous--emerges indeed as horrible.   Lie fights lie,
radical power struggles against capitalist power, blood is
used by the landowners to intimidate, and blood is used by
the strike leaders to stimulate.   The average man ... caught
between these two extremes, suffers and makes his fellows
suffer for no purpose of his own....   The average humanity
of 'In Dubious Battle' is irresolute, vain, calculating in the
individual case, and with his brothers forming the arrogant,
stupid, and cruel mob."[12]

In a more humanistic approach to the novel, Julian
N. Hartt concentrates not on the ostensible dogma of power
politics but the more general theme of man's search for ful-
fillment--a search which may take religious, political, intellectual, financial, or any number of other courses.
Deeming the novel "a striking expression of the optimistic-
realistic eschatological image," Hartt describes the motivat-
ing vision as he sees it: "Steinbeck's novel is more than
a story of social ferment.   It deals seriously with eschatological man.   Eschatological man so imaged is a creature
with a terrible duality of motivations: violent resentment of
the social forces which have cheated him out of his rights;
and passionate attachment to a splendid vision of an age to
come when the furious conflict generated by injustice will
have been resolved forever into the peace of a classless
community."[13]

II.   PLOT SYNOPSIS

Before examining some of the more literary aspects
of this provocative novel which has elicited such a range of
response, it might be helpful to review the basic movement
of the plot.   Although the strike itself, or "group-man" who
is created from the workers' unification, might be regarded
as the true protagonist of the novel, the narrative development is more closely connected to the character of Jim

Nolan, beginning with his "birth" into the Party and ending
with his sacrificial death. Moreover, the reader's point of
view remains with Jim throughout the novel, and although he
does not actually see things through Jim's eyes, he sees
what Jim sees, learns as Jim does, hears, feels, and fears
with Jim and is never supplied with greater insight or additional information by the author.

As the novel opens (like the drawing of a curtain on
a set stage), Jim rises from the chair in which he has been
quietly sitting for a long time, washes up, combs his hair,
packs his meager belongings in a paper bag, and informs
his landlady that he will not be returning to his rented room
even though he is paid up for the next week. A serious,
disenchanted young man without a family and recently released from jail, he is cut off from his previous life and,
indeed, seems almost at the end of life. He remarks several times within the first few pages of the novel that he
feels dead. Keeping an appointment with a radical recruiter,
he describes his past life and states his reasons for wanting
to join "the Party. " "I feel dead, " he repeats. "I thought
I might get alive again. "[14]

The coming-alive of Jim provides a structuring device
for the rest of the action. Shortly after joining the Party,
he is sent with Mac, a seasoned, experienced, hardened
agitator, to organize a strike among apple pickers in a
near-by valley. As Mac outlines the situation, Jim is so
excited that he is unable to eat his supper.

> Here's the layout. Torgas is a little valley, and
> it's mostly apple orchards. Most of it's owned by
> a few men. Of course there's some little places,
> but there's not very many of them. Now when the
> apples are ripe the crop tramps come in and pick
> them. And from there they go on over the ridge
> and south, and pick the cotton. If we can start
> the fun in the apples, maybe it will just naturally
> spread over into the cotton. Now these few guys
> that own most of the Torgas Valley waited until
> most of the crop tramps were already there.
> They spent most of their money getting there, of
> course. They always do. And then the owners
> announced their price cut. Suppose the tramps
> are mad? What can they do? They've got to
> work picking apples to get out even. (IDB, 21)

Mac and Jim ride the rails to Torgas Valley and on the way Mac begins tutoring Jim for his new role as a Party organizer by advising him to take advantage of every opportunity to make contact with workers and to make a conscious effort to gain their goodwill. Take up smoking, Mac suggests, because "it's a nice social habit." Revealing his almost obsessive concern with practical Party methods, Mac explains that even if Jim doesn't enjoy it personally, "it's a good thing to do in our work." "I don't know any quicker way to soften a stranger down than to offer him a smoke, or even ask him for one. And lots of guys feel insulted if they offer you a cigarette and you don't take it" (IDB, 29).

Arriving at a make-shift campsite where some "crop tramps" have gathered, Mac demonstrates the advantage of seizing the moment by falsely claiming medical experience and delivering a baby. He performs this act not because it is desirable as a humane gesture, but because the young woman in labor is the daughter-in-law of the natural, if unofficial, leader of the group--a man whom Mac hopes to use to gather the workers together--and because the focal point of illness, death, or birth is a convenient tool in getting men to work together. Defining their aims and justifying the method, Mac declares to Jim:

> We've got to use whatever material comes to us. That was a lucky break. We simply had to take it. 'Course it was nice to help the girl, but hell, even if it killed her--we've got to use anything... With one night's work we've got the confidence of the men and the confidence of London. And more than that, we made the men work for themselves, in their own defense as a group. That's what we're out here for anyway, to teach them to fight in a bunch. Raising wages isn't all we're after. (IDB, 42)

Finding that the apple pickers are sufficiently angered at the wage reduction to sustain an initial attempt at striking, Mac (with Jim ever at his heels) moves swiftly and expertly to set up supporting machinery. He enlists the aid of Al Anderson, a generous and soft-hearted diner owner whose father lends the strikers a few acres of private property for camping. He sends for Dick, the "bedroom radical," a handsome, boyish Party worker whose specialty is collecting contributions of money and staples from Party

sympathizers. Dr. Burton, a dedicated volunteer but not a
Party member, also arrives to set up an organized, sani-
tary camp area which will satisfy the county health require-
ments.

Realizing that the strike must be fought without guns,
Mac concentrates on group solidarity and organizes his human "equipment." The minor characters are vividly and
concisely portrayed in their diversity of personalities: Lon-
don--the big, personable, natural leader with a volatile
temper and fists to match his anger; Dakin--cool, perceptive, less manipulatable, a fairly successful man who treas-
ures his possessions; Burke--the third group leader, a
suspicious, dangerous man not previously known by London
and Dakin, who had long been acquainted. Although he
hand-picks the leaders, Mac insists that they be "elected, "
and teaches London that the men must vote on everything
they do, but shows him how to sway them to vote as he
thinks best.

It quickly develops that the Torgas Valley Growers'
Association is not without organization of its own, having
perhaps anticipated trouble as a result of the wage reduction. Mac appraises the situation: "It's not so hard to do
when a few men control everything, land, courts, banks.
They can cut off loans, and they can railroad a man to jail,
and they can always bribe plenty" (IDB, 121). The strikers
soon learn the extent of the power massed against them
when they are harassed by officials, assaulted and killed by
vigilantes, maligned in newspaper editorials, denied medical
care by the county, and cut off from the aid of their sup-
porters and sympathizers.

Ironically, it is the owners or their friends who give
the strike the impetus without which it might have quickly
died. When a sniper's bullet kills Joy, a friend of Mac and
Jim, as he attempts to win over a train-load of scabs
brought in by the growers to replace the striking pickers,
Mac has a bloody symbol, a rallying cause, which he char-
acteristically exploits for every spark of indignant hostility
it will bring. The chain of violence is thus begun and, like
a string of firecrackers, continues to explode throughout the
novel with equal brutality and senseless mayhem on both
sides.

Amidst the skirmishes and retreats, the gains and
losses, Mac and Jim remain strangely detached from the

hurts and angers of the men. They may be moved by the
excitement of organizing a huge "group animal" which seems
to come alive with a momentum and power--almost a life--
of its own, but they so divorce themselves from natural human emotion that they can accept without pity the death of
members of their group as calculated losses and the destruction of Anderson's barn and crop as an insignificant by-
product of an essentially praise-worthy venture.   "Don't you
go liking people, Jim," Mac warns.   "We can't waste time
liking people" (IDB, 82).   People may, however, be used
in any way that serves the interest of the Party.   Methodi-
cally, almost surgically, Mac beats up a high school boy as
a warning to his classmates to stay away from the strikers'
camp.

> 'I want a billboard,' said Mac, 'not a corpse. All
> right kid, I guess you're for it.' The boy tried
> to retreat. He bent down, trying to cower. Mac
> took him firmly by the shoulder. His right fist
> worked in quick, short hammer blows, one after
> another. The nose cracked flat, the other eye
> closed, and the dark bruises formed on the
> cheeks. The boy jerked about wildly to escape
> the short, precise strokes. (IDB, 198)

Likewise, at the end of the novel after Jim has been
shotgunned to death in a vigilante ambush, Mac can prop the
body on the stage of the strikers' camp so that the light
purposely falls on the bloody, faceless head. When the new
symbol is visible to all and a small crowd has begun to
gather, Mac begins his call-to-arms again and Steinbeck's
story ceases, not with an end--for there is no end in such
a struggle--but with a continuation or, perhaps, a new beginning.

III.   CRITICAL EXPLICATION

The book, especially the ending, still is exciting and
moving today.   There remains perhaps an overwhelming
temptation to react to In Dubious Battle on emotional or
political grounds.   Although the exploited group may have
changed its name, the relevancy of a novel about individually
weak men uniting to oppose a strong, corporate monster is
still great.   In this age of movements and demonstrations,
modern counterparts could easily be chosen from the evening
news: the Black Panthers, United Farm Workers of

America (Cesar Chavez), Vietnam Veterans Against the War, National Organization of Women, Gay Liberation, Students for a Democratic Society and many others. And perhaps today more so than in the thirties, In Dubious Battle would be admired for its plain rough language and praised for its "radical" philosophy and aggressive violence.

Although the proclivity of today's college students for engaging in student mobilizations and the almost universal passion for "causes" might indicate some immediate rapport with the novel situation, one should avoid regarding In Dubious Battle as essentially a political statement. Frohock accurately appraised such treatment and identified the pitfalls when he stated that "this book has been misjudged by the critics, or rather has gone unjudged, because it involved so many pressing political and social problems that it was generally read as a radical tract rather than as a novel."[15]

In reading In Dubious Battle as a novel, many of the objections of squeamish critics are easily answered. The dismaying violence, for example, is found to be not only intrinsically necessary, but even artistically handled. "There is violence to spare in this book," admits Frohock in his chapter entitled "John Steinbeck: The Utility of Wrath," but he qualifies, "If such a spectacle is tolerable to the reader it is because there is a sort of orderliness in all the violence in the book. The development of the strike forms the frame of In Dubious Battle ... and the development of the strike requires violence.... The orderliness of the violence comes from its absolute double necessity--double in that it is necessary both to the strike and to the growth of Jim's soul."[16]

In like manner, the language of the strikers is extremely important since through it alone does the reader gain his information. "In no other novel," says Joseph Fontenrose, has Steinbeck "so completely avoided subjective statement: in this book we learn everything from actions and conversations."[17] Steinbeck called the book "brutal because there's no author's moral point of view." As Peter Lisca notes, what one has instead is a very objective prose style which relies heavily on dialogue. Steinbeck felt that this was an ideal way of giving a broad perspective without endorsing any particular view: "It is done mostly in dialogue thus permitting many varying opinions but keeping out any author's opinion...."[18] The result is often something

like a play in which the reader does not have access to the
characters' minds, but perceives them "only as they speak
or execute physical movements. "19 This deliberately restricted style may cause the reader to feel himself present
at the scene, knowing no more than the other men standing
around.

　　　Steinbeck's descriptions create a "You Are There"
feeling with his heavy reliance on what a spectator would
see, hear, smell, feel and so on, rather than on authorial
pronouncements. In one early scene, for example, Mac
and Jim join a group of men--all strangers to the two new-
comers--who are subsequently identified by Steinbeck only
by their physical appearances or actions:

> They moved toward the fire, where a ring of
> men sat clasping their knees. 'Can a guy join
> this club?' Mac asked, 'Or does he got to be
> elected?'
> 　The faces of the men were turned up at him,
> unshaven faces with eyes in which the firelight
> glowed. One of the men moved sideways to make
> room. 'Ground's free, mister.'
> 　Mac chuckled. 'Not where I come from.'
> 　A lean, lighted face across the fire spoke.
> 'You come to a good place, fella. Everything's
> free here, food, liquor, automobiles, houses.
> Just move in and set down to a turkey dinner.'
> 　Mac squatted and motioned Jim to sit beside
> him. He pulled out his sack of tobacco and made
> a careful, excellent cigarette; then, as an after-
> thought, 'Would any of you capitalists like a
> smoke?'
> 　Several hands thrust out. The bag went from
> man to man. 'Just get in?' the lean face asked.
> 　'Just. Figure to pick a few apples and retire
> on my income.'
> 　Lean-face burst out angrily. 'Know what
> they're payin', fella? Fifteen cents, fifteen lousy
> cents!' (IDB, 36)

In a later scene, characters identified only by voice or appearance speak as in a play:

> Lantern-jaw: 'No, by God. London can take
> care of himself. London's got a head on him.'
> White-forehead: 'If London has a head on him,

why in hell are we sitting around here?   This
strike's screwy.   Somebody's making money out
of it.   When it gets tough somebody'll sell out
and leave the rest of us to take it on the chin.
(IDB, 160)

In its general objective approach, the novel may be
seen as a demonstration of a philosophical concept which is
discussed within the novel and in other of Steinbeck's works.
As an exercise in "non-teleological thinking, " In Dubious
Battle is an attempt at viewing objectively the total picture
of a given reality without injecting personal bias, assigning
value, or imposing blame.   This important and innovative
concept derives from the philosophical speculations of Steinbeck's close friend, Edward F. Ricketts (a marine biologist
whose essay entitled "Non-Teleological Thinking" was in-
corporated into the book, Sea of Cortez, which he co-au-
thored with Steinbeck).   The aims of open-minded knowledge
are introduced early in In Dubious Battle when Jim characterizes a man who encouraged him to supplement his
rudimentary schooling by extensive reading.   "He was a
crank, he said.   He said he wanted to know things without
believing them" (IDB, 6).

The non-teleological approach to thinking is personi-
fied in the novel by Dr. Burton, a serious, thoughtful young
man who is dedicated not to a cause, but to a receptivity.
He wants to know and see and experience as much as he
possibly can.   "I want to see the whole picture--as nearly
as I can, " he says.   "I don't want to put on the blinders of
'good' and 'bad, ' and limit my vision.   If I used the term
'good' on a thing I'd lose my license to inspect it, because
there might be bad in it.   Don't you see?   I want to be able
to look at the whole thing" (IDB, 103).

In his authorial role, Steinbeck carefully eschews the
blinders of "good" and "bad, " and even though the reader's
sympathy is probably with the mistreated strikers and their
radical leaders, he carefully avoids idealizing or romanticiz-
ing his picture of them and their methods.   The Party's
modus operandi is blatantly opportunistic, the "crop tramps"
are cowardly and cruel, uncooperative and untrustworthy.
Their violence is not quite as bloody as that of the "other
side, " but only because they have no weapons but their
hands.   In burning, kicking, stomping, biting, and so on,
however, they are unsurpassed.

Looking at the whole picture of the strike from a relatively neutral point of view and at a certain distance from emotional involvement, Steinbeck records some strange perceptions about group action. The idea of "group-man," the observation that striking men are different from the individual men who make up the group, is another concept which suggests the author's debt to Ricketts. Steinbeck was, however, an astute amateur biologist and his descriptions of colonial marine animals in Sea of Cortez offer biological comparisons for the human phenomenon discussed in the novel. The angry mob of strikers no longer acts like a body of men collected together, but as "one big animal"-- an animal which can be called into existence whenever emotion, hunger, anger, or hope unite men. Old Dan remarks of the cumulative effect of years of persecution: "It's like the whole bunch, millions and millions was one man, and he's been beat and starved, and he's gettin' that sick feelin' in his guts" (IDB, 48).

It is Doc, however, with his interest in non-teleological thinking, who focuses attention on the appearance of "group-man" in the Torgas Valley and who offers an analytic evaluation of its nature and power. "I want to watch these group-men," he says, "for they seem to me to be a new individual, not at all like single men. A man in a group isn't himself at all, he's a cell in an organism that isn't like him any more than the cells in your body are like you. I want to watch the group, and see what it's like.... It might be worth while to know more about group-man, to know his nature, his ends, his desires. They are not the same as ours" (IDB, 104, 105).

Mac is, in his own less scientific way, aware that group-man is different. As he tells Jim, "It's damn funny about a bunch of men, how they act. You can't tell. I always thought if a guy watched close enough he might get to know what they're goin' to do. They get steamed up, an' then, all of a sudden, they're scared as hell" (IDB, 195). London, another leader of men, has had similar experiences. "Take one guy that you know ever'thing about him, an' take ten more the same, an' you can't tell what in hell they'll do" (IDB, 221).

From long experience, Mac does know a few things about the typical behavior of group-man, although he can not predict with certainty what they will do. "If I could tell in advance what a bunch of guys'd do, I'd be president.

Some things I do know, though. A smell of blood seems to
steam 'em up. Let'em kill somethin', even a cat, an'
they'll want to go right on killin'. If there's a fight, an'
our guys get first blood, they'll put up a hell of a battle.
But if we lose a man first, I wouldn't be surprised to see
them hit for the trees" (IDB, 221).

    In Dubious Battle documents the birth and growth of
"group-man"; it examines his characteristics and motivations, his desires and fears. From this panoramic image,
the reader senses the magnitude and power of the strike.
Yet despite his interest in group-man, Steinbeck realized
the importance of individuals. Man, he has said, is "a
double thing--a group animal and at the same time an individual."20 Thus, In Dubious Battle is also the story of
Jim's birth into the Party, of his growth in knowledge and
power, and finally of his death. Jim's indoctrination in
Party dogma, his realization that his participation in the
strike extends beyond the present reality and links him to
all humanity and all time, and his belief that no sacrifice
would be too great if it helped achieve a better life for
more men lead him from the depths of depression and lack
of self-esteem to a pinnacle of self-realization, dedication,
and almost religious transfiguration. In achieving this degree of ecstatic fulfillment, however, Jim has to harden his
naturally tender feeling for man in particular. After drawing Mac's reprimand about "liking people" too much, Jim
quickly progresses to the point that he can counteract Mac's
growing disgust with the induced violence associated with the
strike. After Mac beats the high school boy, Jim reassures
him. 'It wasn't a scared kid, it was a danger to the
cause. It had to be done, and you did it right. No hate,
no feeling, just a job. Don't worry.... It's just a little
part of the whole thing. Sympathy is as bad as fear. That
was like a doctor's work. It was an operation, that's all"
(IDB, 199). Jim's transition is complete and made even
more extreme by the crossing back of Mac to an attitude of
greater compassion.

    Besides the direct action of the novel and the more
obvious forms of plot and character development, there are
several interesting threads of imagery which should be
noted. The most emphatically stated of these interwoven
and sometimes merging themes is the parallelism of In Dubious Battle and Paradise Lost. Not only does the title
come from the poem, but an epigraph repeats lines 101-109
of Book I which supply the context of the lifted phrase.

Joseph Fontenrose, in his chapter on In Dubious Battle, has
expertly and perceptively detailed much of the specific correspondence between the book and its epic counterpart. He
warns against looking for too great an identity of detail and
points out that one should not expect Steinbeck to "adhere to
the mythical sequence of events."[21]

The main events are, of course, plainly similar: a
strong rebel leader leads other rebels and outcasts in an
insurrection against an omnipotent power. He gathers his
subordinates, groups his army, and proceeds with pitched
and bloody battle. And the battle of the strikers for higher
wages is just as hopeless as that of Satan and his angels
against the ranks of Heaven. Not only is the sympathy for
Satan mirrored in the reader's concern for Jim and Mac,
but many of the characters of Paradise Lost have counterparts in In Dubious Battle. According to Fontenrose:

> Satan's role is obviously played by the Party as a
> collective person, although Jim or Mac or another
> may represent the Party in its Satanic role. In
> contemporary folklore the Devil's color is red.
> The Party secretary who received Jim's applica-
> tion for Party membership is Harry Nilson--the
> Old Harry is a popular name for the Devil.
> Probably the detail of Mac's exhaling steam from
> his mouth as he ate hot stew is meant to illustrate
> the identity of the Party and Satan. Particular
> identifications suggest themselves: London is
> Beelzebub as Satan's right-hand man; Dick, the
> 'bedroom radical,' who employed the social graces
> and masculine charm for the cause, is Belial;
> Sam, direct actionist, is Moloch calling for open
> war; and Burke, dissenter and stool pigeon in the
> strikers' camp, is Abdiel. ... And the camp has‾
> a humble Pandaemonium in the crude wooden plat-
> form from which the strike leaders addressed the
> strikers' assemblies.[22]

The parallelism with Paradise Lost does, of course,
indicate some use of Christian symbolism in In Dubious
Battle, but the detailing of Christian themes extends beyond
those suggested by Paradise Lost. Sometimes it is only a
very minor detail, such as setting the strike in a lush valley
and having the crop to be picked as apples rather than, for
example, cotton. With Biblical stories in mind, it is not
difficult to see Jim as a sacrificial Christ figure who comes

to save the outcasts and does, in fact, give his life. The
novel begins with his rebirth (he gives as his reason for
joining the Party, "I thought I might get alive again. "), and
contains several striking details which link him to Christ.
Doc, seeing him with Lisa and the child, speaks of "the
holy family"; roosters crow at the end of Chapter 13 and
Jim, suffering from his wound, asks for water. In the
final chapter, he is so luminous that his ecstacy is obvious.
"His face was transfigured. A furious light of energy seem
to shine from it" (IDB, 249). And finally, after Jim's
death, Mac utilizes the he-died-for-you theme: "This guy
didn't want nothing for himself--" (IDB, 250).

There is also a general relationship created between
the strikers' feelings and religious fervor and proselytizing.
Doc accuses Jim of being washed in the blood of the Lamb,
and Mac employs the old camp-meeting audience response
participation in his pep-talks. Like the protagonists in the
short story "The Raid, " with whom Mac and Jim share
much in common, neither will admit any association with
religious feeling, seeming not to see that the similarity is
in emotional response rather than in any acceptance of doctrine.

Warren French sees another mythical correspondence
in the book's suggestion of Arthurian legendry. He cites a
"remarkable psychological similarity between Jim Nolan, the
central character of the novel, and one of the principal
knights of the Round Table, Perceval or Parsifal as he is
best known.... " Jim is, says French, "a modern exemplar
of the chivalric ideals of adventurousness (he longs for action and is finally killed by his impetuousness), selflessness,
and chastity. "[23] Although French elaborates his case in
much detail, it must be remembered that some of the char-
acteristics--indeed the very ones which French finds most
striking--fit just as well into the imagery of a Christ
theme.

All of the preceding themes are related to the references to birth and death which permeate the novel. Jim is
born again into the Party; the strike and then group-man
are born of the pickers' anger; violence is born of violence;
and after birth comes death. Mac is cast in the role of
midwife, both to Jim as a productive Party organizer and
to the striker as a whole. He even refers to the strike as
a "baby" and calls the men he must use "babies. "

The act of delivering Lisa's child on his first night in the Torgas Valley is a symbol which radiates out into many aspects of the novel. Not only is the birth itself symbolic of events to come, but on a small scale, group-man is born that night in the cooperative effort of the men who boil water and collect and sterilize cloths to be used in the birth. The unification of the men, Mac plainly tells Jim, is their most important and crucial job. "Every man who gave part of his clothes felt that the work was his own. They all feel responsible for that baby. It's theirs, be-cause something from them went to it. To give back the cloth would cut them out. There's no better way to make men part of a movement than to have them give something to it" (IDB, 43).

There are other threads of imagery which could be detailed also. Animal imagery, for example, ever replete in Steinbeck's novels, is used with great effectiveness to give a backdrop of raw, primitive fury to the anger of the men and a resonance to the violence which is more terrify-ing than simple mechanical destruction. Group-man is never anything but an animal; he does not think, only feel and act, and even then, most of his acts are violent ones.

Animal imagery also figures in character delineation. Jim is trained by Mac just as a new field dog is taught, by allowing him to run with the experienced hunters. Ander-son, who is closely linked with his pointers in feeling, is several times described as moving his hands like puppies playing as he talks to Mac. Dakin becomes a mad dog when his truck is wrecked.

In fact, the more thoroughly one studies In Dubious Battle, the more impressed one will be with Steinbeck's skillful handling of the literary aspects of his story. In Dubious Battle makes a powerful, moving, and accurate documentary statement, but as a literary accomplishment it must be ranked with the best of Steinbeck's writing.

Notes

1. Peter Lisca, The Wide World of John Steinbeck (New Brunswick, New Jersey: Rutgers University Press, 1958), pp. 110-14.

2. Letter from Steinbeck to his agents at McIntosh & Otis,

February 14, 1936. Letter from Steinbeck to Lewis
Gannett, February 3, 1936. Both as quoted by
Peter Lisca, The Wide World of John Steinbeck,
p. 115.

3. Letter from Steinbeck to Ben Abramson, early spring,
1936. As quoted by Lisca, p. 114.

4. Harry Thornton Moore, The Novels of John Steinbeck:
A First Study (Chicago: Normandie House, 1939),
p. 41.

5. F. W. Watt, John Steinbeck (New York: Grove Press,
1962), p. 52.

6. Joseph Fontenrose, John Steinbeck: An Introduction
and Interpretation (New York: Holt, Rinehart and
Winston, Inc., 1963), pp. 42-43.

7. Maxwell Geismar, Writers in Crisis: The American
Novel Between Two Wars (Boston: Houghton Mifflin, 1942), p. 250.

8. Geismar, p. 261.

9. W. M. Frohock, The Novel of Violence in America
(Dallas: Southern Methodist University Press, 1958),
pp. 134-36.

10. Freeman Champney, "John Steinbeck, Californian," in
Steinbeck and His Critics: A Record of 25 Years,
eds. E. W. Tedlock, Jr. and C. V. Wicker (Albuquerque: University of New Mexico Press, 1956),
p. 136.

11. Charles C. Walcutt, American Literary Naturalism, A
Divided Stream (Minneapolis: University of Minnesota Press, 1956), p. 260.

12. Geismar, p. 262.

13. Julian N. Hartt, The Lost Image of Man (Baton Rouge:
Louisiana State University Press, 1964), pp. 74,
76.

14. Steinbeck, In Dubious Battle (New York, Bantam Books,
1961), p. 6. Hereafter, citations will be made

from this edition in the text.

15.   Frohock, pp. 136-37.

16.   Ibid.

17.   Fontenrose, p. 43.

18.   As quoted by Lisca, p. 117.

19.   Ibid.

20.   Steinbeck, "Some Thoughts on Juvenile Delinquency,"
      Saturday Review, 38 (May 28, 1955), 22.

21.   Fontenrose, p. 46.

22.   Ibid., p. 48.

23.   Warren French, John Steinbeck (New Haven: College
      and University Press, 1961), p. 62.

IV.   APPARATUS FOR RESEARCH PAPERS

A.   Ten Questions for Discussion

1.   There are no major women characters in In Dubious
     Battle; in fact, very few women are even mentioned.
     Speculate on the reason for their absence. How are
     those mentioned treated? (Jim's mother, Mrs. Dakin,
     Lisa, the woman combing her hair, the woman who in-
     vites Jim into her tent, etc.) What use is made of
     Lisa's occasional presence?

2.   Old Dan has been said (Howard Levant, "The Unity of
     In Dubious Battle: Violence and Dehumanization," p.
     28) to represent history. How could this idea be sup-
     ported? Has Old Dan a dramatic use beyond what he
     says?

3.   Objections have been raised that the characters of Mac
     and Jim are "unrealistic." How does Steinbeck give
     them life and realism? Are there ways in which they
     are not believable?

4.   Steinbeck himself declared that in In Dubious Battle
     there is "no author's moral point of view." Is this
     really true? Defend or attack the book's objectivity.

5.   The ending of In Dubious Battle, like the work as a

whole, has elicited a wide range of response and interpretation. Consider, for example, the following opinion:
>   The communist's values receive their <u>dramatic</u>
>   evaluation in the scene where the old communist,
>   Mac, uses the body of his young friend and convert
>   to arouse the spirit of the strikers. He appears to
>   have no feeling for the humanity of his dead friend.
>   Such impersonality, one feels, outrages the sense
>   of brotherhood, the transcendental dream of the
>   dignity of man, without which social reform be-
>   comes meaningless. This idea (penetrating indeed
>   for a radical in 1936!) finds significant expression
>   in the note of inconclusiveness which closes the
>   book. The dramatic form has enabled Steinbeck to
>   present an issue, to elaborate some of its ideologi-
>   cal implications, and to pass in the end a judgment.
>   He demonstrates that the battle is fruitless because
>   neither side is right. The love and brotherhood of
>   the workers must be implemented by something
>   closer to the American grain than communism if it
>   is to come into its own and unify the American
>   Dream of a full life for all. Charles C. Walcutt,
>   <u>American Literary Naturalism: A Divided Stream</u>,
>   pp. 261-262.

Will the novel support this interpretation? Is it the
correct view or is this critic "reading ideas into"
Steinbeck's work?

6. Discuss the reasons that the novel was seen as a "tract"
or political propaganda. Do you agree that Steinbeck
achieved his intention of writing without looking through
"the narrow glass of political or economic preconception"?

7. In <u>The Grapes of Wrath</u>, the owners, law officers,
townspeople, etc. are universally portrayed as insensitive, stingy, hardened, uncaring, and even cruel. Is
this also true in <u>In Dubious Battle</u>? Does Steinbeck's
treatment of Anderson, for example, affect the reader's
feeling toward Mac, Jim, and the strike?

8. Describe "group-man," his characteristics and his behavior. How do Mac and Jim, Doc, and other people
who do not become part of the mindless, howling mob
figure into the concept of group-man. Compare the descriptions of group-man in <u>In Dubious Battle</u> with the
descriptions of school-fish <u>in Sea of Cortez</u>, pp. 240-
241.

9. Why did Mac and Jim risk everything for a strike which
they did not even expect to succeed? Give some

examples of their exploitation of the situation. Are
their methods justified? Is their aim really altruistic?
Can you relate this story to any modern or contemporary events? What is your own sense of right and
wrong in such situations?
10. If In Dubious Battle is indeed a novel rather than a
piece of political dogma, how could you prove it? What
makes it art rather than propaganda? Discuss some
of its literary aspects.

B. Topics for Papers

1.   A Study of Non-Teleological Thinking and Its Function
in In Dubious Battle.
2.   A Background Study of Labor Strikes in the Thirties.
3.   A Comparison of In Dubious Battle and "The Raid. "
4.   A Study of Perspective in In Dubious Battle (including
author's point of view and reader's angle of vision).
5.   Christian Symbolism in In Dubious Battle.
6.   In Dubious Battle as an Example of a Proletarian Novel.
7.   The Theme of Sacrifice and the Imagery of Blood in In
Dubious Battle.
8.   Animal Imagery in In Dubious Battle.
9.   Humanity versus Inhumanity: Images and Action in In
Dubious Battle.
10. How a Novel of the Thirties Has Relevance for the
Seventies.
11. Mac and Jim as Satanic Heroes (A comparison of the
figure of Satan in Paradise Lost and Steinbeck's protagonists. Could be expanded to include others.).
12. The Theme of Birth in In Dubious Battle.
13. Of Ways and Means: A Conservative Look at In Dubious Battle (An exercise in preconception, this approach
would require one to try to see what critics have found
condemnatory in the strike story).
14. A Study of the Character of Doc in In Dubious Battle.
15. An Explication of the Ending of In Dubious Battle.

C. An Annotated Bibliography

Degnan, James P. "In Definite Battle: Steinbeck and California's Land Monopolists, " Steinbeck: The Man and His
Work, eds. Richard Astro and Tetsumaro Hayashi. Corvallis, Oregon: Oregon State University Press, 1971,
pp. 65-74.

A reaffirmation and updating of monopolistic economic practices in California.

Fontenrose, Joseph. John Steinbeck: An Introduction and Interpretation. New York: Holt, Rinehart and Winston, Inc., 1963, pp. 42-53.
An extended study emphasizing mythical implications, particularly in relation to Paradise Lost, and discussing imagery as well as examining the meaning of the work.

French, Warren. John Steinbeck. New Haven, Connecticut: College and University Press, 1961. Twayne's United States Authors Series, pp. 62-71.
Deals with Arthurian analogues, analyzes Steinbeck's intention which may be at odds with his objective stance.

Frohock, W. M. "John Steinbeck: The Utility of Wrath," The Novel of Violence in America. Dallas: Southern Methodist University Press, 1958, pp. 124-43.
An enlightening discussion of In Dubious Battle as the artful use of the device of violence.

Geismar, Maxwell. "John Steinbeck: Of Wrath and Joy," Writers in Crisis: The American Novel Between Two Wars. Boston: Houghton Mifflin, 1942, pp. 260-63.
A treatment of the novel as tract first, art second. Seems to underrate the book because of its philosophical and political contentions.

Hartt, Julian N. The Lost Image of Man. Baton Rouge: Louisiana State University Press, 1964, pp. 74-76.
A humanistic view of the changing images of man in the world in modern literature. Although only a couple of pages are devoted to In Dubious Battle, this discussion is worth consulting for its perception of the blend of optimism and violence which the work displays.

Levant, Howard. "The Unity of In Dubious Battle: Violence and Dehumanization," Modern Fiction Studies, 11 (Spring, 1965), 21-33.
A discussion of interwoven images, themes, and the use of language in In Dubious Battle.

Lisca, Peter. The Wide World of John Steinbeck. New

Brunswick, New Jersey: Rutgers University Press, 1958,
pp. 108-29.
    A thorough study of the book, particularly good in the
    description of language and the background of the
    book's writing and publication.

Moore, Harry Thornton. The Novels of John Steinbeck: A
First Study. Chicago: Normandie House, 1939, pp. 40-
47.
    Describes more than any other account the reaction of
    the Left to the ideological content of the novel.

Morsberger, Robert E. "Steinbeck's Zapata: Rebel versus
Revolutionary," Steinbeck: The Man and His Work, eds.
Richard Astro and Tetsumaro Hayashi. Corvallis, Ore-
gon: Oregon State University Press, 1971, pp. 51-54.
    Relates the religious ecstasy of Jim to the leadership
    of Zapata.

Walcutt, Charles C. American Literary Naturalism, A
Divided Stream. Minneapolis: University of Minnesota
Press, 1956, pp. 260-62.
    A treatment of naturalism in Steinbeck's works as
    divided between "spirit and fact, the demands of the
    heart and the demands of the mind."

Watt, F. W. John Steinbeck. New York: Grove Press,
1962. Evergreen Pilot Books, pp. 51-58.
    Depicts the background of In Dubious Battle, puts in
    contrast to previous work, draws on the poles of
    "escapism" and "committment."

Chapter 6

STEINBECK'S THE LONG VALLEY (1938)

by Robert M. Benton

I. BACKGROUND

In an essay especially written to open Tedlock and
Wicker's Steinbeck and His Critics and titled "John Steinbeck: A Literary Biography," Peter Lisca says that "the
most important link between John Steinbeck and his writing
is that he was born and came to maturity in the Salinas
Valley" (3). The long Salinas Valley was to Steinbeck in a
related sense what Yoknapatawpha County was to William
Faulkner. He grew up in it and knew its people. He returned to it when serious writing became an obsession as
well as a vocation. And he drew from it the memorable
scenes, characters, and images which fill The Long Valley.

Although he had published several important novels,
he had not completed The Grapes of Wrath when The Long
Valley was issued in 1938. All but two of the stories in the
volume had been published earlier, however. North American Review carried the first two parts of The Red Pony in 1933,
"The Raid" and "The Murder" the following year, and "The
White Quail" in 1935. "Flight," earlier rejected by Scribner's and Saturday Evening Post, and "The Leader of the
People," a fourth part in The Red Pony sequence, were the
two stories not previously printed.[1] When The Long Valley
was published, Elmer Davis, writing in The Saturday Review
of Literature for September 24, 1938, admired Steinbeck's
refusal "to be back-seat-driven by success," and he called
the volume "certainly some of the best writing of the past
decade" (11). However, Davis viewed Steinbeck as "the
best prospect in American letters" because of all his previous novels only In Dubious Battle dealt with material Davis
believed to be intrinsically worth reading about (11).

69

The first critic who seriously analyzed the stories in
The Long Valley was Edmund Wilson. In The Boys in the
Back Room (San Francisco, 1941), he noted Steinbeck's preoccupation with biology and "his tendency in his stories to
present life in animal terms" (42). Wilson's statement that
"Mr. Steinbeck does not have the effect, as Lawrence or
Kipling does, of romantically raising the animals to the
stature of human beings, but rather of assimilating the human beings to animals" (43) has been frequently quoted by
critics who either failed to see or were outraged by Steinbeck's biological naturalism.

Esteem for The Long Valley steadily increased, however, perhaps because readers have shared the opinions of
Pascal Covici who made the selections for the 1943 Viking
Portable Library edition of Steinbeck. Covici says, "These
are my choices because they stimulated my imagination,
and stirred emotions and thoughts within me which I was
glad to have" (v). He included all four parts of The Red
Pony as well as five additional stories from The Long Valley.

> Apart from the sheer joy of reading these stories
> and selections, the reader will sense in them a
> fresh creative sensibility, a new approach to our
> roots in our own folklore, and social illumination.
> Even in his political and economic concepts Stein-
> beck is thoroughly Jeffersonian, with high hopes
> for a more realistic and riper humanity.   (vi)

In 1946 The Long Valley was published in France and
occasioned critical reexamination of the short-story form.
Steinbeck was called a master of the art, and French
critics echoed André Gide's earlier assessment:

> But Steinbeck, to my mind, has written nothing
> more perfect, more accomplished, than certain
> of the short stories gathered together under the
> title The Long Valley. They are equal to or sur-
> pass the most moving stories of Chekhov. [2]

As an example of the mastery of the short-story form, The
Long Valley serves as a model to readers and writers alike.
Illustrating variations in form and style, the stories are
masterpieces of objective realism, characterization, and
tone. In addition, effect is often achieved through simplicity
of form, and appropriate uses of understatement are

reinforced by powerful symbolic associations. What weaknesses appear in the stories are usually due to Steinbeck's love for dramatic conclusions. For the most part, however, they demonstrate to the reader the sensitive ear and the perceptive eye of one of the most accomplished prose writers of the twentieth century.

II. PLOT SYNOPSIS AND EXPLICATION

The first story in The Long Valley, "The Chrysanthemums," dramatizes a woman's futile attempts to compensate for a disappointing marriage. Elisa Allen loves her husband, but Henry does not fulfill her need for aesthetic companionship. Elisa feels incomplete and has channeled her creative impulses into her garden, especially her prized, long-stemmed chrysanthemums. A strong, competent woman, Elisa is aloof when a tinker asks for work, but she becomes compassionate once the man admires her flowers and tells her a woman down the road asked him to bring her good chrysanthemum seeds if he found some.

Elisa feels close to the tinker through what she believes are shared feelings. She makes work for him and gives him a pot of chrysanthemum sprouts. She reaches for, and almost touches, the tinker's leg. "Then her hand dropped to the ground. She crouched like a fawning dog."3

Later Elisa bathes and dresses to go with Henry into Salinas for dinner and a movie, and on the way she sees the contents of the pot discarded on the road. For a moment she wants to go to the prize fights to see the men punishing one another with gloves "heavy and soggy with blood" (23). The feeling passes, and then she turns away from her husband. "'It will be enough if we can have wine. It will be plenty.' She turned up her coat collar so he could not see that she was crying weakly--like an old woman" (23).

The earlier text of "The Chrysanthemums" was somewhat altered for The Long Valley.4 Changes in spelling give a more homespun flavor: "Chrysanthemums" becomes "chrysantheums." The revised text has less explanation and is more suggestive. Explicit sexual overtones are also added, especially significant in Elisa's crouching in front of the man "low like a fawning dog" (23). At least one critic sees Elisa's devotion to her chrysanthemum bed

as "an attempt to make flowers take the place of a child. "[5]
Obviously, Elisa does see herself as a sexually unfulfilled
and incomplete woman, but she is more completely understood and the story more universally applicable "if we do
not equate sexual fulfillment with a yearning for mother-
hood. "[6] Certainly, Elisa's bathing and dressing for her
trip to Salinas, coming as it does immediately following her
scene with the tinker, appears to be a ritual of purification.
"She felt shame after her display of passion before the
stranger. Now she cleanses herself before returning to her
husband. . . . "[7]

Several elements of irony are apparent in "The Chrysanthemums. " The ironic contrast between the fertility of
the soil and the sterility of human relationships is obvious.
The false interest Elisa shows in the tinker's craftsmanship
is also ironic, but the most salient ironic contrast is that
between Elisa's passionate reaching out to the tinker and the
man's basic insincerity. The story gives a penetrating view
of one who is not fulfilled and who cries "weakly--like an
old woman" for whom hope of romance is a thing of the
past.

"The White Quail" is somewhat less effective than
"The Chrysanthemums" because the symbolism is so explicit
in this second story. Mary Teller does not use her garden
merely to compensate for an incomplete relationship with
her husband. She uses Harry to enable her to actualize her
vision of her garden. Mary evaluates every suitor by her
vision. "She didn't think so much, 'Would this man like
such a garden?' but, 'Would the garden like such a man?'
For the garden was herself, and after all she had to marry
some one she liked" (28). When Harry responded to her
vision of her garden, "she accepted him, and let him kiss
her" (28). Harry feels passion, and Mary passively accepts
his romantic advances. A lot is bought, the house built,
and the garden completed to the last detail of Mary's vision,
but she and her garden make Harry afraid. He admits,
"Well, you're kind of untouchable. There's an inscrutability
about you. Probably you don't even know it yourself.
You're kind of like your own garden--fixed, and just so.
I'm afraid to move around. I might disturb some of your
plants" (30).

Mary works constantly to keep predatory plants and
animals out of the garden, and she is aggressively hostile
about the possibility of a cat who might prey upon the birds

who might visit the garden. She wants to plant poisoned
fish to kill intruders, but Harry soothes her by promising
to buy an air gun. Mary gradually begins to see herself as
two persons, and late one afternoon she sees a white quail
with which she immediately identifies. "She's like the essence of me, an essence boiled down to utter purity. She
must be the queen of the quail. She makes every lovely
thing that ever happened to me one thing" (38). Suddenly a
cat moves out of the bushes, and Mary screams in terror.
Harry comforts her and promises to shoot the cat the following morning. As he waits in the garden, the white quail
appears, and without wavering Harry shoots it and buries it
under a pile of leaves.

The sexual and intellectual chasm between husband
and wife widens when Harry deliberately kills the object of
his frustration rather than attempting to resolve it. Although Harry symbolically kills the Mary who frightened
him, he ends in gloom and despondency. "'I'm lonely,' he
said. 'Oh, Lord, I'm so lonely!'" (42)

In "Flight" Steinbeck achieves one of his most notable
examples of realistic writing. Set fifteen miles below
Monterey on the coast, "Flight" dramatizes the short adult
life of Pepé Torres, the nineteen-year-old son of a widow
whose husband was killed by a rattlesnake. Pepé's moment
of maturity comes when Mama Torres sends him to Monterey for medicine. Pepé is insulted, kills a man, and returns home by night to begin his flight across the mountains.
Mama Torres equips him for his journey as well as she can
and warns him to avoid the dark watchers. Having lost his
innocence in Monterey and having left his knife in the
stranger he killed, Pepé continues to lose articles as he
travels: first his hat, then his coat, and finally his gun.
Stripped of defense and trailed relentlessly into a corner
like a wild animal, Pepé crawls to the top of a rock,
crosses himself, and then stands erect. He is riddled with
bullets and his body rolls down the hill, coming to rest
against a bush.

In "Flight," a story rendered in a prose comparable
to the best of Hemingway, Pepé makes a journey on two
levels. The first, and most obvious, is his trip into manhood. Before he leaves home Pepé says he is a man, but
Mama knows it is not yet so. She later affirms, "A boy
gets to be a man when a man is needed. Remember this
thing. I have known boys forty years old because there was

no need for a man" (50).   The transition has been completed
by the time Pepé returns.

> He was changed.   The fragile quality seemed to
> have gone from his chin.   His mouth was less
> full than it had been, the lines of the lips were
> straighter, but in his eyes the greatest change had
> taken place.   There was no laughter in them any
> more, nor any bashfulness.   They were sharp
> and bright and purposeful.   (51)

His final action also shows him to be a man.   When trapped
and defenseless, he does not cower but shows himself and
stands erect to receive the fusillade of bullets.

On another level "Flight" shows how Pepé becomes
more like a wild animal the farther he goes into the mountains.   As he loses the articles which represent civilization
--the knife, the hat, the gun--he loses his own identity.
An interesting comparison can be made at this point with
Faulkner's Ike McCaslin, in "The Bear," who is not granted
the right to see Old Ben until he has left behind him his
gun and compass--those symbols of civilization.   In both
stories an initiation takes place: Ike into the natural world
and Pepé into manhood with its concomitant responsibility
for one's actions.

In the early sixties Barnaby Conrad produced a short
film based on "Flight" to show at the Edinburgh festival.
In John Steinbeck, a 1970 McGraw-Hill publication, Richard
O'Connor tells the story of Conrad's securing Steinbeck's
permission to show the film (pp. 115-17).   The film, shown
at the 1971 Steinbeck Conference at San Jose State University, is, as Steinbeck proclaimed it to be, a "deeply moving" presentation.

The first fictional portrait of Ed Ricketts, the Doc
of Cannery Row, appears in "The Snake," the fourth story
in The Long Valley.   In "About Ed Ricketts," a profile of
Steinbeck's closest friend published in the Viking Compass
edition of The Log from the Sea of Cortez, Steinbeck notes
that the event described in "The Snake" actually happened.
'I wrote it just as it happened.   I don't know what it means
and do not even answer the letters asking what its philo-
sophic intent is.   It just happened" (xxiii).   In "The Snake"
the fictional Ed Ricketts is Dr. Phillips who operates a
commercial laboratory on Cannery Row in Monterey.   Just

as he begins developing starfish embryos for microscope
slides, a tall woman enters. She waits until he is free
and then asks to buy a male rattlesnake. The woman pays
for the snake and then asks to see it fed. Although obviously repulsed, Dr. Phillips complies, then sickens as he
sees the woman's movements duplicate those of the rattler.
Phillips turns away just as the snake opens its mouth and
unhinges its jaws. "He thought, 'If she's opening her
mouth, I'll be sick. I'll be afraid'" (85). The woman asks
Phillips to keep the snake, promising that she will be back
to feed it soon, but she never returns.

Steinbeck was wise in not attempting to solve the
Freudian puzzle presented by the event. The story serves
as an excellent preliminary portrait of Ed Ricketts which
Steinbeck was to develop in great detail in later novels.
Especially effective is his picture of the white rats in cages
which "scampered up and down the wire" (73), an image
with which he ends Cannery Row.

"Breakfast" was one of the stories picked by Pascal
Covici for the Viking Portable Steinbeck. Covici places it
immediately before the selections from The Grapes of Wrath
and says, "This is one of many working notes made in
preparation for The Grapes of Wrath, which was not used
in the novel" (417). It is the first story in The Long Valley
in which Steinbeck uses a first person narrator and probably
recounts an experience he had while traveling with the migrants before he had written his Pulitzer Prize novel. It
simply tells of a pleasant experience of being invited by a
migrant family to share breakfast. The family speaks with
satisfaction of having had twelve days work, full bellies,
and new dungarees. They are generous, even to offering
to help the narrator get work, and they ask no personal
questions. When breakfast is finished, they leave. "That's
all. I know, of course, some of the reasons why it was
pleasant. But there was some element of great beauty
there that makes the rush of warmth when I think of it"
(92).

Although merely a fragment, "Breakfast" demonstrates
Steinbeck's power in realistic fiction. His descriptions are
clear and clean, with much attention given to color. He
describes the early morning when the mountains "were
black-blue, but behind them the light stood up faintly colored
at the mountain rims with a washed red, growing colder,
greyer and darker as it went up and overhead until, at a

place near the west, it merged with pure night" (89). He
mentions the "lavender grey of dawn" and a tent which was
"only a little lighter grey than the ground" (89). The early
morning color gradations are painted by one who has often
experienced them, and the reader can share in this special
time. The picture of a proud, working family was one
which Steinbeck cherished and would duplicate in other
works.

As "Breakfast" conveys the flavor of The Grapes of
Wrath, so "The Raid" prefigures In Dubious Battle. It is
the story of two party organizers. Dick, an older man
with experience, and Root, a young, fearful neophyte, await
the arrival of workers in an empty hall. Most of the action takes place in Root's mind as he tries to fight off his
fear of a potential raid. Dick maintains a facade of brusque-
ness and impatience with his young companion until a man
runs in to tell them that a raiding party is coming. Dick
tells Root, "if some one busts you, it isn't him that's doing it, it's the System. And it isn't you he's busting.
He's taking a crack at the Principle" (104). The raiding
party arrives, and after Root is knocked down he struggles
to his feet shouting, "It's all for you. We're doing it for
you. All of it. You don't know what you're doing" (107).
Later, in the hospital, Root tells Dick that in the Bible it
says, "Forgive them because they don't know what they're
doing" (108). Dick quickly replies: "'You lay off that
religion stuff, kid.' He quoted, 'Religion is the opium of
the people'" (108).

The battle with fear which Root fights in "The Raid"
is a much more significant fight than that with the raiding
party. Earlier, Dick had said, "You'll be all right, kid.
You got stuff in you. I can tell that. You just never been
under fire" (102). Under fire Root proves his manhood,
and Steinbeck endows him with some of the attributes he
would give to Tom Joad and Jim Casy in The Grapes of
Wrath, and which would tempt critics to call Root a Christ-
like figure.

Steinbeck returns to a study of marital relationships
in "The Harness." Peter Randall, a hard-working, respected farmer of Monterey County, devotes fifty-one weeks
of every year to his sickly wife and his farm. During that
one remaining week Peter leaves on what his wife, Emma,
explains as a "business trip." When Emma dies, Peter becomes hysterical and later explains to a friend that during

that week away from home he "went to fancy houses in San
Francisco. I was drunk for a week, and I went to a fancy
house every night" (119). He also revealed that Emma had
forced him to wear a girdle to hold in his stomach and a
web harness to pull his shoulders back. Peter believes
that Emma's death has freed him, so he takes off the harness and plants his acreage in sweet peas. Peter continues
to put in long hours which result in a bountiful harvest of
the risky crop, but Peter cannot change. He takes his
week in San Francisco again and confesses that Emma
"didn't die dead.... She won't let me do things. She's
worried me all year about those peas.... When I get back,
you know what I'm going to do? I'm going to put in electric lights. Emma always wanted electric lights" (129).

Although "The Harness" is an interesting story, it
lacks irony, and the symbol of the harness is readily apparent. It presents the picture of man capable of frustrated
drunken rages but who has suppressed the fire within. The
American Broadcasting Company produced a filmed version
of "The Harness" for its 1971 "Movie of the Week" series,
and it prompted a reviewer in the Seattle Post-Intelligencer
to affirm that "The best source for great film entertainment
is still great literature" (November 14, 1971, section C,
p. 5).

"The Vigilante" might well have followed "The Raid"
in The Long Valley since it depends on psychological action
rather than physical violence. Mike has helped lynch a
Negro, and the story develops his motivations. Through
conversations with a bartender, and later with his wife,
Mike reveals that the mob action has been for him a kind
of sexual experience. When he goes home and his wife accuses him of being with a woman, Mike admits, "By God,
she was right.... That's just exactly how I do feel" (141).
Peter Lisca relates the story to Steinbeck's development of
group-man theories in that "The vigilante ... fully lives
only for that time when he is part of a group, and when
that group disperses the single man is left a hull" (The
Wide World of John Steinbeck, p. 97).

It is difficult for one not to relate the idiot in the
story "Johnny Bear" to Steinbeck's other portrayals of those
who are mentally unequipped to exist in the society of men--
ones such as Lennie in Of Mice and Men. Steinbeck's ear
for rhythm and repetition, used so effectively in his portrayal of Lennie, is utilized in his characterization of

Johnny Bear, who comes into the bar asking for whiskey.
"It was like a bird call. I don't know what kind of bird,
but I've heard it--two notes on a rising scale, asking a
question over and over, 'Whiskey? Whiskey?'" (152)
Johnny earns his drinks by mimicry, an exact reproduction
of voices he has heard which he often accompanies with
facial contortions. The men in the bar play with the idiot
in the hope of hearing the intimacies of their neighbors.
Like children whose game suddenly results in injury, the
men in the bar are revulsed when the secrets of the community's two aristocratic spinsters are repeated.

Although the story is titled "Johnny Bear," the idiot
is not the focus of the story. Nor are the Hawkins sisters,
one of whom Johnny reveals as having hanged herself after
becoming pregnant by one of her Chinese workers. The
central focus is the community itself, torn between its desire for gossip and its determination to maintain its symbol
of respectability. Steinbeck, for the second time in The
Long Valley, uses a first person narrator who is outside
the established community and can present the story objectively. Like the narrator, the reader can share his feeling
that "Johnny Bear was more monstrous even than I had
known" (157) and can know that the community had caused
its own disintegration. [8]

"The Murder" was apparently an account of an actual
event among valley people similar to those who provide
Steinbeck his subjects in The Pastures of Heaven. "The
Murder" is the story of the Anglo Jim Moore who marries
Jelka Sepic, a Yugoslavian girl whose father says, "He's
not like a man that don't beat hell out of him" (173). Jelka
proves to be a quiet, efficient housekeeper but not a companion. Jim begins to go into town on Saturday nights for
female companionship, but when he returns home early one
night he finds Jelka in bed with her cousin. He kills the
cousin, brutally beats Jelka with a loaded bull whip, then
promises to build them a new house farther down the can-
yon.

Although this story dramatizes the differences of
racial heritage, one cannot fail to note the concepts of
Anglo superiority and male chauvinism. Jim seeks "blond
May at the Three Star in Monterey" (178) in what apparently
is a desire for "his kind." But Jelka is denied this same
outlet. In addition, Jelka is not simply an ignorant immigrant, steeped in the tradition of the old country and

unaware of the ways of the new. She is characterized as a
domesticated farm animal. "She was so much like an animal that sometimes Jim patted her head and neck under the
same impulse that made him stroke a horse" (173). When
he stroked her hair, "she whimpered a little with pleasure"
(174). Even after her beating, she dutifully fixed Jim
breakfast, and "Jim put out his hand and stroked her hair
and the back of her neck" (186). The story weighs heavily
on the mind of a thoughtful reader.

The one story which seems most out of place in The
Long Valley is the fable "Saint Katy the Virgin, " a work in
the beast-epic tradition and reflecting Steinbeck's interest
in medieval life. This farcical tale recounts the life of a
mean, "sinful, " and unrepentant sow who is given to two
monks collecting tithes. Katy is converted by one of the
monks and canonized as St. Katy, the Virgin, since it was
determined that she was "a virgin by intent" (199). She
works miraculous cures and her bones become holy relics.
The story is full of sharp invective against the church and
parodies of typical medieval debates. Peter Lisca, in The
Wide World of John Steinbeck, calls "St. Katy" a "delightful
tale that even Chaucer's Reeve or Miller would have been
proud to present as his claim to the free dinner" (94-95),
and that it is. It does, however, seem an incongruous addition to The Long Valley.

Critics have universally praised The Red Pony as
containing Steinbeck's best writing. Its appeal to both the
young and the old rests upon its general theme of the ma-
turing of a young boy, handled with a deftness seldom
achieved in the twentieth century. The story of The Red
Pony is given in four parts, published at various intervals
between 1933 and 1938. Although each section can stand
alone, it is fitting to consider them consecutively. It is
the story of Jody Tiflin, and it is also the story of John
Steinbeck whose statement concerning the story sets its
context:

> The Red Pony was written a long time ago, when
> there was desolation in my family. The first
> death occurred. And the family, which every
> child believes to be immortal, was shattered.
> Perhaps this is the first adulthood of any man or
> woman. The first tortured question 'Why?' and
> then acceptance, and then the child becomes a
> man. The Red Pony was an attempt, an

experiment if you wish, to set down this loss and
acceptance and growth. [9]

The first story in The Red Pony, "The Gift," is the
best known. Ten-year-old Jody lives on a farm in the
Salinas Valley with his mother, his father Carl who is a
strong disciplinarian, and Billy Buck the hired hand. One
morning his father shows him a red circus pony that is to
be his, if he takes care of him. Jody names the pony
Gabilan, for the ever-present Gabilan Mountains, and Billy
Buck helps Jody train him. Through carelessness, the
pony is left in the rain, gets sick, and dies despite Billy
Buck's tireless efforts to save Gabilan. Jody stays with
the pony almost constantly, but he falls asleep and Gabilan
leaves the barn. By the time Jody reaches the pony it is
too late--the buzzards had already begun their work. In a
frenzy of frustration Jody seizes a buzzard and beats it to
death with a rock.

"The Gift" is moving solely through the physical action of the plot. Few readers can fail to respond to Jody's
suffering, loss, and final acceptance. In addition, Steinbeck's description, especially that of "the grey quiet mornings when the land and the brush and the houses and the
trees were silver-grey and black like a photograph negative" (215), allows the reader to experience morning before
the sun has roused the farm and its inhabitants. Throughout the story, Steinbeck's use of concrete images and his
avoidance of abstractions create powerfully descriptive
passages.

Although "The Gift" is focused primarily on Jody's
education through nature, and death in nature, a secondary
concern is equally evident. Carefully woven into the fabric
of "The Gift" is a quite explicit comparison and contrast
between Jody's father and Billy Buck. Jody's father makes
the rules and demands obedience. "His father was a disciplinarian. Jody obeyed him in everything without questions of any kind" (205). Even Carl's presents "were given
with reservations which hampered their value somewhat. It
was good discipline" (208). But Jody does not learn from
Carl; he learns from nature, and the natural man, Billy,
guides him. Nowhere is this contrast more evident than
the end of the story when Billy and Carl find Jody. Billy
pulls Jody away from the dead buzzard and holds him to
calm him. Carl can only say, "the buzzard didn't kill the
pony. Don't you know that?" (238). No one but natural

man can sense the magnitude of Jody's grief and make an appropriate response.

The second story, "The Great Mountains," provides a counterpoint to "The Gift." It is not the death of a pony but a human with which Jody is confronted. The boy first becomes aware of the mountains which enclose the farm. To the west are the big mountains, described by Carl as "dangerous, with cliffs and things" (241). But to the east are the jolly Gabilans. "People lived there, and battles had been fought against the Mexicans on the slopes. He looked back for an instant at the Great Ones and shivered a little at the contrast" (242). Jody's thoughts are quickly changed by the approach of an old man who proclaims, "I am Gitano, and I have come back" (244). He explained that he was born on that land, and he obviously had come home to die.

Carl's hard nature again is dramatized when he tells Gitano he will have to leave. "Go to your friends. Don't come to die with strangers" (246). Jody is fascinated by the old man and responds with human compassion. He asks Gitano questions about the past and shows him the stock, including the thirty-year-old horse, Easter, that Carl says should be shot. "Old things ought to be put out of their misery.... One shot, a big noise, one big pain in the head maybe, and that's all. That's better than stiffness and sore teeth" (249). The next morning Gitano is gone, having taken old Easter with him into the Great Mountains to die. The story is calm and almost peaceful, with none of the scenes of violence which appear in "The Gift." But Jody learns once more that death comes to all. Regardless of their past usefulness, old men and horses are discarded, and the realization fills Jody with "a nameless sorrow" (256).

The third story, "The Promise," plays upon the same motif as "The Gift." Having lost the red pony, Jody is promised Nellie's foal if he will work all summer to pay the five dollar stud fee. Jody is now involved from the moment of conception when he leads Nellie up the road where he fearfully watches Jess Taylor's stallion savagely mount the mare. He faithfully cares for Nellie, but the birth which he anticipated so long is a terrible experience. When the mare's time has come and she seems not able to give birth, Jody remembers that Billy Buck had failed with the pony too. Suddenly, Nellie is ready, but the foal is turned the wrong way. Jody refuses to leave the barn, but he does turn his head as Billy rips open the mare's belly and drags out the colt.

Billy's face and arms and chest were dripping red.
His body shivered and his teeth chattered. His
voice was gone; he spoke in a throaty whisper.
'There's your colt. I promised. And there it is.
I had to do it--had to. ' (279)

Again Jody has insight into nature and death. The
mare dies to give new life. There is no fault to be rec-
koned in what has happened. In nature life and death are
intimately bound together, and Jody's responsibility for the
new colt is accompanied by his awareness of the interrelatedness of nature.

"The Leader of the People, " the fourth story of The
Red Pony, has a different mood and for some a change in
focus, but it fits compactly with the previous three. Jody
Tiflin's grandfather, his mother's father, appears to be the
central character in "The Leader of the People. " The
talkative old man retells his stories of leading wagon loads
of families across hostile lands to the ocean, much to the
consternation of Carl. As the tales continue, Carl becomes
more irritable until he tells his wife, 'Well, how many
times do I have to listen to the story of the iron plates,
and the thirty-five horses? That time's done.... Nobody
wants to hear about it over and over" (299). But the old
man has overheard.

Carl feebly apologizes, but it does not cure Grandfather's pain. Grandfather admits that the tales are not
what he wants to tell. 'It wasn't Indians that were important, nor adventures, nor even getting out here. It was a
whole bunch of people made into one big crawling beast.
And I was the head" (302). He wants those who hear his
stories to feel, and only Jody can. It is Jody who knows
the old man's deepest needs and who gives Grandfather
reason to hope that at least one person felt as he wanted
him to. In this sense, then, Jody may still be the central
character in the story. "Jody has already become a leader
in showing his people a direction toward better understanding by first accepting the facts that exist. He, too, like
his grandfather, fits Steinbeck's theory of leadership. "[10]

The four stories of The Red Pony are a fitting conclusion to The Long Valley, for they manifest some of the
best writing of Steinbeck as well as some of the best
American writing produced. When Steinbeck was awarded
the Nobel Prize, the Committee said that it was awarded

"For his at one and the same time realistic and imaginative writings, distinguished as they are by a sympathetic humor and social perception."[11] No volume exemplifies the statement of the Nobel Committee as does The Long Valley. The stories in the volume will continue to stimulate readers' imaginations and will evoke thoughts and emotions which will contribute to the celebration of living.

Notes

1. A discussion of the publication history of the various stories in The Long Valley is given by Peter Lisca in The Wide World of John Steinbeck (New Brunswick: Rutgers University Press, 1958), pp. 92-93.

2. Quoted by Thelma M. Smith and Ward L. Miner in Transatlantic Migration: The Contemporary American Novel in France (Durham: Duke University Press, 1955), p. 21.

3. Steinbeck. "The Chrysanthemums," The Long Valley (New York: The Viking Press, 1938), p. 18. Henceforth, all quotations from The Long Valley will be documented by page number in parentheses following the quotation.

4. William R. Osborne. "The Texts of Steinbeck's 'The Chrysanthemums,'" Modern Fiction Studies, 12 (Winter, 1966-1967), 479-484.

5. Mordecai Marcus. "The Lost Dream of Sex and Childbirth in 'The Chrysanthemums,'" Modern Fiction Studies, 11 (Spring, 1965), 55.

6. Elizabeth E. McMahan. "'The Chrysanthemums': Study Of A Woman's Sexuality," Modern Fiction Studies, 14 (Winter, 1968-1969), 454.

7. McMahan, p. 457.

8. Warren French. John Steinbeck (New York: Twayne Publishers, Inc., 1961), p. 85.

9. Steinbeck. "My Short Novels," Steinbeck and His Critics, ed. E. D. Tedlock, Jr., and C. V. Wicker (Albuquerque: University of New Mexico Press, 1957), p. 38.

10. Alfred H. Grommon. "Who is 'The Leader of the People'?: Helping Students Examine Fiction," _English Journal_, 48 (November, 1959), 455.

11. _American Winners of the Nobel Literary Prize_, ed. Warren G. French and Walter E. Kidd (Norman: University of Oklahoma Press, 1968), pp. 221-222.

III.   APPARATUS FOR RESEARCH PAPERS

A.   Ten Questions for Discussion

1. Why is Steinbeck called a writer of realistic fiction?
2. In several stories in The Long Valley Steinbeck uses symbols.   How can symbols enhance realistic fiction? Which symbols are most effective in The Long Valley?
3. Plants and animals are prominent in The Long Valley. Pick three and note the symbolic function of each.
4. Steinbeck often uses description to his advantage.   What special qualities do his descriptive passages possess?
5. How does Steinbeck's writing reveal his interest in biological study?
6. Why does Steinbeck often concentrate on psychological action rather than physical violence?
7. How does Steinbeck use ironic contrast in his works? Note three examples.
8. Looming in the background of "Flight" are "the dark watchers." What purpose do they serve?
9. In "Breakfast" and "Johnny Bear" Steinbeck uses a first person narrator to speak to the reader.   What is the advantage of such a technique in these instances?
10. Some call The Red Pony a story for children.   Can such an assessment be challenged?   On what evidence?

B.   Topics for Research Papers

1. Steinbeck's Use of Color in The Long Valley.
2. Concepts of "Group-Man" in The Long Valley.
3. Steinbeck's Utilization of Violence in The Long Valley.
4. The Image of The Garden in "The White Quail. "
5. Levels of Meaning in "Flight. "
6. "St. Katy The Virgin" and The Beast-Epic Genre.
7. Life and Death: A Constant Cycle in The Red Pony.
8. A Study of the Relationship Between Jody Tiflin and Billy Buck.

C.   Selected Bibliography

1.   Fontenrose, Joseph. John Steinbeck. New York:
     Holt, Rinehart and Winston, Inc., 1963.
         An especially helpful work by a classical scholar
     who shows how traditional myths and legends influence the
     form and content of Steinbeck's fiction. pp. 59-66.

2.   French, Warren. John Steinbeck. New York: Twayne
     Publishers, 1961.
         In one of the better books in the Twayne Authors
     Series, French devotes Chapter Eight to The Long Valley.
     He mentions all the stories and gives special treatment to
     The Red Pony, "The Snake," "Johnny Bear," and "St.
     Katy."

3.   Lisca, Peter. The Wide World of John Steinbeck.
     New Brunswick: Rutgers University Press, 1958.
         For fifteen years the major critical volume on Stein-
     beck's fiction, the book's sixteen pages on The Long Valley
     make it the most comprehensive treatment currently avail-
     able.   Lisca's insights remain valid, and he couples textual
     notations with perceptive analysis.

4.   Modern Fiction Studies, 11 (Spring, 1965).
         Although this journal often carries significant Stein-
     beck criticism, this particular issue is devoted solely to
     Steinbeck.   The articles on "The Chrysanthemums" and
     "Flight" should provoke discussion.

5.   Steinbeck and His Critics, ed. E. W. Tedlock, Jr.,
     and C. V. Wicker. Albuquerque: University of New
     Mexico Press, 1957.
         This is still the best one-volume collection of Stein-
     beck criticism.   Although none of the articles is limited to
     a discussion of a particular story from The Long Valley,
     the general discussions make it a central research tool.

6.   Steinbeck Quarterly [Special Numbers: 5(Summer-Fall,
     1972) and 6(Winter, 1973)]
         These two special issues, just recently published,
     carry analyses of all the works in The Long Valley except
     "Breakfast."   Fourteen critics from all sections of the
     country are represented, including Fontenrose, French,
     and Lisca.

7.   Watt, F. W. John Steinbeck. New York: Grove

Press, 1962.
    The last eight pages of the second chapter cover
stories in The Long Valley. Watt does little more than
trace the action in selected stories.

8. West, Ray B. , Jr. The Short Story in America 1900-
    1950. Chicago: Henry Regnery Company, 1952.
    West compares Steinbeck with Sherwood Anderson in
the use of underlying symbols to achieve control. West's
discussion of irony in "The Chrysanthemums" is perceptive.

9. Wilson, Edmund. The Boys in the Back Room. San
    Francisco: Colt Press, 1941.
    This is one of the earliest works to include The
Long Valley in a critical evaluation of Steinbeck's work.
Wilson's comments helped shape early Steinbeck criticism.

Chapter 7

THE TURNING POINT:
THE PASTURES OF HEAVEN (1932)

by Richard Peterson

I. BACKGROUND

The critical position of The Pastures of Heaven in
John Steinbeck's development as a writer and the question
of the short story-novel as a viable art form in fiction are,
to a great extent, the key factors in determining the value
of Steinbeck's second major publication. [1] Many of Steinbeck's critics believe that in The Pastures of Heaven Steinbeck first establishes his proper donnée as he also develops
the narrative techniques and major themes which define
Steinbeck's dimensions as a writer. The people of Las
Pasturas del Cielo, for example, represent the minor and
major characters that will now dominate Steinbeck's stories.
Their lives are intimately connected with the land, and they
inevitably tend to create their values out of their strong
faith in the natural process of renewal and continuity. John
Whiteside has the most respect of all the farmers in the
valley because he has the strongest sense of the power of
the land to fulfill and perpetuate man's finest dreams and
visions. His great house becomes the symbol of his desire
to create a family dynasty; but for the families of the valley it embodies permanence and tradition as well as good
judgment and manners. The people of the Pastures also
represent those Steinbeck characters with a simple and direct approach to their daily lives based on the need for
group or community relationships. The mark of prestige
in the community is being elected to the school board.
The means of survival for a man as lonely as Pat Humbert
is to participate in every group meeting, whether it be an
informal gathering at the country store or a picnic or
dance.

Steinbeck's technique in The Pastures of Heaven reflects the nature of the world he now creates. His approach
is simple, direct, and objective. On the one hand, he can
achieve a sense of warmth and vitality by sympathetically
drawing out the life of his characters. Yet, at the same
time, Steinbeck creates a sense of balance or objectivity
in The Pastures of Heaven through his use of irony. He
avoids the danger of creating a sentimentalized fable of
simple country folk living in organic harmony with the land
and in social harmony with each other by also revealing the
hypocrisy of community life and the self-interest which
sometimes exists in acts of good will. By exposing the
shallowness and selfish actions of certain outwardly respectable members of the Pastures as he creates other individuals who live in simple harmony with the land, the community, and their own private visions, Steinbeck establishes
the counterbalancing themes--the evils of social respectability and the virtues of individual adaptability--which form the
basic conflict in much of his fiction.

On one level, Steinbeck portrays the respectable
Munroes who strive to be accepted in the community by becoming exactly like their neighbors in thought, action, and
appearance. Yet, the Munroes, in their quest for security
and respectability, manage to destroy the hopes of several
sensitive individuals who desire little more than to pursue
their simple and harmless visions. The danger of middle-
class virtue, as it appears for the first time in The Pastures of Heaven, is that it stifles individual growth and often
destroys individual talent. What remains, after the Munroes inflict their damage, is a world dominated by mediocrity and insensitivity. There is no place in a respectable
society for a Tularecito or a Junius Maltby and his son or
for the Lopez sisters, as there will be no place for a
Lennie or a Danny and his friends or the Joad family.

The form of The Pastures of Heaven presents critical
problems of classification and approach. Like Joyce's Dubliners and Anderson's Winesburg, Ohio, Steinbeck's work
may be approached as a collection of short stories that are
tightly unified by theme and the device of a single or collective persona. On the other hand, Steinbeck has carefully developed the thematic interrelationship between the
stories so that The Pastures of Heaven has the general
range and design of the novel, much in the same manner as
Faulkner's Go Down, Moses. The need to fit The Pastures
of Heaven into one of the literary genres seems, however,

more a matter of convenience than anything else. What is
important in appreciating the book's value is to arrive at
some sense of Steinbeck's purpose in selecting a form that
has the basic characteristics of the novel, but also has
units or "chapters" which easily stand as individual and
complete in story, characterization, and theme.

Perhaps the most advantageous approach to form in
The Pastures of Heaven is to compare it to Anderson's
Winesburg, Ohio, the work of fiction it most clearly resembles. In both works, the stories are studies of characters who are united externally by their contact with an
individual or group of individuals. The appearance of this
figure, George Willard in Winesburg, Ohio or various members of the Munroe family in The Pastures of Heaven, provides a unity for the entire collection of stories that brings
it close to the novel form. Neither George Willard nor any
of the Munroes, however, is as individually important as
the character that is at the center of the story. In this
respect, George Willard may appear as a major character,
as a sympathetic listener, or as simply a disinterested observer; while a Munroe may act directly and consciously
upon an individual's life or may function only as unconscious
catalyst for a character's loss of hope without ever knowing
what has come about.

Steinbeck and Anderson's mutual dependence on characterization for idea and technique is further emphasized by
the way in which they build their themes around character.
Each writer uses the characters who appear in separate
stories to develop a major theme, but he also employs his
"outsider" to stress an alternative or conflicting theme.
Anderson weaves the theme of human isolation from story
to story in Winesburg, Ohio, but he also suggests the possibility of emotional growth and human understanding through
George Willard. In The Pastures of Heaven, Steinbeck
portrays individuals united by the need for some dream or
illusion to give their life purpose, but the Munroes, with
their middle-class virtues and realities, constantly appear
to destroy their hope.

Sherwood Anderson's comments on the form of Winesburg, Ohio offer the best insight into Steinbeck's purpose in
creating a similar form in The Pastures of Heaven. Anderson, in his Memoirs, stated his belief that he had created
a novel form which was closer to the constant change and
flow of the American experience than the more traditional

form of the novel: ''I have even sometimes thought that the
novel form does not fit an American writer, that it is a
form which has been brought in. What is wanted is a new
looseness; and in Winesburg, I have made my own form. ''
Steinbeck achieves the same unity of form and life in The
Pastures of Heaven. His stories unite each character on
the basis of a common need or common experience, but
they also reveal the depth and diversity of individual lives.
The Pastures of Heaven marks a level of accomplishment
in craftsmanship for Steinbeck that matches Anderson's in
Winesburg, Ohio, and it reveals the perceptiveness into the
complexities of human nature which will continue to expand
in Steinbeck's later works. Out of this work comes Steinbeck's sense of the interrelatedness of form and the lives
of his characters. Also anticipated in The Pastures of
Heaven is Steinbeck's growing need to study individual lives
not only as isolated cases, but as a part of a group phenomenon as well.

II.   PLOT SYNOPSIS

        The Pastures of Heaven consists of ten ''chapters''
which are framed by two brief vignettes that function as
ironic prologue and epilogue for the major and specific
stories.   The irony of the prologue is self-contained.   It
tells the story of the original discovery and naming of the
land.   A Spanish corporal, in pursuit of a small deer, accidentally finds a long valley so beautiful and serene that
he is stricken with wonder and names the valley after ''the
green pastures of Heaven to which our Lord leadeth us'' (p.
2). 2 The irony lies in the appointed task of the corporal
''whose rapacious manhood was building a new race for
California, this bearded, savage bearer of civilization'' (p.
2).   He has captured a group of twenty Indians who have
abandoned Christianity (and the redeeming work of moulding
adobe bricks in the clay pits) and returned to their pagan
ways.   The discovery of the valley happens while the corporal is leading the chained renegades back to the Mother
Church and a chance at repentance in the clay pits.   The
corporal, whose cherished hope is to return to Las Pasturas del Cielo to live out his last days, adds the final note
of irony by contracting the pox from an Indian woman and
dying alone, locked in a barn by his friends to prevent the
infection of others.

        The epilogue re-establishes the wonder and the hope

expressed by the Spanish corporal, as a group of individuals
touring the peninsula aboard a sight-seeing bus halt long
enough to gaze down into the valley and yearn for the happiness, tranquility, and success they believe exist in the
Pastures of Heaven. Their feeling that the good life exists
in the valley and the bus driver's desire to someday own
"a little place down there" re-state the corporal's hope and
form a mythic pattern of promise and eventual peace naturally associated with the land. What functions as an ironic
counterpoint to the myth of Las Pasturas del Cielo is the
reality of the lives of those actually living on and working
the land. The irony remains essentially outside the epilogue
itself, but the fate of those citizens of the Pastures of
Heaven whose stories comprise the main body of Steinbeck's
work leaves no doubt that the myth of promise may be far
more illusory than real.

The first story provides the connecting link between
all the other stories in The Pastures of Heaven. The ominous and potentially evil nature of the link is evident almost
immediately. We are told the history of the Battle farm,
a place that has well watered and fertile land but a place
associated in the minds of the people with a curse. Since
1863, two generations of Battles have stayed on the farm,
but their stay ended with the bizarre death of John Battle,
a man stricken by "epilepsy and the mad knowledge of God,"
who died trying to strangle a rattlesnake that he believed to
be a devil incarnate. In 1921, the Mustrovic family arrived suddenly and mysteriously to take possession of the
farm after it had lain fallow for ten years. In two years
the land was restored to productive health by the son of the
old couple; but without any warning or any indication of a
reason for their actions, the Mustrovics left the farm
abruptly and without a trace. Their actions confirmed for
the people of the Pastures of Heaven their belief in the
curse of the Battle farm: "'It's good land,' they said, 'but
I wouldn't own it if you gave it to me. I don't know what's
the matter, but there's sure something funny about that
place, almost creepy. Wouldn't be hard for a fellow to believe in haunts'" (p. 8).

When Bert Munroe and his family move onto the Battle farm, they seem determined to rid the place of any
unusual and individual characteristics and to make it "look
like a hundred thousand other country houses in the West"
(p. 9). Their reasons, however, have nothing to do with
the curse of the farm, for they believe in a curse all their

own. Bert Munroe made the decision to come to the Pastures of Heaven because of numerous business failings,
which he attributes not to any shortcomings on his part but
to accidents or even to a "nameless thing" that prevents
him from success. He seeks an immunity from the curse
by turning to the land and becoming the same as everyone
else in the valley. When he finally hears about the Battle
curse he is so confident and happy that he feels that perhaps his own curse and the farm's curse have killed each
other off. The reaction of T. B. Allen, who appears as a
resident storyteller in the community, runs counter to Bert's
optimism and sets the stage for what is to come in the remaining stories: "Maybe your curse and the farm's curse
has mated and gone into a gopher hole like a pair of rattle-
snakes. Maybe there'll be a lot of baby curses crawling
around the Pastures the first thing we know" (p. 15).

The succeeding chapters of The Pastures of Heaven
uncover the baby curses spawned by the Munroes. Despite
the fact that they commit no action that is deliberately
malicious or designed to harm anyone, the Munroes afflict
considerable damage on the reputation and lives of several
individuals. Even though most of their actions are actually
taken with the public welfare in mind, their touch drives
people into despair, exile, and even murder. Each of the
Munroes takes an unwitting part in the destruction of some
hope or dream. Jimmie Munroe, Bert's seventeen-year-old
son, is the catalyst that leads to the exposure of "Shark"
Wicks' fake business deals simply because of his inflated
reputation as the town rake and his misunderstanding of
Wicks' daughter's mental slowness as a subtle invitation for
a romantic adventure. Bert Munroe becomes the unknowing
instrument that sends the strangely gifted Tularecito to an
asylum for the criminally insane. On another occasion, he
is the unwitting catalyst that sets in motion a series of
events which leads Mrs. Van Deventer to murder her insane daughter. Mrs. Munroe destroys the idyllic life of
Junius Maltby and his young son by giving the boy a package
of new clothes and making father and son aware of the social reality that their pastoral existence is a life of poverty
in the eyes of a respectable and well meaning community.
Bert Munroe returns to destroy the excitement and dreams
of the Lopez sisters, Molly Morgan and Ray Banks with two
innocently inspirited but devastating jokes that drive their
unintended victims from the valley and a morbid curiosity
about hanging that falters when Bert Munroe has the opportunity to witness one. Mae Munroe, Bert's attractive

daughter, innocently inspires Pat Humbert to rid himself of
a lonely and past-haunted life by expressing the wish to
visit Pat's house; but his obsessive efforts to re-model the
house become meaningless when he discovers that she will
soon marry young John Whiteside.

Mae's marriage to John Whiteside coupled with Bert
Munroe's ill-timed desire to be a good neighbor lets loose
the final curse on the Pastures. When John Whiteside's
son marries and leaves home to work in Monterey, where
Mae's friends are, John Whiteside's hopes for a family
dynasty are shattered. When Bert Munroe decides that it is
a good time to burn off some bothersome brush on the
Whiteside farm, he inadvertently helps to start a fire that
destroys the house which has stood as the symbol of John
Whiteside's dream of immortality. Steinbeck has saved his
most admirable character for the last cruel turn of the dis-
ruptive influence of the Munroes on the dreams and ambitions of the people of the Pastures of Heaven. John Whiteside has the noblest vision and the most disinterested goals
of all those affected by the Munroes; but his fall, though
greater than the others, is as inevitable as the collapse
forced on the Munroe's less visionary and sometimes less
intelligent victims who, nevertheless, do have their own
personal hopes or private worlds shattered. In each case,
an unwitting comment or action by a Munroe or an act intended as a neighborly gesture becomes the intrusive element which destroys the desired peace and happiness that
the tourists feel does exist in the Pastures of Heaven.

III. CRITICAL EXPLICATION

In 1931, Steinbeck wrote a letter to McIntosh and
Otis in which he stated his purpose in The Pastures of
Heaven. He decided to set his novel in a valley about twelve
miles from Monterey called Corral de Tierra whose name
he had changed to Last Pasturas del Cielo:

> The valley was for years known as the happy val-
> ley because of the unique harmony which existed
> among its twenty families. About ten years ago
> a new family moved in on one of the ranches.
> They were ordinary people, ill educated but hon-
> est, and as kindly as any. In fact, in their whole
> history, I cannot find that they have committed
> a really malicious act or an act which was not

dictated by honorable expediency or out-and-out
altruism. But about the M___s there was a
flavor of evil.... There have been two murders,
a suicide, many quarrels and a great deal of un-
happiness in the Pastures of Heaven, and all of
these can be traced to the influence of the M___s.
So much is true. I am using the following method. The manuscript is made up of stories, each
one complete in itself, having its rise, climax
and ending. Each story deals with a family or
an individual. They are tied together only by the
common locality and the common contact with the
M___s. I am trying to show this peculiar evil
cloud which follows the M___s.[3]

While Steinbeck's letter adequately summarizes his
basic plan in The Pastures of Heaven, it greatly oversimpli-
flies the thematic purpose behind the destructive influence
of the Munroes on certain members of a normally peaceful
and happy community. If taken quite literally, the letter
reads like the open confession of a writer taken by a bad
dose of naturalism caused by a mixed reading of Emile
Zola, the Goncourt brothers, and Edgar Allan Poe. What
gives richness and depth to The Pastures of Heaven is the
way in which Steinbeck establishes the basic conflict between
the Munroes and those who come in contact with the Munroes. He assigns a particular meaning to the actions and
motivations of the Munroes, which in the letter he refers to
as a peculiar evil cloud. At the same time, he unites the
individuals influenced by the Munroes by their common approach to life, which works in opposition to the life style
of the Munroes. This conflict of meaning is treated
uniquely in each of the stories. The character who provides the focal point of the story responds to the realities
of life in his own particular way; and, in turn, he is influenced by a Munroe in a way that either reinforces the goodness of his vision or exposes its weakness.

The story of Junius Maltby and his son best reveals
the basic conflict between the life style of the Munroes and
the simple, dream-like existence of the individuals whose
lives are changed by their contact with the Munroes. Junius, despite his indolence, is one of the most sympathetic,
and, to a degree, one of the most admirable characters in
the novel. Before he moves to the Pastures of Heaven, his
life resembles that of such fictional counterparts as Walter
Mitty and Little Chandler. His cultured background and

liberal education have stimulated his imagination, but in the
real world he performs the duties of a clerkship "against
which he struggled for ten years" (p. 65).   At the age of
thirty-five he is struck down by a serious lung condition
which forces him to seek a warm, dry climate.   When he
hears of the Pastures of Heaven, for the first time in his
life he feels that something has personal meaning for him:
"The name pleased him.   'It's either an omen that I'm not
going to live,' he thought, 'or else, it's a nice symbolic
substitute for death'" (p. 65).   He soon discovers that the
name of the valley signifies a new life.   He moves into a
boarding house owned by the widow Quaker and, in a short
time, he sheds the old, dead skin of ten years as an ac-
countant.   A year later, when Mrs. Quaker expresses her
fear that the neighbors are whispering about the single man
living in her house (an ominous foreboding of what the Munroes will do to Junius and his son), Junius quickly and
gladly marries her: "Now he had a home and a golden future....   Junius sent for his books, his morris chair with
the adjustable back, and his good copy of Velasquez' Cardinal.   The future was a pleasant and sunshiny afternoon to
him" (p. 66).

        Junius, too busy with his readings of Robert Louis
Stevenson, fails to take care of the farm, and the Maltby
family, in the eyes of the community, grows very poor.
Later, his wife dies in childbirth, and leaves him with an
infant son; but Junius, his son, fittingly named Robert Louis,
and a hired hand continue to live in a manner which the
people of the valley find impossibly unproductive.   Steinbeck's view of Junius, however, is not the same; his irony,
usually a means to achieve balance in the stories, is directed more at Junius' innocent blunderings (he buys a
"normal" male goat to provide milk for his child) than at
his life style, which grows and blossoms within its own
domain: "They didn't make conversation; rather they let a
seedling of thought sprout by itself, and then watched with
wonder while it sent out branching limbs.   They were surprised at the strange fruit their conversation bore, for they
didn't direct their thinking, nor trellis nor trim it the way
so many people do" (p. 71).   What the people of the valley
fail to comprehend, Steinbeck states as directly as possible:
Junius Maltby, living an unreal, unimportant, romantic
existence, is happy.

        The dark cloud hovering over Junius' paradisiacal
life is one that he is completely unaware of: his neighbors

find his poverty a fearful burden on an otherwise productive
valley, and both the men and the women resent his idleness
and his complete lack of pride, which they interpret as
savagery and degeneracy. Since Junius owns his Eden, the
good people of the valley have no immediate way of doing
anything about him. They can, however, disguise their
contempt for Junius as a more socially respectable pity for
Junius' son, and, as Mrs. Banks states it, "wait until he's
school age.... He belongs to that father of his. But just
as soon as the child is six, the county'll have something to
say, let me tell you" (p. 73). Being socially respectable,
Mrs. Banks and her allies cannot invade Junius' paradise
and drag him out to face his retribution for social evils
done, but they can, by law--which, as Junius points out to
his son, has a "self-protective appendage called penalty"--
force Robbie out into their world. Ironically, once Robbie
attends school, he displays a maturity and self-possession
which assures him the position of king of the school yard.
Junius' downfall, which is to be brought about through the
public exposure and public ridicule of his son, fails to
materialize on the childhood level. Among school children,
the concern for outward appearance and social position is
not yet strongly entrenched. The key to the destruction of
the happy and self-contained world of Junius Maltby lies in
the phrase from Robert Louis Stevenson that Robbie slightly
misuses in a handwriting exercise: "There is nothing so
monsterous [sic] but we can believe it of ourselfs" (p. 76). 4

     For the public world of Mrs. Banks to triumph over
the private world of Junius Maltby, his son has to be made
aware of the social reality of his poverty. This task is
accomplished by the well-meaning Munroes and their peculiar
evil cloud. On the day of terror when the school board
members and a few of their wives visit the local school,
Mrs. Munroe brings a mysterious package with her. After
the dreadful formalities are concluded, Mrs. Munroe presents Robbie with the package. When Robbie opens it and
discovers shirts and new overalls the effect is immediately
devastating. As Mrs. Morgan, Robbie's teacher, tries to
explain, "I think, you see--why, I don't think he ever knew
he was poor until a moment ago" (p. 85). Mrs. Munroe's
single act of charity does what all the ill-feeling and cruel
remarks directed against Junius Maltby could not accom-
plish. Her conviction that Robbie's "health is more important than his feelings" is as damning as God's wrath
against Adam. Junius and his son are now aware of their
poverty and Eden is lost forever. Mrs. Morgan sees the

Maltbys for the last time as they board a bus for San Francisco. His last words to her summarize the loss of his
dream and what brought about that loss: "I didn't know I
was doing an injury to the boy, here. I hadn't thought
about it. I suppose I should have thought about it. You
can see that he shouldn't be brought up in poverty. You
can see that, can't you? I didn't know what people were
saying about us" (p. 86).

What Steinbeck establishes in the story of Junius
Maltby and his son are the dimensions of good and evil in
his fiction. In the final parallel between the evicted Junius
and the fallen Adam, the story actually assumes allegorical
proportions. The good in the story exists in the simple
and happy lives of the Maltbys. Their qualities of self-reliance and adaptability and their simple and heroic faith in
the visionary power of words are the basic values found in
Steinbeck's world. The evil in Steinbeck's fiction is also
clearly defined in the defeat of Junius Maltby. Steinbeck
indicts middle-class respectability as the real enemy to
individual thought and behavior. The desire of a Mrs.
Banks or a Mrs. Munroe for a public morality based upon
appearance and a social order based upon ownership and
upkeep works against the natural community that exists between
people and the natural harmony that exists between the people
and the land. What is so threatening about the world of the
Munroes is that the natural group instinct for survival has been
perverted into an obsessive need to preserve the status quo.
Anything beyond the norm is to be feared and destroyed, usually
by law or social pressure. In this particular story, the innocent
and harmonious existence of the Maltbys threatens the self-as-
sumed authority and smug assurance of the respectable members
of the Pastures of Heaven. The end result is the triumph of
middle-class respectability and mediocrity over the values evident in the life style of Junius and his son.

The other stories in The Pastures of Heaven, which
form a pattern with the narration of the fall of Junius Maltby functioning as the focal point, present variations on
Steinbeck's major theme. The insensitivity and mediocrity
of the Munroes, the "average" family in the valley, are
constant factors in bringing about changes in individual lives
which appear to be for the worse. Steinbeck, however,
deliberately complicates his attack on middle-class respectability by creating a series of characters whose interest in
life is based upon a questionable dream or unnatural life
style. The crassness of the Munroes is constantly evident

in Bert Munroe's ill-timed good-neighborliness and his
disastrous sense of humor and curiosity as well as the remarkable shallowness of his two late adolescent children.
Yet, several individuals affected by the Munroes are already
seriously handicapped by their particular visions of life.
Not all the "different" individuals have a convenient Eden
where they can dangle their feet in the stream of life and
allow a seedling of thought to sprout by itself. Some, in
an effort to avoid personal failures or harsh memories,
create a safer world for themselves within their own minds
which, unfortunately, crumbles when accidentally exposed
to social realities. Steinbeck's sympathies are with these
characters rather than with the world of the Munroes, but
his interest is in exploring the values or weaknesses contained within their dreams.

        The most unusual case of the individual who is com-
pletely cut off from the realities of the people of the Pastures of Heaven, and the most difficult case to approach
and evaluate, is that of Tularecito, the little frog. Tularecito, the precursor of Lennie in Of Mice and Men, is a
gnome-like creature whose mental slowness is compensated
by special gifts of natural sensitivity and strength. In one
respect, Tularecito is the victim of the same insensitive
forces which drive Robbie from the sanctity of his home.
Franklin Gomez accepts the abandoned misshapen baby into
his house, and treats the child, whose brain never develops
beyond a fifth-year mentality, with a compassionate understanding which lies beyond the grasp of his neighbors, who
feel uncomfortable and resentful in the presence of someone
so odd and obscure. Because of Gomez's care, Tularecito
remains relatively protected from the outside world and his
own dangerous tendency to become violently angry when
anyone carelessly breaks one of the marvelous carvings of
animals which he creates with his hands. It is only when
the relentless school board forces him to attend school that
the series of events occur, triggered to a great extent by
a well-meaning but bewildered school teacher, which lead
to the public action to commit Tularecito to an asylum for
the criminally insane. Once Tularecito hears Miss Morgan
read about fairies, changelings, and gnomes, he decides to
find the little people that live in the earth. Unfortunately,
his quest leads him onto Munroe property where he nearly
clubs to death Bert Munroe when he begins to refill the
hole dug by Tularecito. The ironic fate of Tularecito is
to spend his life in the special world of the asylum when
all he sought was the chance to find a world which he could

call home: "I am not like the others at the school or here.
I know that. I have loneliness for my own people who live
deep in the cool earth.... My own people are like me,
and they have called me" (p. 45).

Steinbeck tempers both the injustice of Tularecito's
fate and the view he establishes that society should allow
individuals of feeling, the Franklin Gomezes, to care for
the Tularecitos so that they may live within their own private worlds. In the next story in The Pastures of Heaven,
Helen Van Deventer cares only too well for her mentally ill
child, and she refuses to send her to a hospital for the insane. The problem, however, is that Hilda is seriously
disturbed; her private world is a nightmarish version of
Tularecito's land of gnomes: "Terrible creatures of the
night, with claws and teeth, tried to kill her while she
slept. Ugly little men pinched her and gritted their teeth
in her ear..." (p. 51). Helen Van Deventer's own sickness
further compounds the problem. She discovers a self-satis-
fying pleasure in pain and misery, and she thrives upon the
tragic. Her reason for not committing her daughter is that
Hilda's insanity serves as a constant ordeal for Helen, her
tragic raison d'être. When Bert Munroe pays a neighborly
visit to the valley's newest inhabitants, he unknowingly instigates actions which end when Helen hunts down and kills
her own daughter. Yet, Hilda's murder, an ironic twist on
the doctor's warning that it is Hilda who exhibits the homi-
cidal tendencies, serves a purpose other than to expose,
once again, the destructive mediocrity of the Munroes.

By juxtaposing the stories of Tularecito and Helen
and Hilda Van Deventer, Steinbeck illustrates his belief in
two different types of abnormal individuals. Tularecito
represents the sub-human, mentally deficient, animal-like
creatures who, nevertheless, remain what Franklin Gomez
calls "good animals." On the other hand, Hilda and, eventually, Helen Van Deventer are mentally unbalanced or de-
mented individuals who, as "disturbed animals," remain a
constant threat to do serious harm. Whereas Steinbeck
points out the need to give understanding and compassion to
the Tularecitos, he also shows the effect of the infectious
and destructive nature of dementia if it is not contained.
In Steinbeck's world, however, society confines the primitive
but uniquely gifted, and permits madness to flourish if it
can disguise itself with a mask of respectability.

Several of the stories in The Pastures of Heaven are

concerned with relatively normal individuals who are united
by their desire to live in response to a dream or vision.
The Munroes are constantly around to alter individuals by
destroying their hopes, but their secondary position in the
stories (they often appear as deus ex machina to perform
their dubious tasks) indicates that Steinbeck's primary interest lies in the illusory world of the Munroes' victims.
Steinbeck, on the one hand, consistently portrays the failure
of each character to sustain his dream within the Pastures
of Heaven, but he also varies the meaning of each story
according to the degree to which the individual is at fault
and the intensity and ambition of his dream.   Characters
such as Shark Wicks, Molly Morgan, and Pat Humbert share
a common failure, their inability to cope with time.   Shark
Wicks is unwilling to accept his limited position in the valley, so he creates an imaginary financial empire.   He also
fails to adjust to the physical maturity of his daughter and
develops a fanatical interest in preserving her virginity.
Molly Morgan and Pat Humbert are caught more by their
allegiance to the past than by any deliberate attempt to stop
the movement of time.   Molly wants to protect her childhood memory of her father as a modern Galahad, even at
the cost of losing a pleasant home and a rewarding teaching
position.   Pat does try to escape the nagging ghosts of his
mother and father, but his hope to win the admiration and
love of Mae Munroe has no basis in reality, and he remains an attendant-in-residence of a haunted house.   In all
three cases, either by trying to stop the flow of time or by
deliberately or passively preserving the past, the individual
is unable to accept change and becomes a victim of the inevitable flow and mutability of life.

The stories of the Lopez sisters and Raymond Banks
are contrasting studies of human nature that are united by
the interference of Bert Munroe, but neither situation seems
as critical for the characters involved as those concerning
individuals more deeply committed to their dreams.   The
Lopez sisters are so filled with the simple joy of living
that they can recover from the crisis of their public exposure as prostitutes.   They "tragically" accept the life of
the "bad woman" who peddles sex without the moral façade
of selling "tortillas, enchiladas, tamales and some other
Spanish cooking" (p. 89).   Raymond Banks, the owner of a
chicken ranch, loses the enjoyment of an occasional trip to
watch an execution at San Quentin prison when Bert Munroe
forces him to see the hanging from the viewpoint of the
prisoner; but it is difficult to lament the end of Raymond

Banks' busman's holidays, even though the stronger inclination is to condemn Bert's morbid curiosity.   The Lopez
sisters leave the valley and Raymond Banks will never see
a good hanging again, but the natural goodness and moral
resiliency of the sisters and Raymond's seriousness and
lack of imagination are sufficient to see them through their
losses.

The final story in The Pastures of Heaven presents
the most visionary of all the hopes and dreams exposed to
the peculiar evil cloud which follows the Munroes.   John
Whiteside's dream of founding a dynasty parallels the ambition of Joseph Wayne in To a God Unknown and their visions and their subsequent failures are equally profound,
even though no parallel exists between Whiteside's fall and
the death of the Frazerian fisher king.   The Whiteside
house embodies the sense of tradition that exists among the
people of the valley, and the Whiteside family represents a
deep and enduring faith in the immortality of man which
exists in the natural process of renewal and continuity within the family structure.   Again, the culprit in the story is
the Munroe family.   Mae Munroe's desire to live near her
friends in Monterey after she marries John Whiteside's son
ends the unity and hope of continuity in the Whiteside family; and Bert Munroe's good-neighborliness instigates the
project which ends when the Whiteside house accidentally
burns down.

The destruction of the most far reaching dream that
appears in The Pastures of Heaven by the forces of mediocrity strongly suggests the possibility that the world belongs
to the Munroes even if the victory is by default.   Steinbeck
qualifies that possible conclusion, however, by focusing on
the nature of the vision.   John Whiteside's fall borders on
tragedy because he fails to accept the nature of reality when
he creates his grand design.   He is a saner version of
Faulkner's Thomas Sutpen in Absalom, Absalom!; but, unfortunately, he shares Sutpen's flaw, his inability to adapt
his vision to natural and human factors.   Steinbeck does not
deny the value of the dream in any of the stories in The
Pastures of Heaven any more than Fitzgerald does in The
Great Gatsby.   He does, however, suggest that men of
imagination and feeling have to be aware of the forces which
threaten them.   They will have to accept the cruel twists of
fate and overcome the human mediocrity and idiocy which
exist in ominous abundance in the world if they are to succeed in fulfilling their visions of the harmony and peace

which the tourists mistakenly believe exist in the Pastures
of Heaven. The battle for that harmony and peace is portrayed in the novels which follow The Pastures of Heaven.

Notes

1. Even though The Pastures of Heaven was published in
    1932, a year before the publication of To a God Un-
    known, Steinbeck had finished a version of the latter
    work, entitled "To an Unknown God," before he
    started serious work on The Pastures of Heaven.
    The difficulty that Steinbeck's agents, McIntosh &
    Otis, had in finding a publisher is the apparent rea-
    son To a God Unknown appeared after The Pastures
    of Heaven. Peter Lisca points out in his study of
    Steinbeck manuscripts that the many deletions and
    additions in the first draft of The Pastures of Heaven
    indicate that Steinbeck also struggled with this work
    before arriving at a final version. See Peter Lis-
    ca's The Wide World of John Steinbeck (New Bruns-
    wick, N. J.: Rutgers University Press, 1958), pp.
    57-58.

2. The Pastures of Heaven (New York: Viking, 1952).
    All quotations that appear in the study are taken from
    this edition.

3. This version of the letter, not quoted completely here,
    appears in Lisca, pp. 56-57.

4. The significance of the line was made even more obvi-
    ous when Steinbeck published the story of Junius
    Maltby in 1936 as a monograph with the title, Nothing
    So Monstrous. Steinbeck uses the line ironically in
    the story, for Stevenson's "monstrous" vision is the
    hope and vitality of youth. Steinbeck also made his
    viewpoint more obvious in the later monograph by
    writing an epilogue in which he expresses his own
    hope that Junius would not "go under" and one day
    may have come back to the Pastures of Heaven.

IV. APPARATUS FOR RESEARCH PAPERS

A. Ten Questions for Discussion

1. Steinbeck uses irony in The Pastures of Heaven rather forcefully in some of his stories, while in others he employs it with more precision and sharpness. In which of the stories does the irony appear more obvious than in some of the others? Is this forcefulness important thematically?

2. Does Steinbeck's interest in the organic relationship between man and nature affect the development of character in The Pastures of Heaven? In what way does a perversion of this relationship give authority and prestige to the respectable people of the valley?

3. Katherine Wicks feels that her husband has never had the opportunity to fulfill his dream of wealth. Based on the evidence in the story do you agree with her that, once properly inspired, Shark Wicks will achieve in the real world of business what he accomplished in his imaginary financial dealings?

4. How relevant to the meaning of The Pastures of Heaven is Miss Morgan's view that American cultural starvation is "due to its boorish and superstitious denial of the existence of fairies" (p. 42)?

5. Is it possible to see Helen Van Deventer as the real victim in the story of her mad pursuit of pain and tragedy? What possible significance do Hubert's dying words have in determining the drives behind Helen's mad actions?

6. On the one hand, membership on the school board represents a mark of prestige in the valley. John Whiteside, the most respected farmer in the valley, holds the board's most important position. The board, itself, however, is responsible for damaging the lives of Tularecito and Robbie Maltby. What purpose does Steinbeck have in assigning a dual function to the school board in The Pastures of Heaven?

7. How seriously does Steinbeck treat the moral issue of the Lopez sisters' function in the valley? Is it possible that seriousness is one of the moral problems in The Pastures of Heaven?

8. How sympathetic is Steinbeck in portraying Molly Morgan's compelling need to preserve the image of her dead father? What is his purpose in providing the reader with sufficient evidence to know that Molly's vision is a distortion of the truth?

9. The story of Raymond Banks could be seen as a parody
    of the non-thinking Hemingway hero who thrives on the
    religion of doing something well and feeling good about
    it. How seriously does Steinbeck treat the subject of
    professional killing in the story?
10. Compare Steinbeck's use of the house as symbol in the
    stories of Pat Humbert and John Whiteside. Does either
    of the stories develop the image of house in a way com-
    mon to American literature (some examples, for a com-
    parative discussion, might be Poe's "The Fall of the
    House of Usher," Hawthorne's The House of the Seven
    Gables, James' "The Jolly Corner," and Faulkner's
    Absalom, Absalom!)?

B. Suggested Topics for Research Papers

1. The dimensions of Steinbeck's ironic realism in The
    Pastures of Heaven.
2. John Whiteside and the theme of patriarchy in Stein-
    beck's fiction.
3. Steinbeck's use of time in The Pastures of Heaven.
4. Junius Maltby, Molly Morgan's father, and the Lopez
    sisters: mapping out the territory for Tortilla Flat.
5. The myth of prophecy and curse in The Pastures of
    Heaven.
6. The Pastures of Heaven and Winesburg, Ohio: studies
    of the frustrated and lonely American.
7. The dreamer or the dream in The Pastures of Heaven.
8. Tularecito and Lenny: Steinbeck's good animals.
9. Steinbeck as social reformer in The Pastures of Heaven.
10. Fate in The Pastures of Heaven: Steinbeck and the
    problem of Naturalism.
11. Evidence of Steinbeck's non-teleological thinking in The
    Pastures of Heaven.
12. The Pastures of Heaven and the vision of Eden in Stein-
    beck's fiction.
13. Steinbeck's women: matriarchy and dementia in The
    Pastures of Heaven.
14. Social respectability: the snake in Steinbeck's Pastures
    of Heaven.
15. Steinbeck's unorthodox morality: madness and death in
    The Pastures of Heaven.

C.   Selected Bibliography

1.   Fontenrose, Joseph.   John Steinbeck: An Introduction
     and Interpretation.   New York: Holt, Rinehart and
     Winston, 1963.
          Fontenrose's book is an indispensable tool for seri-
     ous readers of Steinbeck's fiction.   Its particular contribu-
     tion to Steinbeck scholarship lies in the area of myth.
     Fontenrose traces Steinbeck's major interest in myth and
     how he incorporates fables and mythic patterns into his
     work.   He points out that Steinbeck's The Pastures of Heav-
     en has elements of folktales and fables dealing with curses,
     changelings, and chivalry among other things.

2.   French, Warren.   John Steinbeck.   New York: Twayne,
     1961.
          Warren French is one of the leading Steinbeck
     scholars in the world, and his book is an example of his
     sensitive understanding of Steinbeck's writings.   His chapter
     on The Pastures of Heaven is of particular value in stress-
     ing the various thematic patterns in the book, and, most
     importantly, it develops in detail the negative theme of
     middle-class respectability which Steinbeck associates with
     the Munroe family.

3.   Lisca, Peter.   The Wide World of John Steinbeck.
     New Brunswick, N.J.: Rutgers University Press, 1958.
          The chief value of Peter Lisca's impressive study of
     John Steinbeck is its information on Steinbeck manuscripts.
     Lisca points out that The Pastures of Heaven went through
     a variety of manuscript changes before it reached its final
     form.   Lisca views The Pastures of Heaven as more loosely
     developed thematically and structurally than do other Stein-
     beck critics.

4.   Moore, Harry Thornton.   The Novels of John Steinbeck:
     A First Critical Study.   Port Washington, N.Y.: Ken-
     nikat Press, 1968 (1939).
          This study, originally published in 1939, is a pioneer
     work in Steinbeck scholarship.   It provides a sensitive early
     reading of The Pastures of Heaven, and traces several of
     Steinbeck's developments as a major writer to directions in
     character, setting, and theme taken in this work.

5.   Watt, F. W.   Steinbeck.   London: Oliver and Boyd,
     1962.
          F. W. Watt offers the British view of John Steinbeck.

His comments on The Pastures of Heaven emphasize the
humanizing trend in Steinbeck's interest in character.   The
particular value in this study lies in Watt's appraisal of
the American critics' approach to the works of John Steinbeck.   He offers an excellent review of the basic approaches
in Steinbeck scholarship.

Chapter 8

STEINBECK'S THE PEARL (1947)

by Martha Heasley Cox

I. BACKGROUND

In The Log from the Sea of Cortez, Steinbeck's account of the scientific junket which he, Ed Ricketts, and their companions made in 1940 to the Gulf of California, Steinbeck tells of their visit to the fascinating and venerable city of La Paz. Indians are proud to have been born in that city with its magic carpet name, renowned throughout the area and once the great pearl city of the world. Steinbeck recounts an event which occurred there in recent years, a story of an Indian boy and a pearl, which, he says, seems to be true, though "it is so much like a parable that it almost can't be," a story that "is far too reasonable to be true" (103).

> An event which happened at La Paz in recent
> years is typical of such places. An Indian boy
> by accident found a pearl of great size, an unbe-
> lievable pearl. He knew its value was so great
> that he need never work again. In his one pearl
> he had the ability to be drunk as long as he
> wished, to marry any one of a number of girls,
> and to make many more a little happy too. In
> his great pearl lay salvation, for he could in ad-
> vance purchase masses sufficient to pop him out
> of Purgatory like a squeezed watermelon seed.
> In addition he could shift a number of dead rela-
> tives a little nearer to Paradise. He went to La
> Paz with his pearl in his hand and his future
> clear into eternity in his heart. He took his
> pearl to a broker and was offered so little that
> he grew angry, for he knew he was cheated.
> Then he carried his pearl to another broker and

was offered the same amount. After a few more
visits he came to know that the brokers were only
the many hands of one head and that he could not
sell his pearl for more. He took it to the beach
and hid it under a stone, and that night he was
clubbed into unconsciousness and his clothing was
searched. The next night he slept at the house
of a friend and his friend and he were injured
and bound and the whole house searched. Then
he went inland to lose his pursuers and he was
waylaid and tortured. But he was very angry
now and he knew what he must do. Hurt as he
was he crept back to La Paz in the night and he
skulked like a hunted fox to the beach and took
out his pearl from under the stone. Then he
cursed it and threw it as far as he could into the
channel. He was a free man again with his soul
in danger and his food and shelter insecure. And
he laughed a great deal about it. (Log, 102-3)

Steinbeck completed the manuscript for The Log from
the Sea of Cortez in 1941, using the two journals he and
Ed Ricketts had kept on the trips. Not until 1944, four
years after the visit to La Paz, did Steinbeck write his
version of the "true story," which, under the title "The
Pearl of the World," appeared in Woman's Home Companion
in December, 1945. The book version, with its title
shortened to The Pearl, was published by Viking Press in
1947; at the same time the RKO picture based on the short
novel was released.

II.   PLOT SYNOPSIS

Kino, a fisherman, lives with his wife Juana and
their baby son Coyotito in a brush house near the beach.
The peaceful awakening of Kino and his world on one perfect morning is disrupted by the enemy, who in the form
of a scorpion, invades the hut and stings the baby. Juana
attempts to suck the poison from the puncture, then insists
upon seeing the doctor, a cruel, ignorant, and avaricious
man, who never visits the brush houses. Knowing that the
doctor will not come to them, they go to his home, followed by all the neighbors. The doctor's servant, after
ascertaining that Kino has no money, tells them that the
doctor is out. Kino is angry and humiliated, but they return to the beach and go out in their canoe, hoping to find

a pearl of sufficient value to entice the doctor to treat their son. While Juana prays in the canoe, Kino searches for the pearl to the accompaniment of a barely perceptible inner song, The Song of the Pearl That Might Be. Under a little overhang, Kino finds a very large and old oyster; he brings it to the canoe, opens it, and discovers the greatest pearl in the world, perfect, and as large as a sea gull's egg.

The town vibrates with the news; the priest, the shopkeepers, the doctor, the beggars, the pearl buyers contemplate the pearl's worth and their own interests. People of the town, jealous of Kino's good fortune, become his enemy. But Kino and Juana, unaware of the evil about them, share their joy and plan their future: they will be married in the church, dressed in fine new clothes; Kino will buy a new harpoon and a rifle, Coyotito will go to school. When the priest comes to the hut, Kino hears the music of evil. When the doctor arrives to examine the baby, who is now nearly recovered, the parents, afraid to take any chances with their son, permit his treatment. After they leave, Kino buries the pearl in the dirt floor of their brush house. During the night an intruder comes searching for the pearl; Kino plunges his knife into him and receives a bruised forehead in the encounter. When Juana pleads with Kino to destroy the pearl before it destroys them, Kino insists that they must have the future the pearl will bring them. He digs up the pearl, and its loveliness and promise so comfort them that they begin the second day with hope.

Dressed in their best clothes, they lead a procession of neighbors, beggars, and other townspeople into La Paz where they intend to sell the pearl to the buyers, all of whom in reality represent one man. The first buyer they approach, a man skilled in the trade, says that the pearl is too large, a curiosity of little value, worth no more than a thousand pesos. When Kino refuses to sell it for that price, the buyer summons three confederates, all of whom disparage the pearl and offer even less. Kino leaves, determined to sell his pearl elsewhere, perhaps even in the capital. Kino's brother, Juan Tomás, warns Kino that he has defied not only the pearl buyers but the whole structure of life and will know its retribution. Always afraid of the city, Kino is now also afraid at home where unknown dark things lurk in the shadows. When he is attacked again that night, Juana pleads once more that he throw the pearl back into the sea. Kino, determined to give them their chance in the world, says that they will leave the next morning for the capital and sell the pearl there.

When morning comes, Juana, in an attempt to divert disaster, takes the pearl and runs to the beach. Kino hears her leave and reaches her just in time to wrench the pearl from her hand as she prepares to throw it into the water. Enraged, he strikes her, then kicks her after she falls among the boulders. When, sick with disgust, he walks up the beach, he is attacked once again and kills his unknown assailant. Juana knows that they must flee since Kino is now a murderer and hurries back to the hut for Coyotito. Kino goes to prepare the canoe, to find that it has been destroyed; he returns to the brush house, to find it in flames. The family takes refuge in Kino's brother's house until nightfall, when they leave quietly, going north where Kino has heard there were cities.

They walk all night, attempting to conceal their footprints, and hide at dawn in a little clearing near the road. There Kino looks into the pearl seeking his vision of a rifle, a church wedding, and an education for Coyotito. Instead he sees the reality of memory: a dark body with blood dripping from its throat, Juana crawling toward home after her beating, Coyotito's feverish face after the doctor's treatment. The music of the pearl has now become sinister and is interwoven with evil.

Kino awakes from an uneasy sleep to see three figures approaching; two of them, whom he recognizes as trackers, are on foot bent low to the ground and one is on horseback, carrying a rifle. Kino tells Juana that he should surrender, but she says that the pursuers would then spare neither her life nor that of the child. As they flee frantically toward the mountains, Kino sees Juana's cut and bruised feet and tries to persuade her to hide with the baby while he leads the trackers on, but she insists on going on with him. Gaining strength from her resolution, he heads toward a shadowy cleft where they find a spring and little pools of water. They hide in a small erosion cave near the spring when Kino sees the trackers approaching in the distance. He tells Juana to keep the baby quiet as the trackers pass by. They stop to rest by the pool, however, and one watches with the rifle in his lap while the others sleep. Kino, knowing that they will be found in the morning, sees that their only hope is for him to attack the man on guard while it is still dark. He edges carefully

down the rock shoulder and hides behind a dwarf palm only
twenty feet from the enemy.   Just as he starts to attack,
the moon rises.   It is now too late, for he will be seen.
With no alternative, Kino prepares to leap just as soon as
the man turns his head.   At that moment Coyotito cries,
alerting the watcher and awakening one of the sleepers, who
thinks the cry may have been that of a coyote pup.   When
the baby cries again, the watcher raises his rifle and fires
just as Kino is in mid-leap.   Maddened, Kino kills the
watchman and one of the seated men with his knife, then
grabs the rifle and shoots the third as he tries to climb the
cliff.   Only then does he hear the hysterical cry of death
from the little cave in the mountain.

Kino and Juana return late in the afternoon, walking
side by side down the country road.   Kino carries a rifle
and Juana a small heavy bundle in a shawl over her shoulder.   They walk through the city and down among the brush
houses to the water's edge.   Kino holds the pearl in his
hand.   In it he sees the frantic eyes of the man he has
shot and Coyotito with the top of his head blown away.   The
music of the pearl is distorted and insane.   Kino offers the
pearl to Juana, who refuses it, saying softly, "No, you."
Kino flings it into the ocean and they watch it disappear in
the setting sun.   The music of the pearl disappears too as
it settles down on the floor of the sea.

III.   CRITICAL EXPLICATION

While Steinbeck has based his novella on the "true
story" he heard, he has expanded its meaning, ordered and
controlled its action, and focused the reader's attention on
the aspects of the story he wishes to stress.   The seed
story, as Steinbeck records it, is less than 350 words and
fills about one page; the novella Steinbeck wrote contains
six chapters and fills, in the Bantam edition, 118 pages.

The original story has no indication of time limitations; Steinbeck's version takes five days to lead its victims from happiness and hope to desolation and despair.
It begins with daybreak and ends with sunset.   In the first
sentence, we are told that Kino awakens in the near dark,
but it is the dark that precedes the light of day; in the conclusion, he stands beside Juana in the setting sun, but it
is already dark night in his soul.   At the outset, Kino and
Juana are young, in love, and happy with each other and

their son; they have a canoe in which to earn their liveli-
hood, a grass hut they have made into a home, and the respect of the neighbors.   At the end they have lost the good
will of the community, their coral, their home, and their
son.   They have made a journey from innocence to awareness, both in the sense of an intellectual experience and
an actual excursion, a trip planned first to sell the pearl,
then a nighttime flight necessitated by the committing of a
murder, and finally a nightmare effort to escape the trackers who are in pursuit of both the pearl and their lives.

Such a journey is frequently employed in allegory
and many allegories and parables, stories told to teach
moral or religious lessons, contain stock characters,
stereotypes who stand for qualities or ideas or classes and
have little or no individuality.   Kino is, no doubt, man in
his dual role as protector and provider; Juana is woman
as both wife and mother; Coyotito is the first-born son, the
pride and hope of his parents.   The doctor is avarice; the
pearl buyers, deceit and collusion.   The whole community,
with the exception of Juan Tomás and his family, becomes,
through jealousy, the enemy.   Juan is brother, friend, and
counselor.   Insects, animals, inanimate objects also assume additional planes of meaning.   The scorpion is evil,
which can bring crippling or death; the pearl is promise,
which can bring wealth, freedom, knowledge, power, and
life--or sin, evil, destruction, and death.   In such a reading, Kino is Everyman and La Paz, Everywhere.

But Steinbeck's sense of place is so strong, even in
the structure of parable or allegory, that his settings are
particularized.   Several of the characters too are sufficiently developed to attain some complexity and credibility as
individuals.

The story is told from the point of view of an omniscient narrator, who is not only the central intelligence
through whose mind and eyes we see the story but who also,
it seems safe to assume, speaks for Steinbeck.   This narrator tells us what characters do and say, observing them
and their surroundings with the accuracy and detail of the
eye of a camera.   But he also reads the minds of all,
even such minor characters as the beggars in front of the
church, and reveals secret dreams, inner music, and mur-
mured prayers.   In addition he interprets action and comments on behavior, sometimes making authorial judgments.
He tells us, for example, about the efficacy of a seaweed

poultice and what the tilt of a man's hat reveals.

The tone changes as the story progresses, reflecting at first the happiness Kino feels as he and his world awaken to a bright new day, "a morning like other mornings and yet perfect among mornings," (The Pearl, 14) but becoming increasingly solemn, and culminating in the somberness of the stalking long shadows, the tower of darkness, and the pillars of black fear that Kino and Juana carry with them as they return to La Paz, removed from human experience and on the other side of pain.

The story occurs in an atmosphere of illusion and unreality, qualities engendered by the uncertain light of the Gulf. All sights are unreal and vision can not be trusted. The air vibrates in a hazy mirage, obscuring some things and magnifying others so that people of the Gulf do not rely on their eyes to show them correct distances or clear outlines. Perhaps, the narrator speculates, they learn to trust things of the spirit and imagination instead.

When Steinbeck wrote The Pearl, he had worked extensively with film and been long absorbed with cinematic techniques. The year before, he had been in Mexico working on the impressive documentary The Forgotten Village, for which he wrote the script. It is not surprising, then, that much of The Pearl seems to be written from the point of view of the camera. His description of La Paz, for example, begins with a long or establishing shot of the town on the estuary; then the camera moves in closer in a medium shot to reveal the sand on the beach; then in a close-up pauses to observe the activities of the crabs and the lobsters, before going undersea to record life there:

> The town lay on a broad estuary, its old yellowed plastered buildings hugging the beach. And on the beach the white and blue canoes that came from Nayarit were drawn up, canoes preserved for generations by a hard shell-like waterproof plaster whose making was a secret of the fishing people. They were high and graceful canoes with curving bow and stern and a braced section midships where a mast could be stepped to carry a small lateen sail.
>
> The beach was yellow sand, but at the water's edge a rubble of shell and algae took its place.

> Fiddler crabs bubbled and sputtered in their holes
> in the sand, and in the shallows little lobsters
> popped in and out of their tiny homes in the rub-
> ble and sand. The sea bottom was rich with
> crawling and swimming and growing things. The
> brown algae waved in the gentle currents and the
> green eel grass swayed and little sea horses
> clung to its stems. Spotted botete, the poison
> fish, lay on the bottom in the eel-grass beds, and
> the bright-colored swimming crabs scampered over
> them. (The Pearl, 17-18)

The same photographic quality and attention to detail
is sustained throughout the novella, which begins in Kino's
brush hut, located in a tuna clump near the water. The
hut has a ground floor and, like all the other brush houses,
"leaked light and air" (82). Furnished with the greatest
simplicity, it contains the sleeping mat of woven tules for
Kino and Juana, the hanging box for Coyotito, and the fire-
pit which serves for cooking, heat, and light. A rutted
path leads to the city, which, with its stone and plaster
houses, its blinding plaza and church, its pearl buyers' offices with barred windows all clustered together on a narrow street, begins where the brush houses stop. The
houses have harsh outer walls, but cool inner gardens where
birds are caged and water splashes on flagstones. The doctor's chamber with its heavy dark furnishings, religious
pictures, and delicate china and silver is in sharp contrast
to the austerity of the brush house.

In more description akin to underwater photography,
we go with Kino and see through his eyes the beds where
he gathers the gray oysters "with ruffles like shirts on the
shells" (21) and the "hummock of rubbly rock" (24) beside
which he finds the ancient oyster and first glimpses the
ghostly gleam of the great pearl.

We accompany the little family as they walk all
night, their flight lit by stars, to hide at daybreak in a
roadside covert, "a little clearing where deer might have
lain ... curtained thickly with the dry brittle trees that
lined the road" (91). When the approach of the trackers
necessitates further flight, we see, in a long shot, the
mountains toward which the family flees, "the naked granite
mountains, rising out of erosion rubble and standing monolithic against the sky" (99). Then we return to such close
range that we observe the horned toads watch them pass as

they head for a dark, shadowy cleft in the range, where a hint of foliage presaged water. There indeed a water bubbles out of a stone forming little pools. Nearby is the platform of stone and sand where the pursuers will stop to rest and sleep. On the gray shoulder behind the cleft are shallow erosion caves, scoops hollowed by the wind, where they hide until Kino climbs down the mountain face to attack the pursuers, and where Coyotito is killed. Then Kino and Juana return to La Paz, walking through the stone and plaster city, by the site where their house once stood, to the water's edge. They, the pearl, and the story are back where all began as the pearl sinks into the floor of the sea.

The brief original story of the pearl contains several characters, all of whom Steinbeck uses in some form in his novella: an Indian boy, a number of girls, dead relatives, pearl brokers, a friend, attackers, and pursuers. The unnamed Indian boy is transformed into Kino, named, as the Priest tells him, for a great man and a great father of the church, who "tamed the desert and sweetened the minds of thy people" (35). That man was the seventeenth-century Jesuit, Eusebius Kino, a missionary and explorer in the Gulf region. Kino, Steinbeck's protagonist, is a young married man with a child, who is respected in the community. He has black hair; a thin, coarse moustache; and warm fierce eyes. Over his clean white clothes which have been washed a thousand times, he wears an ancient blanket and a large straw hat, properly tilted. A fisherman and pearl diver, he owns his own canoe, inherited from his father and grandfather before him, and his brush hut, but can offer the doctor what is seemingly his total wealth otherwise-- eight ugly, misshapen almost valueless seed pearls in payment for treating his son.

Kino is a quiet sensitive man, who has great strength and courage. His sigh of satisfaction is to him conversation, and his account of the future he sees in the pearl is the longest speech Juana has ever heard him make, causing her to wonder at his courage and imagination. He listens continually to an inner music, not knowing whether he alone or all of his people hear it. He speaks softly to his timid dog and always touches his canoe tenderly. When he leaves the cave to attack the pursuers, he lays his palm on Coyotito's head in farewell and touches Juana's cheek. But he fights fearlessly when his family is threatened, snarling and bearing his teeth when he destroys the scorpion; leaping, striking, and spitting at the dark thing in his house; and

moving with the strength of a terrible machine as he kills
the three pursuers. Yet when he encounters the brokers,
his only defense is a slight slitting of the eyes, tightening
of the lips, and a reticence. Angered at their collusion,
he strides away, with blood pounding in his ears, and decides, though he has never been away from home and fears
strangers and strange places, to go to the capital to sell
his pearl. Beset by conflicting emotions of fear and anger
when he approaches the doctor, his actions show the ambivalence he feels: his lips draw tight in anger as he knocks
but he simultaneously raises his other hand to take off his
hat. After his public shaming when the doctor refuses to
see him, he, like Billy Budd, can only strike out. In the
absence of his adversary, he strikes the gate such a crushing blow that the blood flows from his split knuckles.

Kino possesses a native shrewdness which serves
him well: he instinctively knows his dramatic effect when
bargaining with the broker; he hears the music of evil when
the priest visits; he refuses to give the pearl to the doctor
for safekeeping; he knows that the pearl is valuable because
of the attempted thefts.

Kino changes after the discovery of the pearl. He
feels trapped by his own ignorance and by the doctor's
greed and duplicity. He becomes cautious and suspicious,
fearing everyone, knowing that even the gods are hostile to
his plans. His brain burns "even during his sleep" (47-48).
He is determined, however, to give his family a future, to
see that his wishes for them, which are both modest and
admirable, have a chance for fulfillment. He resists,
therefore, Juana's pleadings that he throw the pearl--and
the future he envisions--back into the water. When she
defies him, and tries to throw the pearl away herself, he
beats her brutally before he turns away in sick disgust.
Later, however, he decides twice to sacrifice himself for
his wife and son, once through surrender to the pursuers,
once as a decoy to lead the trackers on while Juana hides
with Coyotito. Only Juana's insistence that his surrender
would be futile, since they would all be killed anyway and
she wishes to stay with him, prevents either action. Finally, when Coyotito is dead, he returns to the city, as
"dangerous as a rising storm" (116).

The number of girls the Indian boy wishes to marry
or "to make . . . a little happy" (Log, 102) coalesce in
Juana, whose name means "woman" and who, in the

novella, is Kino's only romantic interest. She has dark
eyes which make "little reflected stars" (2) and wears her
black hair in two braids tied with ribbons. When the story
opens she wears an old blue skirt and torn shawl, but
changes to her wedding skirt and waist for the trip to the
pearl brokers.

Juana is the idealized woman, obedient, respectful,
cheerful, patient, and courageous. She is a good mother,
caring for Coyotito and reassuring him with soft songs to
make him feel warm and safe. When Coyotito is wounded,
it is Juana who sucks the poison from his puncture, then
insists that he be treated by the doctor. She keeps the baby
quiet on the flight until, after many hours of silence, his
murmuring cry alerts the pursuers to their presence. Then
it is her "keening, moaning, rising, hysterical cry ... of
death" (114) that reveals Coyotito's fate to Kino and to us.

A helpmate to Kino, she shows surprising strength
and courage. In the canoe she rows like a strong man and
withstands hunger and fatigue almost better than Kino himself. Her prayers in time of trouble are a mixture of ancient magic and a Hail Mary. It is she who first senses
the evil in the pearl and twice pleads with Kino to destroy
it. When he refuses, she tries to throw it back into the
water herself. She tends Kino when he is wounded, rushes
to help when he is attacked, and drags the body of the man
he murdered into the bushes. It is Juana who then decides
that they must flee. On their return "her wide eyes stared
inward" and she was "as remote and removed as Heaven"
(115).

The relationship of Kino and Juana undergoes subtle
changes as the story progresses, indicated, at least in part,
by their relative standing or walking positions: when they
go to see the doctor, Juana walks first, carrying Coyotito,
with Kino following behind; on the way to and from the pearl
brokers, Kino goes first and Juana follows; when they begin
their flight, Kino again leads, while Juana, carrying the
baby, trots after him. But in times of sorrow, shame, or
renunciation, they stand or walk side by side: when they
are humiliated by the doctor they stand side by side in rejection; when they return to La Paz, they walk not in single
file but side by side; when Kino throws the pearl into the
water, they stand side by side for a long time.

Whatever the specific and local cultural and ethnic

patterns which at least help determine their relationship,
they are also influenced by the man-woman syndrome, a
pattern of behavior dictated by their, and perhaps Steinbeck's, attitudes toward their respective sexes. The narrator tells us that though Juana is puzzled by the differences
between a man and a woman, she knows, accepts, and
needs them. In reply to her repeated pleading that he destroy the pearl, Kino's face grows crafty and he refuses,
saying twice, "I am a man" (74); and Juana is silenced,
"for his voice was command" (74). When, exercising her
"quality of woman" (77) for reason, caution, and preservation, she attempts the deed herself the next morning and
receives a severe beating for her efforts, she neither resists nor tries to protect herself. When Kino said "I am
a man, " that "meant that he was half insane and half god"
(77); and "Juana had need of a man; she could not live
without a man" (77). Though in her "woman's soul" (77)
she knew she would be destroyed, she would follow him
without question, and sometimes her "quality of woman ...
could cut through Kino's manners and save them all" (77).
She does preserve the family unit twice on the flight; once,
when she goads Kino out of surrender, and again, when he
takes strength from her refusal to stay behind while he
goes on alone. In the final scene, she softly refuses when
he offers her the pearl; maintaining the man-woman roles,
she leaves the gesture of renunciation to him.

Hints of catharsis, on their emergence from the valley of the shadow of death after the sacrifice of their first-
born in the mountains, occur when the narrator tells us
that as Kino and Juana return, walking side by side, they
seem removed from human experience, as if they "had gone
through pain and had come out on the other side" (116) and
"that there was almost a magical protection about them"
(116).

Other characters mentioned in the seed story are the
pearl brokers, the pursuers who were presumably also the
attackers, a friend, and dead relatives. Four pearl buyers
appear in Steinbeck's version, without names but with distinct personalities, all differentiated in some way from one
another, but all alike in their desire to perform their duty
to their common employer, conniving to convince Kino that
the pearl is of little value and to buy it as cheaply as possible. In the novella, the attackers, even more ominous
because they are without form or name, are assailants who
creep in the night, identified as "the sound" or "the thing. "

The pursuers on the flight are three, the dark horseman carrying the rifle and the two inhuman trackers, who scutter, crawl, and whine "like excited dogs on a warming trail" (96). The closest parallel to the friend of the seed story is Kino's brother, Juan Tomás, who offers counsel about selling the pearl and caution about defying the way of life of the fishermen. Like the Indian boy's friend, Juan Tomás shields Kino in his home after Kino has killed his unknown assailant. Although the dead relatives the Indian boy "could shift ... a little nearer Paradise (Log, 102) do not appear in Steinbeck's version, the Masses of the seed story are mentioned in the sketch of the doctor, whose dead wife "if Masses willed and paid for out of her own estate could do it, was in Heaven" (14).

The doctor; Coyotito; Juan Tomás's wife, Apolonia, and their four children; the doctor's servant; the priest; the neighboring fishermen; the four beggars; the shopkeepers; and the Chinese grocery store owners are not suggested in the seed story. Some are only supernumeraries; some more; but all add color and verisimilitude to the story.

The most fully developed is the doctor, a fat and lazy man, who is cruel and avaricious. A member of a race which has starved, robbed, frightened and despised Kino's people for nearly four hundred years, he is the chief antagonist of the novella. His clothing, a Parisian dressing gown of red watered silk; his appearance, eyes which rest in puffy little hammocks of flesh, and mouth drooping with discontent; his breakfast, chocolate and other sweets served in silver and fine china--all delineate his position and character and differentiate between his life and Kino's. Though the doctor battens on the suspicion, fear, and ignorance of the fishermen, he tends their sick only when assured of ample recompense, feigning the need for his services when none exists, and practicing subterfuge rather than the healing art to attain his ill-gotten wealth.

Coyotito, the baby, serves chiefly as catalyst. His scorpion sting necessitates the visit to the doctor and, in turn, the search for the great pearl. Kino's desire to give his son an education is a major reason for retaining the pearl. Juana's concern for his welfare and safety help define her role as woman, even in defiance of her husband. His death is the ultimate pain, the death of hope, which leads to the return of his parents and the rejection of the pearl. His name, the diminutive of the Mexican-Spanish

word for Coyote, derives from the Nahuatl word "coyotl."
Steinbeck emphasizes the connection when he has one of the
pursuers speculate that the baby's cry from the cave may
be a coyote, for he has heard "a coyote pup cry like a
baby" (113).

Steinbeck's suggestions that the story is parable encourage readers to search for symbolic interpretations, for
elements or characters that suggest a range of meaning
beyond themselves. The most obvious symbol is, of course,
the pearl, itself an accident, the result of a grain of sand
that so irritated the oyster that in self-protection it created
a layer of smooth cement. This particular pearl, however,
is unique. As perfect as the moon and as large as a sea
gull's egg, it is the greatest pearl in the world. Its significance and appearance and effect vary with the beholder,
the time, and the place. For Kino, it is a crystal ball
which reveals fortune and future, forming promising pictures of things hitherto considered impossible. The beauty
of the pearl cozens his brain and promises a "poultice
against illness and a wall against insult" (51). It closes
"a door on hunger" (51). Eventually he says "it is my mis-
fortune and my life and I will keep it" (86), and in a
Faustian declaration: "This pearl has become my soul....
If I give it up I shall lose my soul" (87). For Juana, who
comes to believe the pearl has destructive power, it is
evil, like a sin, and the devil is in it. In the town, the
pearl stirs up black and evil, for when the essence of the
pearl mixed with the essence of men "a curious dark resi-
due was precipitated" (30). Then the symbol of the pearl
merges with the symbol of the scorpion, which, accompanied by the song of evil, had invaded the idyllic setting
and struck the child. Now the pearl-scorpion has struck
the town: "the black distillate was like the scorpion" (30)
and the "poison sacs of the town began to manufacture
venom, and the town swelled and puffed with the pressure
of it" (30).

The pearl, its promises having proved as deceptive
and illusory as those of the witch's brew in Macbeth, no
longer projects the future for Kino but reflects instead the
reality of past nightmares: his wife beaten; his enemies
killed; his son ill, then dead. By the end of the novella,
the pearl's silver incandescence has become gray and ul-
cerous like malignant growth. When Kino flings it back into
the ocean, it winks and glimmers in the setting sun, as if
to reinforce its illusory qualities, before it disappears.

Both the canoe and the rifle have symbolic overtones too. The canoe, which Kino always touches tenderly, is "at once property and source of food" (19) and "the bulwark against starvation" (19). Its destruction is murder, murder most foul: "This was an evil beyond thinking. The killing of a man was not so evil as the killing of a boat. For a boat does not have sons, and a boat cannot protect itself, and a wounded boat does not heal" (80). When Kino saw a rifle in the pearl, his neighbors nodded at his wild imaginings, for to own a rifle was an impossibility. His wish for one "broke down the barriers" (32); yet, ironically, it is the one wish granted. When Kino and Juana return, he carries the rifle, the instrument of death for his son, across his arm; she carries the dead baby in her shawl crusted with dried blood. It is almost as if one has been exchanged for the other.

Symbols less well integrated into the story, and obvious in their meaning, are the school of small fishes slaughtered by the great fishes and the little mice who creep about on the ground while the night hawk hunts them silently.

In addition to fowls and fishes, Steinbeck uses insect and animal imagery throughout the novella, often for reasons other than symbolic. The skinny black puppy, for example, who appears three times, helps show the change in Kino, who speaks to it softly on the first morning but ignores it on subsequent appearances even though it "threshed itself in greeting like a wind-blown flag" (37) or "nearly shook his hind quarters loose" (43). A list, no doubt incomplete, includes goats, moths, ants, roosters, wild doves, the scorpion, caged birds, sea birds, small gray birds, dawn birds, fiddler crabs, lobsters, sea horses, spotted botete, pigs, crickets, tree frogs, toads, fishes, hawks, cats, coyotes, horned toads, jack rabbits, wild sheep, deer, pumas, racoons, water-skaters, water-worms, and cicadas.

These images frequently appear in similes and metaphors: when Kino strikes Juana, he hisses at her like a snake, and she stares at him "with wide unfrightened eyes, like a sheep before the butcher" (76); and later Kino edges "like a slow lizard down the smooth rock shoulder" (110). Such images enforce the dehumanization process that occurs as the story progresses, as well as the animal-like existence the family leads while hunted and at bay in the mountains. After the destruction of the canoe, Kino became an

animal "for hiding, for attacking" (80); when they left La
Paz "some animal thing was moving in him" (90); and they
run "for the high place, as nearly all animals do when they
are pursued" (99).

But this is man forced into an animal existence when
he is pushed beyond the bounds of human endurance. In an
earlier passage, the narrator is careful to distinguish between the two species and asserts the superiority of man:
"... it is said that humans are never satisfied, that you
give them one thing and they want something more. And
this is said in disparagement, whereas it is one of the
greatest talents the species has and one that has made it
superior to animals that are satisfied with what they have"
(32).

Steinbeck has used animal and insect imagery frequently, and perhaps most effectively, to provide sound effects in the novella, and has indeed written a sound track
into his story. Here is one of numerous examples: "The
coyotes cried and laughed in the brush, and the owls
screeched and hissed over their heads. And once some
larger animal lumbered away, crackling the undergrowth as
it went" (91). Similar onomatopoeic passages sometimes
contain visual, auditory, and olfactory imagery, as in this
instance:

> He heard every little sound of the gathering night,
> the sleepy complaint of settling birds, the love
> agony of cats, the strike and withdrawal of little
> waves on the beach, and the simple hiss of dis-
> tance. And he could smell the sharp odor of ex-
> posed kelp from the receding tide. The little
> flare of the twig fire made the design on his
> sleeping mat jump before his entranced eyes. (71)

The most discussed and, initially, most obvious of
the sound effects are the songs which accompany all action,
warning, celebrating, comforting; roaring, soaring, inter-
mingling, rising and falling until the symphony ends: the
Song of the Family, the Song of Evil, the Song of the Enemy, the Song of the Undersea, the Song of the Pearl That
Might Be. For Kino's people had been great makers of
songs and "everything they saw or thought or did or heard"
(2) became a song; they made songs "to the fishes, to the
sea in anger and to the sea in calm, to the light and the
dark and the sun and the moon" (22).

Lighting effects are handled subtly throughout the novella, often emphasizing the uncertain, illusory quality, as in this passage with its pattern of moon and clouds and dark and light: "A flight of herring clouds had moved over the sky from the south. The pale moon dipped in and out of the strands of clouds so that Juana walked in darkness for a moment and in light the next" (78).

Critics have interpreted The Pearl in a number of ways. It has been called a search for values, man's search for his soul, a study of the vanity of human wishes, the struggle of one man against a predatory community, a lesson showing that man must stay in his own niche and not encroach on others, and, most often, a rejection of materialism. Though the omniscient narrator guides the reader toward an interpretation or, at least, toward several thematic statements, Steinbeck, in the prefatory comment, invites every reader to take his own meaning from the story, to read his own life into it.

IV. APPARATUS FOR RESEARCH PAPERS

A. Ten Questions for Discussion

1. Steinbeck differentiates between the qualities of man and woman, calling man "half insane and half god" and saying that he may be saved at times by the quality of woman--reason, caution, and self preservation. Do Kino and Juana exemplify these respective qualities? If so, when and how? Do you consider the qualities typical of generic man and woman? How would a woman's liberationist view Steinbeck's depiction of woman and her place, as exemplified by Juana?

2. Peter Lisca says that Steinbeck is unwilling to assign absolute blame and create villains in The Pearl. Are there characters you consider villainous? the doctor, the priest, the pearl brokers, the trackers, the assailants? If so, why? If not, why not?

3. Harry T. Moore says: "We cannot describe Kino or his people as in despair, for they have never known any life other than the one they lead; neither are they in hopelessness, for they are not aware that there is anything for which to hope." Do you agree? If so, how do you account for Kino's wishes?

4. Do characters develop and change in the novella? If so, who does, and how?

5. What is the climax of the novella? What are the major
   complications? How are they resolved?
6. Why does Kino return to La Paz? Under what conditions? What awaits him there? Warren French feels
   that Steinbeck leaves too many questions unanswered.
   He says: "Steinbeck leaves the impression at the end
   of The Pearl that all is forgiven and will be forgotten.
   But is it? ... Kino has killed several agents of his
   pursuers. Can he be expected to go unpunished? Even
   more important, can he really suppress his ambitions
   and accept his former humble place?" How would you
   answer his questions?
7. While discussing The Pearl as allegory, Harry T.
   Moore poses several questions: "What are the results
   of Kino's particular search...? What is the nature of
   Kino's soul? its disposition? in grace? or reprobation?
   What set of values did he arrive at? What is the precise nature of the materialism which he rejected?"
   How would you answer each question?
8. Steinbeck wrote in the Preface: "If this story is a
   parable, perhaps everyone takes his own meaning from
   it and reads his own life into it." What does the parable mean to you?
9. Joseph Fontenrose calls The Pearl "a morality set to
   music." Discuss the use Steinbeck makes of the Songs.
   Do they supply meaning? If so, how? Do you find
   them successful? Why, or why not?
10. Comment on the following:
    a. Kino's decision comes, of course, when he realizes
       the destructive nature of material wealth, since in
       order to keep his pearl he must be willing to ex-
       ploit his own people, the Indians of the Gulf. So
       Kino rejects his newly-acquired fortune but not until
       an avaricious society has burned his home and
       killed his baby. --Richard Astro
    b. To say that in throwing the pearl into the sea Kino
       is symbolically divesting himself of false values is
       to sentimentalize his character by attributing to
       him qualities which are inconsistent with his earlier
       actions and statements. --Roland Bartel
    c. This gesture [flinging the pearl into the sea] has
       been widely admired as symbolizing a rejection of
       materialism. Unfortunately, that is not all it sym-
       bolizes. The reader is led to believe that Kino
       has not only rejected materialism but accepted the
       whole way of life he hoped to escape. The gesture
       may be interpreted not only as noble renunciation,

but also as defeatism.   --Warren French
d. Kino becomes incredibly sophisticated.   --Harry T.
    Moore
e. The Pearl offers lyrical beauty and a simple action
    leading to a sombre and pathetic conclusion.
    --F. W. Watt
f. This [The Pearl] is a non-teleological tale.   This
    is the way things are.   --Joseph Fontenrose
g. But although Steinbeck may have brought together
    a Mexican folk tale and a passage from the "Acts
    of Thomas" to create a pattern of man's search for
    his soul, that search takes place in a context which
    gives it also a materialistic and a practical mean-
    ing, one related to Steinbeck's concepts of non-
    teleological thinking and ecology.

B.   Suggested Topics for Research Papers

1. The novella begins: "Kino awakened in the near dark."
    Discuss the significance of the word "dark" in this sen-
    tence.   Then trace the words "dark," "darkness," and
    "night" throughout the story, commenting on their mul-
    tiple meanings in varying contexts.
2. Discuss the reactions of the following characters to the
    pearl: Kino, Juana, Juan Tomás, the priest, the doc-
    tor, the pearl buyers.   How does the response of each
    reflect his character?
3. Discuss the use of dialogue in The Pearl.   Is it con-
    sistent, credible, effective?
4. Much of The Pearl is lyrical.   The ending, in particu-
    lar, employs a number of poetic devices: repetition of
    phrases, balanced sentences, simile and metaphor,
    symbolism and imagery.   Write a paper analyzing the
    use of poetic techniques in the conclusion.
5. Discuss the role of religion in the novel, considering
    the part of the priest, the content and context of Juana's
    prayers, and Kino's attitude toward God or the gods.
6. In his prefatory comment, Steinbeck says, "as with all
    retold tales that are in people's hearts, there are only
    good and bad things and black and white things and good
    and evil things and no in-between things anywhere."
    Analyze the novel in the light of the author's comment.
    What things are good?   What evil?   Do you find any
    that are in-between?
7. Assessment of Steinbeck's achievement in The Pearl
    varies.   Warren French calls the novella turgid and

over-inflated, a melodramatic soap-opera which is "not just a disappointment, but a betrayal." Peter Lisca says that "one of the distinguishing marks of Steinbeck's genius is his ability to fuse the realistic and the lyric into a fable-like texture and structure" and that "The Pearl is perhaps his greatest success with this strategy." Write a paper in refutation or support of either assessment.

8. Steinbeck's short story "Flight" [available in The Long Valley or in The Portable Steinbeck] affords an interesting study in relation to The Pearl. Read "Flight," then write a paper tracing the parallels between the short story and the short novel.

9. Critics have suggested that Steinbeck may have been influenced by both "The Hymn of the Soul," sometimes called "The Hymn of the Pearl," from the Gnostic Acts of Judas Thomas and by Matthew 13:45-46. Read both possible sources and see what parallels you can draw.

10. Discuss the symbolic uses of The Pearl in other contexts, other cultures, other times. Consult an unabridged dictionary, a thesaurus, a book of quotations, an encyclopedia, a dictionary of symbolism, and a Biblical concordance. What similarities do you find between Steinbeck's use of The Pearl and that of others?

C. Selected Bibliography

Primary Sources

1. Steinbeck, John. The Log from the Sea of Cortez. New York: The Viking Press, 1941. Steinbeck's Log contains the seed story for The Pearl and additional information about La Paz. The Log was also published in Sea of Cortez (in collaboration with Edward F. Ricketts). New York: The Viking Press, 1941.

2. _____. The Pearl. New York: The Viking Press, 1947. The first book version published. The novella has been reissued in several paperback editions, by Viking and other publishers, and in an edition with The Red Pony (1965) and with five other novellas in The Short Novels of John Steinbeck, both published by Viking.

3. _____. "The Pearl of the World," Woman's Home

Companion, 72 (December, 1945), pp. 77 ff. The first
published version of the novella, which was subsequently
published separately as The Pearl.

Secondary Sources

1. Astro, Richard. "Steinbeck's Post-War Trilogy: A
    Return to Nature and the Natural Man," Twentieth Cen-
    tury Literature, 16 (April, 1970), 109-122. A discus-
    sion of The Pearl as one of a trilogy in which Steinbeck
    treats man and his relationship to nature, specifically
    in The Pearl man's choice of the benign natural order
    over the materialistic man-made world.

2. Bartel, Roland. "Proportioning in Fiction: The Pearl
    and Silas Marner," English Journal, 56 (April, 1967),
    542-546. An argument that attention to the relative
    space allotted to different episodes, characters, and
    themes is one important step in correct interpretation
    and that such attention should help correct many popular
    but erroneous interpretations of The Pearl.

3. Fontenrose, Joseph. John Steinbeck: An Introduction
    and Interpretation. New York: Holt, Rinehart and Win-
    ston, Inc., 1963, pp. 111-114. A discussion of The
    Pearl as "a morality set to music. "

4. French, Warren. John Steinbeck. New Haven: Col-
    lege and University Press, 1961, pp. 137-142. In a
    chapter entitled "The Defective Pearl," French calls
    the novella "not just a disappointment, but a betrayal, "
    and explains the reasons for his assessment.

5. Hamby, James A. "Steinbeck's The Pearl: Tradition
    and Innovation," Western Review, 7 (1970), 65-66. An
    argument that an understanding of Steinbeck's theme in
    The Pearl requires a study of analogous detail, detail
    which shows that cultural innovation must develop within
    tradition and cannot overthrow that tradition.

6. Lisca, Peter. "Steinbeck's Fable of the Pearl," in
    Steinbeck and His Critics. Albuquerque: The Univer-
    sity of New Mexico Press, 1957. An analysis of The
    Pearl as a successful blending of "the realistic and the
    lyric into a fable-like texture and structure. "

7. _____ . The Wide World of John Steinbeck. New

Brunswick: Rutgers University Press, 1958, pp. 218-
230. An analysis of The Pearl with particular attention
to Steinbeck's prose style which "becomes technique as
well as medium. " The chapter on The Pearl in this
book contains much of the same material as the essay
listed above.

8. Metzger, Charles R. "The Film Version of Steinbeck's
The Pearl, " Steinbeck Quarterly, 4 (Summer, 1971, 88-
92. An analysis of the differences between book and film,
with the suggestion that one view and judge the film with the
recognition that it was made in Mexico, by Mexicans, and
primarily for Mexican viewers.

9. Morris, Harry. "The Pearl: Realism and Allegory, "
English Journal, 52 (October, 1963), 487-95, 505 (reprinted in Steinbeck: A Collection of Critical Essays.
Englewood Cliffs, New Jersey: Prentice-Hall, 1972,
pp. 149-162). An explication of the allegorical mode,
followed by a discussion of the problems Steinbeck encounters in combining allegory with realism in The
Pearl.

10. Sugrue, Thomas. "Steinbeck's Mexican Folk-Tale, "
New York Herald Tribune Weekly Book Review, December 7, 1947, p. 4. A detailed comparison of Steinbeck's novella with the passage from "Acts of Thomas, "
known as "The Song of the Pearl" or "The Song of the
Soul. "

11. Vanderbeets, Richard. "A Pearl Is a Pearl Is a
Pearl, " CEA Critic, 32 (1970), 9. An argument that
Steinbeck warns against attempting to assess a natural
object at more than its real essence, that the pearl is
only a pearl and, as such, is inherently neither good
nor evil.

12. Watt, F. W. John Steinbeck. New York: Grove
Press, 1962, pp. 84-87. A brief analysis of the short
novel as a critical attack on the ways and values of
American civilization, an attack presented in a simple
story with lyrical beauty.

Chapter 9

STEINBECK'S OF MICE AND MEN (NOVEL) (1937)

by John F. Slater

I. BACKGROUND

The publication of Of Mice and Men in January of
1937 opened an impressive new horizon in the course of
Steinbeck's literary development and brought about significant alterations, not entirely welcome, in his personal situation. Especially during his early years as a writer,
Steinbeck had shown restless attraction to imagery that focused on the activity of learning. When he wrote, in Tortilla Flat, "the waves gently practiced at striking and hissed
a little," he seemed to amplify his private concern with the
laborious reiterations needed to establish the wave-length of
a distinctive voice. In Of Mice and Men, Steinbeck continued to learn through practice. True to the scientific attitude he adopted toward the procedures of his craft, he
viewed the novel as a kind of laboratory, a theater of operations where he could master innovative dramatic skills.
Such skills had occasionally been absent from In Dubious
Battle, the novel that preceded Of Mice and Men, but they
were outstandingly present in the novel that followed, The
Grapes of Wrath. Steinbeck himself later repeatedly referred to Of Mice and Men as an "experiment."

The "experiment," he said, was an attempt to make
"a play that can be read or a novel that can be played."[1]
What he achieved was a union of competing genres that reflects simultaneously his respect for formal order and his
suspicion of it, his need for design without the expense of
yielding to any one orthodoxy. The surfacing at this time
of Steinbeck's overt interest in dramatic modes indicates
another, related conflict as well. His emergence as a public figure was threatening to impinge on his role as artist.
Of Mice and Men was an immediate popular and critical success. The novel, with the play and movie adaptation that
followed, brought financial security and engendered lasting

respect among critics who have treated few other of Steinbeck's works as kindly with the passage of time. But even
during the two-year period when he was working on Of Mice
and Men, Steinbeck was already troubled by the prospect of
wide recognition and acceptance: "I am scared of popularity. It has ruined everyone I know. "[2] Steinbeck welcomed
a moderately sized audience and subscribed to "the recent
tendency of writers ... to deal in those themes and those
scenes which are best understood and appreciated by groups
of people. "[3] An unbridled reception, however, could be as
harmful as a formless novel, and consequently Steinbeck declared his intention of "holding an audience, " necessarily
imagined as a finite one if the book were to become a play,
and of creating intimate, "almost physical contact"[4] with
his readers. For Steinbeck, the readership equivalent to a
packed house was a few tens of thousands, and he addressed
himself to them, not to the millions who eventually mate-
rialized in the wake of The Grapes of Wrath.

    An amusing sequence of anecdotes, involving the vari-
ous dogs that frequented the Steinbeck household from time
to time, serves to measure the rapidly changing circumstances he experienced during the mid-1930s. When writing
Cup of Gold, his first novel, Steinbeck had commented on
the dog-eat-dog aspect of canine life in a letter to his publishers, who were having difficulty promoting his books in
a hotly contested market: "Tillie Eulenspiegel the Airedale
has puppies, as sinful a crew as ever ruined rugs. Four
of them found your letter and ate all of it but the address.
I should imagine they were awed by the address if I had
not learned that they could hold nothing in reverence. At
present they are out eating each other. "[5] Cup of Gold is
about Henry Morgan and his "sinful crew" of pirates, a
subject genially reflected in Steinbeck's domestic milieu.
By 1933, dogs offered an audience, rather than a theme.
Steinbeck was more determined than ever to support himself as a writer, but his books had been such financial
disappointments that he could no longer afford a pet. Drawing on the only resource available, he outfitted himself in
the same dream of success with a dog and an audience:
"Even a little money would be better than a bundle of paper. We are very happy. I need a dog pretty badly. I
dreamed of great numbers of dogs last night. They sat in
a circle and looked at me and I wanted all of them. Apparently we are headed for the rocks. The light company
is going to turn off the power in a few days but we don't
care much. The rent is up pretty soon and then we shall
move, I don't know where. "[6] The ingredients of this

passage--a circle of admirers, a soon to be extinguished
light--compose a mock, beast fable version of a scene that
recurs many times in Steinbeck's work. A group clusters
around a campfire, spellbound by the illuminations of their
best story teller. Even in jest, Steinbeck gravitated to the
images of audience control that inform Of Mice and Men.

   The final incident, to be taken no more facetiously
than its predecessors, was a disaster that befell the initial
manuscript of Of Mice and Men. Steinbeck now wrote his
publisher about the dog-as-critic because, with the mixed
reactions stirred by In Dubious Battle, hostile reviews, rather than indifferent sales, were his current preoccupation:
"Minor tragedy stalked. My setter pup, left alone one
night, made confetti of about half of my manuscript book.
Two months' work to do over again. It sets me back.
There was no other draft. I was pretty mad, but the poor
little fellow may have been acting critically. I didn't want
to ruin a good dog for a manuscript I'm not sure is good at
all. He only got an ordinary spanking."[7] Commenting on
this event, Lewis Gannett reports that, "After the Book-of-
the-Month Club had accepted Mice, and critical enthusiasm
began to boil, Steinbeck still felt that Toby might have been
right. 'I'm not sure Toby didn't know what he was doing
when he ate the first draft,' he wrote. 'I have promoted
Toby-dog to be lieutenant-colonel in charge of literature.
But as for the unpredictable literary enthusiasms of this
country, I have little faith in them.'"[8] Readers who enjoy
fetching conclusions from afar will note that the mercy killing of a pathetically decrepit cur figures prominently in the
plot of Of Mice and Men.

   Prefatory comments that link Of Mice and Men to the
decade that produced it must issue a precautionary note. To
the extent that the book is a documentary account as well as
an artistic tour de force, it touches on Steinbeck's private
history more than the contemporary public history of his
country. Despite the continuation of the era's great event,
the Depression, Steinbeck was relatively unencumbered, at
least by 1936, in the management of his family affairs. On
the other hand, he had become reflective and inward-looking
about the direction his career increasingly promised to take.
Correspondingly, Of Mice and Men, unlike the two novels
that embraced it, is not about the alignment of massive
economic forces. Certainly the story is interested in how
modular groups of people, even two men together, formulate
effective myths of social cohesion; but the emphasis is on

individual performance or its failure, not monolithic external
factors.   In Of Mice and Men, Steinbeck is steadfastly sympathetic toward men less fortunate than himself.   On this
occasion, however, the overwhelming power that leads to the
prosperity of those who harness it while maiming countless
unenfranchised victims is represented, not by titanic accumu-
lations of economic might but by the supremacy of Steinbeck's
own verbal and imaginative faculties.   The twentieth-century
subculture in which Lennie and George find themselves is
no doubt a diminished source of romantic fantasy or its fulfillment, but Steinbeck goes out of his way to indicate that
the realization of what dreams they can salvage is economically well within their grasp.   Lennie, by virtue of his
psycho-physical abnormality, and George, by virtue of his
fatally dependent, self-defeating temperament, represent re-
grettable limitations of personal talent more than the defects
of a nation divided into warring factions.   Their world is a
hard one, inhospitable to pastoral visions drawn from the
American past, but it does not deny a place to people like
Slim, ordained by special accomplishments, any more than
the demanding world of American literature withheld ac-
clamation from the novel Of Mice and Men and its author.

II.   PLOT SYNOPSIS

Section I

        The novel begins outdoors.   The scene is a wooded
enclosure near a pool formed in the Salinas River "a few
miles south of Soledad, " California.   The time is sunset,
Thursday.   George and Lennie appear.   George is "small
and quick, dark of face, with restless eyes and sharp,
strong features. "   Lennie trails behind, shapeless, a huge
gangling puppet, George's "opposite. "   Impulsively, he drinks
from the pool despite George's warning that he will make
himself "'sick like you was last night. '"   Lennie has forgotten that he and George have plans to work on a nearby
ranch.   All he can remember is "'about the rabbits. '"   His
only verbal defense is literalness: "'Ain't a thing in my
pocket, ' Lennie said cleverly.   'I know there ain't.   You
got it in your hand. '"   Lennie has been concealing a mouse.
He has petted it, and it is dead.   Angrily, George throws
it away.

        George coaches Lennie how to act when they arrive
at the ranch next day.   Lennie will remain silent, "'An' you

ain't gonna do no bad things like you done in Weed, neither. '"
As George starts supper, Lennie tries to retrieve the mouse
but George prevents him. In the past, at his Aunt Clara's,
Lennie has always ended up killing his pets. In Weed, too,
Lennie '"Jus' wanted to feel that girl's dress--jus' wanted
to pet it like it was a mouse. '" The girl panicked, and the
two men fled an ugly mob.

George complains, '"When I think of the swell time I
could have without you, I go nuts. I never get no peace. '"
Sorrowfully, Lennie offers to leave, and George's temper
subsides. To soothe Lennie, he recites a tale they know by
heart. Most farm laborers are the '"loneliest guys in the
world, '" but with George and Lennie things are different.
'"We got somebody to talk to that gives a damn about us. '"
They have each other. George repeats their dream of own-
ing a farm. They will '"live off the fatta the lan', '" and
Lennie will tend the rabbits.

Their meal completed, George issues further instructions: '"If you jus' happen to get in trouble like you always
done before, I want you to come right here an' hide in the
brush. '" The sun sets, the men prepare for sleep, and the
section ends.

Section II

Throughout, the scene is the ranch bunkhouse. The
time is ten o'clock, Friday morning. George and Lennie
are greeted by an "old swamper" who has lost his hand in
an accident and been relegated to housekeeping chores. The
boss enters. He becomes suspicious when George does all
the talking but is reassured when George boasts of Lennie's
great strength. He leaves, warning George not '"to put
nothing over. '"

George and Lennie begin to make friends with the old
man when Curley, the boss's son, suddenly enters. A former boxer, he is small and belligerent, especially toward
larger men, who make him feel inferior. When he leaves,
George expresses contempt for '"tough little guys'" and
adds, '"he better watch out for Lennie. Lennie ain't no
fighter, but Lennie's strong and quick and Lennie don't know
no rules. '"

The conversation turns to Curley's wife of two weeks,

a "'tart'" who already has "'got the eye'" for Slim, the best
teamster on the ranch. The old swamper reports that Curley is obscenely possessive of his wife and jealous of all the
hired men. George deals a hand of solitaire and talks to
Lennie about Curley: "'Don't let him pull you in--but--if
the son-of-a-bitch socks you--let 'im have it.'" As an af-
terthought, he repeats his instructions to "'hide in the brush
by the river'" if Lennie gets in trouble.

Curley's wife appears in the doorway and assumes a
seductive pose. "She wore a cotton house dress and red
mules, on the insteps of which were little bouquets of red
ostrich feathers." George sends her off and is furious at
Lennie, who has been entranced. "'She's a rat-trap if I
ever seen one,'" George warns.

The workers return from the fields for lunch. Slim
enters "with the majesty only achieved by royalty and master craftsmen. He was a jerkline skinner, the prince of
the ranch." Displaying the ease of total self-confidence, he
introduces George and Lennie to the other men. One of
them, Carlson, remarks that because Slim's bitch has
thrown a litter of pups, it is now time for the old swamper, Candy, to shoot his own woebegone old sheepdog and
take a new pet. Lennie's eyes light with the idea that he,
too, may get a puppy. Before the section ends, Curley
twice more looks in the bunkhouse door, searching for his
wife.

Section III

The scene remains the same. It is Friday evening.
George and Slim discuss Lennie over a game of cards.
Slim is astounded by the strength Lennie has displayed during the afternoon's work. Warming to Slim's cordial manner, George tells of Lennie's early life with Aunt Clara.
He mentions Lennie's almost suicidal loyalty and obedience
to his commands. Lennie is "'a nice fella,'" not in the
least "'mean.'" Becoming confessional, George reports the
recent trouble in Weed and the narrow escape he has made
with Lennie. "'I'd be scared too if he grabbed me. But
he never hurt her. He jus' wanted to touch that red dress,
like he wants to pet them pups all the time.'"

Lennie enters, hiding a puppy beneath his coat, but
George makes him return it to the barn so that Lennie will
not injure it. The rest of the men come in after finishing a

game of horseshoes. Carlson again urges Candy to dispose
of his dog and volunteers to shoot it himself. Everyone is
impressed to learn that a former ranch hand, Bill Tenner,
has had his letter of appreciation published in a popular
magazine: "'I think your mag is the best dime's worth I
ever spent.'" Not to be sidetracked, Carlson once more
presses his point with Candy. "Candy looked a long time at
Slim to try to find some reversal. And Slim gave him
none." Carlson exits with the dog and a pistol. The rest
gossip uncomfortably about Curley's wife and the merits of
local prostitutes until they hear a shot and Carlson returns.

Slim has gone to the barn to doctor one of his mules.
Curley enters in a rage, seeking his wife. Fearful she is
with Slim, he leaves with most of the men, who sense an
entertaining ruckus. To divert Lennie and revive Candy's
spirits, George elaborates his pipedream of a farm of their
own. Candy offers to contribute a large stake in order to
purchase the actual place George has in mind, and for the
first time George begins to take himself seriously.

All of the men return. Curley has challenged Slim
and been forced to back down. Exasperated, he viciously
attacks Lennie, who is still chuckling over the picture George
has drawn of the future. "'Get 'im, Lennie!'" George
shouts. "The next minute Curley was flopping like a fish
on a line and his closed fist was lost in Lennie's big hand."
Curley's hand is crushed. The section closes with George
apprehensive about their jobs but doing his best to comfort
the bewildered Lennie.

Section IV

The scene is the stable, converted into a room for
Crooks, a Black handyman. It is Saturday night, and
Crooks is alone, applying liniment to his crippled spine.
Lennie appears in the doorway, having been with his puppy.
Begrudgingly, Crooks invites him to sit down, even though
by custom his room is off limits to the other men. Talking
more to himself than to his guest, Crooks muses about the
relationship between George and Lennie. "'If I say something, why it's just a nigger sayin' it.'" Similarly, "'George
can tell you screwy things, and it don't matter. It's just
the talking. It's just bein' with another guy.'" Crooks
teases Lennie, suggesting that George may not return from
town, where he is spending the evening; but like George in

the past, he relents in the face of Lennie's complete vulner-
ability. Crooks himself is much alone and passes the time
reading, unsatisfactory recreation because the man who
reads in solitude "'got nothing to measure by. '"

Lennie begins his story of the farm and the rabbits
as Candy enters and takes a seat. Crooks knows the story
and cynically dismisses it; but Lennie's faith is infectious
and Crooks momentarily thinks that he, too, might find a
place at the farm. The mood is shattered when Curley's
wife appears. She is bored and resentfully unveils her own
fruitless dream of Hollywood success. Brutally, she returns
the three men to reality: "'Listen, Nigger, ' she said.
'You know what I can do to you if you open your trap?'"
"Crooks sat perfectly still, his eyes averted, everything
that might be hurt drawn in. " The section ends with
George's return from town. He takes Lennie to task for
having intruded on the Black man.

Section V

It is Sunday afternoon. The scene is the manger
where Lennie is with his puppy. He has petted it, and it is
dead. Curley's wife enters. "She wore her bright cotton
dress and the mules with the red ostrich feathers. " She
compliments Lennie's strength and congratulates him for
hurting Curley's hand. She repeats her dream of Hollywood
success and invites Lennie to stroke her hair--as he has
stroked the puppy. She panics when Lennie holds on too
tightly. "'Don't go yellin', '" he said, and he shook her;
and her body flopped like a fish. And then she was still,
for Lennie had broken her neck. " Lennie vanishes.

The men find the body of Curley's wife, and Curley
organizes a searching party. The section ends with his instructions, "'When you see 'im, don't give 'im no chance.
Shoot for his guts. That'll double 'im over. '"

Section VI

The novel ends outdoors. The scene is the wooded
enclosure by the Salinas River. The time is late Sunday
afternoon. Lennie appears. He sits by the river and is
tormented by visions of his Aunt Clara and an enormous
rabbit. George arrives, and once more he comforts Lennie

with the story of a farm of their own.   He sits behind Lennie.   Concealed in his hand is Carlson's pistol.   At the end
of his story, "George raised the gun and steadied it, and
he brought the muzzle of it close to the back of Lennie's
head.   The hand shook violently, but his face set and his
hand steadied.   He pulled the trigger."

Curley's party arrives.   George explains that he has
taken the pistol from Lennie and shot him in self-defense.
Slim understands: "'You hadda, George.   I swear you hadda.   Come on with me.'"   He takes George off to get a
drink.   The rest remain behind, uncomprehending: "Curley
and Carlson looked after them.   And Carlson said, 'Now
what the hell ya suppose is eatin' them two guys.'"   The
novel is finished.

III.   CRITICAL EXPLICATION

Although Of Mice and Men is not the best case in
point, one of the most prominent characteristics of the
Steinbeck phenomenon is that his reputation among academic
critics has fluctuated drastically during the past three dec-
ades.   The general tide has flowed and ebbed, and some
individuals, such as Harry T. Moore, have gone so far as
zealously to recant previous commendations.   Given Steinbeck's rather special status among the writers of his era,
such shifts in opinion have been inevitable.   In the first
place, Steinbeck made himself hard to grasp.   His technical
variations are incessant and programmatic, and yet he
seems to return, time and again, to the same motifs, the
same types of characters, the same landscape.   What is
more, Steinbeck addressed literary critics, responsible to
uncompromising artistic standards, at the same time that
he consistently attracted a very broad popular audience,
readers who looked for entertainment, inspiration, information, but were under no obligation to weigh Steinbeck's stylistic nuances as consciously as trained professionals.   The
scene was further complicated by Steinbeck's receiving the
Nobel Prize when his best work was behind him.

On the other hand, Steinbeck's career has been pawn
to historical developments operating beyond the sphere of his
personal influence.   These developments may well have reduced scholarly interest in Of Mice and Men.   Most obviously, World War II and its aftermath made the Depression and
its byproducts seem outmoded and thus deprived Steinbeck of

a most fertile subject matter. More subtly, the 1950s, the
decade during which enthusiasm for Steinbeck suffered its
greatest decline, witnessed an intellectual climate on American campuses which was alien to the very qualities Steinbeck
most prized--stylistic flexibility and daring, and close engagement with public, frequently universal issues. Among
professors of literature, the 1950s were the high-water
mark of T. S. Eliot, the principles of New Criticism, and
the ascetic technique of close critical analysis. Metaphysical poetry, with its stress on psychic interiors and elegant
design, was much in vogue. Fiction that accommodated itself to the reigning method of inquiry usually received the
highest praise; but many writers, including Steinbeck, were
not interested in conforming to the favored prescriptions,
although Of Mice and Men certainly could have satisfied the
most fastidious disciples of Eliot's school.

Students, on their part, were profoundly introverted,
skeptical about the effectiveness of political action, defen-
sively elitist in their literary tastes. There was a great
revival of interest in theater--in some instances the number
of self-supporting productions during any one semester was
prodigious--but the most ambitious undertakings were largely
in behalf of the dramatists for whom Eliot was the most eloquent apologist, the Elizabethans and the Stuarts, rather
than experimental new talent. It was as though undergradu-
ates had relinquished any claim on the idiom of their own
future and were content to enact their dreams of progress
accompanied by the ringing cadences of centuries-old blank
verse. The retreat was away from the dynamic arena of
contemporary concern into the relatively immobile inheritance of the proscenium arch. Dramatic art promised a
world distinctly different from daily life, a world that was
austere, patrician, pure, and students vigorously moved to
occupy it. Such a climate afforded little space to Steinbeck
and Of Mice and Men, a novel animated by the premise that
all men possess the dramatic impulse and exhibit it in their
commonest pursuits.

In terms of literary criticism, Leslie Fiedler's controversial book Love and Death in the American Novel ush-
ered in the revolution of the 1960s. The controversy cen-
tered on Fiedler's thesis that the American novel is distinguished by an archetypal sequence of close relationships between "male pairs," such as Huck Finn and Jim, that border
on what Fiedler now calls, with some reservations, the
"homoerotic." Fiedler's contention helps place Of Mice and

Men in an important historical tradition, although no one
would quarrel with Burton Rascoe's early assessment that
"the relationship between George and Lennie is a paradigm
of all the nonphysical, nonsexual (let us use the so tritely
inadequate and now almost meaningless word 'spiritual' to
help out in indicating the meaning) emotions, concerns, and
aspirations in the world. "[9] But Fiedler provided another
kind of access, as well, to the reader who sought to base
his admiration of Steinbeck on the solidest possible ground.
Fiedler impatiently rejected the strictures of New Criticism
and reasserted the right, even of academic critics, to share
the motivations of general readers who view factors other
than artistic performance--factors such as the light a given
novel might shed on cultural continuities--as valid if not indeed essential dimensions of reading activity.

     In our own time, as much in consequence of an ever
lengthening thaw in the academic environment as of relaxed,
exploratory preferences among the young, it is possible to
view Steinbeck from every available perspective without inhibition.   Of Mice and Men is relevant to current concerns,
including the concern of students to be subjective, even sentimental, free from fear of recrimination while reserving
the right to be tough-minded about immutable realities when
occasion requires.   A generation of students that introduced
the word "scenario" to the lexicon of political activism can
appreciate Steinbeck's abiding interest in the wellsprings of
social drama.   Furthermore, powerful sympathy has revived
for the downtrodden protagonists Steinbeck chronicled.   Like
George and Lennie, many young people profess to "give a
damn, " and their experience often vindicates the use of the
slogan.   Thoreau's vision of a life uncluttered by academic
sophistication has won new adherents--and has its counterpart in Lennie and George's dream of a farm of their own.
Salinas remains the scene of economic and social friction,
and even Soledad has lent its name to the headlines.   Of
Mice and Men proves no exception to the renewed timeliness
of Steinbeck's work.

     In invoking the much abused word "relevant, " how-
ever, it is necessary to observe the caution as well as the
courage that Richard Poirier displays when he discusses the
word in his recent book The Performing Self.   "The term, "
he writes, "is in itself a cause for confusion.   For if English studies is to become more 'relevant' to anything,
shouldn't it be first of all made more 'relevant' to English
literature?"[10] One function of Poirier's language must be

to sanction study of the relationship between Of Mice and
Men and appropriate American works that preceded or, in
some instances, followed it, including of course Steinbeck's
own. So unusual a book scarcely runs the risk of appearing
derivative; on the contrary, much benefit can accrue from
showing that Steinbeck's novel, however unorthodox, is
nevertheless responsive to what D. H. Lawrence called the
"classic" American tradition.

   In his groundbreaking book Studies in Classic American Literature, D. H. Lawrence talks at length about The
Deerslayer. Cooper's novel is probably a remote source of
the yearning for peaceful independence that infects Of Mice
and Men, although so many other prominent writers, such
as Emerson and Whitman, have perpetuated the theme that
no single source is outstanding. Elsewhere in his work,
most notably in To a God Unknown, Steinbeck returned to
the legend of founding a dynasty in the wilderness that Cooper had initiated in another of The Leatherstocking Tales,
The Pioneers. It is worth noting in anticipation of further
discussion that the image of the "trap" so pervasive in Of
Mice and Men is also active in The Deerslayer. One aspect
of The Deerslayer Lawrence found especially absorbing was
the difference between the two Hutter sisters: "The two
girls are the inevitable dark and light. Judith, dark, fear-
less, passionate, a little lurid with sin, is the scarlet-and-
black blossom. Hetty, the younger, blonde, frail and innocent, is the white lily again. But alas, the lily has begun
to fester. She is slightly imbecile."[11] The rhetorical
means Cooper devised to communicate Hetty's simpleminded-
ness was her constant confusion of the literal and figurative
meanings of words. "Mother used to call heaven the future,
but you seem to think it means next week, or tomorrow!"[12]
she laments to Judith at one point. The relationship of such
confusion to Of Mice and Men starts to be apparent when
Steinbeck explains what he intended Lennie to convey to
readers. He mentions Lennie's "earth longings" and then
goes on to say that Lennie "was not to represent insanity at
all but the inarticulate and powerful yearning of all men."[13]
The passage from Cooper suggests an incipient version of
the much blunter exchange Steinbeck was to compose in order
to dramatize Lennie's inarticulateness:

        'Don't let him pull you in--but--if the son-of-a-
    bitch socks you--let 'im have it. '
        'Let 'im have what, George?'

Hetty's literalistic response to the Bible also finds some
analogy in Lennie's trusting response to George's visions or,
for that matter, in Tularecito's naive responses to stories
in The Pastures of Heaven: "But Tularecito continued his
careful drawing, only pausing now and then to blink at the
teacher and to try to understand how these distant accounts
of the actions of strangers could be of interest to anyone.
To him they were chronicles of actual events--else why were
they written down. The stories were like the lessons. "[14]

Lawrence's discussion of Cooper concludes that the
white man, like the two phases of white womanhood symbolized by Hetty and Judith, "is divided against himself.
He plays off one side of himself against the other side, till
it is really a tale told by an idiot, and nauseating. "[15]
Lawrence ends the Cooper chapter by saying, "This is the
very intrinsic-most American. He is at the core of all the
other flux and fluff. And when this man breaks from his
static isolation, and makes a new move, then look out,
something will be happening. "[16] In terms of literary history, the "something" that happened was startling. As if in
reaction to Lawrence's hint about "a tale told by an idiot, "
William Faulkner, in 1929, published The Sound and the
Fury.

Steinbeck's own novel "Something That Happened," the
original title of Of Mice and Men, bears some resemblance
to Faulkner's work although, as several commentators have
rightly stated, the general similarities between the two men
and their works are surprisingly slight. In its opening section, The Sound and the Fury is in fact a tale told by an
idiot, not about one, and therein lies a crucial distinction.
Even so, the novel from the onset exploits verbal confusion
of the sort observable in Cooper and Steinbeck. Benjy
Compson, the imbecile through whose eyes the story is
viewed, mistakes a nearby golfer's cries of "caddy" for the
name of his beloved sister, "Caddy. " And the confusion is
aggravated by the Black youngster, Luster, who teases Benjy
in somewhat the same fashion that Crooks for awhile teases
Lennie. Furthermore, Benjy, like Lennie, has a history of
frightening girls in a way misconstrued as sexual assault,
and his downfall occurs on Easter Sunday, when his brother
Jason finally decides to commit him to an institution. Lennie's fate on the weekend when Of Mice and Men takes place
only dimly parallels the events of the Crucifixion, probably
because Steinbeck chose not to oppress his narrative with
symbolic allusions far beyond the capacity of his characters

to invent or detect. The presence of the parallels is still
undeniable and offers further testimony that Steinbeck, in
his own manner, was attuned to the same literary rhythms
that interested Faulkner at the time.

Another writer who deserves special comment in reference to Steinbeck and Of Mice and Men is Eugene O'Neill.
Writing about his play Burning Bright, Steinbeck mentioned
his efforts to suggest a "universal language": "While I had
eminent authority for this method from Aeschylus down
through O'Neill, it was still problematical whether audiences
used to the modern realistic theater would accept such expression."[17] Of Mice and Men is an example of the "realistic theater" Steinbeck referred to, and in any case his experiment with "a novel that can be played" finds its prece-
dent at least as far back in American literature as the "Mid-
night, Forecastle" chapter of Moby Dick. In light of Lennie's nature, it is worthwhile recalling that Melville's drama
revolves around Pip, Ahab's mentally retarded protégé.
Melville based Pip on Lear's fool in Shakespeare, but in
Billy Bud he produced his own quite independent version of
a character who, at least under stress, is pathologically inarticulate and expresses himself through violent physical action with disastrous consequences. Like Melville, O'Neill
often wrote of the sea, and several of his plays show Melville's influence. In turn, O'Neill anticipated certain aspects
of Steinbeck. To a God Unknown, for example, is somewhat
reminiscent of Desire Under the Elms, and The Hairy Ape
foreshadows Of Mice and Men with prisonlike stage settings
that symbolize the self-imposed limitations of dramatic method as well as the restricted lives of the characters, so that
technique and theme reinforce each other with compounded
incisiveness.

Throughout Steinbeck, in fact, rhetorical arrange-
ments, however liberated compared with ordinary ones, com-
plement the victimization of characters by uncontrollable,
even unrecognizable imperatives latent in nature and in man-
made systems like the rudimentary verbal ones the characters themselves put together. Thus when the reader of Of
Mice and Men submits to the exciting flow of unfolding
events, he also perceives himself in the presence of an
architectural scheme analogous to the rise-and-fall trajectory
of classical drama. This recognition of the novel's structural integrity reveals that, even as they manipulate one
another, Steinbeck's characters are as subservient to the
dictates of his master plan as to the urgencies of natural
impulse.

To implement the economy of an "experiment" in
dramatic form, Steinbeck communicated the parallels he
sensed between natural and rhetorical forces by focusing on
a specific image in Of Mice and Men, the image of a "trap."
Most obviously, he used the slang word for "mouth," "trap,"
to suggest that even apparently casual utterances can hem
men in. He did this repeatedly at salient moments in other
books also, demonstrating his care, shared with O'Neill,
for the all-important metaphors of colloquial speech. At
the start of The Grapes of Wrath, Tom Joad, just released
from prison--one kind of "trap"--related imprisonment to
the traps of ordinary discourse: "'But look, when you been
in stir a little while, you can smell a question comin' from
hell to breakfast. You telegraphed yours the first time you
opened your trap.'"[18] Earlier in the conversation, the
truck driver Tom has been talking to "knew he was being
trapped" by Tom's words, "but couldn't see the way out."[19]
In In Dubious Battle, Jim complains to Doc, "'You build a
trap of words and then you fall into it.'"[20] And in To a
God Unknown, an exchange between Thomas and Joseph implies that the dangers endemic in common talk may well
multiply in an atmosphere of conscious artifice, "ceremony"
or "ritual":

'... I was afraid there was some ceremony.'
'You are afraid of every kind of ritual, Thomas. Do you know why?' Joseph slowed his horse
so that Thomas could come closer.
'No, I don't know why,' Thomas admitted slowly, 'it seems a trap, a kind of little trap.'[21]

An explicit "trap" reference occurs in Of Mice and
Men when Curley's wife says to Crooks, "'Listen, Nigger,
... You know what I can do to you if you open your trap?'"
The reference seems insignificant in isolation, but in the
context of George's warning Lennie that Curley's wife is
"'a rat-trap if I ever seen one,'" it elevates sensitivity to
the trap of racial discrimination that imprisons Crooks.
Given the title of the novel, George's comment about a
"rat-trap" also brings to mind Burns' couplet, "The best
laid schemes o' mice an' men/Gang aft a-gley," and its
implication that destiny, chance, is a trap set for men,
mice, and perhaps rats too. Of Mice and Men is as much
concerned with references to "chance," often in connection
with games, as it is with traps. George's "rat-trap" comment also shows how rhetorical and natural threats coincide
in Of Mice and Men. Women, and by extension human

sexuality, are a biological trap for Steinbeck's characters.
The Salinas bordellos trap men's money and sap their will
power. Steinbeck perhaps intended an oblique disparagement
of Lennie's Aunt Clara when he bestowed the name Clara on
the more expensive of the town's two madams. References
to Curley's "glove fulla vaseline" disagreeably symbolize the
entrapment of husband and wife in mutual sexual exploitation.
These references supplement Candy's loss of his hand, prepare the ground for the crushing of Curley's hand and, again
by extension, show the meaning of Crook's crippled spine.
Crook's infirmity is emblematic of his handicapped racial
status, a brand of impotence cruelly thrust home by what
Curley's wife says to him.

Thus far, we have noticed historical factors that have
influenced the reception of Of Mice and Men, and we have
also seen that the novel clearly participates in the main-
stream of historically important American fiction. The history of critical reactions to the book also deserves attention.
The conclusions that critics have drawn about Of Mice and
Men can best be summarized by quoting one of Steinbeck's
astutest readers, Peter Lisca, who accepts the lead of Antonia Seixas in his finding that "the simple story of two migrant workers' dream of a safe retreat, a 'clean well-lighted
place,' becomes itself a pattern or archetype which exists
on three levels. "

"There is the obvious story level on a realistic plane,
with its shocking climax. There is also the level of social
protest, Steinbeck the reformer crying out against the exploitation of migrant workers. The third level is an allegorical one, its interpretation limited only by the ingenuity
of the audience. "22 Referring to Burns' poem, Lisca goes
on to identify a final, fourth level: "In the poem, Burns
extends the mouse's experience to include that of mankind;
in Of Mice and Men, Steinbeck extends the experience of two
migrant workers to the human condition. 'This is the way
things are, ' both writers are saying. On this level, perhaps
the most important, Steinbeck is dramatizing the non-teleological philosophy which had such a great part in shaping In
Dubious Battle and which would be fully discussed in Sea of
Cortez. "23 Lisca's comments are definitive, and his chapter on Of Mice and Men in The Wide World of John Steinbeck
is the indispensable point of departure for any survey of the
novel's critics.

The current explication has sought to show that the

"inevitableness" Lisca notices in Of Mice and Men is the effect of the novel's rhetorical components, not just of the
superficial course of events. Lennie's actions repeat themselves with a regularity that soon becomes predictable, and
Steinbeck similarly marshals his artistic resources to produce a cyclical, rather than linear dramatic action. In addition to the recurrent elements already discussed at some
length, the reader will probably have recognized several others in the synopsis and in the novel itself. Apparently
minor details often serve to buttress the novel's taut, in-
terlocking arrangement. When George tells Lennie, "'You
ain't gonna put nothing over on me,'" his language forecasts
the boss's parting shot in the following section. The color
red repeatedly signifies feminine allure. A great, mysterious fish, at home in the natural surroundings of the novel's
opening, ironically anticipates the desperate human "fish,"
Curley and his wife, that Lennie maims and kills. Larger
rhetorical units form patterns, too. The end of the novel
recapitulates almost verbatim the description at the beginning, although by the end Steinbeck has progressively edu-
cated his audience about the symbolism of incidental detail.
The unassailable dispassion with which a water bird swallows
a snake throws in starkest contrast George's agonized res-
ignation to Lennie's death. Less overtly, the series of
references to the characters' literary tastes draws attention
to the much greater capability and complexity of Steinbeck's
own. Even the mechanical procedure of noting the length of
the novel's six sections illuminates Steinbeck's self-conscious
artistry. The initial sections expand at a measured tempo
into the spacious central episodes; then follows the compres-
sion and acceleration that leads to the denouement.

        In closing, it is worthwhile reemphasizing an issue
raised in the introduction: in every way, Of Mice and Men
reflects Steinbeck's exceptional concern for the implications
of his craft at the time he wrote the novel. The novel ar-
bitrates between an urgent need for freedom and a no less
importunate need for control, personal needs that appertain
more to the universal history of artists than to the passing
history of the mid-1930s. Steinbeck's characters are equally
engrossed in the private dilemmas and decisions common to
untutored creativity in every age. George has the faculty
of creating dream worlds that seem real as long as he can
improvise an audience. With Lennie's death, he falls from
grace. Recognizing that his audience, like his fable, has
been ephemeral, the captive of circumstances, he accommo-
dates himself to a more mundane version of reality than the

one he has made in his mind.   The importance for any story
teller of a suitable audience is a principal theme of the
novel.   Crooks cannot read without a companion; George
cannot sustain his story without Lennie.   In this respect,
the end of Of Mice and Men seems purposefully equivocal.
George has located a new audience in Slim, a man whose
consummate elan and professional composure is the clearest
surrogate for the finesse Steinbeck's literary proficiency
represents.   Vicariously, George is compensated for Lennie's
loss by participating in the special amalgam of stylistic ingenuity and compassionate sensibility, the blend of pragmat-
ism and idealism, that Steinbeck displays at his very best.
Unlike the ending of Tortilla Flat when, after the death of
Danny, "no two walked together,"24 George is not alone.
But unlike the ending, too, of the opening section of Of Mice
and Men, when "a coyote yammered, and a dog answered
from the other side of the stream," Lennie has gone "acrost
the river," but the final question, "'Now what the hell ya
suppose is eatin' them two guys?'" remains unanswered.
Steinbeck had won an audience, but its understanding was
not necessarily proportionate to its size.

        In retrospect, it may turn out that our own times
will prove Steinbeck's apprehensions groundless.   Truman
Capote's In Cold Blood, the book in which Capote returned
from esoteric fiction to journalistic verisimilitude and a revived interest in men violently incompatible with the institu-
tionalized regimens of twentieth-century America, offers recent testimony that Steinbeck's artistic and philosophical assumptions possess hitherto unsuspected durability.   Capote's
real-life protagonists, Hickock and Smith, as they wander
through the Southwest, resemble literary migrants from the
American past more than atrocious murderers; like Lennie's
death, their execution draws a curtain on sadly depleted
American dreams as well as personal ones, and leaves the
reader with little recourse other than protest as futile as it
is strident, or existential acceptance of a bleak modern
panorama.   But with the same tension evident at the end
of Steinbeck's book, Capote's pyrrhic victory in the abolition
of capital punishment is poised against the apocalyptic visions of personal liberty proposed, however tentatively, in
Of Mice and Men, visions that the more outspoken of our
contemporary voices have reaffirmed: "As dawn began to
break I lay flat on my back in the lawn of the town square
and kept saying over and over again, 'You won't tell what
he done up in Weed, will you?   What'd he do up in Weed?
You won't tell will you?   What'd he do up in Weed?.   This

was from the picture Of Mice and Men, with Burgess Meredith talking to the foreman of the ranch. "[25] Sal Paradise
and his various literary descendants obstinately refuse to
abandon hope in George and Lennie's dream, any more than
his creator, Jack Kerouac, abandoned Steinbeck's protean
gestures of stylistic freedom.

Notes

1. As quoted in Lewis Gannett, "John Steinbeck's Way of
    Writing, " in E. W. Tedlock, Jr. , and C. V. Wick-
    er, eds. , Steinbeck and his Critics: A Record of
    Twenty-five Years (Albuquerque: The University of
    New Mexico Press, 1957), p. 30.

2. Gannett, p. 28.

3. As quoted in Peter Lisca, "Of Mice and Men, " The
    Wide World of John Steinbeck (New Brunswick, N. J. :
    Rutgers University Press, 1958), p. 133.

4. Ibid.

5. Gannett, p. 26.

6. Ibid. , pp. 26-27.

7. Ibid. , p. 30.

8. Ibid.

9. Burton Rascoe, "John Steinbeck, " Tedlock and Wicker,
    p. 61.

10. Richard Poirier, The Performing Self (New York: Ox-
    ford University Press, 1971), p. 65.

11. D. H. Lawrence, Studies in Classic American Litera-
    ture (1923; rpt. New York: Viking, 1964), p. 61.

12. James Fenimore Cooper, The Deerslayer (1841; rpt.
    New York: Signet, 1963), p. 366.

13. Gannett, p. 30.

14. Steinbeck, The Pastures of Heaven (1932; rpt. New

York: Viking, 1963), p. 55.

15. Lawrence, p. 62.

16. Ibid. , p. 63.

17. Steinbeck, "Critics, Critics, Burning Bright, " Tedlock
     and Wicker, pp. 43-44.

18. Steinbeck, The Grapes of Wrath (New York: Viking,
     1939), p. 19.

19. Ibid. , p. 11.

20. Steinbeck, In Dubious Battle (1936; rpt. New York:
     Viking, 1963), p. 231.

21. Steinbeck, To a God Unknown (1933; rpt. New York:
     Bantam, 1955), p. 152.

22. Lisca, pp. 138-139.

23. Ibid. , pp. 139-140.

24. Steinbeck, Tortilla Flat (1935; rpt. New York: Viking
     1963), p. 179.

25. Jack Kerouac, On The Road (New York: Viking, 1957),
     p. 76.

IV.   APPARATUS FOR RESEARCH PAPERS

A.   Ten Questions for Discussion

1.   Steinbeck said he wanted to write "a play that can be
     read or a novel that can be played. " What aspects of
     his literary program point in the direction of such an
     "experiment"? Does the "experiment" suggest a logi-
     cal relationship between In Dubious Battle, Of Mice
     and Men, and The Grapes of Wrath? Could factors in
     American history and the history of American litera-
     ture have prepared Steinbeck's readers for his at-
     tempt? In general, how does the historical profile of
     any given era dictate the literary forms that will be
     produced and favorably received?
2.   American writers often seem especially troubled about

their status as literary men and women. What do you make of Steinbeck's statement that "I am scared of popularity. It has ruined everyone I know"? How might widespread academic attention affect a work like Of Mice and Men? Judging from characteristics within the novel itself, what would be an ideal audience for it? What assumptions should the audience share?

3. Are there similarities between Steinbeck's manipulation of his characters and the characters' manipulation of each other? How can Steinbeck's frequent celebrations of human liberty be reconciled with the authority he exercises over his characters? What differences are there between the story George tells Lennie and the story Steinbeck tells his readers?

4. Several critics have found fault with Of Mice and Men because of its alleged "sentimentality." What is "sentimentality" and what is wrong with it? Do American culture in general and American literature in particular supply illustrations of sentimentality? How might a writer depict sentimentality without becoming sentimental himself?

5. There are historical precedents for George and Lennie's dream of a farm of their own. One is suggested by Thoreau's experiences recorded in Walden. What modern writers besides Steinbeck have created characters who try to "get away from it all"? How do the dreams of the other characters in Of Mice and Men compare to George and Lennie's? Would other dreams be more likely to succeed in practice? Where does responsibility for the failure of dreams lie? In people? In the dreams themselves? In environment?

6. Analyze the connection between Lennie's inarticulateness and his evidently inferior mental endowment. Must these two defects always accompany each other? In Of Mice and Men, what are the assets and liabilities of verbal power? What other kinds of power does Steinbeck suggest? Comment on the quality of each character's talk. How does it compare to the quality of language in the book as a whole? A sign of Lennie's weakness is his faulty memory, his need for repetition. Why, then, does Steinbeck repeat himself?

7. What is the significance of the following motifs and images: contests of strength and skill; chance; animals (consider the title); the river; caves?

8. To what extent does the structure of Of Mice and Men resemble the structure of classical or Shakespearian drama? What are the effects of this resemblance?

9. When discussing Steinbeck's characters in <u>Of Mice and</u>
   <u>Men</u>, consider their similarity to characters in other of
   his works you have read. Which characters does Steinbeck seem to like or dislike, for what reasons? The
   characters often express opinions about each other.
   Does Steinbeck always agree with these opinions?
10. Steinbeck's original title for <u>Of Mice and Men</u> was
    "Something That Happened." Why do you suppose he
    changed his mind?

                B. Suggested Topics for Research Papers

1. The "Questions for Discussions" can of course suggest
   material and critical points of view for research essays
   of varying length, and they have been presented with
   this potential use in mind.
2. Steinbeck wrote other works in the play-novel form of
   <u>Of Mice and Men</u>. A worthwhile project would be to
   read one or more of these later works and study their
   relationship to <u>Of Mice and Men</u>. See <u>The Pearl</u> (a
   short novel that became a film), <u>Burning Bright</u> and <u>The</u>
   <u>Moon is Down</u> (plays), and <u>The Forgotten Village</u> (a documentary film script).
3. For the student of <u>Of Mice and Men</u> interested in general theories about American literature, works like Leslie Fiedler's <u>Love and Death in the American Novel</u> and
   R. W. B. Lewis's <u>The American Adam</u> have much to
   offer. The very fact that Fiedler, for example, has almost nothing specific to say about Steinbeck leaves a
   clear field for imaginative thinking.
4. A survey of the varieties of critical commentary <u>Of Mice</u>
   <u>and Men</u> has generated is valuable not only because of
   the light it sheds on the novel but also because it puts
   on display the shifts in critical styles and interests that
   have occurred over the past thirty-five years.
5. Lennie is but one of several characters in Steinbeck's
   works who are marked by mental peculiarities and a
   close attraction to animals. Prototypes exist in <u>The</u>
   <u>Pastures of Heaven</u> and <u>To a God Unknown</u>, for example.
   These characters have inspired considerable critical response. Study of such characters and of the appropriate
   criticism (start with Edmund Wilson) could lie at the
   heart of an ambitious, rewarding investigation of <u>Of</u>
   <u>Mice and Men</u>.
6. Warren French has commented extensively on Steinbeck's
   explanation that <u>Tortilla Flat</u> is based on Arthurian

legend.   French argues further that traces of the legend
reappear in Of Mice and Men.   The direction a substantial project might take should be self-evident.

7.   Our explication has suggested several American works
prior to Of Mice and Men that are in some way related
to it.   Any one of these relationships could provide the
theme of a research essay.

8.   Peter Lisca and Antonia Seixas, in the works cited in
the bibliography, stress the relationship between
Sea of Cortez and Of Mice and Men.   Read Sea of
Cortez and write an essay on the relationship.

9.   Our introductory comments have contended that Of Mice
and Men reflects Steinbeck's private history more than
public events of the mid-1930s.   Read about Steinbeck's
life at the time he wrote the novel and draw your own
conclusions.

10.   Of Mice and Men is both a novel and a play.   Study
Steinbeck's remarks about this mixed form (in Lisca,
especially), and then write an essay on how his ideas
work out in practice.   A comparison with the play would
be in order.   Give special attention to the two endings.

11.   Most critics agree that Of Mice and Men contributes to
the great American theme of dream versus reality.
Some think the novel is a tragedy.   Some call it realism.   Consideration of such open-ended critical proposi-
tions leads to the most demanding and perhaps the most
profitable kind of research effort.   (Are "tragedy" and
"realism" mutually exclusive?)

C.   Selected Bibliography

A checklist of articles on Of Mice and Men should be
consulted in the Spring, 1965, issue of Modern Fiction
Studies, p. 100.   Tetsumaro Hayashi's John Steinbeck: A
Concise Bibliography (1930-65) (Metuchen, N. J. :   The Scarecrow Press, 1967), pp. 126-129, is exhaustive.
See also: Hayashi's A New Steinbeck Bibliography (1929-
1971) (Scarecrow Press, 1973).

Burgum, Edwin Berry.   "The Sensibility of John Steinbeck. "
E. W. Tedlock, Jr. , and C. V. Wicker, eds. , Steinbeck and His Critics: A Record of Twenty-five Years.
Albuquerque: University of New Mexico Press, 1957,
pp. 104-118.   See especially pp. 109-112.   Burgum argues that George and Lennie are compelling as personalities, rather than as symbols of massive economic forces.

Carpenter, Frederic I. "John Steinbeck: American Dreamer. " Tedlock and Wicker, pp. 68-79. See especially
pp. 76-77. Of Mice and Men is a "tragedy of idea, "
p. 76.

Dusenbury, Winifred L. "Steinbeck: Of Mice and Men. "
The Themes of Loneliness in Modern American Drama.
Gainesville: University of Florida Press, 1960, pp.
45-50. The author stresses that Of Mice and Men is a
personal drama and that Steinbeck's technique and plot
are the suitable means to express the theme of loneliness.

Fontenrose, Joseph. John Steinbeck: An Introduction and
Interpretation. New York: Holt, Rinehart and Winston,
1963, pp. 53-59. Fontenrose examines possible sources
of the sense of inevitability the novel conveys and views
the catastrophe as the product of individual failure.
"The individual's desire for carefree enjoyment of
pleasures is the serpent in the garden, " p. 59.

French, Warren. "End of a Dream. " John Steinbeck. New
York: Twayne, 1961, pp. 72-79 [rpr. in Robert Murray
Davis, ed. , Steinbeck: A Collection of Critical Essays.
Englewood Cliffs, N. J. : Prentice-Hall, 1972]. In this
excellent essay, French discerns in Of Mice and Men
remnants of the Arthurian legend so prominent in Tortilla Flat. He emphasizes George's need for Lennie
and his accommodation to reality after Lennie's death.
"This is a story not of man's defeat at the hands of an
implacable nature, but of man's painful conquest of this
nature and of his difficult, conscious rejection of his
dreams of greatness and acceptance of his own mediocrity, " p. 76.

Gannett, Lewis. "John Steinbeck's Way of Writing. " Tedlock and Wicker, pp. 23-37. See especially pp. 26-33.
Gannett supplies details about the composition and publication of Of Mice and Men and recounts the "dog" incidents.

Geismer, Maxwell. "Of Mice and Men. " Writers in Crisis.
Boston: Houghton Mifflin, 1942, pp. 237-270. Geismer
levels the charge of sentimentality but acknowledges the
realism Steinbeck achieved.

Jackson, Joseph Henry. "Introduction. " Of Mice and Men.

New York: Random House, Modern Library, 1937. A
chatty biography covering the period of Steinbeck's life
prior to Of Mice and Men.

Lewis, R. W. B. "John Steinbeck: The Fitful Daemon."
Carl Bode, ed., The Young Rebel in American Literature. London: William Heinemann, 1959, pp. 121-41;
[rpt. in Steinbeck: A Collection of Critical Essays, pp.
163-75.] Given Lewis's generally unfavorable assessment of Steinbeck, his opinion that Of Mice and Men is
"the one work in which his trapped daemon did squirm
out and get almost completely into the language" (p.
172) is especially significant.

Lisca, Peter. "John Steinbeck: A Literary Biography."
Tedlock and Wicker, pp. 3-22. See especially pp. 11-
13 for an account of the novel's history.

_____. "Of Mice and Men." The Wide World of John
Steinbeck. New Brunswick, N.J., 1958, pp. 130-143.
Lisca tells how the novel came into being, discusses
Steinbeck's stylistic intentions, and finds four levels of
meaning in Of Mice and Men. This article is one of
the very best available.

Marks, Lester. "A Few Words about 'Something That Happened.'" Thematic Design in the Novels of John Steinbeck. New York: Humanities Press, 1969, pp. 58-65.
This essay includes an informative contrast between Of
Mice and Men and In Dubious Battle. Unlike its pred-
ecessor, Of Mice and Men "focuses upon two individuals who, while they serve allegorical purposes, retain
their individuality," p. 63.

Moore, Harry T. "Of Mice and Men." The Novels of John
Steinbeck: A First Critical Study. Chicago: Normandie
House, 1939, pp. 47-53. An important early negative
view of the book. Moore views Of Mice and Men as an
attempted tragedy that merely results in sentimentality.

Rascoe, Burton. "John Steinbeck." Tedlock and Wicker,
pp. 57-67. A congenial, perceptive reaction to the first
presentation of the play Of Mice and Men.

Seixas, Antonia. "John Steinbeck and the Non-teleological
Bus." Tedlock and Wicker, pp. 275-280. See especially pp. 276-277 for a succinct reaction to the novel in

light of Steinbeck's non-teleological philosophy.

Steinbeck, John. "My Short Novels." Tedlock and Wicker,
    pp. 38-40. Steinbeck tells how his dog ate the initial
    manuscript of the novel.

Tedlock, E. W., Jr., and Wicker, C. V. "Perspectives in
    Steinbeck Criticism." Steinbeck and His Critics, pp. xi-
    xii. The editors map the course of Steinbeck criticism
    during its first quarter century. See especially pp.
    xvii, xviii, xxiii, and xxiv for significant references to
    Of Mice and Men.

Wilson, Edmund. "The Californians: Storm and Steinbeck."
    New Republic, 103 (December 9, 1940), 784-787. Wil-
    son began an adverse strain of Steinbeck criticism with
    his comment that an "interest in plants and animal life
    was a pernicious influence in Steinbeck's works" and his
    charge that Steinbeck presents "human beings so rudi-
    mentary that they are almost on the animal level."
    Lennie was one of his examples.

Chapter 10

OF MICE AND MEN (PLAY) (1937)

by Franklin E. Court

I. BACKGROUND OF THE WORK

Of Mice and Men, published in 1937, was Steinbeck's first attempt to write in the play-novelette form, the "novel which can be played," as he claimed.[1] It was also the first of his works to gain wide national recognition; and in its treatment of the plight of itinerant workers, it foreshadows his most widely acclaimed novel, The Grapes of Wrath, published just two years later in 1939.

Although the play was probably in progress two years before its publication, it was not finished until after the novel version had become a best-seller. The money that Steinbeck made on the novel enabled him to leave San Francisco in the spring of 1937. He traveled by freighter to the Panama Canal and then on to New York. In May, he sailed to Europe, visiting England, Ireland, Sweden, and Russia. He returned to the United States in August and stayed for a time with George S. Kaufman at Kaufman's farm in Pennsylvania. With advice from Kaufman, Steinbeck finally finished the play. It opened on November 23, 1937 at the Music Box Theater in New York, directed by Kaufman and presented by Sam H. Harris. The roles of George and Lennie were played by Wallace Ford and Broderick Crawford, respectively.

The play was a success; it won for him the Drama Critics' Circle Award. Steinbeck, however, did not wait for the play to be produced. He bought a car in Detroit and drove to Oklahoma where he joined a group of migrant laborers heading for California.[2]

II. PLOT SYNOPSIS

Act I, scene I: Thursday night;
                 a bank of the Salinas River.

        The curtain rises on an empty stage. George enters,
followed by Lennie, a half-wit whom George cares for. The
two are itinerant workers on the way to a ranch job. Lennie is fond of animals. Although he has forgotten where he
is going, he remembers "about the rabbits."[3] In his coat-
pocket, he carries a dead mouse to pet as they walk along.
Lennie's "petting" has killed the mouse. George reminds
Lennie of the job they have just come from "up north" in
Weed, and he warns Lennie not to say a word when they
get to the ranch. George decides that they will sleep out
in the open tonight. He hands Lennie a can of beans; Lennie wants ketchup with them. George, angry, tells Lennie
there is none and proceeds to lament over his situation:
without Lennie tagging along, he could keep a job, "stay in
a cat house all night," eat anywhere he wanted, and buy a
gallon of whiskey a month. He reminds Lennie of the time
in Weed when he wanted to feel a girl's dress, to "hold onto
it like it was a mouse" (p. 647); they had to run to keep
from being shot. As he watches the expression of terror
growing on Lennie's face, his anger subsides. Lennie offers to leave, but George apologizes. "First chance I get
I'll find you a pup," he tells Lennie (p. 647). Lennie then
asks George to tell him "about the rabbits" again. George
repeats a speech he has made for Lennie many times before: someday they will buy a ranch and Lennie will be
able to raise rabbits. George asks Lennie to remember the
spot where they are now camped, and in case he should get
into trouble, he should hide there. Lennie agrees.

Act I, scene II: late Friday morning;
                  the interior of a bunkhouse.

        George and Lennie are talking with Candy, a stoop-
shouldered old man with a missing right hand, who tells
them about the boss and life in the bunkhouse. The boss
enters and begins to question them about their late arrival.
When he leaves, George warns Lennie about bosses. Candy
returns, leading an old, blind sheep dog. Curley, the
boss's son, enters and begins to badger Lennie with questions; Lennie remains mute. Curley gets angry and George
and he threaten each other. When Curley leaves, Candy

tells George that Curley is a "little guy" who hates "big
guys" (p. 653). Curley's temper has grown worse because
his new wife is a flirt. Candy leaves; Curley's wife enters
looking for Curley. She makes a number of sexually provocative gestures; Lennie watches, fascinated. She leaves
and Slim enters. Carlson enters and asks Slim if his dog
had pups. Slim had to drown four, but five are still alive.
Carlson suggests giving one to Candy as an incentive for
getting rid of the old dog he leads around. Lennie asks
George to ask Slim for a brown and white one. George
agrees.

Act II, scene I: about seven-thirty Friday
                   evening; same bunkhouse.

        Slim and George enter. George thanks Slim for hav-
ing given a puppy to Lennie. Candy enters with his dog;
Carlson enters and tries to convince Candy that he should
shoot the old dog in the head and take a puppy from Slim.
Carlson even offers to do it; Candy finally agrees. Candy,
overhearing George telling Lennie once again about the
ranch they will buy, offers to help pay part of the cost.
George agrees; they will have the necessary money within a
month. Meanwhile, Curley's wife has been looking in
through the window in the back. She exits when George in-
sults her, but she leaves the heavy carnation smell of her
perfume behind. Curley enters with the other men and
recognizes the smell. Insanely jealous, he tries to pick a
fight with Lennie who cries out in terror to George. George
tells Lennie to fight back. Lennie smashes Curley's hand
before the others can pull him off. To protect George and
Lennie, Slim tells Curley to say that his hand was caught in
a machine, or else Slim and the men will tell everybody
what really happened, and Curley will be laughed at. The
men leave; Lennie asks George if he can still tend the rabbits.

Act II, scene II: ten o'clock Saturday evening;
                    Crooks' room in the barn.

        Crooks is the black stableman. He sits rubbing him-
self with liniment when Lennie appears in the doorway.
Crooks asks if he always understands what George says to
him; Lennie, paying no attention, asks about the pups.
Crooks comments on how important it is for people to talk

to each other.   He tells Lennie that if George does not come
back from town, Lennie will have no one to talk to and will
be forced to live, like himself, in a kennel.   Crooks complains about his inability to live similarly to the white men
on the ranch.   Lennie still pays no attention.   He tells
Crooks about the farm.   Crooks replies that the dream of
getting a farm someday is in the minds of hundreds of itin-
erants; nobody ever gets it, he adds.   Candy enters; this is
the first time that he has ever been in Crooks' room.
Crooks listens disdainfully to Candy's talk of the farm and
then asks if they could use a hired hand.   George enters.
Curley's wife comes in to ask Crooks what really happened
to Curley's hand.   Seeing the bruises on Lennie's face, she
assumes Lennie did it; she begins to stroke his shoulder,
George whirls her around; she defies him, and George lifts
his hand to strike her.   The boss's figure appears in the
door.   She leaves.

Act III, scene I: mid-afternoon Sunday;
                    one end of a great barn.

        Lennie strokes a puppy that he has killed.   He wor-
ries that now George certainly will not let him tend the rabbits.   Curley's wife enters and secretively hides a suitcase
in the hay.   Seeing Lennie, she asks him not to tell Curley;
she plans to leave tonight.   They talk, neither listening to
the other, until she asks Lennie to feel the soft texture of
her hair.   Lennie strokes too hard; she screams.   He
closes his hand over her mouth and nose, begging her to
stop.   Her neck snaps; Lennie runs.   Candy finds the body
and calls George.   George will now never buy that ranch.
Discovering his luger missing, Carlson assumes that Lennie
has it.   The men, armed, set out to kill Lennie.

Act III, scene II: evening; the river bank.

        Lennie enters; George follows, slightly ahead of the
men, and pushes Lennie into the tules.   The men enter;
Slim realizes what George has done and urges the men to
leave the scene and spread out.   George asks Lennie to re-
move his hat and to look across the river while he explains
what the ranch is going to look like.   George pulls Carlson's
luger out of his pocket and fires into Lennie's head.

III. CRITICAL EXPLICATION

Steinbeck has the kind of dramatic imagination that is
at its best when viewing life symbolically. Of Mice and
Men, for instance, reads best on the level of semi-allegory.
There are obvious elements of social protest in the play:
the plight of migrant workers, a theme that is later developed more fully in The Grapes of Wrath (1939); race discrimination, revealed in the abuse and ostracizing of Crooks,
the black stableman, by the other ranch hands; and the insensitive treatment of old Candy who tells George, "They'll
can me pretty soon. Jest as soon as I can't swamp out no
bunkhouses they'll put me on the county" (p. 665). Elements
of social protest, however, are slight when compared with
the more universal message of the play, a lack underscored
by the fact that the characters have no visible social awareness.

Steinbeck intended that the play, as well as the novel,
should be a microcosm. 4 The little world is cruel; Nietz-
schean in the sense that the weak and the innocent perish,
and it seems they are given every possible assistance. The
strong survive, but only because they are the strong, and
not necessarily the best. From the beginning, it is evident
that a person with Lennie's sensitivity and lack of intelligence cannot live in this world; he is victimized by forces
beyond his or George's, his guide and protector's, control.
Lennie's sensitivity and innocence are most dramatically revealed through his obsessive attraction to soft, furry things.
In the opening scene, he carries a dead mouse in his jacket
pocket. When George asks what he wants with a dead
mouse, Lennie replies that he only wanted to pet it with his
thumb as they walked. The mouse symbolizes the theme of
innocence and frailty destroyed that pervades the play. Reference to it establishes in the play's opening scene a symbolic motif that reappears in the dogs, Curley's wife, and
Lennie's dream of tending rabbits on the ranch that he and
George will buy someday.

As the play progresses, Lennie's feeling for the dead
mouse is transferred to the soft, furry pups that Slim's dog
has borne. The theme of innocence destroyed reappears
when Lennie unintentionally kills the pup Slim has given him.
Candy is also given a pup as recompense for his old, blind
sheep dog who is shot by Carlson. The old dog is too frail
and weak to survive any longer in this world; he must be
led around by a string. Carlson, one of the play's more

brutal and insensitive characters, insists that he knows
"nothing that stinks as bad as ole dogs" and convinces Candy
that the ancient dog should be shot (p. 660). When Candy
finally relents, Carlson leads the old dog out and shoots him
in the back of the head with the luger that George will later
use to shoot Lennie. The parallels between Candy's dog and
Lennie are obvious: both must be led, depending for their
existence on guardian figures; and like the dog, Lennie is
also shot with the same pistol in the back of the head. The
motif of the destruction of the innocent and frail, introduced
through the mouse, is repeated therefore in the deaths of
the pup, Candy's dog, and Lennie. There is no place on
the ranch for those who are not self-sufficient. This is one
reason why the men find it strange that Lennie and George
should get along traveling together. Ranch hands are "lon-
ers," key figures in the tradition of American rugged indi-
vidualism. That they should find it strange for the strong
to care for the weak is Steinbeck's subtle criticism of a
tradition that breeds insensitivity.

There is no place on the ranch either for Curley's
wife. Her frailty is emphasized by her incessant need for
male companionship and by the smell of the flowered perfume
that identifies her to the men. She is never as "bad" as
they think. They object to her not because she acts flirta-
tious (these are the men, remember, who spend week-ends
at "old Susy's place") but because she is a threat. She is
overshadowed by Curley, her domineering and brutal husband, who is also the boss's son. The men are afraid of
Curley because he can have them fired and because he is
also a vicious character prone to fighting. Curley means
trouble, not his wife. She has been forced into this environment and is made to live in a way that is alien to her frail
nature: all that she really desires is to have someone to
talk to and to be taken dancing occasionally.

The similarities between Lennie and Curley's wife
are emphasized in act three when they sit together in the
barn and talk. Although they carry on separate conversations, they seem, nevertheless, as Steinbeck points out, to
grow closer together. They are both alien to the world of
the ranch; Lennie frequently asks to leave; and in this scene,
Curley's wife informs Lennie that she is leaving in the
evening. The symbolic motif introduced by the mouse is repeated as Lennie begins to stroke the softness of her hair;
for she too is a soft, furry thing, frail and in her own naïve
fashion, innocent. She is destroyed. Her frailty and naïvete

combine to effect her death: she innocently asks Lennie to
feel the soft texture of her hair; when he grabs her by the
nose and mouth to keep her from screaming, her neck
snaps.

One of the underlying ironies of the play is that Curley's wife, an innocent, should be killed by Lennie, another
innocent. But it must be remembered that Lennie puts his
hand over her face to keep her from screaming because he
is afraid of angering George by doing another "bad" thing.
In a sense, he therefore acts to protect himself and George
from those social forces, similar to the one they encount-
ered in Weed, that have terrorized him.   Lennie does not
actually know what a "bad" act is; he must be told by George
who interprets "badness" in the terms dictated by a society
that George can understand but that Lennie cannot.   The
initial moves that Lennie makes (feeling one girl's dress or
another's hair) are not essentially bad, but they are interpreted that way by the people that Lennie is forced to live
with.

In the end, the ranch world triumphs: Lennie is
dead, and George can no longer hold on to the dream of
buying a piece of land. As he predicts, he will grow old
working for fifty dollars a month and visiting "old Susy's"
until, someday, he will be too broken to work; and then,
like Candy and the old dog, he too will be "put away. "

By his own admission, Steinbeck used the play-novelette form in order to keep the work terse and concise. [5]
The play, however, is a much better demonstration of that
concern than the novel.   Its structure is tight and unified;
no dialogue is wasted; the action is integrally related.   The
exchange between Crooks and Lennie, for example, in act
two, scene two, might seem to have little to do with the
drama's development, but Crooks' observation--"I seen it
over and over--a guy talking to another guy and it don't
make no difference if he don't hear or understand.   The
thing is they're talkin'" (p. 669)--is directly related to
another of the play's major themes: the need for companionship.

It is companionship that keeps George and Lennie
together, a knightly loyalty that recalls Steinbeck's earlier
Arthurian experiments;[6] and it is equally the lack of companionship that underscores Crooks' resentment, Candy's
loneliness, and Curley's wife's decision to leave the farm.

Crooks is not permitted to play cards with the white hands
and envies George's good fortune at being able to share his
life with Lennie, even if Lennie is a half-wit. Candy symbolizes the loneliness of old age; his last hope is to form a
bond of comradeship with George and Lennie when they buy
the farm, a hope that is shattered, as both he and George
realize, when Lennie kills Curley's wife. Curley's wife is
so hungry for the companionship denied her by her overbear-
ing husband (she has no name; she is always "Curley's
wife") that she risks traveling to the bunkhouse to see the
men. When George calls her a tart, she replies, "I got
nobody to talk to. I got nobody to be with. Think I can
just sit home and do nothin' but cook for Curley? I want
to see somebody. Just see 'em an' talk to 'em" (p. 666).
Steinbeck is suggesting, through Crooks, who is probably
the loneliest man on the ranch, that people need people,
even if they cannot always understand each other; at least
they are together--"the thing is they're talkin'."

     The theme of companionship also helps to illuminate
George's role in the play. Lennie is a symbol of the primeval and fundamentally innocent yearning for the earth that is
found in all men. He dreams of finding his peace tending
rabbits on a ranch. Twice, he expresses a desire to lose
himself in a cave when he realizes that he has done some
"bad thing." His dream of the ranch, his plan to seclude
himself in a cave, and even his return to the river bank at
the end of the story suggest a ritualistic return to the womb,
a point that underscores the symbolic nature of his role as
an earth symbol. 7 George's presence in the play is explained largely in terms of his relationship to this symbolic
Lennie. George's function in the drama is puzzling. He
cares for Lennie; he serves as the instrument of Lennie's
death; but the play is Lennie's. Lennie as an earth symbol
keeps the dream of a ranch alive in George. In other
words, George must have Lennie in order to have the
ranch. He believes, however, on the surface, that without
Lennie he could get along much better: "God Almighty, if
I was alone, I could live so easy. I could go get a job of
work and no trouble. No mess ... and when the end of the
month come, I could take my fifty bucks and go into town
and get whatever I want. Why, I could stay in a cat-house
all night. I could eat any place I want. Order any damn
thing" (pp. 646-47). George could "get along" better, but
without Lennie, the hope of buying a farm of his own would
be gone. After Lennie kills Curley's wife, George realizes
that the dream has indeed ended. He tells Candy: "I'll

work my month and then I'll take my fifty bucks.   I'll stay all night in some lousy cat-house or I'll set in a pool room until everybody goes home.   An' then--I'll come back an' work another month.   And then I'll have fifty bucks more" (p. 676).   His life offers nothing now but the promise of monotonous routine.

George can verbalize the dream of the ranch, but Lennie manifests it physically in his very being.   When George kills Lennie, he kills that part of himself that believed the dream could come true.   It is significant that George's character should change at the end of the play, for he is the play's only developing character.   The pattern of his development is downward from hope and optimism to despair: all he has left now is the thought of working for "fifty bucks" and staying all night in a "cat-house."   In order to realize a dream, one must be whole in mind and body.   George's mind can intellectualize the dream; but in Lennie, the physical embodiment of the dream, is found the blood force, the vital energy necessary to make it come true.   Steinbeck might also be suggesting here that the primeval urges of the body, as symbolized by Lennie, are ultimately stronger than the things of the mind.   Now, without his physical counterpart, George fades.

Central to the play's pathos is the fact that George does not deserve this fate; he has done nothing to bring it upon himself.   Lennie, on the contrary, happily retains the dream until the very end.   George asks him to look across the river and to listen as he describes the scene so vividly that Lennie will actually see it.   When Lennie exclaims, "I can see it, George.   I can see it!   Right over there!   I can see it!"   George shoots him (p. 680).   Lennie dies happily, even triumphantly, with the vision of the farm before him.   Ironically, Lennie, who has killed the woman, dies fulfilled, while George, who has done nothing, must now endure a twofold torment: one, as a result of having killed his friend, leaving himself companionless; the other, at no longer having even the promise of the dream to look forward to.   But George's fate is not Lennie's fault either.   He still has the option of buying the farm and accepting the companionship of Candy.   He refuses both.   The reason, aside from a symbolic interpretation of his lack of "wholeness" now that Lennie is gone, remains one of the most perplexing questions posed by the drama.

Structurally, the play is unified.   The questions that

remain in the mind of the audience are solely within the
province of character development. The tightness of the
play's structure is emphasized by the three-act, two-and-a-
half-day time lapse in the action and the fact that the play
ends where it began, on the bank of the Salinas River, suggesting that the action has indeed come full circle. Like
their two forerunners in Mark Twain's Huckleberry Finn,
Lennie and George leave the safety of the river and venture
inland to realize their dream in accordance with the demands
of civilization; the effort is thwarted, and they are forced to
retreat once again for safety to the river--the natural world.
Just as there was no future for Huck and Jim in a civilization dominated by the bigoted, hypocritical, and generally insensitive townspeople who lived along the Mississippi, there
is now no future along the Salinas, a long way west of the
Mississippi, for George and Lennie. The civilization they
find is dominated by the Curleys and the Carlsons. Lennie
is dead; George will dissipate. But the Curleys and the
Carlsons, to be sure, will survive and prosper because
their insensitivity fosters the kind of cruel strength that is
needed to survive. They are the strongest, but, as the
drama makes clear, they are not the best.

Notes

1. See the article that Steinbeck wrote for Stage, 15 (Janu-
    ary, 1938), 50-51.

2. I am indebted to Peter Lisca, The Wide World of John
    Steinbeck (New Brunswick, N.J.: Rutgers University
    Press, 1958), for most of the biographical data in-
    cluded in this sketch.

3. Of Mice and Men, in Twenty Best Plays of the Modern
    American Theatre, ed. with an intr. by John Gassner
    (New York: Crown, 1939), p. 644. All subsequent
    references are to this edition.

4. Letter to his agents, quoted in The Wide World of John
    Steinbeck, p. 134.

5. Stage, pp. 50-51.

6. See Warren French's discussion of the Arthurian ele-
    ments in the story in John Steinbeck (New York:
    Twayne, 1961), p. 73.

7. See Peter Lisca's discussion of Lennie's desire for the
    "safe place"; The Wide World of John Steinbeck, pp.
    135-36. Compare Joseph Fontenrose's discussion of
    Lennie's and George's vision of Eden in John Stein-
    beck: An Introduction and Interpretation (New York:
    Barnes and Noble, 1963), pp. 58-59.

IV. APPARATUS FOR RESEARCH PAPERS

A. Ten Questions for Discussion

1. What can you assume about George's character from his
    comments on "sleeping out" in act I, scene II? Why is
    it important to the play's development that the two pre-
    fer spending the night by the river instead of going to
    the ranch? Do you attach any special significance to the
    fact that the play ends by the river?
2. What is the relationship between Lennie and the earth?
    Does he symbolize anything in particular?
3. Discuss the significance of Candy's story in act I, scene
    II about the fight between Smitty and Crooks, the stable-
    man. How is the story related to the play?
4. Account for George's attitude toward "bosses" in act I,
    scene II. What do his statements reveal about his char-
    acter? Is the "boss" symbolic of anything in the play?
5. On a number of occasions, the men remark that two
    men traveling together like George and Lennie is strange
    and rather uncommon. How do you account for this at-
    titude? What might Steinbeck be suggesting about the
    relationship between people in American society? Why
    do you think George does remain with Lennie?
6. What role does Candy, the clean-up man, play in the
    development of the drama? Do you attach any particular
    significance to the fact that Candy leads an old, blind
    dog around by a string and that the dog is finally shot
    in the head?
7. Is Crooks' one-sided discussion with Lennie in act II,
    scene II relevant to the play's action? Why does Stein-
    beck have Crooks lament over his place in life to a half-
    wit who pays no attention? Is the act symbolic? What,
    if anything, do Crooks and Lennie have in common?
8. What role does Slim play in this drama? He seems to
    have superior insight and compassion. Does he repre-
    sent anything in particular?
9. Is Curley's wife as bad as the men think? What do she
    and Lennie have in common? Account for the exchange

between them in act III, scene I.
10. Are there any developing characters in the play? What
    of George and Lennie, particularly? Do their charac-
    ters change as the play progresses? What do you make
    of the exchange between Candy and George immediately
    after finding the body of Curley's wife? Is Lennie re-
    sponsible for George's bad fortune?

B. Suggested Topics for Research Papers

1. One critic has suggested that there are similarities between Of Mice and Men (play) and Eugene O'Neill's early
   dramas of vagabondage, such as Bound East for Cardiff,
   The Long Voyage Home, and The Moon of the Caribbees.
   Read any one of O'Neill's early dramas and write a paper comparing it with Of Mice and Men.
2. Write a comparative study of theme, characterization,
   and technique in Of Mice and Men and The Moon Is Down,
   the play-novelette that Steinbeck published in 1942.
3. Lennie, in his innocence and attachment to the earth, is
   very much like Jim in Huckleberry Finn. Write a comparative analysis. Can George safely be compared to
   Huck?
4. The theme of madness is common in much twentieth century American literature. Using Of Mice and Men and
   the character of Lennie particularly, discuss the similarities in theme found in any of the following: Faulkner's The Sound and the Fury, Albee's The American
   Dream, and Kesey's One Flew Over the Cuckoo's Nest.
5. Of Mice and Men was originally intended to be called
   "Something That Happened." Find out why Steinbeck
   chose that title originally and where the title, Of Mice
   and Men, came from. Explain in your paper why both
   titles are appropriate.
6. Trace Steinbeck's use of the Arthurian legend through
   his earlier works to Of Mice and Men.

C. Selected Bibliography

1. French, Warren. John Steinbeck. New York: Twayne,
   1961.
   French discusses the Broadway and motion picture success of Of Mice and Men; he reads the story as "dark
   comedy"; the allegorical base of the story is less clear
   in the play than in the novel.

2.   Fontenrose, Joseph.   John Steinbeck: An Introduction
     and Interpretation.   New York: Barnes and Noble, 1963.
     The author discusses the adaptation of the play from the
     novel.   The play is like a tragedy of Sophocles or Ibsen.

3.   Lisca, Peter.   The Wide World of John Steinbeck.   New
     Brunswick, N. J.:   Rutgers University Press, 1958.
     Lisca includes in his analysis of the story many references
     pertinent to the history of the play's progress.

4.   Steinbeck, John.   Stage, 15 (January, 1938), 50-51.
     Steinbeck discusses using the play novelette form in order
     to keep the work concise.

Chapter 11

STEINBECK'S SEA OF CORTEZ (1941)

by Richard Astro

I. BACKGROUND OF THE WORK

Sea of Cortez: A Leisurely Journal of Travel and Research (1941) is among the most important, if least understood, works in Steinbeck's literary canon. A published record of the scientific expedition by Steinbeck and marine biologist Edward F. Ricketts to the Gulf of California in the spring of 1940, it is a comprehensive phyletic catalogue of life in the Gulf's faunal province preceded by a philosophic-scientific narrative which was published separately in 1951 as The Log from the Sea of Cortez. The Log, which is the main concern of this study (the scientific half of Sea of Cortez has long since gone out of print), is the end result of Steinbeck's developing interest in the habits and habitats of the animals living on the rocky shores and in the tide pools of the Pacific Coast, an interest which dates back to the summer of 1923 when he took the formal course in general zoology from C. V. Taylor at the Hopkins Marine Station in Pacific Grove, California. Working under Taylor, Steinbeck was exposed to the ideas of biologist William Emerson Ritter, whose notion of the organismal conception of life (the doctrine that a whole is more than the sum of its parts and that "the whole exercises a measure of determinative control over its parts"[1]) was currently in vogue among west coast naturalists. Steinbeck thought a good deal about Ritter's notion of the superorganism and applied the basic precepts of the organismal conception to relationships between characters and between groups of characters in much of his early fiction.

Steinbeck met Ed Ricketts in 1930, and their friendship was solidified by the fact that Ricketts, who had recently immigrated to the Monterey Peninsula from the University of Chicago where he had studied biology under the eminent

168

marine ecologist, W. C. Allee, gave impetus and professional insight to the ideas about man and his social and natural
environment that Steinbeck was attempting to work out in his
novels and short stories.

Although he was hard at work during the 1930s on
such minor gems as Tortilla Flat, Of Mice and Men and In
Dubious Battle, as well as on his undisputed masterpiece,
The Grapes of Wrath, Steinbeck maintained an abiding interest in Ricketts' research of the animals of the intertidal
zones, and on occasion accompanied his friend on collecting
expeditions. Through Ricketts, he became acquainted with
the literature of the seashore since the marine biologist had
in his laboratory on the waterfront in Pacific Grove "probably
the finest library outside of Stanford and U.C. Berkeley on
the marine ecology of the Pacific Coast."2 Certainly Steinbeck was familiar with the materials which went into Between
Pacific Tides (1939), the published record of Ricketts' years
of reading about and observation of the ecological nature of
tidepool life, which the marine biologist wrote in collaboration with Jack Calvin and for which Steinbeck wrote the Foreword to the second edition (1948).

The Grapes of Wrath was published within months of
Between Pacific Tides, and both men, having marked important milestones in their careers, felt the need for some
breathing space. Accordingly, they agreed to collaborate on
a small handbook about the marine invertebrates of San Francisco Bay. According to Ricketts' plan for the project,
Steinbeck was to write a small guidebook, "specifically designed for beginning biology classes but [it] will be written
and ordered so that it may be used by the sea coast wander-
er who finds interest in the little bugs and would like to know
what they are and how they live. Its treatment will revolt
against the theory that only the dull is accurate and only the
tiresome, valuable."3 Steinbeck wrote a preface for the
handbook which runs slightly less than 2,000 words. Although incomplete and as yet unpublished, it is extremely interesting in that Steinbeck pinpoints the ecological and rela-
tional cast of his (and Ricketts') thinking by noting that it is
as pointless to study tidepool life by isolated investigations
of individual marine organisms as it is to study patterns of
family life in New York City simply by examining one New
York family in detail.

Steinbeck and Ricketts developed a format for their
proposed Bay Area handbook and travelled to collecting

stations at Tomales Point and Moss Beach, but the project
was abandoned early in 1940 in favor of a more extensive
venture to the largely uncharted regions of the Gulf of California. Both men helped to organize the Sea of Cortez expedition, but Ricketts was clearly the driving force behind
what began a year earlier as a modest study of marine life
in San Francisco Bay. Already a novelist of reputation,
Steinbeck had some money (Ricketts always lived below subsistence level), and while he was interested in the project,
his main reason for financing it was his desire to enable
Ricketts to continue his research of the North American lit-
toral.

Through the generous efforts of Webster F. (Toby)
Street, a Monterey attorney, Steinbeck chartered Anthony J.
Berry's seventy-six foot purse-seiner, the Western Flyer,
and ordered most of the necessary supplies. Ricketts ar-
ranged the collecting materials and obtained port clearances
from the Consul General of Mexico who alerted local officials
of the Western Flyer's "proposed yachting trip into Mexican
waters."4 And on March 11, 1940, Steinbeck, Ricketts and
a crew of five (not four as is suggested in the Log--Carol
Steinbeck, the novelist's first wife, made the entire trip, although she is never mentioned in the text) sailed from Monterey harbor for the Gulf of California, returning six weeks
later on April 20.

II. PLOT SYNOPSIS

"The design of a book is the pattern of a reality controlled and shaped by the mind of the writer,"5 insist Steinbeck and Ricketts in the introduction to the narrative section
of Sea of Cortez. Speaking of their proposed plan for writing the Log, the authors note that "we could do one of several things about its design," "but we have decided to let it
form itself: its boundaries a boat and a sea; its duration a
six weeks' charter time; its subject everything we could see
and think and even imagine; its limits--our own without
reservation" (1).

Herein Steinbeck and Ricketts pinpoint the unique format and structure of The Log from the Sea of Cortez. Since
it is not a work of fiction, it has no plot in the usual sense
of the term, and as non-fiction, it is held together only by
the geographical and chronological order of the accounts reported, and by the fact that almost every chapter is divided

into two-parts: a narrative of events that happened and reflections upon those events. The narrative traces the voyage
of the Western Flyer from Monterey Bay down the west
coast of California and the Baja peninsula to Cabo San Lucas
(March 11-17), then north up the west side of the Sea of
Cortez to La Paz (March 20), Loreto (March 25), and Angel
de la Guardia (April 3), eastward across the Gulf to Tiburon
Island (April 3) and south to Guaymas (April 5), and then
back to Monterey via the Agiabampo estuary and Cedros Island (April 11-20).

        In the absence of a formal plot, the Log does have a
very definite "design" which is crucial to an understanding
of the book's real meaning and its importance to an understanding of Steinbeck's fiction. This "design" grew out of
the authors' curiosity, which they suggest "was not limited,
but was as wide and horizonless as that of Darwin or Agas-
siz or Linneaus or Pliny. We wanted to see everything our
eyes would accommodate, to think what we could, and, out
of our seeing and thinking, to build some kind of structure
in modeled imitation of the observed reality" (2).   This
"structure" is a picture of life in the Gulf, qualified by the
authors' awareness that since permanent objective reality is
"only available in pickled tatters or in distorted flashes" (3),
the knowledge reported is warped by "the thrust of our individual personalities" and by "the collective pressure and
stream of our time and race" (2).

        There are, of course, the factual reports about the
animals collected and about commensal and symbiotic relationships between individual marine organisms which led
Ricketts to affirm that "this little trip of ours is proving to
be an important expedition, and that out of it are coming
some fairly significant contributions to invertebrate zoology,
to marine sociology and even--I wouldn't be surprised--to
human thought. "[6] But these reports are accompanied by
speculations about the organismal basis of life in the Gulf
"which the early Church would have been forced to call a
mystery" (165), and about the ecological unity of life as a
whole in which "species merge into species, " "groups melt
into ecological groups, " so that "all things are one thing and
that one thing is all things" (217).   And built into Steinbeck
and Ricketts' accounts of the life-styles of the simple Indians
living in the remote fishing villages along the shores of the
Sea of Cortez are thoughts about what we in the United States
call progress, which may ultimately lead to our extinction
while the Indians of the Gulf sit dreamily in their dugout

canoes and recall a "great and godlike race [of Northameri-
canos] that flew away in four-motored bombers to the accompaniment of exploding bombs, the voice of God calling
them home" (89).

There are highly serious (at times almost homiletic)
discussions of birth and death, history, navigation, and the
scientific method in the Log, carefully sandwiched between
less solemn reflections about sea myths, big-horn sheep
hunting, the idiosyncrasies of the crew members, temperamental outboard motors, lemon pies, drinking (the authors
did a considerable amount on the trip), and aphrodisiacs (in
which it is concluded that sexual intercourse "is the only
good one"). Indeed, the "design" of the Log is punctuated
by a blend of genial humor and high seriousness. And the
reader is given relief from the lofty philosophical speculations by remarks about a new species of a genus of parasite
(Proctofilus) which lives in the anus of the sea-cucumber and
which Steinbeck and Ricketts named Proctofilus winchelli after Walter, whom they both detested. There is also the
tongue-in-cheek observation as to how one of the crew members collected some specimens of Phthirius pubis which are
"members of the common species so widely distributed
throughout the world" (125).

Blending humor with intense seriousness, scientific
fact with metaphysical speculation, Steinbeck and Ricketts
created in The Log from the Sea of Cortez a cohesive narrative unified around their fundamental assumption that all
forms of inquiry are valid since "the laws of thought must
be the laws of things...." "Thought and things are part of
one evolving matrix," insist Steinbeck and Ricketts, "and
cannot ultimately conflict."[7]

Lashing out at scientific specialists, at those "dry-
ball" scientists who create "out of their own crusted minds"
a "world wrinkled with formaldehyde" (29), Steinbeck and
Ricketts proliferate in all directions as they study the teem-
ing, boisterous life of the Gulf. Their trip (and the written
record of that trip) had "dimension and tone." Its "boundaries seeped through itself into some time and space that
was more than all the Gulf and more than all our lives"
(270). The "design" of The Log from the Sea of Cortez is,
as the authors remark about their trip, "an integrated nucle-
us from which weak strings of thought stretched into every
reachable reality" (270). It is a biological record firmly
anchored in scientific fact, but "bright with sun and wet with

sea water" and "the whole crusted over with exploring thought" (270).

III. CRITICAL EXPLICATION

What Scott Newhall called a chioppino of travel, biology and philosophy[8] is an extremely valuable creation in its own right. The scientific second half with its excellent plates of pink murex and brown cowry which records about 550 different species--ten percent of which had not been previously described--is an indispensable aid to students studying the marine invertebrates of the Gulf of California. And the narrative section is a completely lucid and poetic fusion of science and philosophy, art and ethics, by two uniquely intelligent men who proved that the complicated life of the tidepool could be described by persons other than the scientific pickler and the museum drone.

Much of the Log is pure poetry and its creators are poets of Nature. The best passages in the narrative are those in which Steinbeck and Ricketts depict the sea and the tide, the wind and the calm, the reefs and beaches, the Indians and the little animals, the cold stirring waters of the Pacific and the warm brackish lagoons of the Gulf. And in those brief but memorable glimpses of the war between the pigs and vultures on the beach at San Lucas and of the dogs of La Paz barking into the night, one encounters the best results of the collaboration by artist and biologist.

But over and above its intrinsic worth, The Log from the Sea of Cortez is, if read properly, also valuable for the light it sheds on the thematic design of Steinbeck's greatest fiction. At the same time, it is a mistake to insist, as most of Steinbeck's critics have done, that the Log contains a concise statement of Steinbeck's basic beliefs. For such an assumption disregards the very substantial role played in the writing of the narrative by Ricketts, whose ideas sometimes parallel but rarely imitate and in one instance clearly oppose those of the novelist.

It has generally been supposed that, as Joseph Fontenrose suggests, "Steinbeck wrote the first part, the narrative of the trip" while "Ricketts wrote the second part, a phyletic catalogue,"[9] and that "the materials for the narrative and speculative portion came in part from two journals, one kept by Ricketts and the other by Steinbeck."[10] Neither

assumption is accurate. There were two journals kept during the expedition, but neither was written by Steinbeck.
Rather they were written by Ricketts and by Tony Berry,
captain of the Western Flyer, and much of the published
narrative is taken directly from Ricketts' log.

The lengthy discussion of navigation (chapter five in
the Log) is a slightly condensed version of an entry in
Ricketts' journal. Reflections about the cemetery at San
Lucas and about the "borrego" hunt at Puerto Escondido appear in similar form in Ricketts' text, as does most of the
scientific theorizing and those sections of the narrative (but
particularly chapter twenty-six) which question "that factor
of civilization" we call progress. In addition, a section of
chapter eleven of the Log which contains information about
tidal patterns and some Jungian observations about man's
"sea-memory, or sea-thought, which lives deep in the mind"
(32) is a slightly altered transcription of part of an unpublished essay written by Ricketts based on reflections he
made on a collecting expedition to Southeastern Alaska in
1932. [11]

"Originally a journal of the trip was to have been
kept by both of us," wrote Steinbeck and Ricketts in a joint
memorandum to Pascal Covici (Steinbeck's editor) to the
editorial board of the Viking Press (the book's publisher),

> but this record was found to be the natural expres-
> sion of only one of us. The journal was subse-
> quently used by the other chiefly as a reminder of
> what had actually taken place, but in several cases
> parts of the original field notes were incorporated
> into the final narrative, and in one case a large
> section was lifted verbatim from other unpublished
> work. [12]

The Steinbeck-Ricketts memorandum refutes the idea that Sea
of Cortez is two books, the first by Steinbeck and the second
by Ricketts. Rather, as Ricketts suggested in a brief document he titled "Morphology of the Sea of Cortez," "the
structure is a collaboration, but mostly shaped by John.
The book is the result."[13] And the reference in the memorandum to "a large section [which] was lifted verbatim from
other unpublished work" refers directly to the crucial Easter
sermon on non-teleological thinking which was originally an
essay written by Ricketts during the late 1930s.

Certainly, as Ricketts insists, Steinbeck "shaped" the narrative and added a good deal to it himself, and Jack Calvin's suggestion that "Sea of Cortez might be thought of as by Ricketts, ghostwritten by Steinbeck,"14 is, as Calvin concedes, an overstatement. But to maintain that the metaphysical speculation and social theorizing in the Log are Steinbeck's alone, to insist that the novelist created the entire narrative from scratch, is to distort the facts in the worst possible way.

The essential question, then, that must be answered is how Steinbeck and Ricketts' views of the world coincide and how they differ. Then, having determined these similarities and differences, one must ascertain how the Log can best be employed as a guide to understanding Steinbeck's fiction.

Most of the writings of both men (Steinbeck's novels, short stories and works of non-fiction, and Ricketts' Between Pacific Tides and his unpublished essays, journals, and extensive correspondence) indicate that Steinbeck and Ricketts are naturalistis in the sense that they are painstaking in acquiring knowledge of nature and eager to integrate their beings with the holistic basis of natural life. Both embrace an ecological view of the natural world which they admire and study because of their faith in it as that through which their own lives have meaning and worth. And both draw responses from that world which lead them to celebrate a higher principle of cosmic order.

> And it is a strange thing that most of the feeling we call religious, most of the mystical outcrying which is one of the most prized and used and desired reactions of our species, is really the understanding and the attempt to say that man is related to the whole thing, related inextricably to all reality, known and unknowable.... It is advisable to look from the tide pool to the stars and then back to the tide pool again. (216-217)

Where Steinbeck and Ricketts ardently disagree is on their respective attitudes toward the value of social change and material progress. For whereas the many statements in the Log which suggest that "our tremendous drives, our great drives, the fantastic production of good that can't be sold, the clutter of possessions which enslave whole populations with debt ... the defence of the country against a

frantic nation of conquerers, and the necessity for becoming
frantic to do it" (208) may really be "our mutation, of which
the assembly line, the collective farm, the mechanized army,
and the mass production of food are evidences or even
symptoms" (88) are squarely consistent with Ricketts' attitude toward "progress" as it appears in virtually all of his
other writings, they conflict sharply with Steinbeck's ringing
affirmation of man's ability to "walk up the stairs of his
concepts" and "emerge ahead of his accomplishments" in
The Grapes of Wrath, the book which directly precedes Sea
of Cortez.

Ricketts recognized this ideological clash between himself and Steinbeck and even went so far as to write an essay
about their differing views.   During the summer of 1940, the
novelist took time off from his work on "shaping" Sea of
Cortez to write the screenplay for a film entitled The Forgotten Village.   Ricketts accompanied Steinbeck to Mexico
for the filming, and while the novelist championed progress
and social change in his account of a small Mexican village's
struggle against disease and outmoded medical practices,
Ricketts wrote an essay entitled "Thesis and Materials for
a Script on Mexico" in which he selects "a motif diametri-
cally opposite to that of John's 'Forgotten Village.'"[15] In
short, Ricketts seeks to preserve "the deep smile" and ad-
vocates a simple appreciation of what is as opposed to what
might be or could be.   "The chief character in John's
script," wrote the marine biologist, "is an Indian boy who
becomes so imbued with the spirit of modern medical progress that he leaves the traditional way of his people to associate himself with the new thing."

> The working out of a script for the 'other side'
> might correspondingly be achieved through the
> figure of some wise and mellow old man, who has
> long ago developed beyond the expediences of eco-
> nomic drives and power drives ... and who ap-
> propriately might point out the evils of the en-
> croaching mechanistic civilization to a young per-
> son.[16]

In his desire to appreciate what is, instead of what
might be or could be, Ricketts is a monist who carefully
worked out a method by which he might understand the essence of the cosmic whole and acquire a personal emotive
relationship with that whole.   This method is what he called
non-teleological thinking, and its precepts are contained in

his essay of the same name which appears in the Log. In
this essay, which, incidentally, Joseph Fontenrose suggests
is "the philosophical center of the book,"[17] Ricketts insists
that the non-teleological method of thinking can enable man
to break through to an understanding of "the whole world of
fact and fancy, body and psyche, physical fact and spiritual
truth." "The whole picture is portrayed by is, the deepest
word of deep ultimate reality, not shallow or partial as reasons are, but deeper and participating, possibly encompass-
ing the Oriental concept of being" (151).

        In contrast to what he calls teleological thinking,
which "considers changes and cures--what 'should be' in
terms of an end pattern" (134) and which often leads to "a
fierce but ineffectual attempt to change conditions which are
assumed undesirable" (135), Ricketts prefers non-teleological
ideas which "imply death, fundamentalism and clarity--see-
ing beyond traditional or personal projections" (135).

        Despite some severe problems in his handling of
philosophical terminology (particularly with the words "teleological" and "non-teleological"), what the marine biologist
seems to be talking about in his essay on non-teleological
thinking is an open, non-blaming, non-causal approach to
life by the man who looks at situations and events and accepts them as such. In so doing, the beholder perceives
the whole picture and becomes an identifiable part of that
picture. "The method extends beyond thinking even to living
itself," insists Ricketts, "in fact, by inferred definition, it
postulates 'living into'" (147).

        Steinbeck respected and was, as a writer, deeply in-
terested in Ricketts' desire to "live into life," and many of
his finest novels and short stories (among them "Flight,"
"The Leader of the People," and Of Mice and Men) reflect
his use of Ricketts' gospel of non-teleological thinking as
fictional method, if not as thematic design. Moreover, there
are several Ricketts-like characters in Steinbeck's fiction
(most particularly Doc Burton of In Dubious Battle) who view
life non-teleologically and who, like Burton, refuse "to put
on the blinders of 'good' or 'bad,' and limit my vision" in
their quest "to see the whole picture," to "look at the whole
thing."[18]

        But Steinbeck was at the same time a thorough teleo-
logist. And although he placed a high premium on the con-
templative function of the human mind, he insisted that for

this function to have real meaning, it must serve some socially responsible end. From the time when he was first
exposed to Ritter's organismal conception of life, which postulates the notion that any organism (including man) must
work toward recognizable ends and goals if it is to survive,
Steinbeck was a steadfast believer in meaningful change and
progress. And while he writes about his non-teleologists as
well as his escapees and drop-outs with understanding and
affection, they are rarely his personae and never his heroes.
After witnessing first-hand the ruthless tyranny by greedy
land monopolists and agri-businessmen over California's
migrant poor, the novelist turned to political fiction, and he
created as his fictional hero, not the detached visionary who
disparages progress in favor of understanding things as they
are, but that unique individual who combines philosophical
wisdom and social commitment and acts to benefit the social
order.

        Jim Casy, the unorthodox ex-preacher in The Grapes
of Wrath, is at first a Rickettsian non-teleologist who dismisses traditional codes of behavior, and concludes that
"there ain't no sin and there ain't no virtue. There's just
stuff people do. "[19] But as time progresses and situations
worsen, the non-teleological visionary turns social reformer
who gives his life to end the oppression of the dispossessed.
Whereas Burton, who wants no more than to see "the whole
thing, " is unable to help a group of striking apple pickers
work toward meaningful social change and ends up a lonely
man, by his own admission, "working all alone, toward
nothing, " Casy dedicates himself to "go where the folks is
goin'" and becomes a Christ who directs his disciples from
need to concept and finally to action. Whereas In Dubious
Battle ends in self-neutralizing ambivalence, The Grapes of
Wrath ends in triumph.

        Ricketts' doctrine of non-teleological thinking was very
much on Steinbeck's mind in the late 1930s as he worked,
first in In Dubious Battle, and then in The Grapes of Wrath,
to plot a course by which the man of vision could, while
"living into life, " employ the principles of his vision to effect worthwhile change without falling into blind political
partisanship which is an open door to prejudice. So, putting together the narrative section of Sea of Cortez in the
summer of 1940 with Ricketts' journal and the essay on non-
teleological thinking before him, the novelist noted that the
Log "is a good clearing-out of a lot of ideas that have been
working on me for a long time. "[20]

Indeed, the final form of the Log stands as it is largely because of Ed Ricketts. And if the world-view contained in that volume seems sometimes paradoxical and at odds with the thematic design of Steinbeck's fiction, it is because the book combines the thoughts and observations of two individuals with parallel but hardly identical philosophies of life. The Log contains Ricketts' fundamental notions about man and about the world as a whole (some Steinbeck shared, others he rejected). On Steinbeck's part, it is a lasting testament of affection for the person and a sincere statement of respect for the ideas of his closest friend.

Early in 1951, as Steinbeck was preparing a separate edition of the Log for publication by the Viking Press, he noted in a letter to Pascal Covici that "a good writer works at the impossible. " "And if he is a writer wise enough to know it can't be done, then he is not a writer at all. "21 Indeed, Steinbeck states that "there is another kind [of writer] who pulls in his horizons, drops his mind as one lowers rifle sights. "22

Steinbeck and Ricketts do not "lower their rifle sights" in the unique blend of science and philosophy they called The Log from the Sea of Cortez. It is true, of course, that they worked at the impossible if what they intended was to present a clear picture of their respective world views. But out of the attempt came as important a work as any book which bears John Steinbeck's name. Ricketts and Steinbeck teach us a good many things in Sea of Cortez. They teach us more about the faunal province of the Gulf of California than any previous study of the region, and they instruct us in a highly valuable, if now nearly forgotten, method of scientific inquiry which reverses the modern process "of looking quickly at the whole field and then diving down to a particular" (60). If we recognize that Ed Ricketts had a large hand in the writing of the narrative as well as the phyletic catalogue, we can explore the ideas of a truly unique individual whose notions about man and the world, while not always philosophically satisfying, are always interesting. And, having determined which of Ricketts' views Steinbeck shared and which he rejected, we may better employ the narrative section of Sea of Cortez as a key to understanding the thematic design of Steinbeck's fiction.

Notes

1. William Emerson Ritter and Edna W. Bailey, "The Organismal Conception: Its Place in Science and Its Bearing on Philosophy," University of California Publications in Zoology, 31 (1931), 307.

2. Edward F. Ricketts, "Contents of PBL Destroyed Nov. 1936," p. 6. This is an unpublished list of possessions lost in the fire which gutted Ricketts' laboratory on Cannery Row.

3. Ricketts, "Suggested Outline for Handbook of Marine Invertebrates of the San Francisco Bay Area," unpublished and undated manuscript, p. 2.

4. Hector M. Escalona to Edward F. Ricketts, March 21, 1940.

5. Ricketts and Steinbeck, The Log from the Sea of Cortez (New York: Viking Compass, 1962), p. 1. All further citations from the Log refer to this edition and are identified by page number in the text.

6. Ricketts to Steinbeck, August 22, 1941.

7. Actually, Ricketts and Steinbeck are quoting from John Elof Boodin's book, A Realistic Universe. See the Log, p. 257.

8. Scott Newhall, "John Steinbeck's Chioppino of Biology and Philosophy," San Francisco Chronicle, "This World" section, December 14, 1941.

9. Joseph Fontenrose, John Steinbeck: An Introduction and Interpretation (New York: Holt, Rinehart and Winston, 1962), p. 85.

10. Peter Lisca, The Wide World of John Steinbeck (New Brunswick, N. J.: Rutgers University Press, 1958), p. 181.

11. Ricketts' essay is entitled "The Tide as an Environmental Factor." Although never published, it was of great value to graduate students as well as to resident and visiting faculty at the Hopkins Marine Station during the mid-1930s.

12. Ricketts, "Memorandum from Steinbeck-Ricketts to Pat Covici and to the Editorial Board of Viking, " August 25, 1941.

13. Ricketts, "Morphology of the Sea of Cortez, " unpublished and undated one page manuscript.

14. Jack Calvin to Richard Astro, July 14, 1969.

15. Ricketts, "Thesis and Materials for a Script on Mexico, " unpublished manuscript written in Mexico during the summer of 1940, p. 3.

16. Ibid. , p. 5.

17. Fontenrose, p. 87.

18. Steinbeck, In Dubious Battle (New York: Viking Compass, 1963), p. 130.

19. Steinbeck, The Grapes of Wrath (New York: Viking Compass, 1958), p. 32.

20. Lewis Gannett, "Steinbeck's Way of Writing, " The Portable Steinbeck, revised edition (New York: Viking, 1946), p. xxv.

21. Steinbeck, Journal of a Novel (New York: Viking, 1969), p. 4.

22. Ibid.

IV. APPARATUS FOR RESEARCH PAPERS

A. Ten Questions for Discussion

1. Discuss the "scientific method" employed by Steinbeck and Ricketts on the Gulf of California expedition. In what ways does it differ from the procedures employed by most scientific specialists? In short, how do Steinbeck and Ricketts differ as "scientists" from those individuals whom they describe as "dry-balls"?
2. Although she is never mentioned in the narrative, Carol Steinbeck (the novelist's first wife) made the entire voyage aboard the Western Flyer. Forgetting any possible personal considerations by Steinbeck, and concentrating

only on the theme of the text itself, why do you suppose
Steinbeck kept his wife out of the Log?

3. Steinbeck and Ricketts' chief interest in tidepool life in
    the Log concerns the relationships between species of
    marine organisms. This leads them to use such terms
    as "commensal" and "symbiotic" to describe and analyze
    these relationships between organisms. What precisely
    do these terms mean and how do they help to define the
    relationships between tidepool organisms?

4. Discuss the "bawdiness" of the Log. Why do Steinbeck
    and Ricketts insist that their account must be bawdy "if
    it is to be true"?

5. Steinbeck and Ricketts express some highly unorthodox
    religious views in the Log. But they also understand
    and are certainly moved by the traditional religious ob-
    servances by the people in the region of the Gulf. Dis-
    cuss this strange combination of religious heterodoxy
    and understanding. How does it fit into the overall
    world view expressed in the Log?

6. Define the term "non-teleological thinking" as it is used
    in the Log. How specifically would this method of think-
    ing serve to explain the attitude expressed about the life-
    styles of the simple villagers Steinbeck and Ricketts en-
    countered during their voyage?

7. Discuss Steinbeck and Ricketts' analysis of the relation-
    ship between the individual organism and the group ani-
    mal in the Log. What do they say about possible anal-
    ogies between marine invertebrates and men, and be-
    tween the collective animal and collective man?

8. Define as concisely as possible Steinbeck and Ricketts'
    use of the term "ecology." What precisely do they mean
    by "the ecological picture"?

9. Sr. Manuel Madinabeitia (see the Log, p. 159) recently
    told this writer (3/24/72) that when he accompanied
    Steinbeck and Ricketts on the "borrego" hunt in the
    mountains near Puerto Escondido, neither the novelist
    nor the biologist had any intentions of killing a "bor-
    rego." On the basis of the overall world view expressed
    in the Log, why do you suppose Steinbeck and Ricketts
    felt this way?

10. Talking about their trip, Steinbeck and Ricketts note that
    "the Gulf does draw one.... And since we have re-
    turned, there is always in the back of our minds the
    positive desire to go back again." They go on to state
    that "if it were lush and rich, one could understand the
    pull, but it is fierce and hostile and sullen." Having
    read their account, why do you think Steinbeck and
    Ricketts wanted so much to return to the Gulf?

B. Suggested Topics for Research Papers

1. Discuss the Log in the light of the modern ecology move-
    ment. What specifically did Steinbeck and Ricketts tell
    us in 1941 about problems of conservation and depletion
    that we are only beginning to think seriously about to-
    day?

2. Compare The Log from the Sea of Cortez with Stein-
    beck's other travelogue, Travels with Charley (1962).
    How did the passage of time alter Steinbeck's view of
    man and the world in which he lives?

3. When The Forgotten Village was published in 1941,
    Ricketts told a close friend, "I don't think it's much
    good. " Read Steinbeck's screenplay and then decide
    why, on the basis of the world view expressed in the
    Log, you feel Ricketts found fault with The Forgotten
    Village. Avoid overly-simple explanations by remember-
    ing that Ricketts thought The Grapes of Wrath a great
    work of fiction.

4. In "About Ed Ricketts, " Steinbeck's personal portrait of
    the marine biologist which precedes the Viking Compass
    edition of the Log, the novelist notes the unique nature
    of Ricketts' thinking, which "was as paradoxical as his
    life. He thought in mystical terms and hated and dis-
    trusted mysticism. " Bertrand Russell has pointed out
    in Mysticism and Religion that mysticism may be a
    creed or simply an attitude toward life--and if the latter
    --can suggest a perception of reality which builds upon
    rather than ignores the analytic and discursive method.
    Discuss the mysticism in the Log in this regard. Is it
    a creed or an attitude toward life? And if the latter,
    does it build upon the discursive and analytic method?

5. In 1923, when Steinbeck enrolled for the summer course
    at the Hopkins Marine Station in Pacific Grove, he was
    exposed to the ideas of William Emerson Ritter whose
    doctrine of the organismal conception of life (defined
    most succinctly in his article with Edna W. Bailey en-
    titled "The Organismal Conception: Its Place in Science
    and Its Bearing on Philosophy, " University of California
    Publications in Zoology, XXXI [1931], 307-358) was then
    in vogue among west coast naturalists. Ricketts, on the
    other hand, studied under W. C. Allee, the famous Chi-
    cago ecologist, whose ideas about the universality of so-
    cial behavior among animals and whose theory of social
    transition formed the basis of his classic study about
    patterns of social behavior in Animal Aggregations
    (1931). Ritter's idea and Allee's views on the behavior

patterns among animals, while similar, are by no means
identical. And a knowledge of the differences between
the ideas of these two men helps to determine the differences in thinking between Steinbeck and Ricketts.
Study the differences between Ritter's organismal conception of life and Allee's notions about animal aggregations and then indicate how these differences are recorded and reconciled in the Log.

6. Above all, the Log contains ample evidence that Steinbeck's interest in biology was pervasive and genuine and
that he shared with Ricketts a tendency to view life bio-
logically and ecologically. Using In Dubious Battle, The
Grapes of Wrath, Cannery Row and Burning Bright as
representative examples, decide how the biological view
of life in the Log is reflected by the manner in which
Steinbeck handles character and situation in his fiction.
Finally, decide whether or not Steinbeck views man as
he views marine invertebrates.

C. Selected Bibliography

1. Astro, Richard. "Steinbeck and Ricketts: Escape or
Commitment in the Sea of Cortez, " Western American
Literature 6 (Summer, 1971), 109-21.
A detailed account based on previously unavailable
and as yet unpublished essays and journals by Edward F.
Ricketts about how Sea of Cortez was written and published
as well as facts about what actually happened on the Gulf of
California expedition.

2. Bracher, Frederick. "Steinbeck and the Biological View
of Man, " Pacific Spectator (Winter, 1948), reprinted in
Steinbeck and His Critics, eds. E. W. Tedlock and C.
V. Wicker. Albuquerque: University of New Mexico,
1957, pp. 183-96.
Perceptive discussion of the relationship between the
ideas expressed in the Log and Steinbeck's early fiction.
Ricketts, who had read Bracher's article soon after it appeared, called it "the best evaluation yet of Jn [sic] anywhere, the deepest understanding of non-tel-think [sic], the
first tying up of those ideas. " (Ricketts to Antonia Seixas,
2/4/48)

3. Duffus, R. L. The New York Times Book Review, De-
december 28, 1941.
A brief but interesting synopsis of Sea of Cortez

which leads the reviewer to conclude that "Mr. Steinbeck's
novels will be better for the experience. One hopes that he
and Mr. Ricketts get another trip together."

4. Fadiman, Clifton. "Of Crabs and Men," New Yorker,
    17 (December 6, 1941), 133.
        Insists that Sea of Cortez is proof positive that Stein-
beck is a biological novelist; that he is "an intellectual anti-
isolationist" and is "anti-teleological in his thinking, as all
good biologists should be."

5. Fontenrose, Joseph. "Sea of Cortez" in John Steinbeck:
    An Introduction and Interpretation. New York: Holt,
    Rinehart and Winston, 1962, pp. 84-97.
        Clearly the best in-depth analysis of the philosophical
network of ideas in the Log. The discussion of non-teleological thinking is particularly valuable even though Fontenrose did not have access to the Ricketts document.

6. Hedgpeth, Joel W. "Philosophy on Cannery Row,"
    Steinbeck: The Man and His Work, eds. Richard Astro
    and Tetsumaro Hayashi. Corvallis: Oregon State Uni-
    versity, 1971, pp. 89-129.
        A comprehensive study of the life and works of Ed-
ward F. Ricketts with particular attention to Between Pacific
Tides and Sea of Cortez. The most factual account of the
marine biologist to date.

7. _____. "The Scientific Second Half of the Sea of
    Cortez," San Francisco Chronicle, "This World" sec-
    tion, December 14, 1941.
        A lively review of the book's phyletic catalogue which
points to the scientific successes of the Steinbeck-Ricketts
expedition.

8. Hyman, Stanley. "Some Notes on John Steinbeck,"
    Antioch Review, 2 (June, 1942). Reprinted in Steinbeck
    and His Critics, pp. 152-66.
        Short-sighted essay which sees Sea of Cortez as un-
fortunate evidence that Steinbeck abandoned his social compulsion and emerged "into a perfect scientific vacuum."

9. Ingels, Beth. "Sea of Cortez, New Picture of Stein-
    beck," Monterey Peninsula Herald, December 6, 1941.
        Little known but superbly honest review by a friend
of both authors who insists that Sea of Cortez is "one of the
most unusual books ever published in this country."

10.   Lisca, Peter.   "Sea of Cortez" in The Wide World of
      John Steinbeck.   New Brunswick, N. J. :   Rutgers Uni-
      versity, 1958, pp. 178-85.
         A good but brief summary of the ideas in the Log,
chiefly valuable in relation to the thematic design of Steinbeck's fiction.

11.   Lloyd, Francis L.   "The Steinbeck-Ricketts Expedition
      to Mexico," The Carmel Pine Cone, March 15, 1940.
         Neglected and highly interesting account of the back-
ground of the Steinbeck-Ricketts expedition with particular
attention to previous collecting trips by both men.

12.   Marks, Lester Jay.   Thematic Design in the Novels of
      John Steinbeck.   The Hague: Mouton, 1969, pp. 16-18,
      20-24, 55-57, 128-30.
         Competent analysis of the philosophy of life expressed
in the Log, but with too great a tendency to relate this philosophy directly to almost all of Steinbeck's fiction.

13.   Newhall, Scott.   "John Steinbeck's Chioppino of Biology
      and Philosophy," San Francisco Chronicle, "This World"
      section, December 14, 1941.
         A distortive account of Sea of Cortez by a reviewer
who feels that Steinbeck was badly battered by his attempt
"to write a book about anything as prosaic as voyaging to
the Gulf of California. "

14.   Peattie, Donald Culross.   Saturday Review of Litera-
      ture, 24 (December 27, 1941), 5.
         Stuffy review insisting that "one-tenth of this rabbit-
out-of-hatting would have sufficed this reader" by a critic
bothered by the fact that Steinbeck "never wrote a book like
this before. "

Chapter 12

STEINBECK'S <u>TO A GOD UNKNOWN</u>

by Robert DeMott

I. BACKGROUND

John Steinbeck wrote Wilbur Needham in 1934 expressing great pleasure and relief that Needham had grasped
Steinbeck's intention in <u>To a God Unknown</u>.[1] The novel
searches the darkness and vicissitudes of primitive natural
and human processes in its movement toward personal and
natural resolution. It swings between human and animal,
pagan and Christian, sacred and profane, conscious and unconscious values. Through it all the protagonist-hero,
Joseph Wayne, seeks reconciliation, unification, and understanding in a world of bipolar opposites, projected in great
part, especially toward the end of the book, on a symbolic
landscape.

II. PLOT SYNOPSIS

The novel can be summarized briefly. The story
opens in Vermont in 1903. Joseph Wayne, the protagonist
of the novel, is one of four brothers. He has received his
father's blessing and migrated to California, where he ac-
quires land in the Valley of Nuestra Senora. When he learns
of the death of his patriarchal father, he imagines that his
father's spirit has come to California and has lodged itself
in a large oak tree close to Joseph's house.

Next, Joseph's brothers, Thomas, Burton, and Benjamin, come to California to live and work with Joseph on
his farm. In a pine grove on a ridge in back of the farm,
Joseph and Thomas discover a glade which contains a huge
rock and an ever-flowing spring which issues from a small
cave in the rock. Increasingly, the oak tree and the

mysterious glade become focal points for Joseph's procrea-
tive and spiritual energies. Joseph marries Elizabeth Mc-
Greggor, a schoolteacher, who delivers a baby boy the following year. Joseph initiates his son, John, by placing him
in the great oak tree, despite his pious brother Burton's
protests. Burton, outraged and offended by Joseph's acts
of paganism, girdles the oak tree then moves away to Pacific Grove.

        The winter which follows the death of the tree is
sterile and dry. Elizabeth dies when she falls from the
rock in the glade. The drought continues to decimate the
land until the Waynes have to leave their home and drive
the cattle to greener pastures near the San Joaquin River.
Joseph, however, stays on at the ranch, later moving up to
the glade. Finally, the spring dries up. On New Year's
Day Joseph climbs the rock and sacrifices himself by slash-
ing his wrists. As he dies he becomes identified with the
rain, and immediately rain begins to fall on the parched
land.

III.   CRITICAL EXPLICATION

        Generally, it has been thought that the Unknown God
Steinbeck addresses in his novel, and to whom he repeats a
paean (modelled on the Hindu Rig Veda) at the beginning of
the novel, is a "God over Gods," a transcendent and spiritual ideal to whom man not only prays for salvation, but with
whom he yearns for identity and association. Peter Lisca
has written: "To a God Unknown is concerned not only with
the problem of 'Who is He to whom we shall offer our sacrifice?' (as the poem's [Rig Veda] refrain indicates), but also
with the nature of man's proper relationship to that God."2
Joseph Fontenrose has carried this further. "All Gods are
finally one god," he says; "the whole world is one living being." Steinbeck's paganism became pantheism, "the World-
God is the God-Unknown."3 Lester Marks, too, is convinced that the Unknown God is the "Creator of all things."4
The dramatic movement of Joseph Wayne, the protagonist-
hero, has been considered outward and upward toward a
transmigratory identification with a Universal Godhead, a
movement to an Oversoul. Thus, the novel has often been
branded "mystical."5 Yet Steinbeck was upset by that label,
as he told Needham. Why? Because the novel is not transcendent or mystical. It does not open outward but inward.
It does not move toward God, but toward man. In short,

the Unknown God is not an extra-terrestrial ideal, but is, as Steinbeck explained to Needham, the powerful, fruitful and moving unconscious of man. His novel attempts to demonstrate how the unconscious impinges upon and often crosses into the conscious realm of man. [6]

Joseph Wayne, "a grand ungodly god-like man, " to use Melville's description of Ahab, follows an internalized and mythic route, one leading away from structured society and religion, back into projections of his psychic life, to the symbolic Center of the World. There, coexistent with his self-sacrifice, he gains a moment of individuation and understanding, successfully fulfilling his dual role as "creator" and "savior" of the land he has become. The process of individuation is the individual's search for his own fruitful relationship with his unconscious. That relationship cannot be purchased by someone else's system of symbols. For example, Joseph Wayne assumes the imagery of Christ numerous times in the novel, but nearly always through the eyes of others. This is important, I think, because Steinbeck is subtly establishing Joseph's realization of his own uniqueness as the goal of the process of individuation. "From one point of view this process takes place in man ... by itself and in the unconscious; it is a process by which man lives out his innate human nature. Strictly speaking ... the process of individuation is real only if the individual is aware of it and consciously makes a living connection with it. "[7]

Joseph Wayne is a hero and a god-like man, but it is a mistake to associate him with the historical Jesus Christ. He is the symbolic type of a Christ-like individual who signifies psychologically the self. He represents the projection of an important and central archetype, as Jung has shown; the archetype of the self which has functionally the significance of a ruler of the inner-world, the realm of the unconscious. Nevertheless, Joseph is not a purely conceived Christ symbol as his worshippers, Rama, Juanito, and Elizabeth would have him. The Christ symbol, Carl Jung writes, lacks "wholeness in the modern psychological sense since it not only fails to include the dark side of things but specifically excludes it in the form of a Luciferian opponent. "[8]

Joseph's process of individuation, his transformational journey, I take to be the subject of the novel. It is a journey in which the man' must first move into his darker half before he comes to symbolize the ideas, forms and forces which hold and shape the unconscious of man, and by

recognition of which, a wholeness can be effected. Joseph
Wayne's actions and his final sacrifice may be explainable
by historical and mythical precedents to Christ, the Biblical
Joseph, and Joseph of Arimathea, but they are also made
fuller and more comprehensible once it is agreed that Steinbeck is exploring an individual's unconscious and is seeking
to explain the psychic energy he finds there, an energy necessary to reconcile the opposition between warring contrary
states, particularly man and nature. In teaching this novel,
then, these mythic aspects are my starting point.

   To a God Unknown is not a mystical novel, but it is
a visionary one. Much like the dance Joseph witnesses in
Chapter 17, the book attempts to be "timeless ... a thing
eternal, breaking through to a vision...."9 The novel is
written in the Visionary Mode, which Jung distinguishes from
the Psychological Mode. Where the latter "takes its materials from the vast realm of conscious human experience--
from the vivid foreground of life," the Visionary Mode
"arises from the timeless depths ... the disturbing vision
of monstrous and meaningless happenings that in every way
exceed the grasp of human feeling and comprehension," making quite "other demands upon the powers of the artist," allowing a glimpse into "the unfathomed abyss" of the self. 10

   This vision is Steinbeck's transferred to Joseph
Wayne. It provides us ultimately with a view of restorative
wholeness arising from a symbolic conjunctive heiros gamos,
the archetypal wedding of opposites, between Joseph Wayne
and the earth, which results from his sacrifice in Chapter
25. In the climax of the novel mother earth and primal
man are reunited with each other into a purified juncture
without tension which is both essentially incorruptible and
naturally good. Joseph's blood nourishes the moss at the
center of the world, bringing rain that assures an end to the
drought plaguing the land. Thus the proper balance is re-
gained in a world of bipolar opposites, and the earth's natural fruitfulness is restored. Jung reminds us that without
the experience of opposites there can be no wholeness. 11
It is necessary, therefore, that Joseph Wayne experience the
dry years and the decimation of the land that comes with
drought. Steinbeck presents us with a projected vision of
wholeness effected by the process of individuation in Joseph's
psyche. Once Wayne realizes he can become whole only
through self-sacrifice, and that only through sacrifice can
the land he loves be saved, then the climax and goal are at-
tained simultaneously.

Most commentators on To a God Unknown have accepted Harry Moore's claims that the novel was based on an
earlier story by Steinbeck called "The Green Lady."[12] In
that version, "the protagonist falls in love with a forest,
identifies the forest with his daughter and kills himself by
walking into the forest while it is ablaze."[13] J. R. Le-
Master rightly asserts that the story reveals Steinbeck's
early bent for myth. There is, however, more to the situation than meets the eye. Richard Astro has learned "The
Green Lady" was an "unfinished play written not by Steinbeck, but by one of his closest friends."[14] That close
friend was Webster Street, now a lawyer in Monterey, California. In the original version of the play, Street set the
action in Mendocino County, during the late 1920s. He
wrote two acts and prepared a series of character sketches
but could not complete the play, probably because he could
not avoid implications of incest between the protagonist and
his daughter. He gave the typescript to Steinbeck, hoping
to collaborate with Steinbeck on it, but the latter declined.
Steinbeck had the play available to him when he began working on the novel and there are some striking similarities
between the two pieces, for instance, in the names of the
protagonists. Where Street called his Andy Wane, Steinbeck
has used Joseph Wayne. Whatever Steinbeck's dependence
on Street's work was, it was less important than the awakened interest Steinbeck had in Jungian psychology and in
myth.

In the early 1930s both Steinbeck and Ed Ricketts
were visitors at the office of Dr. Evelyn Ott, a psychologist
working on the Monterey Peninsula. Ott had been a student
of Jung's and the three--Ott, Steinbeck and Ricketts--con-
versed on Jungian matters. Steinbeck's interest in myth
was solidified by Joseph Campbell, one of America's leading
scholars in that area of investigation. Campbell was in
California in 1932 where he saw Steinbeck's early version of
the novel.[15] The book was almost wholly myth, without
very much plot. Campbell suggested Steinbeck flesh out the
story, which he did, achieving its final form in early 1933.

The structure of the novel is triadic, chapters 1-13,
14-21, and 22-26 comprising separate sections in which the
hero's condition corresponds to a new cycle or a new cir-
cumstance in the natural world itself. The first 13 chapters
are introductory and go far in setting the scene and the tone
of the book. Joseph Wayne leaves the family farm near
Pittsford, Vermont, and travels to California in search of

new land to farm. The first movement of the novel, then,
is from society and family to isolation; a fact which will be
repeated in the last section of the novel when the hero seeks
a condition of isolation which is a prerequisite for his fulfillment. Joseph's trip to California is an act of divestment
which is necessary for him to emerge as a hero. He is tot-
tering at the edge of a threshold between memory of home,
the past and familial security, which all represent conscious
attributes of his heritage; and the desire for land and love
for the earth which he can only gain in the future, thus
gratifying his unconscious needs:[16]

> Far in the back of his mind lay the feeling that he
> was being treacherous. The past, his home, and
> all the events of his childhood were being lost and
> he knew he owed them the duty of memory. This
> land might possess all of him if he were not care-
> ful. To combat the land a little, he thought of
> his father, of the calm and peace, the strength
> and eternal rightness of his father, and then in
> his thought the difference ended and he knew that
> there was no quarrel, for his father and this new
> land were one. (p. 5)

Gradually cutting himself away from the old memories
of home and family, Joseph is pleased when he imagines his
father's spirit has accompanied him to California, proving
an earlier benediction and promise the old man had given
Joseph before leaving Vermont. To consummate his new
birth into the first stage of fulfilling his dynastic dream, he
enacts a literal heiros gamos when he "flung himself face
downward on the grass and pressed his cheek against the
wet stems. His fingers gripped the wet grass and tore it
out, and gripped again. His thighs beat heavily on the
earth" (p. 8). Joseph's first act on his newly acquired land
is to copulate with Mother Earth, a primordial act of pro-
pitiation and "dying" which prefigures his ritual sacrifice at
the novel's end. At this point in his development Joseph's
consciousness impinges on his passionate act and he is left
"bewildered and frightened at himself" (p. 8). He is embarrassed by his action and immediately realizes he must
channel his demonic sexual energy into a socially acceptable
symbol--"'I'll need a wife,'" he tells himself, "'It will be
too lonely here without a wife'" (p. 8). Thus far he has
not been able to free himself of the imposed vestiges of
guilt. In Psychology and Alchemy Jung has written that "the
essence of the conscious mind is discrimination; it must if

it is to be aware of things, separate the opposites, and it does this <u>contra naturam</u>. In nature the opposites seek one another ... and so it is in the unconscious, and particularly in the archetype of unity, the Self. Here, as in the deity, the opposites cancel out."17 Much of Joseph Wayne's psychic journey gradually places him in a position where he can act out the drama of his unconscious without fear, guilt or shame.

Before Joseph can pursue a wife, however, he must establish an order on the land which reflects his balanced use of it. First he put up his tent; next he must build his house. Both are acts of creation in the proper order necessary before he can call his place a farm; a composite result of the fusion between Wayne's projection of a farm, and the land itself, out of which the farm must come. To be fruitful the farm must employ the strength and energy of the land in a suitable structure and harmony, one that takes account of process, growth, and change. But in constructing his world Joseph overlooks the possibility of detrimental change which is foretold in the accounts of the great drought in the Solon Valley which have occurred, as one Indian said, "twice in the memory of old men" (p. 12). Potentially, Wayne's <u>hubris</u>, his pride in asserting "'It [the dry years] won't come again'" (p. 13), is another example of his discriminating consciousness asserting a condition his unconscious will not accept.18 Later on, when Joseph realizes that natural change can just as easily lead to dryness and sterility as well as to fruitfulness, he rectifies the situation by his own sacrifice and restores a proper balance to the land. Again, we are reminded that he must experience opposites before he can attain wholeness.

Significantly, Joseph builds his house under the branches of an enormous oak tree, a mythological symbol for long life and strength, associated here with the Tree of Life. The oak tree is equally a symbol of the world axis, a zone of intersection between heaven, earth and hell thought to be a sacred zone in numerous mythologies.19 While these mythological connotations adhere to the Wayne Oak it is primarily the function of the tree to house the spirit of Joseph's dead father and act as a beneficial mediator between himself and the land. Though Ramos, a driver who delivers lumber to the farm, warns him "'that's not good. One of those limbs might crack off and take your roof with it, and smash you, too, some night while you're asleep'" (p. 9), Wayne assures him it is a strong tree meant to be protective rather

than menacing, and soon lodges the spirit of Joseph's dead
father.

After Joseph's brothers leave Vermont to come to
Joseph's homestead, they begin to build a dynastic farm just
as Joseph planned. One day Joseph, Thomas Wayne, and
Juanito are riding on the ridge behind the house looking for
stray cattle. They turn their horses into a thickly forested
grove where everything is quiet, the birds do not sing and
the pine needles on the ground "muffled the sound of walking
creatures" (p. 29). The three men move toward the true
center of the world, and Steinbeck's treatment of the scene
bears relating.

> They had come to an open glade, nearly circular,
> and flat as a pool. The dark trees grew about it,
> straight as pillars and jealously close together.
> In the center of the clearing stood a rock as big
> as a house, mysterious and huge. It seemed to
> be shaped, cunningly and wisely, and yet there was
> no shape in the memory to match it. A short,
> heavy green moss covered the rock with soft pile.
> The edifice was something like an altar that had
> melted and run down over itself. In one side of
> the rock there was a small cave fringed with five-
> fingered ferns, and from the cave a little stream
> flowed silently and crossed the glade and disap-
> peared into the tangled brush that edged the clear-
> ing. Beside the stream a great black bull was
> lying, his front legs folded on his forehead. When
> the three men entered the glade the bull had been
> chewing his cud and staring at the green rock.
> He turned his head and looked at the men with
> red-rimmed eyes. He snorted, scrambled to his
> feet, lowered his head at them, and then, turning,
> plunged into the undergrowth and broke a passage
> free. The men saw the lashing tail for a moment,
> and the long, black swinging scrotum, which hung
> nearly to the knees; and then he disappeared and
> they heard him crashing in the brush. (p. 29)

It all happened in a moment, Steinbeck tells us. The force
of the scene, the glade and the bull, have an awesome effect
on the three men.

> 'Be still a moment, Tom, ' he said languidly.
> 'There's something here. You are afraid of it but

> I know it. Somewhere, perhaps in an old dream,
> I have seen this place, or perhaps felt the feeling
> of this place.' He dropped his hands to his sides
> and whispered, trying the words, 'This is holy--
> and this is old. This is ancient--and holy.' (p.
> 29)

There is no answer to Joseph's proclamation. The glade
was silent and a buzzard swept across the circular sky.

The mysterious circular glade, the moss-covered
rock and the phantom black bull are all the stuff of archetypal primitivism. The glade and the rock, with its re-
cessed cave and flowing stream, represent the sacred Center
of the World, a zone of intersection between the worlds.
This axis mundi, as Mircea Eliade has established, is sacred. "Every microcosm, every inhabited region, has what
may be called a 'Centre'; that is to say, a place that is sacred above all. "[20] The center is pre-eminently "the zone
of the sacred, the zone of absolute reality"[21] where regen-
erative and creative acts take place that mimic the original
creation of the world. Usually the sacred zone is characterized by a Fountain of Youth. The glade is provided with
a flowing stream, a symbolic fountain and cosmogonic symbol of life. The stream is a source of energy, which in
conjunction with the mysterious altarlike rock, will provide
Joseph with knowledge and vitality when his tree is killed
and his land wasted.

The suffusing circle of the pine glade has other connotations: the Indian mandala, for example, is an imago
mundi of vast importance, as is the philosophical World Egg,
a symbol of roundness which implies perfection, continuity,
unity and harmony. The circle in all of its guises is "a
container of opposites," a uroboros of monumental influence
and significance in the psyche of primitive man. [22] Appro-
priately, the black bull (glimpsed but once in the novel) is
a demonic symbol of fecundity and masculine power which
looks back to Joseph's copulation with the curiously "female"
earth, and looks forward to the eventual fertility the Wayne
ranch will abound with. The men have been in touch with
the unconscious where mythological forms abound. These
primordial images are overwhelming in their force and power, so much so that now the three men are at a loss to explain the experience. Yet with time these cosmic images
will be translated into a viable and usable symbolic language
making it possible for Joseph to find the deepest sources and
springs of his life, otherwise closed off to him.

Joseph's marriage is the next significant event in section one and occupies Chapter 10. The church wedding between Elizabeth McGregor and Joseph is only a prelude to their real marriage when they pass through a mountain cut above the Nuestra Senora Valley where Joseph's farm is located. Elizabeth is afraid to go through the dark pass and over the other side of the mountain into the sunlit valley, but Joseph summons his strength and speaks:

> 'Listen, Elizabeth, do not be afraid. I tell you I
> have thought without words. Now let me grope
> among the words, tasting them, trying them. This
> is a space between the real and the clean, unwav-
> ering real, undistorted by the senses. Yesterday
> we were married and it was no marriage. This
> is our marriage--through the pass--entering the
> passage like sperm and egg that have become a
> single unit of pregnancy. This is a symbol of the
> undistorted real. I have a moment in my heart,
> different in shape, in texture, in duration, from
> any other moment. Why, Elizabeth, this is all
> marriage that has ever been, contained in our
> moment. ' (p. 52)

Note here that for Joseph it is the un-Christ-like sexual and erotic imagery of penetration and resultant pregnancy that is most important in the marriage passage, because it is most "natural. " Again Steinbeck has brought us to the threshold between past and future, memory and desire, a symbolic moment of transformation and rebirth enacted in a meta-phorical heiros gamos. This time Elizabeth is reborn.

In Chapter 11 Joseph and Elizabeth arrive back at his ranch where Joseph learns that Benjy, his younger brother, has been killed by Juanito. The latter found Benjy molesting Juanito's wife, Alice, and he killed him. Normally, this would be a sad beginning for any marriage, but for Joseph it makes little difference. He is neither sad nor glad that Benjy is dead. "'All things are one, and all a part of me'" (p. 61), he remarks. His attitude here is central to the novel because Joseph is a hero whose individuation process represents a "dialectical interaction between the contents of the unconscious and of consciousness; symbols provide the necessary bridges, linking and reconciling the often seemingly irreconcilable contradictions. "[23] It is not God who recon-ciles life and death, but Joseph Wayne. He is both literally and symbolically the central source in the Wayne family, the

man of imagination who can create symbols and fictions
which explain the cosmogonic whole.

Joseph comes to signify a secular kind of godhead in
the eyes of his family members. Rama, Thomas' wife, a
woman of earthy knowledge, tries to explain her view of Joseph
to his new bride. In terms vividly akin to a description of the
unconscious, she says, "'a door is open in me, and partly open in
you. Thoughts that hide deep in the brain, in the dark, un-
derneath the bone can come out tonight'" (p. 65). Rama
worships Joseph and considers him "all men," a man totally
un-selfconscious (one might add a man of the unconscious),
yet with a mastery and a power. She tells Elizabeth:

> ... I tell you, this man is not a man, unless he
> is all men. The strength, the resistance, the
> long and stumbling thinking of all men, and all the
> joy and suffering, too, canceling each other out
> and yet remaining in the contents. He is all these,
> a repository for a little piece of each man's soul,
> and more than that, a symbol of the earth's soul.
> (p. 66)[24]

While Joseph is concerned with natural increase and
has been known to "cut off barren creatures mercilessly"
(p. 22), he is also a judicious man to whom most acts of
nature are acceptable. In the last episode of the first major
section of the novel, Joseph proves his extraordinary dis-
pensatory powers when he talks Juanito out of wanting to be
punished and killed for Benjy's death. The two men meet
at the sacred glade. Approaching the great rock at the center of the glade, Joseph feels a foreboding sense of fear;
everything is dreadfully silent, signalling the onset of precious intuitive knowledge. Joseph is momentarily confused
and lost; then he looks to the rock for "strength and understanding." Joseph then tells Juanito his action in killing
Benjy was a natural one so that he cannot take it upon himself to punish Juanito. At this point, Juanito runs to the
rock and drinks water flowing in the stream. "'This water
is good,'" he claims; the Indians have said "'it comes out
of the center of the world'" (p. 71).

Both Joseph and Juanito have returned to the source
of the land--the everflowing stream that symbolizes life and
which contains restorative power for men. Though Joseph
has no need to drink from the stream, he is profoundly affected by its counterpart, the great rock brooding at the

center of the glade. The rock denotes "permanence, solidity and integrity."[25] It is equally a numinous object reminiscent of the church, but also because the object "appears as the receptacle of an exterior force that differentiates it from its milieu and gives it meaning and value. This force may reside in the substance of the object or in its form; a rock reveals itself to be sacred because its very existence is hierophany: incompressible, invulnerable.... It resists time; its reality is coupled with perenniality."[26] After Juanito leaves, Joseph walks to the rock and draws his "hand over the heavy fur of moss. 'Out of the heart of the world'" (p. 72). His first visit to the glade was one of discovery. Though Joseph didn't know its meaning he predicted someday he would return. On his second visit he dispensed Juanito and arrived at a further understanding of his own evolving power as a reconciler of men and their actions. What he will ultimately become, however, is a reconciler of men and nature, a situation only his eventual sacrifice atop the sacred rock will prove.

Between the end of chapter 13 and the beginning of chapter 14 a confluence of new events, both from the human and the natural worlds, occur which move the narrative ahead and create new turnings of the cycle: (1) a new day begins as Joseph leaves the glade; (2) the season progresses rapidly toward the new year; (3) Joseph has a new awareness of his relationship with the earth: "his nature and the nature of the land were the same" (p. 72); and (4) Joseph, already forgetting what Benjy looks like, anticipates returning to the ranch house to see his new bride, thus turning his thoughts from the dead to the living. "All the mythological processes of nature ... are symbolic expressions of the inner unconscious drama of the psyche which becomes accessible to man's consciousness by way of projection--that is, mirrored in the events of nature."[27] In other words, when the imaginative and the real events of the human psyche coincide and are in balance with the natural world, then growth, fruition and increase can be expected. Thus, the first section of the novel conspires to bring Joseph, a newly emerged hero, to a point of equilibrium based on his interaction with nature. The second portion of the novel will see Joseph's fortunes rise higher, but will also reveal the reasons for his paradoxical demise and triumph.

The second division of To a God Unknown begins in chapter 14 with the winter season rapidly approaching and the Wayne farm correspondingly busy at getting their crops out and preparing for the new year. Jennie, Benjy's widow, leaves the ranch to return to her home. Alice, Juanito's wife, waits pregnant for him to return from his penitent wanderings. Rama, Thomas's wife, emerges as the chief ethnic figure in this section. She acts as a spiritual guide for Elizabeth, much as Juanito had done for Joseph earlier in the book.

Soon the seasonal rains begin in November. By Christmas the grass is ankle high and it appears to Joseph that it will be a good year. In order to celebrate the Wayne family success, Joseph plans to hold a fiesta for New Year's Day. The fiesta occupies nearly the whole of chapter 16, and is central to the novel. J. R. LeMaster notes that one of the "most definitive myths about man and the Life Principle is found in the fiesta of the New Year. Such a celebration is important because death of the Old Year (the life-death-resurrection pattern) is at the very heart of the primitive ritual."[28] All of the people of the valley attend the event begun by Father Angelo holding a Catholic mass at 8 A.M. on New Year's morning. However, as might be expected, the real ritual beginning is yet to come. Joseph begins the fiesta by drinking a full draught of wine. Father Angelo approves of Joseph's ritual enactment, but when Joseph "walked to the tree and poured a little wine on its bark" (p. 86), Father Angelo admonishes him '"That it is not a good thing to do, my son'" (p. 86). Joseph, embarrassed at being confronted, whirled on the priest and asks, '"What do you mean?--There was a fly in the cup!'" (p. 86).

The fiesta continues all day, capped by a dance of Dionysian frenzy as the participants are demonically transported by the magic of the moment and the power of the guitars. Joseph is pleased with the ritual. Standing apart (the condition of the hero is isolation), he feels tied to the dancers, yet he does not join them. '"We have found something here, all of us,'" he thinks. '"In some way we've come closer to the earth for a moment'" (p. 88). Both myth and ritual, it should be noted, "satisfy the needs of a society, and the relative place of one or the other will depend upon the particular needs (conscious and unconscious) of the individuals in the particular society at a particular time."[29] At this moment, despite the Catholic epilogue to the feast, it is the older pre-Christian rituals which emerge to take their place in the light of day.

Near the end of the fiesta a thunderstorm scatters the

revelers but delivers moisture necessary for proper growth
of the crops. Nature seems well pleased with Joseph at this
point and rewards him accordingly, not only with rain, but,
as he learns later that day, with a child to complete the
fertility cycle and carry it over to the human realm. Dramatic enactments of mythological events are a projection of
the psychological processes going on in the hero, and the
connection between creation, New Year's ritual and birth or
rebirth is an apparent part of the mimicking of the origin of
the world of New Year's day. The child will be precious,
Joseph tells Elizabeth, "'but not so precious as the bearing
of it. That is as real as a mountain. That is a tie to the
earth ... It is a proof that we belong here ... that we are
not strangers'" (p. 92). What better or more appropriate
day could Joseph have learned of his child's impending birth,
than on the first day of the new year?

     After learning Elizabeth's good news Joseph slips out
of their bed and goes to the great oak near the house. As
a symbolic Tree of Life the oak insures fertility because it
is a part of nature in tune with natural cycles. By participating in the life of the tree, by naming it father, Joseph
partakes of its power as a mediator between man and nature.
For many months he has given the tree offerings to propiti-
ate and encourage it. Now he promises to put his own child
in the tree when it is born. Joseph's "fiction" of his father-
tree comforts him and helps him explain the natural workings
of the universe. "'This thing is growing strong,' he thought.
'I began it because it comforted me when my father was
dead, and now it is grown so strong that it overtops nearly
everything. And still it comforts me'" (p. 94). It is evident that Joseph Wayne both creates myths and enacts them,
a forceful testimony to the power and fertility of his imagination and symbol-producing proclivity.

     The second section of the novel coincides with Jo-
seph's deeper and deeper involvement with the chthonic and
numinous symbols of nature and his increasing openess about
his relationships to those symbols. As soon as "the collective human core of the archetype, which represents the raw
material provided by the collective unconscious, enters into
relation with the conscious mind and its formgiving character, the archetype takes on 'body' ...; it becomes repre-
sentable, and only then does it become a concrete image--an
archetypal image, a symbol."[30] Joseph, of course, becomes
increasingly bolder in his communion with the archetypes and
symbols of the natural world and the rites associated with

them, until finally in the last section of the novel when he is most in touch with his potency and has most shed his guilt, he will move entirely (at the glade) into a symbolic landscape.

The intense heat of summer holds sway over the Wayne farm when Elizabeth gives birth to a baby boy which Joseph delivers himself. The child is named John after the tradition of the Wayne family to name all the sons of Joseph John, and the sons of John, Joseph. Joseph fulfills his promise to the oak tree and places the child in the crotch of the tree as an initiatory rite. Joseph and his pious brother Burton argue over this act, Burton accusing Joseph of paganism, though this time in the presence of Elizabeth.

Burton leaves the ranch within a week and moves to Pacific Grove with his wife. Shortly after he departs Joseph becomes anxious about the condition of the oak. Elizabeth, now coming to understand more and more the nature of Joseph's unconscious projections, cautions him not to play his game too hard and Joseph responds that she may be right, though his fearful premonition about the tree proves true, and the tree, an ambassador between Joseph and the land (p. 116), begins to die. Joseph's foreboding sense of having done something wrong, his belief that he is the reason "'an evil is hanging over the land'" (p. 117) is dispelled when Thomas discovers that Burton girdled the tree. Joseph is shocked but not vengeful, thinking Burton will punish himself for having acted contra naturam. He realizes he must return to the glade. "'I'll be needing the sweetness and the strength of that place,'" he says (p. 119), echoing his unconscious thought much earlier in the novel that the glade would be "'a place to run to, away from pain or sorrow or disappointment or fear ... if ever there's need to lose some plaguing thing, that will be the place to go'" (p. 39).

Chapter 21 brings to a close the second movement of the novel. The oak has died and the land and its inhabitants will soon suffer gradual decrease and sterility. The death of the tree is matched by the coming of the winter season and the eventual death of Elizabeth. November arrives, cold and foggy, but without its fruitful rain. Head colds and illnesses break out on the farm, all symptoms of "unnaturalness" and further manifestations of the upset balance between man and nature. While Joseph grows quietly

worried about that failure of the rain, Elizabeth has greater
longings to return to the glade. No longer pregnant, as she
was in Chapter 17 when she first visited the glade, Elizabeth wants to face the great rock and discover for herself
its meaning and its hold over her, which has caused her to
love the rock more than Joseph or herself. Of her earlier
experience at the glade, she tells Joseph, "'While I sat
there I went into the rock. The little stream was flowing
out of me and I was the rock ...'" (p. 123).

        This moment in the novel is a transitional one. Jo-
seph, faced with the death of his life-giving tree, has recognized in himself the need for another source of counsel in
his life to help combat the sterility that is beginning to lay
waste the land. "'If only it [the tree] were alive,' he
thought. 'I would know what to do. I have no counsel any
more'" (p. 124). With the tree gone he thinks of the glade,
but as yet the glade's meaning and significance are untested
and unformulated in his mind. What he needs (and what
Steinbeck provides) is an episode that will return him to the
glade. The opportunity comes when Elizabeth asks him to
go there with her. At the glade Elizabeth conquers her previous fears and mounts the rock as if to triumph over her
unconscious. Accidentally she slips off, breaks her neck
and dies. The event is unfortunate in a physical sense, but
immediately Steinbeck reveals its hidden fortunate purpose
in the lesson it provides Joseph.

        Shocked at the accident, Joseph's mind cannot fathom
what has happened. "'All the stories, all the incidents that
made the life were stopped in a second,'" he thinks; "'opinions stopped, and the ability to feel, all stopped without any
meaning'" (p. 129). Yet a meaning does emerge. Looking
down at his dead wife, suddenly Joseph feels the "calm"
settling on himself. "He said, 'Good bye, Elizabeth,' and
before the words were completely out he was cut off and
aloof" (p. 129). A light rain falls and Joseph knows instinctively the rock and Elizabeth "'are two, and you are
here. Now I will know where I must come'" (p. 129). The
transitional moment is complete. A turning point has been
reached after which Joseph will live out his unconscious projection in a symbolic landscape. "'The forces gather and
center and become one and strong,'" he thinks. Now he
must "join the center," and "he knew how he loved the rock,
and hated it" (p. 130).

        Joseph returns with Elizabeth's body to the farm,

depositing her with Thomas before going off alone to a great
pool, the only source of water left in a nearby dried-up
river. The pool, a common image of the unconscious, is
"deep and brown and ill-smelling. In the dusklight he could
see the big black eels moving about in slow convolutions"
(p. 130). Atop one of the streamside boulders he stares
down into the water where "the whole day passed before him,
not as a day, but as an epoch. He remembered little gestures he had not known he saw" (p. 131). Joseph, of course,
is seeking justification for the death of his tree and for the
death of Elizabeth. Deep in thought, plunged in his unconscious, he discovers the primal archetypal pattern for all of
life: "'This is the beginning of the thing I knew. There is
some cycle here, steady and quick and unchangeable as a
fly-wheel.' And the tired thought came to him that if he
gazed into the pool and cleaned his mind of every cluttering
picture he might come to know the cycle" (p. 131). The
cycle has manifested itself variously in Joseph's life--for
good in the creation of his dynastic ranch, in the abundance
of nature, his marriage and his child; and for bad in the
sudden sterility of the land, the death of Elizabeth, and the
death of his tree. Now that he understands the cyclical opposition of life and death, now that he grasps their significance by mentally diving into himself, nature provides a
testimony of his insight.

As he gazes Narcissus-like into the water he witnesses a savage spectacle. Five wild pigs and "a great
curved-tusked boar" come to the pool to feed on the eels.
They, in turn, are attacked by a magnificent Mountain Lion,
which kills one of the pigs. Joseph's coincident recognition
of the cycle of nature and his witnessing the slaughter gives
him a new bond with the earth. "He thought how a new bond
tied him to the earth, and how this land of his was closer
now" (p. 131).

Chapters 22-26 constitute the last division of the book.
January comes, a new year begins, and still there has been
no rain. By April the ground is dried out "and the hope of
the country was gone. The cattle were thin and laced with
ribs ... there were few calves born. Two sows died with a
mysterious illness before they littered.... The game was
going away from the hills. The quail came no longer to sing
in the evening.... It was an odd thing to see a rabbit" (p.
137). By May some rain falls but it is too little and too
late, a false hope destroyed within weeks when the grass
withers and droops and the dust chokes the air again. The
dry years have arrived at last.

In Joseph's mind he makes a direct connection between the dry land and himself. "'I'm failing to protect the
land,' he thought sadly. 'The duty of keeping life in my
land is beyond my power'" (p. 140). However, just when
conditions seem bleakest Joseph receives another sign. With
Thomas he discovers an old man, living on the coast side
of the mountains, a "seer" whose ritual of daily sacrifice
is performed when the sun goes down. Both animal and sun
"die" at the same time. The old man has abandoned reasoning about his action--he does it because he likes it and
because he becomes the sun at the moment of sacrifice.
More than this, the old man hints at the ultimate sacrifice--
his own, when the time is "perfect" for such self-immola-
tion. Joseph responds eagerly to the old man, a like soul
responding to its kin: "'It is not thought safe to open a
clear path to your soul for the free, undistorted passage of
the things that are there,'" he says admiringly (p. 148).

The old man's "crazy" action gives new life to Joseph, who now decides against accompanying Thomas on a
100-mile cattle drive to greener pastures. "'I'll have to
stay,' Joseph said. 'If I went with you, I'd be wanting to
start back every moment to see if the rain had fallen yet,
or if there was any water in the river. I might as well not
go away'" (p. 150).

Thomas leaves to be with the cattle at the San Joaquin River and Rama will go with him. John, Joseph's son,
has been cared for by Rama since Elizabeth died. Joseph
wants her to take the child forever, knowing he will not see
John again.

With Thomas, Rama and John gone, Joseph tidies up
the farm, puts his lands in order, then finally moves up to
the glade to live. The rock is no longer separate from himself, and the glade, he feels, is the heart of the land, still
breathing and alive. The oppressive heat continues in autumn, even passing into November without rain. To combat
the effects of the dryness Joseph begins a daily ritual of
watering the moss on the rock, restoring it to greeness.
With the new year approaching Joseph keeps his vigil at the
rock, now joined by Juanito who has returned from his penitent wanderings to be with Joseph. Together they watch the
rock and stream until at one point the stream begins to rise
and Joseph is filled with great hope. Juanito tells him that
"'before a spring goes dry it grows a little'" (p. 169). Unless God interferes, he adds, the spring will stop.

Tenaciously remaining with the glade for months, Joseph
keeps his vigil at the rock, ritually watering it each day.
As long as he could keep the stream-source flowing and
prove its vitality by nourishing the moss on the rock, then
he had no need for an ultimate decision. Once the water
ceased to flow, however, only the hero's sacrifice could re-
store proper balance to himself and the land. When Joseph
returns from a visit to Father Angelo's he finds the stream
dried up. Desperately he sacrifices a weak calf, but nothing
happens. Then he accidentally cuts his wrist on a saddle
buckle. As he bleeds he becomes progressively calmer.
With his calmness comes a knowledge of what he must do.

> 'Of course, ' he said, 'I'll climb up on the rock. '
> He worked his way carefully up its steep sides
> until at last he lay in the deep soft moss on the
> rock's top. When he had rested a few minutes,
> he took out his knife again and carefully, gently
> opened the vessels of his wrist. The pain was
> sharp at first, but in a moment its sharpness
> dulled. He watched the bright blood cascading
> over the moss, and he heard the shouting of the
> wind around the grove. The sky was growing
> grey. And time passed and Joseph grew grey too.
> He lay on his side with his wrist outstretched and
> looked down the long black mountain range of his
> body. Then his body grew huge and light. It
> arose into the sky, and out of it came the streak-
> ing rain. 'I should have known, ' he whispered.
> 'I am the rain. ' And yet he looked dully down the
> mountains of his body where the hills fell to an
> abyss. He felt the driving rain, and heard it
> whipping down, pattering on the ground. He saw
> his hills grow dark with moisture. Then a lancing
> pain shot through the heart of the world. 'I am
> the land, ' he said, 'and I am the rain. The grass
> will grow out of me in a little while. '
>
> And the storm thickened, and covered the world
> with darkness, and with the rush of waters. (p.
> 179)

Earlier Joseph had identified the rock with Elizabeth. In
this penultimate scene he enacts his final heiros gamos,
both with the earth, his mother, and with the rock, now become his wife. The latter part of the novel, pervaded with
images of darkness and dream, constitutes the final

interiorization of Joseph's journey and his movement away
from traditional figures of society and religion into a symbolic landscape which is more surreal than real. It is a
landscape presided over by the cold pale moon of indefinite-
ness rather than the hot sun of sharpness and clean outline:

> The land was unsubstantial under the misty,
> strained light; the dry trees seemed shapes of
> thicker mist. He left the town and took the river
> road, and his contact with the town dropped behind
> him. He smelled the peppery dust that arose un-
> der the horse's hoofs, but he couldn't see it.
> Away in the dark north there was a faint flicker
> of aurora borealis, rarely seen so far south. The
> cold stony moon rose high and followed him. The
> mountains seemed edged with phosphorus, and a
> pale of cold light like a glow-worm's light seemed
> to shine through the skin of the land. The night
> had a quality of memory. (p. 176)

Later, he compounds his surrealism. Joseph "glanced over
his shoulders at the bone-white moon, sailing and hovering
in the blown dust. 'In a little while, ' he said, 'it will fly
down and eat the world'" (p. 177).

Steinbeck's description leaves us with the impression
that Joseph is traversing not a real landscape, but a figurative one upon which the projections of his psyche have been
blown up to a proportion which he must at last account for.
The whole novel brings us to this point. Everything now
conspires in this figurative place of death to lead him irre-
vocably to sacrifice because his unconscious now demands it
as the only method for attaining a new beginning. Thus the
glade is a natural and geographical place of death and vivi-
fication where the cycle of nature begins and ends; yet it is
also the symbolic equivalent of Joseph's unconscious, where
his awareness of reality and his place in the world also begins and   ds. Every hero, Erich Neumann writes, achieves
"a syntl. ɔis between consciousness and the creative unconscious. He has found within himself the fruitful center, the
point of renewal ... which, in the New Year fertility festival [Joseph sacrifices himself on New Year's day], is identified with the creative divinity, and upon which the continued
existence of the world depends."[31] The unconscious is that
known god within upon which the cyclical continuance of man
and nature depends. "The birth, life, and death of the individual may be regarded as a descent into unconsciousness
and return."[32]

Joseph's moment of death restores fertility to the land, and certainly fulfills mythical and historical precedents in cultures thousands of years old. Equally, his death is his moment of personal triumph when he has reached the goal of the process of individuation where he can act according to his fullest potency. Thus, the drama, which is both exterior and interior, is concluded.

Notes

1. Steinbeck's letter to Wilbur Needham, dated April 4, 1934, is in the Clifton Waller Barrett Library of the University of Virginia. Permission cannot be obtained from Steinbeck's agents to publish the letter, although they are not averse to allusions to it.

2. Peter Lisca, The Wide World of John Steinbeck (New Brunswick, New Jersey: Rutgers University Press, 1958), p. 42.

3. Joseph Fontenrose, John Steinbeck: An Introduction and Interpretation (New York: Holt, Rinehart and Winston, 1963), p. 17.

4. Lester Marks, Thematic Design in the Novels of John Steinbeck (The Hague: Mouton, 1969), p. 35.

5. Maxwell Geismar, Writers in Crisis (New York: Dutton, 1942; rptd., 1971), p. 248.

6. In his letter to Needham Steinbeck revealed that he considered all the demons, mysticism, and religious symbolism in the world to be generated by the collective and personal unconscious of man. Jung has differentiated between the two terms in The Archetypes and the Collective Unconscious, trans. R. F. C. Hull (New York: Pantheon Books, 1959). He writes, "A more or less superficial layer of the unconscious is undoubtedly personal. I call it the personal unconscious. But this personal unconscious rests upon a deeper layer, which does not derive from personal experience and is not a personal acquisition but is inborn. This deeper layer I call the collective unconscious. I have chosen the term 'collective' because this part of the unconscious is not individual but universal; in contrast to the personal

psyche, it has contents and modes of behavior that
are more or less the same everywhere and in all
individuals" (pp. 3-4).

7. Joseph Henderson, "Ancient Myths and Modern Man, "
    in Carl Jung, ed. , Man and His Symbols (Garden
    City, New York: Doubleday, 1964), p. 162. Toward
    the end of the novel Steinbeck has Juanito cross
    himself in Joseph's presence and build "a tall blaze
    to see Joseph's face clearly" (p. 168), to see the
    disappointment and weariness of Christ's face in
    Joseph. Steinbeck notes, however, that "Joseph
    was not dead, " and there the analogy breaks down
    somewhat.

8. Carl Jung, Aion, trans. R. F. C. Hull (New York:
    Pantheon Books, 1959), p. 41. To be a new Christ,
    Joseph would have to purchase the symbolism of
    Christ. This is second-hand and therefore inau-
    thentic.

9. Steinbeck, To a God Unknown (New York: Bantam
    Books, 1960) p. 92. Subsequent references to this
    text will be incorporated parenthetically into my es-
    say.

10. Quoted in Morris Philipson, Outline of a Jungian Aes-
    thetics (Evanston: Northwestern University Press,
    1963), pp. 104-106.

11. Carl Jung, Psychology and Alchemy, trans. R. F. C.
    Hull (New York: Pantheon Books, 1968), p. 20.

12. Harry Moore, The Novels of John Steinbeck (Chicago:
    Normandie House, 1939), p. 30.

13. J. R. LeMaster, "Mythological Constructs in Stein-
    beck's To a God Unknown, " Forum, 9 (Summer
    1971), 8.

14. Richard Astro, "John Steinbeck: Prospectus for a
    Literary Biography, " Steinbeck Quarterly, 4 (Sum-
    mer 1971), 77.

15. My information is from a letter from Richard Astro,
    dated May 14, 1971. Joseph Campbell told Astro
    that he helped Steinbeck with myth as much as he

and Ricketts helped Campbell. It is not difficult to imagine that their discussions coincided with what Campbell established in The Hero with a Thousand Faces (New York, 1949; reprinted Cleveland: World Publishing Company, 1956), that the modern intellectual can "concede that the symbolism of mythology has a psychological significance ... Sigmund Freud, Carl G. Jung, Wilhelm Stekel, Otto Rank, Karl Abraham, Géza Róheim ... developed a vastly documented modern lore of dream and myth interpretation" (p. 255).

16. On the concept of the hero's necessary confrontation with a threshold of literal or metaphorical manifestation, see Joseph Campbell, "The Crossing of the First Threshold," in The Hero with a Thousand Faces, pp. 77-89.

17. Carl Jung, Psychology and Alchemy, p. 25.

18. Joseph Henderson, "Ancient Myths and Modern Man," in Man and His Symbols, notes "The myth of the hero is the most common and the best known myth in the world," and he sketches briefly a pattern from the hero's birth, rise to prominence "his fallibility to the sin of pride, and his fall through betrayal or a 'heroic' sacrifice that ends in his death" (p. 110). Obviously Steinbeck has used this pattern, though what makes his example of it interesting is his particular working out of the hero's fate in terms of his unconscious.

19. See Mircea Eliade, Images and Symbols, trans. Philip Mairet (New York: Sheed and Ward, 1969), pp. 42-46 for more on this idea.

20. Ibid., p. 39.

21. Mircea Eliade, Cosmos and History, trans. Willard Trask (New York: Harper and Row, 1959), p. 17.

22. Erich Neumann, The Origins and History of Consciousness, trans. R. F. C. Hull (Princeton: Princeton University Press, 1970 (1954), p. 8.

23. Jolandi Jacobi, Complex/Archetype/Symbol, trans. Ralph Manheim (New York: Pantheon Books, 1959), p. 115.

24.   Cf. Carl Jung, Symbols of Transformation, trans. R.
      F. C. Hull (Princeton: Princeton University Press,
      1967). "The religious figure cannot be a mere
      man, for it has to represent what it actually is,
      namely the totality of all those primordial images
      which express the 'extraordinary potent,' always
      and everywhere. What we seek in visible human
      form is not man, but the superman, the hero or
      god, that quasi-human being ..." (pp. 177-78).

25.   J. E. Cirlot, A Dictionary of Symbols, trans. Jack
      Sage (New York: Philosophical Library, 1962),
      p. 262.

26.   Mircea Eliade, Cosmos and History, p. 4.

27.   Carl Jung, The Archetypes and the Collective Uncon-
      scious, p. 6.

28.   LeMaster, "Mythological Constructs in Steinbeck's To
      a God Unknown," p. 11.

29.   Clyde Kluckhohn, "Myths and Rituals: A General The-
      ory," in John Vickery, ed. Myth and Literature
      (Lincoln: University of Nebraska Press, 1966), p.
      39.

30.   Jolandi Jacobi, Complex/Archetype/Symbol, p. 75.

31.   Erich Neumann, The Origins and History of Conscious-
      ness, p. 212.

32.   Joseph Campbell, The Hero with a Thousand Faces, p.
      259.

IV.   APPRATUS FOR RESEARCH PAPERS

A.   Ten Questions for Discussion

1.   Do you think To a God Unknown is a believable novel?
     Why or why not?
2.   Some critics have said To a God Unknown is faulty be-
     cause its dialogue is stiff and unrealistic and the char-
     acters often speak in language which is above their level
     of education and social station. Do you agree?
3.   What is the importance of Steinbeck's use of nature,

animals, birds, natural cycles, and elemental forces?
Is his use of these elements related to the book?

4. A great number of male novelists of this century have
   had difficulty creating believable women characters. Do
   you think this can be said of Steinbeck's portrayal of
   Rama and Elizabeth?

5. What do you suppose Steinbeck's view toward organized
   religion is in this novel?

6. What purposes do the minor characters Juanito, Burton
   and Thomas Wayne serve in the novel?

7. What does Joseph Wayne come to understand after he
   meets the old Seer in the Mountains?

8. One of Steinbeck's strongest virtues as a novelist is his
   descriptive power. Choose 5 or 6 examples of descriptive passages in the novel and decide what elements they
   contain that make them exceptional writing.

9. The ending of the novel is somewhat ambiguous. When
   rain returns to the valley it could be the result of one
   of three things: a natural end to the drought, Father
   Angelo's praying to God for rain, or Joseph Wayne's
   sacrifice of himself. Which do you think the answer is?

10. Father Angelo is an important "foil" to Joseph Wayne.
    How do you think Steinbeck characterizes Father Angelo?

B. Suggested Topics for Research Papers

1. John Steinbeck was fascinated by mythical and legendary
   tales all of his life. We have seen how certain primitive mythical elements conspire to form the substance of
   To a God Unknown; now examine some of Steinbeck's
   other novels to determine what legendary, mythical or
   artistic sources form their bases. Begin with Cup of
   Gold, Tortilla Flat, or East of Eden.

2. Compile a catalog of important natural mythical symbols
   used by Steinbeck in To a God Unknown. Choose one
   which appeals to you, for instance, the Tree of Life
   symbol, then investigate the history of its development
   and use in other societies and cultures.

3. Imagine that you are a young writer who has just published a successful first novel. Your publisher has given
   you an advanced contract for a second book. You would
   like to utilize a mythical framework upon which to base
   your new book. Which myth would you use? How would
   you use it? Prepare a brief "treatment" of your version of the myth.

4. To a God Unknown has not always fared well with

Steinbeck's readers or his critics.   Prepare a detailed
essay in which you either defend the book against its de-
tractors, or you agree with the criticism of the novel.
In either case, whether you argue pro or con (or some
shade between the two), you will have to familiarize
yourself with the criticism of the novel.

5. Joseph Wayne's three brothers, Thomas, Burton, and
Benjy, are minor characters in To a God Unknown who
operate chiefly as "foils" to Joseph's actions.   Nevertheless, they do have personalities uniquely their own.
Examine their presence in the novel and determine the
effectiveness of Steinbeck's portrayal of them.

C.   Selected Bibliography

I.   On Steinbeck's To a God Unknown

1.   Fontenrose, Joseph.   John Steinbeck: An Introduction
and Interpretation.   New York: Holt, Rinehart and Winston, 1963.   See especially pages 13-19.
     An excellent, though brief, introduction to the novel.
Concerned with mythical, Biblical and historical elements in
novel.

2.   French, Warren.   John Steinbeck.   New York: Twayne,
1961.   See especially pages 47-52.
     Brief analysis of the novel, though not as provocative
as Fontenrose.

3.   LeMaster, J. F.   "Mythological Constructs in Steinbeck's To a God Unknown, " Forum (University of Hous-
ton), 9 (Summer 1971), 8-11.
     Concerned with mythical elements in the novel but too
brief and sketchy to be effective.

4.   Lieber, Todd.   "Talismanic Patterns in the Novels of
John Steinbeck, " American Literature, 44 (May 1972),
262-275.
     See especially pages 168-69 for comments on To a
God Unknown where he examines Steinbeck's use of talismanic
devices, such as the tree and the rock, and links them to
Steinbeck's mythic imagination.

5.   Lisca, Peter.   The Wide World of John Steinbeck.   New
Brunswick, New Jersey: Rutgers University Press,
1958.   See especially pages 39-55.

An extensive and balanced treatment of the novel.
Very good.

6.   Marks, Lester.   Thematic Design in the Novels of John
     Steinbeck.   The Hague: Mouton, 1969.   See especially
     pages 34-46.
         Interesting and readable analysis, though he does not
consider scholarship after 1960.

II.   General Introduction to Myth and Work of Carl Jung

1.   Campbell, Joseph.   The Hero with a Thousand Faces.
     New York, 1949; rptd.   Cleveland: World Publishing Co.,
     1956.
         Excellent introduction to the hero figure in various
mythologies.

2.   Jung, Carl, ed.   Man and His Symbols.   Garden City,
     New York: Doubleday, 1964.
         Heavily illustrated introduction to various aspects of
Jungian-mythical symbology.   Very readable and clear.

3.   Jung, Carl.   The Portable Jung,   ed. Joseph Campbell.
     New York: Viking Press, 1971.
         The best short compendium of Jung's various writ-
ings.

4.   Murray, Henry, ed.   Myth and Mythmaking.   New York:
     George Braziller, 1960.
         Impressive collection of essays on myth by a variety
of outstanding scholars.

5.   Vickery, John, ed.   Myth and Literature.   Lincoln,
     Nebraska: University of Nebraska Press, 1966.
         Good introduction to mythic criticism of literature.

Chapter 13 *

STEINBECK'S TORTILLA FLAT (1935)

by Arthur L. Simpson, Jr.

I. BACKGROUND OF THE WORK

Critics and scholars generally agree on the signal importance of Tortilla Flat in Steinbeck's development as a novelist for several reasons. It was the author's first full-scale novel which drew on his contemporary Southern Californian environment for character and event, indicating a turn away from involvements with the romantic legendary materials of Cup of Gold (1929) and the heavy-handed mythic allusiveness of To a God Unknown (written c. 1930-32, published 1933). Tortilla Flat certainly deals with some of the same types of themes and characters that appeared in the group of thematically related stories on aspects of American life, The Pastures of Heaven (written c. 1931, published 1932), a work which also reflects a growing "preoccupation with fresher materials much closer at hand--the ordinary people of his [Steinbeck's] 'long valley.'"[1] But Tortilla Flat (published 1935) is different, not only in being the first novel to deal with immediately contemporary materials, but also in that it announces a special concern for and interest in people who are socially and economically dispossessed, a concern and interest to be elaborated in the major works of Steinbeck's middle period--In Dubious Battle (1936), Of Mice and Men (1937), and The Grapes of Wrath (1939).[2] Finally, Tortilla Flat was Steinbeck's first significant popular and financial success. It made the best seller lists, became a stage play, and was sold to a motion picture studio.

Steinbeck tentatively planned Tortilla Flat as a collection of short stories. While in January of 1933 he was finishing the last draft of the final version of To a God Unknown, he wrote to his publisher:

> I think that when this is sent off (this new novel)
> I shall do some short stories. I always think I
> will and they invariably grow into novels but I'll
> try anyway. There are some fine little things
> that happened in a big sugar mill where I was as-
> sistant chief chemist and Majordomo of about sixty
> Mexicans and Yuakis taken from the jails of
> northern Mexico. ...
>
> There was the ex-corporal of Mexican cavalry,
> whose wife had been stolen by a captain and who
> was training his baby to be a general so he could
> get even better women.... There is the saga of
> the C---- family. The son hanged himself for the
> love of a chippy and was cut down and married to
> the girl. His father aged sixty-five fell in love
> with a fourteen year old girl and tried the same
> thing, but a door with a spring lock fell shut and
> he didn't get cut down.... These are a few as
> they really happened. I could make some little
> stories of them I think. [3]

Professor Lisca notes that this letter shows that after The Pastures of Heaven almost all of Steinbeck's works
drew heavily on first-hand experience or accounts and that
an episodic approach to plot and action, although later structured in various ways, became one of the trademarks of
Steinbeck's later novels. [4]

The episodic quality of Tortilla Flat no doubt contributed to Steinbeck's difficulty in finding a publisher for the
book. One publisher found no "important story or argument"
in the work, and Steinbeck's literary agents complained that
the book needed "something to hold it together."[5] During
the year and a half it took to find a publisher, Steinbeck
wrote to his agents to give them some structural selling
points:

> The book has a very definite theme. I thought it
> was clear enough. I had expected that the plan of
> the Arthurian cycle would be recognized. Even
> the incident of the Sangreal in the search of the
> forest is not clear enough, I guess. The form is
> that of the Malory version--the coming of Arthur,
> and the mystic quality of owning a house, the
> forming of the Round Table, the adventures of the
> knights and finally, the mystic translation of Danny.

The main issue was to present a little known and
to me delightful people.

Is not this cycle or story or theme enough? Perhaps it is not enough because I have not made it
clear enough. Then I must make it clearer.
What do you think of putting in an interlocutor,
who between each incident interprets the incident,
morally, aesthetically, historically, but in the
manner of the paisanos themselves? This would
give the book much the appeal of the Gesta Ro-
manorum, those outrageous tales with monkish
morals appended, or of the Song of Solomon in
the King James Version, with the delightful chapter headings which go to prove that the Shulamite
is in reality Christ's Church. It would not be as
sharp as this, of course. But the little dialogue
would at least make clear the form of the book,
its tragi-comic theme, and the strong but different
philosophic-moral system of these people.

A cycle is there. You will remember that the association forms, flowers and dies. Far from having a hard theme running through the book, one
of the intents is to show that rarely does anything
in the lives of these people survive the night. [6]

In view of the contents of this letter--particularly 'I
must make it clearer"--it seems possible that Steinbeck may
have taken steps to clarify his structural principle. Professor Lisca reports that the handwritten manuscript of Tortilla
Flat does not contain the chapter headings (modeled after
those in Malory's Morte D'Arthur--such as 'How Danny,
home from the wars, found himself an heir, and how he
swore to protect the helpless"[7]) or the Preface, which
spells out the Arthurian allusion (1-3)--but that they were
present in the typescript received in May, 1935 by the
eventual publishers, Covici-Friede. [8]

In spite of Steinbeck's concern (and/or efforts) to see
that the structure and theme of Tortilla Flat be understood,
he was to be disappointed. The instant reaction of reviewers and critics was generally negative; they saw the book as
a celebration of the animal side of man, as unreflective
praise of primitive humanity, and as an unstructured escapist insult to traditional forms of prose fiction (see annotated
bibliography). Steinbeck was able to live with critical

attacks, distortions, and praise. By his own accounts, at
least, he tried not to overreact to critics, for whose activities he never had excessive respect. [9] More recent critics
have been able to place the question of his "primitivism" in
a broader and more intelligent context of his total work
(again, see annotated bibliography), and Steinbeck didn't respond to attacks on his Arthurian structural principle, since
he was still affirming it as late as 1957. [10]

The very popularity of Tortilla Flat did bother him.
He seems to have been convinced that the public was reading
his book for all the wrong reasons, as a condescending portrayal of quaint and curious irresponsible inhibition. Professor Warren French has suggested that the book's initial
success is attributable to the desire of readers in the depths
of the depression to read about irresponsible characters who
were "happy with even less than they had, "[11] but Steinbeck,
rightly or wrongly (as I will discuss in the next section),
felt an outrage at the popular reaction, which he expressed
in his foreword to the 1937 Modern Library edition:

> I wrote these stories because they were true
> stories and because I liked them. But literary
> slummers have taken these people up with the vul-
> garity of duchesses who are amused and sorry for
> a peasantry. These stories are out, and I cannot
> recall them. But I shall never again subject to
> the vulgar touch of the decent these good people of
> laughter and kindness, of honest lusts and direct
> eyes, of courtesy beyond politeness. If I have
> done them harm by telling a few of their stories,
> I am sorry. It will not happen again. [12]

Whatever the author's regrets, Tortilla Flat gave him
assurance of financial success and of status as a major writer whose basic concerns in Tortilla Flat were to receive
fuller and more complex treatment in his still to come major works.

II.   PLOT SYNOPSIS

The preface to Tortilla Flat, reflecting the concern
described in the preceding discussion that the episodic quality of the book might give the impression of a lack of structure, takes care to give an overview of plot, of setting, and
of character. We learn that the characters are paisanos

Study Guide to Steinbeck

(the current term is chicano)--members of that disadvantaged
and victimized group of Americans who are "a mixture of
Spanish, Indian, Mexican and assorted Caucasian bloods, "
whose "ancestors have lived in California for a hundred or
two years, " and who speak both English and Spanish with a
paisano accent. (2)

The setting is Tortilla Flat, the "other-side-of-the-
tracks" section of Monterey, which is not flat at all. Monterey occupies the slope of a hill above the bay and Tortilla
Flat is farther up the hill where the forest of dark pines in-
termingles with the town. It is Monterey's Chicago ghetto,
"where the streets are innocent of asphalt and the corners
free of street lights, " where the paisanos live "in old wooden
houses set in weedy yards, and the pine trees of the forest
are about the houses" (2). For a brief overview of plot,
Steinbeck's opening paragraph is eminently useful:

> This is the story of Danny and of Danny's friends
> and of Danny's house. It is a story of how these
> three became one thing, so that in Tortilla Flat if
> you speak of Danny's house you do not mean a
> structure of wood flaked with old whitewash, over-
> grown with an ancient untrimmed rose of Castile.
> No, when you speak of Danny's house you are un-
> derstood to mean a unit of which the parts are
> men, from which came sweetness and joy, philan-
> thropy and, in the end, a mystic sorrow. For
> Danny's house was not unlike the Round Table, and
> Danny's friends were not unlike the knights of it.
> And this is the story of how that group came into
> being, of how it flourished and grew to be an or-
> ganization beautiful and wise. This story deals
> with the adventuring of Danny's friends, with the
> good they did, with their thoughts and their en-
> deavors. In the end, this story tells how the
> talisman was lost and how the group disintegrated
> (1).

Steinbeck's mention of the Round Table--to be discussed
more fully in the next section--functions importantly at this
point as an invitation to encounter the plot of Tortilla Flat
at a more complex level of meaning than that of an entertaining series of picaresque episodes and to see in the adventures of the paisanos significant human values in dramatic
conflict and tragic resolution.

Three main sections of the book recount the establishing, the flourishing and the disintegrating of Danny's household as a group committed to an ideal of realizing (although
the paisanos never put it this way) their best affective and
cognitive potential in a limited social context dedicated to
freedom and friendship.

The main characters are introduced in the Preface
and the early chapters. Danny--the protagonist--is small,
dark, energetic, and bow-legged. He is related to almost
everyone in the Flat "by blood or romance" (2); he had a
wealthy (by Tortilla Flat standards) grandfather but valued
his freedom more than any wealth. Pilon--the name means
"something to boot"--is the philosopher, logician, and casu-
ist of the group and has a marked ability to rationalize any
motive of even grossest self-interest into idealistic and altruistic impulses. Pablo is a nondescript intermittent jail-
bird. The Pirate (called so because of his beard) is a
simple-minded kindling-gatherer and lover of his six dogs.
Jesus Maria Corcoran is a soft-hearted, sensual doer of
good deeds. The characters share a number of conflicting
and complementary traits: they are hedonistic--valuing the
pleasures of the flesh (women, wine)--and idealistic--anxious
to take the side of the underdog. They disregard and stand
outside of--as much as they can--the establishment's law;
yet they are fiercely devoted to their privately developed
ethics of friendship. And they share an unquestioning assumption of the theological truths of Catholicism, along with
a very relaxed practice of that religion.

The first section of Tortilla Flat (preface and Chapters I through VII) present the establishing of Danny's household. Danny returns from World War I to find himself the
inheritor (from his grandfather) of two small houses in Tortilla Flat. The inheritance poses two problems to Danny:
the first is that he fears that being a property owner will
complicate his life by limiting his freedom. The second is
more serious and turns out to be an obstacle that must be
overcome before the household can be established: it is the
danger that Danny's higher social status may alienate him
from his friends. After meeting Pilon, who points out this
danger, Danny swears to share his property with him (Chapter I). Pilon moves into one of the houses with Danny but
becomes both jealous of Danny's status and fearful of losing
his own freedom as Danny's errand boy or slave. They find
a temporary solution as Pilon agrees to rent the other house
(Chapter II).

Both Pilon and Danny move up on the social scale as landlord and tenant; they continue to share food, women, and wine; but tenancy responsibilities--he can't pay any rent-- worry Pilon. He relieves his moral burden by renting part of his house to Pablo ("I will pay when Pablo pays" [21]) (Chapter III). But Danny's role as landlord requires him to ask for rent money. Pilon and Pablo encounter Jesus Maria Corcoran and rent him part of their house for $2.00. But the money goes for wine, and in the night the rent house burns down (Chapters IV and V).

Danny was secretly glad the house burned ("If it were still here, I would be covetous of the rent, ... my friends have been cool toward me because they owed me money. Now we can be free and happy again" [43]). Pilon, Pablo, and Jesus Maria go to Danny and confess their fault "like little children to a father" (44), and after a ritual castiga- tion, Danny accepts them into his house in the name of friendship, on the sole condition that they stay out of his bed. Danny's responsibilities are diminished with only one house; the others' responsibility is gone, with their change in status from tenants to guests. In gratitude, Pilon, Pablo, and Jesus Maria affirm eternal loyalty in an oath that they would see that Danny never go hungry (Chapter VI).

The household is set up on a basis of friendship, loyalty, and commitment; yet it is not complete without some positive goal or reason-for-being beyond its own self-per- petuation. The Pirate is the source of this binding and solidifying goal.

Pilon was worried about how to keep his oath to sup- port Danny. He knew that the Pirate gathered enough fire- wood to sell for a quarter each day. The pirate supported himself and his dogs on the charity of restaurant cooks and lived free in an abandoned chicken house. Unable to dis- cover the Pirate's hoard of quarters, Pilon and the others-- rationalizing over their concern for the Pirate's well-being and inability to handle money--invite him to live with them. Convinced finally of their true friendship, the Pirate turns over to Danny's household for safekeeping the nearly $300.00 in quarters he had been saving for a brass candlestick he had promised to St. Francis for healing a sick dog he once had (the dog was killed by a truck right after that).

Danny's house was now established. Since the money was for St. Francis, it could not be spent, and it was safe

under the group's guardianship. The bag of quarters became
"the symbolic center of the friendship, the point of trust
about which the fraternity revolved" (110), and a symbolic
quest--a reason for being--which was bigger than the group
itself and was normatively and spiritually superior to mere
self-preservation (Chapter VII).

With the household established, the second section
(Chapters VII through XIV) of the novel goes on to deal with
the "adventuring of Danny's friends, with the good they did,
with their thoughts and endeavors" (1). This is the most
episodic section of the novel, and it reaches a climax (Chapter XII) when Big Joe Portagee (who is the most bestial of
the group and who joined it after the house was established
and didn't share fully in its founding ideals) stole the Pirate's
nearly completed treasure hoard, after which the group recovered it and the candlestick was given the church--events
culminating in the pirate's dog seeing a "mystic" vision of
St. Francis. Buying the candlestick was the culmination of
the group's quest.

The episodic chapters of this second section function
importantly to unify the plot of the novel by contrast with
previous and following events. For example, immediately
after Pilon (in Chapter VII) had tried to find a real treasure,
failed, and then had it entrusted to him for a spiritual purpose, in Chapter VII Pilon and Big Joe set out to find a
legendary treasure, the burial place of which was supposed
to be revealed to the spiritually pure on St. Andrew's Eve.
What they find is a geodetic survey marker, and after several mutual deceptions, the adventure turns to nothing.
Chapter IX is a lively parody on society's materialistic
pride and greed in which Danny buys a (motorless) vacuum
cleaner for the favors of (electricity-less) Sweets Ramirez.
Pilon, worried that Danny's commitment to the group might
waver with his affection for Sweets, steals the machine and
trades it for wine so that Danny will return. The whole incident anticipates Danny's abandoning of the group at the end
of the book. Chapter X, in which the group befriends a
Mexican corporal with a dying child, suggests some relationships between society and violence which are dramatized in
the concluding section of the novel. In Chapter XI the comic
portrayal of Big Joe Portagee's insensitive and animal qualities prepares for his theft of the Pirate's money in XII.
In Chapter XIII the group chivalrously attends the needs of
the starving children of Teresina Cortez, and for a while,
this endeavor functions as a kind of surrogate for the quest

for the candlestick, but the real "symbolic center" of the
fraternity has gone with the Pirate's money; and Chapter
XIV, with its (still comic) reflections on man's capacity for
inhumanity, prepares for the concluding section.

In the final section (Chapters XV through XVII) Danny
finds the weight of his responsibility to the fraternity too
much. He abandons the group, steals from it, reverts to
the unrestrained violence of his pre-fraternal youth, and
sells the house to a bootlegger. The group is able to steal
the house back (by destroying the unfiled, although legal,
deed of transfer), and Danny returns exhausted and changed.
He lies (for the first time) to his friends about having sold
the house.

But this is only symptomatic of a deeper malaise.
The "symbolic center" is gone, and the quality of its mutual
commitment (especially Danny's) is gone: "the good life, "
as Steinbeck wrote, "lay in ruins" (151) (Chapter XV).

The group tries to regain the old Danny by having
Tortilla Flat's historic party (they even work for a day to
buy food and drink). At the ensuing Saturnalia Danny
achieves legendary status as a drinker, lover, and brawler.
But violence is his undoing, and when no one else will fight
him, he charges into the night looking for "The One who can
fight. . . . The Enemy who is worthy of Danny" (170) and
falls into a gulch to his death (Chapter XVI).

After Danny's funeral, the group comes together one
last time for drinking and reflection. But with the leader
dead and the commitment lost, there is no going back.
They burn the house and "walked slowly away, and no two
walked together" (170) (Chapter XVII).

III.   CRITICAL EXPLICATION

Critical achievement of a more complete understanding
of Tortilla Flat has been hindered not only by a too common
and sometimes facile assumption that the novel was a primitivistic celebration of uninhibited life or an ironic rendition
of the Arthurian myth, but also because the central thematic
concerns of the book have been obscured by complexities and
failures in its satiric form.

Peter Lisca[13] documented what Warren French later

described as "two successive stages of misinterpretation" of Tortilla Flat. [14] No doubt the public read this depression best-seller as a literature of escape into a world simpler and poorer, yet happier, if more quaint and curious, than their own. The concurrent reaction of many reviewers and early critics was to see the book as a simplistic glorification of the animal side of man. Typical comments of this sort affirmed that the book "had the virtue of being unmoral without apology, "[15] that the characters were "not quite human beings, " but were "cunning little living dolls who amuse us like pet guinea pigs or rabbits, "[16] and that the book was a "celebration" of "man as animal" who was "without any other pretensions. "[17] Other early critics objected to the loose episodic quality of the book: it was called "little more than a sketch book" that insulted "literary genres, "[18] and "a gay trifle" not to be taken seriously "if the author had not invited such treatment. "[19]

According to Warren French, the second stage of misinterpretation of Tortilla Flat began with Lewis Gannett's publication in 1943, in the introduction to the Portable Steinbeck, of a letter Steinbeck had written to his agents in 1934 [see section on "Background of the Work"]. In answer to criticisms that the novel was formless, Steinbeck had explained that it followed a definite pattern based on the Malory version of the Arthurian legends. [20] Minimizing lapses between Tortilla Flat and Malory's tale, certain critics have endorsed Steinbeck's use of the Arthurian frame, calling Tortilla Flat "the best Arthurian story for which modern society can serve as a basis"[21] and a novel which "both illuminates the Dark Ages and dignifies the paisanos. "[22]

From the beginning of critical reaction, various interpreters of Tortilla Flat have correctly appraised the novel's central concerns as dealing with a kind of conflict between the values of Danny's paisano fraternity and those of 20th century civilization. [23] Such thematic concerns tended to be neglected in Arthurian readings, and more recently, some critics have objected to overconcentration on the Arthurian frame, arguing that this emphasis tends to obscure important elements of the novel's theme and form. [24]

Avoiding preoccupation with the Arthurian reference has allowed for what might be a third and more adequate stage of interpretation of Tortilla Flat. Such a stage is marked by close attention to the satire that pervades and informs the total structure of the book. Warren French

sounded the keynote of such a reading in 1961 when he insisted that satiric thrusts at the respectable middle class
and at the organized church were strictly incidental in Tortilla Flat--that the target of the book's satire was "the very
group Steinbeck has been accused of glamourizing," Danny's
paisano fraternity. 25

But sympathy and satire make an uneasy mix, and
readers' reactions (I see this in my own students' responses)
to Tortilla Flat often reflect a peculiar feeling of malaise--
they may feel delighted, but they seldom feel instructed by
it. Something is uncomfortable about the book that is difficult to describe. I think the wide disparity of critical opinion that I have described is indicative of some such malaise
operating at the critical level, and I believe it is attributable
to the fact that Tortilla Flat distinctively draws upon two
genres--novel and satire--which ultimately are not compatible. We speak, of course, about "satiric novels," but
when we do we are usually talking about novels of which
satire is only one aspect and usually not definitive of structure. Huckleberry Finn contains satiric thrusts, for example, at middle-class bad taste and sentimentality (the Grang-
erford episode) and at gullibility founded in mindless pride
(the Peter Wilks episode), but such thrusts are not the central concerns of the novel. Without trying to be definitive,
it is probably a safe generalization that while novels utilize
varieties of realism in making a portrayal of and comment
on human experience, satire involves the deliberate use of
varieties of artifice (different kinds of narrators, personae,
mock-heroic, burlesque, hyperbole, invective, and the like)
for purposes which are intentionally judgmental and norma-
tive. Tortilla Flat tries to do both things at once: it
makes a realistic presentation of obviously sympathetic characters; at the same time the book's satiric artifice doesn't
quite take them seriously, judges these characters, and finds
them seriously flawed. Thus conflicts of content and form
produce a parallel jolt between the reader's affective and
cognitive responses to the book.

I want to suggest that Tortilla Flat can best be understood as a work which uses novelistic techniques--such as
character development, incident, setting, and symbol--to
make a dramatic presentation of a flawed society (Danny's
fraternity, as French said) which becomes the target of the
satire that is the defining principle of the book. Further, I
want to suggest that an understanding of the complexities in
the book's satiric form--and of lapses of control of the

satire--can contribute to a more complete and more accurate
estimate of what Tortilla Flat is, does, and says.

The Impossible Society of Danny's House

In 1942 Maxwell Geismar commented that Tortilla
Flat missed a chance for "a more serious social appraisal"
of the "positive human values in the paisano society" because the book "ignores the more realistic significance of
the paisano existence." He complained that this flawed the
book as a comment on the "pressing social problems of
[Steinbeck's] time."26 The comment was correct, but the
complaint was inappropriate because Tortilla Flat's portrayal
of Danny's society functions at a level more satiric and
philosophical than realistic and sociological. That is, the
realistic significance of paisano existence is not the book's
major concern: Tortilla Flat's portrayal of Danny's household is part of a satiric construct of an impossible society,
containing from its inception the seeds of its destruction.

Danny's fraternity is a unit founded on a social ideal
of friendship--loyalty, commitment, and tolerance toward
immediate comrades. It was also founded on more individ-
ualistic ideals of absolute freedom, total security, complete
absence of restraint of impulse, and full sensual self-gratification. These latter were also the ideals of Danny and
his friends when they lived much more in a state of nature--
sleeping in the woods, subsisting by considerable wit and
little work--prior to coming into fuller contact through Danny's inheritance with the broader civilization of Tortilla Flat
and Monterey. Getting the security and comradeship of the
fraternity required only a minimal compromise of the paisanos' prior "natural" values--a fact that is paralleled by
the partial and tangential relation of the household to the
rest of society, as the book's topography suggests: Monterey merges into Tortilla Flat, the area where the "forest
and the town intermingle" (2), and Danny's household is an
enclave in the closer-to-nature environment of Tortilla Flat.

For one brief shining moment, Danny's society tentatively grasps a realization that a fully human (and social)
life involves more than physical security and free self-gratification. In the preservation of the Pirate's money for the
purchase of the candlestick, the fraternity finds a reason for
being that is bigger than individual self-interests. But this
doesn't last, and the basic causes of the downfall of Danny's

society are dramatized in three themes that run concurrently
through the plot of Tortilla Flat. These are the themes of
violence, of stasis, and of the self-interested objectification
of others.

The centrality of violence in the experience of Danny
and his friends becomes a clear indication that they fail to
see the restraint of violent impulse as either necessary or
desirable if a society is to provide genuine security for free
and full human development. Tortilla Flat presents violence
as part and parcel of the paisano way of life: "love and
fighting, " Pilon generalized, "and a little wine. Then you
are always young, always happy" (136). Violence was the
major point of contact between Danny's group and the Monterey establishment--the physical violence of the paisanos
paralleling the exploitive financially violent tactics of the
respectable. Danny's first reaction to his being "raised" in
society by his inheritance was a drunken spree of vandalism.
Violence was also part of the ritual of friendship in the paisano household: part of the celebration of the inheritance
that led to the fraternity was a "really fine, " if casual,
fight between Danny and Pilon (17).

Violence is more than a habitual response for the
fraternity. It is a ritual in the true sense of a symbolic
reenactment of patterns of behavior that have social value
and significance. In two central episodes the paisanos are
satirically presented as viewing violence as an appropriate
and even necessary legal and moral means of organizing society.

When the paisanos are sure that Big Joe Portagee
had stolen the Pirate's money, they thoroughly extract his
confession. Danny knocks him out; then

> They did not speak to him at all. Danny meas-
> ured his distance carefully, like a golfer address-
> ing the ball. His stick smashed on Big Joe's
> shoulder; then the friends went about the business
> in a cold and methodical manner. Jesus Maria
> took the legs, Danny the shoulders and chest.
> Big Joe howled and rolled on the floor. They
> covered his body from the neck down. Each blow
> found a new space and welted it. The shrieks
> were deafening. (113)

After they bruise the "whole front of the body, " they are

about to go to work on head and bare foot with can-opener
and stick when Big Joe confesses the money's whereabouts.
And after he has confessed, we learn that

> Danny leaned down, took him by the shoulder, and
> rolled him over on his face. Then the friends
> went over his back with the same deadly precision.
> The cries grew weaker, but the work only stopped
> when Big Joe was beaten into unconsciousness.
> (113)

Next they cross-hatch Joe's back and rub in salt, and Danny
finally decides, "I think he will be honest now" (114). That
this violence was a morally pedagogical tactic becomes clear
from the friends' subsequent treating of Joe's wounds. But
even given the Portagee's animal stupidity and the narrator's
comment that although his morals were probably untouched,
Joe would never again steal from Danny's house (114), all
this might seem like excessive and gratuitous cruelty had it
not been for a prior episode which spelled out the paisanos'
rationale of violence.

Peter Lisca has called the episode of the corporal
and his son (Chapter X) a "parable" of the book's theme,
but I think it is presented as much more than an "allegory
of the basic tenets of the predatory social system which the
paisanos have successfully avoided."27 The incident is actually a satiric presentation of the paisano's philosophy of
violence as a social tool.

The friends befriend a Mexican corporal whose baby
is dying and whose wife had been stolen by a captain. The
paisanos assume that violent revenge is necessary, and they
offer to help. Pilon's recollection at this point of how his
cuckolded grandfather dealt with a licentious priest (by tying
him naked to a post in a corral and turning a little calf in
with him) indicates the historical background of this kind of
"social tool" in paisano tradition (101). But the corporal
declines help at this sort of revenge, saying that his plan
had been to make his son a general, because "if that capi-
tán, with the little epaulets and the little sash, could take
my wife, imagine what a general with a big sash and a gold
sword could take!" (103). The corporal does not abjure
violence per se: he has a better idea. He would try to
work within the system by maximizing its use and effectiveness. And the narrator's comment that the paisanos "were
proud to have known such a man" (103) tells us more about

the paisanos and their rationale of violence than it does
about the corporal.

Perhaps Tortilla Flat is suggesting that a society
burdened with a violent tradition and not-so-latent violent
propensities cannot maintain its form.   Certainly Danny's
couldn't.   It is true that under the civilizing influence of
the household he had not fought so often or been "adventur-
ously drunk" (147).   But in spite of all the previous talk
about the "responsibilities" of ownership, the narrator tells
us that it was not the weight of property (147) that led to
Danny's abandoning and ultimately destroying the household.
It was his longing for freedom from the order he had established with his society--a longing for a freedom he defined
in terms of "storm and violence, sweet violence!" (147).
Danny abandoned his household and turned his violence
against it, and his final act of violence--supposedly against
the cosmos, God, the broader social framework, nature, or
whatever--was actually an act of self-destruction: a man
destroyed by the prime principle of his life, an end that
could have been tragic in some other than a satiric context.

Danny's final self-defeating affirmation of violence
grew out of another self-defeating quality of his society--its
stasis.   Nature may flourish in its seemingly unchanging
cycles, but a society that allows for a full realization of
human potential must also allow for change and growth as
potential is realized.   But Tortilla Flat dramatizes Danny's
society as one that came to a state of stasis--as one whose
time became like that of nature: no clocks, no watches but
"the great golden watch of the sun" (133).   Actually, even
during the time of its growth when seeking non-self-inter-
ested ends, the whole tendency of the society had been to
preserve the status quo.   The tasks it took on had a static
quality--to preserve the Pirate's treasure, to maintain the
traditional way of life (and the diet) of the Cortez family.
The static quality the society achieved is made quite explicit.
The narrator speaks of even the Monterey establishment as
having a changeless "quality. "   More strongly, he says that
Tortilla Flat had a changeless "routine, " and still more
strongly, "in Danny's house there was even less change"
(146).

Leaving the state of nature and entering into a society, Danny had briefly experienced a potential for moral and
social growth (the candlestick, the Cortez children) which
transcended immediate self-gratification, but which he could

not continue to sustain. French has suggested that the story
of Danny is an "extended illustration of Harry Morgan's observation in Cup of Gold that 'civilization will split up a
character, and he who refuses to split goes under. '"28
Danny goes under only partly because he refuses or is unable to split away from his totally free, organically unified
"natural" propensities. The other part of the reason is that
the society he established was only a partial one--flawed in
that it had not sufficiently removed itself from nature to
function fully as a human society, as the repeated linking of
natural (cyclic, static) time and the time of Danny's society
shows. Further, it was not the weight of property (the
"talismanic bond" of the society and the prime symbol of
its civilized status) that Danny tried to escape; it was the
"beating of time" (147) he began to feel--time as a static,
cyclic routine that the society had reverted to (146) when it
had ceased to grow. The society wasn't far enough removed from nature's time ("[Danny] looked at his friends
and saw how with them every day was the same" [147]) to
continue to grow, and Danny wasn't far enough removed
from nature's freedom, expressed in terms of violence, to
get it growing again. Under the beating of nature's time,
Danny reverted to nature's freedom and violence. Thematically, Tortilla Flat seems to be saying more than "he who
refuses to split goes under. " It suggests that once a man
has split from nature, he cannot go back again. Danny's
reversion to nature led to his betrayal of his one significant
human achievement--his household. Danny's natural "freedom" had certainly not been just another name for nothing
left to lose, for in returning to his society, spiritually
devastated but unable to leave behind nature's freedon/vio-
lence, he lost everything.

        A final and most important internal feature of Danny's
society which led to its dissolution was its tendency to objectify almost every person it contacted and to use them as
means of its own self-gratification.

        Except in the instances of refusing to abscond with
the Pirate's money (it became the "symbolic center" [110]
for the fraternity's spiritual values) and the saving of the
Cortez family, Danny's group had very little conception of
society as a "kingdom of ends. " Of course, the group was
tolerant of the foibles of others, and they were capable of
sporadic disinterested acts toward people outside their immediate household, such as the befriending of the corporal.
But the internal organization of the fraternity never went

beyond a primitive version of a Rousseauesque social contract based on the abstraction that isolated in a state of nature, a man has unlimited rights. The friends "contracted"
to give up certain "rights" (to steal from the household or
to sleep in Danny's bed, for example) in order to secure
the values of comradeship and security and the free exercise
of their remaining "rights" (the right not to work, for example). In one sense Tortilla Flat might be read as an
exemplum of an operational failure of the contract theory of
government. Danny's society never went beyond such a
theory toward any real appropriation of the more complex
idea that the function of society is to secure equally for
everyone the right to his full human development and that to
be a member of society in the fullest sense, a man must
see that his own good--his own full human development--
requires his endorsing of this function of society to secure
the right of all men to be treated as ends and not as means.

     Tortilla Flat's portrayal of the tendency of Danny's
paisanos to objectify people dramatizes the inadequacies of
the group, both as a self-contained social unit and as a social unit in relation to other such units. There is no significant difference between the ways Danny's society relates
to the Monterey establishment and to the rest of Tortilla
Flat. The group preys on both, using them as objects--
means to achieve its ends. The fraternity recognizes no
property rights except its own; Mrs. Morales isn't Danny's
neighboring human being; she is simply a source of chickens.
The Pirate's money may have been sacrosanct, but the Pirate himself was used as a means--of getting food. The
fraternity has been described as an ecological community,
illustrating the "ecological principle" that "some kind of
creature will adapt itself to every possible source of subsistence."29 It may be fine for "creatures" (parasites are
an example of such "creatures") to objectify their source of
subsistence, but it is hardly an admirable tactic for humans
consciously to perfect for use on other humans. Pilon's
rationalizations are the repeated examples of such a tactic,
and for all their critically touted complexities, 30 they remain nothing more than satiric presentations of amusing
pieces of casuistry that never obscure the self-gratification
at the expense of others that occasioned them.

     Perhaps the clearest instances of the tendency to ob-
jectify others occur in the paisanos' relations with women,
who, in Danny's society are objects, not people. Big Joe
Portagee's insensitive, mindless, and muddy use of Tia

Ignacia (Chapter XI) is different only in degree and not in
kind from the objectification of women seen in the relations
of Danny with Mrs. Morales and Sweets Ramirez or in Pilon's with Mrs. Torrelli: "a lively one, that Butter Duck ...
it is seldom that one finds all things in one market--wine,
food, love, and firewood" (36).   Lively, perhaps; but neither
butter nor ducks (or markets) are human.

        As was the case with violence, the fraternity's ten-
dency to objectify others boomeranged, contributing to its
destruction.   When he abandons the household and steals
from it to sustain his violent escapades, Danny is obviously
using it as a means for his own private ends.   But the
friends could excuse such thefts as pranks.   Even a "crime
against friendship" (152), such as stealing Pilon's shoes,
could be attributed to temporary madness.   But it was Danny's supreme act of objectifying his own society by selling
the house (the group's symbolic "talismanic bond" and its
literal center) to Torrelli that led to the disintegration of the
fraternity, following Danny's realization that the ties that
held it together were coming apart.   This realization is
presented in a key passage describing Danny's return to the
house after the paisanos had destroyed Torrelli's unrecorded
deed to the house.   It is worth quoting at length:

> 'Danny,' he said, 'that pig Torrelli came up here
> this morning with lies.   He had a paper he said
> you signed.'
>   Danny looked startled.   'Where is that paper?'
> he demanded.
>   'Well,' Pilon continued.   'We knew it was a
> lie, so we burned that paper.   You didn't sign it,
> did you?'
>   'No,' said Danny, and he drained his jar.
>   'It would be nice to have something to eat,'
> observed Jesus Maria.
>   Danny smiled sweetly.   'I forgot.   In one of
> those bags are three chickens and some bread.'
>   So great was Pilon's pleasure and relief that
> he stood up and made a little speech.   'Where is
> there a friend?' he exclaimed.   'He takes us into
> his house out of the cold.   He shares his good
> food with us, and his wine.   Ohee, the good man,
> the dear friend.'
>   Danny was embarrassed.   He looked at the
> floor.   'It is nothing,' he murmured.   'It has no
> merit.' (159)

The fine dramatic irony here constitutes a deft satiric touch.
We and Danny know something the paisanos don't: he actually did sell the house.   And at this point Danny is objectifying his friends much more seriously than when he was
stealing from them.   In lying about having signed away the
house, he is manipulating not just their possessions, but
their future lives and expectations, by letting them think
things will go on as before.   Telling a lie while knowing it
will be believed and acted upon is to assume a god-like
stance, moving people around like pawns.   After Danny did
this, the friendship, marked by the ritual of the sharing of
the food and wine, literally turned to "nothing. " Manipulated
objects can't be comrades, and Danny is dead right in saying of an outward sign of communion in such a context that
"it has no merit. "

Tortilla Flat as Satire

Edmund Wilson's comment in 1940 that the characters
of Tortilla Flat were "not quite human beings, " but were
"cunning living little dolls who amuse us like pet guinea-pigs
or rabbits"[31]--while approved by many subsequent critics as
an appraisal of the book's primitivism--actually provided a
clue for a more complete understanding of Tortilla Flat, not
as a primitivistic novel but as a satiric social commentary.
What Tortilla Flat does is to present a unique kind of society (comparably to the presentation of those of the Lillipu-
tians, Brobdignagians, and Houyhnhnms in Gulliver's Travels)
as a vehicle for satire.

Read as a novel, Tortilla Flat contains obvious lapses
in realistic portrayal of character.   Wilson was right: the
characters, except possibly Danny, are one-dimensional and
predictable.   Their trademarks--Pilon's casuistry, Big Joe's
animal stupidity, Jesus Maria's sensual soft-heartedness--
don't change.   But such a comment is not a legitimate negative criticism of a satire, a genre defined largely by its
rhetorical quality and its use of artifice.

Satire is rhetorical in the classical sense of language
used for a persuasive purpose.   In satire this purpose is to
encourage reader agreement with the judgment the work ren-
ders on its object.   The element of artifice is basic: "all
good satire, " Maynard Mack reminded us, "exhibits an ap-
preciable degree of fictionality.   Where the fiction inheres
in familiar elements like plot ... its presence is

unmistakable. "[32]   One of the main artifices of satire is a
kind of exaggeration (for example, of character--like Pilon's
elaborate casuistry; of attitude--like the paisanos' attitude
toward women; or of incident--like the final party), especially functioning to indicate the contrast between the values being attacked and the norms by which judgment is to be made.
These norms are seldom announced in satire; they are most
often implicit and are often reflected in another satiric artifice, the use of a persona--an assumed personality (a narrator or a certain character) through which the satire is revealed.   The sometimes genial, sometimes mock-heroic, and
always ironic narrator of Tortilla Flat is the primary distinguishing mark of the work as a satire.

Readers of satire have been repeatedly cautioned not
to ignore the rhetorical quality of the genre by confusing
persona with author[33]--by attributing, for example, the attitudes and character of the persona and A Modest Proposal
to Jonathan Swift, who didn't really want to kill and eat children, but who put this sentiment into his persona for satiric
purpose.

"New" or "objective" critics have properly made us
guarded about inquiring into an artist's intention.   But in the
case of satire, such inquiry is not only legitimate but also
necessary.   No one really doubts that Swift intended to write
a satire in A Modest Proposal.   But how do critics account
for a book like Tortilla Flat that is basically satiric, with
the paisanos as target, when the author later claimed he
didn't intend to hold them up for ridicule at all?[34]

It seems unreasonable to doubt Steinbeck's sincerity
in his disclaimer.   One quality that comes across in a reading of all his prose is a stringent attempt at honesty.   On
the other hand, critical honesty seems to require acknowl-
edgment of the basic satiric form of Tortilla Flat.   And the
plot of Tortilla Flat does present a flawed society, as I have
tried to show, which the narrative persona makes a satiric
target.   It is hard not to have a satire when the narrator repeatedly resorts to mock-heroic to highlight the incongruity
between the paisanos' professed ideals and their actual life-
style, when he invokes Arthurian heraldic legendry to under-
cut the validity of their actual quests by comic contrast, or
when he uses the language of superior denigration of assumed "racial" differences.   The narrator's condescension
is apparent in comments like "two gallons is a great deal of
wine, even for two paisanos" or "the friends had sunk into a

routine which might have been monotonous for anyone but a
paisano [my italics]" (20, 146). Such comments differ only
in degree from the dialogue in Huckleberry Finn about a
steamboat accident: "We blowed out a cylinder head. "/
"Good gracious! anybody hurt?"/"No'm. Killed a nigger. "/
"Well, it's lucky; because sometimes people do get hurt. "35

An early critic, not distinguishing between Steinbeck
and narrator, saw the incongruity between Steinbeck's professed liking for real paisanos and his way of talking about
them in Tortilla Flat, and suggested that the "humanities"
of the book weren't "any too secure" and that the author's
"social sympathies" hadn't been "awake all the time. "36
Even if we assume they were (while acknowledging that they
may not have been--Americans today are a little more likely
to be aware of the possibility of unconscious racism than in
1937), the critical question remains, of how an author writes
a satire without intending to.

Professor Stanley Alexander has recently suggested
an approach to an answer, describing how Steinbeck's affinity
for pastoral portrayal of character and setting was in conflict with the mock-heroic form he imposed in Tortilla
Flat. 37 Alexander points out how both mock-heroic and
pastoral are condescending stances: the first commenting
on the foolish incongruity of unheroic people trying to act
that way, and the second suggesting an admiration of a simple peasantry for having the same human virtues that the
rest of us (narrator and readers) have38 (remember Huck's
astonishment that Jim cared as much for his family as
"white folks does" for theirs?39). Steinbeck may have been
adopting the mock-heroic narrator for comic effect, without
realizing the total satiric implications of such a narrator.

In Tortilla Flat Steinbeck was experimenting with an
unfamiliar satiric form with which he was later never really
successful. 40 The book is flawed as a satire because Steinbeck's affective position of concern for the paisanos, presented in pastoral terms, clashed with his narrator's negative cognitive appraisal of their society, presented in terms
of satire. The sympathetic treatment of an object of satire
requires full control of the mock-heroic form. Pope's treatment of Belinda in The Rape of the Lock is an example of
such control; and Steinbeck wasn't in Pope's satiric league,
as his failure to develop a consistent narrative persona in
Tortilla Flat demonstrates. Mack describes three basic
types of satiric personae--the genial man of good character

whose sense of duty calls him reluctantly to satiric correc-
tion of folly, the ingênu or naïf whose amazement at what he
sees is a satiric vehicle, and the morally secure, indignant
public defender who attacks vice wherever he finds it. 41
The problem with Tortilla Flat as satire is that the narrator assumes all of these stances, along with several others,
at seeming random.   The narrator's voice at various points
is indignant, genial, sentimental, ironic, and pastoral.

Steinbeck may have liked the paisanos and tried to
write true stories about them, but Tortilla Flat remains a
flawed satire on a fictional flawed society.   And the lasting
value of a careful study of the book may be that the unique
disjunction of its affective and cognitive concerns will continue to remind us that neither in literary creation nor in
literary criticism can life and art be totally merged.

Notes

1.   Peter Lisca, The Wide World of John Steinbeck (New
     Brunswick, N.J.: Rutgers University Press, 1958),
     p. 71.

2.   Good accounts of the place and importance of Tortilla
     Flat in the Steinbeck canon are in Lisca, pp. 6-9,
     72-82; Maxwell Geismar, Writers in Crisis (Boston:
     Houghton Mifflin, 1942), p. 252; and Lewis Gannett,
     "Introduction," The Portable Steinbeck (New York:
     The Viking Press, 1943), pp. xii-xv (reprinted in
     E. W. Tedlock, Jr. and C. V. Wicker, eds.,
     Steinbeck and His Critics (Albuquerque: University
     of New Mexico Press, 1956), pp. 23-37.   Steinbeck
     and His Critics is hereafter cited as SHC.

3.   Cited in Lisca, pp. 72-73.   Lisca's publication history
     of the book is good.

4.   Lisca, pp. 73-74.

5.   Lisca, p. 74.

6.   Cited in Gannett, pp. xiii-xiv.   Also in SHC.

7.   John Steinbeck, Tortilla Flat (N.Y.: The Viking Press,
     1935), p. 1.   All subsequent references to this work
     will be indicated by page numbers in parentheses
     following quotes.

8.   Lisca, pp. 78, 300 (n. 5).

9.   See the section "Steinbeck on Criticism" in SHC, pp. 43-56.

10. Lisca, pp. 78-79. Also in SHC.

11. Warren French, John Steinbeck (N. Y.:   Twayne Publishers, 1961), p. 53.

12. John Steinbeck, "Foreword," Tortilla Flat (N. Y.: Random House, 1937).

13. Lisca, pp. 6-9, 75, 81, 89.

14. French, p. 53.

15. Harry T. Moore, The Novels of John Steinbeck (Chicago: Normandie House, 1939), p. 39.

16. Edmund Wilson, "The Californians: Storm and Steinbeck," New Republic, 103 (December 9, 1940), 784-787.

17. Freeman Champney, "John Steinbeck, Californian," Antioch Review, 7 (Fall 1947), 355.   Also in SHC. See also Woodburn Ross, "John Steinbeck: Earth and Stars," University of Missouri Studies in Honor of A. H. R. Fairchild, ed. Charles T. Proudy (Columbia: University of Missouri Press, 1946). Also in SHC. Also, Stanley Edgar Hyman, "Some Notes on John Steinbeck," Antioch Review, 2 (Summer 1942). Also in SHC.

18. Carlos Baker, "Steinbeck of California," Delphian Quarterly, 23 (Spring 1940), 40.

19. Lincoln R. Gibbs, "John Steinbeck: Moralist," Antioch Review, 2 (Summer 1942). Also in SHC. See also Moore, p. 39: "Even though Tortilla Flat does not at the last provide the sense of harmony which a more smoothly proportioned story should, it makes pleasant piecemeal reading, and is a charming comedy."

20. French, pp. 53-54.

21. Arthur F. Kinney, "The Arthurian Cycle in Tortilla
     Flat," Modern Fiction Studies, 11 (1965), 11-20.
     Reprinted in Robert Murray Davis, ed., Steinbeck:
     A Collection of Critical Essays (Englewood Cliffs,
     N.J.: Prentice-Hall, 1972), pp. 36-46.

22. Joseph Fontenrose, John Steinbeck: An Introduction and
     Interpretation (N.Y.: Holt, Rinehart, and Winston,
     1963), p. 40.

23. Frederick I. Carpenter, "John Steinbeck: American
     Dreamer," Southwest Review, 26 (July 1941),
     454, 466. Also in SHC. See also Fontenrose, pp.
     32-35. (Fontenrose described the fraternity as an
     "organismic" and "ecological" community adapting
     itself to a unique "source of subsistence" in the so-
     cial environment, but he felt the Arthurian theme
     was "more important".)

24. Peter Lisca, for example, says that "more important
     than any unity of action given the book by a super-
     ficial resemblance to the Morte D'Arthur is the unity
     of tone and style which makes clear and effective
     what Steinbeck called 'the strong but different philo-
     sophic-moral system of these people' and the book's
     tragicomic theme'" (Lisca, p. 79). And Howard
     Levant has recently argued that "it is true that
     Tortilla Flat has a cyclic rhythm, but the resulting
     type of structure is too universal to be identified
     readily as a debt to Malory, at least in as close a
     parallel as Steinbeck's opening sentence would indi-
     cate" ["Tortilla Flat: The Shape of John Steinbeck's
     Career," PMLA, 85 (1970, 1088]. See also French,
     p. 56.

25. French, pp. 56-57.

26. Geismar, pp. 254-56.

27. Lisca, pp. 89-90.

28. French, p. 57.

29. Fontenrose, p. 29.

30. See, for example, Lisca, pp. 36-38.

31. Cited by and commented on in Lisca, p. 7.

32. "The Muse of Satire," Yale Review, 41 (1951), 84.

33. Mack, pp. 83, 88-90. See also W. O. S. Sutherland,
     Jr., The Art of the Satirist (Austin: University of
     Texas Press, 1965), pp. 12-15.

34. I refer to Steinbeck's disclaimer in his Foreword to
     the 1937 Modern Library edition of Tortilla Flat,
     cited previously.

35. Chapter 32.

36. Barker Fairley, "John Steinbeck and the Coming Liter-
     ature," Sewanee Review, 50 (June 1942), 153-
     154.

37. Stanley Alexander, "The Conflict of Form in Tortilla
     Flat," American Literature, 40 (March 1968),
     59.

38. Ibid., p. 61.

39. The Adventures of Huckleberry Finn, Chapter 23.

40. See French, pp. 144, 158-159. French describes speci-
     fic failures of Sweet Thursday and The Wayward
     Bus as satires.

41. Mack, pp. 88-89.

IV. APPARATUS FOR RESEARCH PAPERS

                A. Ten Questions for Discussion

1.   The critical explication made the point that there was
     no essential difference between the relations of Danny's
     fraternity to Tortilla Flat and to Monterey. Do you
     agree or disagree? Give examples to support your
     contention.

2.   Is the attitude of the narrator consistent throughout the
     book? Is it different toward different events, charac-
     ters, and subject matters? Is the narrator's language
     consistent? Is there any change in the narrator toward
     the end of the book?

3.   The episode of the Pirate's dogs' vision has been ac-
     cused of sentimentality.   What is sentimentality?   Is
     this episode an example of sentimentality?   Are there
     others?
4.   Like real people, fully realized fictional characters have
     their positive and negative qualities.   Are the major
     characters of Tortilla Flat fully realized?   Which ones
     are and aren't?
5.   Is there a balance or imbalance on the part of the pai-
     sanos in terms of self-interest and altruism?
6.   Is there any character development in Tortilla Flat?
     Which characters change and which remain constant?
     What is the effect of character development, or lack of
     it, on the novel?
7.   If satire is an intentionally judging literary type, and if
     Tortilla Flat is a satire, what are the norms according
     to which its judgments are made?   Are they explicit?
     Or implicit?   Or both?
8.   Is there anything to be learned from the Danny-Sweets
     Ramirez episode?   Do parts of it relate to other parts
     of the story?   How?
9.   How is the episode in which Joe Portagee finds love re-
     lated to the rest of the story?
10. Is there a relation between the narratives of Tall Bob
     Smoke and that of the Viejo Ravanno?   Between these
     two narratives and the other incidents in Tortilla Flat?

B.   Suggested Topics for Research Papers

1.   Read Malory's Morte D'Arthur, or selected portions of
     it (a good starting point might be Eugene Vinaver, ed.,
     King Arthur and His Knights: Selected Tales by Sir
     Thomas Malory [Boston: Houghton Mifflin Company, rev.
     Riverside ed., 1968], which contains a workable begin-
     ning bibliography) and write a paper giving your thesis
     concerning the Arthurian theme in Tortilla Flat and your
     appraisal of other critics' comments on the subject.
2.   Steinbeck's various treatments of paisanos in Tortilla
     Flat, The Pearl, "Flight," (LV), and Pastures of Heaven.
3.   Tortilla Flat as a novel of social protest, considering
     the relationship of the paisanos to the establishment's
     law, commerce, religion, political structures, and con-
     ventions.
4.   Rhetorical patterns in the speech (of characters and of
     narrator) depicted in Tortilla Flat.
5.   Get a working idea of some various theories of satire

(a good starting point is Alvin B. Kernan, ed., Modern
Satire [New York: Harcourt, Brace and World, 1962]),
and write a paper showing how Tortilla Flat might be
related to such theories.
6. The view of women in Tortilla Flat.
7. The significance of names in Tortilla Flat.
8. The use of plant and animal symbols in Tortilla Flat.
9. The strengths and deficiencies of early reviews and
   criticisms (up to 1943) of Tortilla Flat.
10. Is Tortilla Flat a racist book?

C. Selected Bibliography

The starting point for any working bibliography of
Steinbeck is Tetsumaro Hayashi's John Steinbeck: A Concise
Bibliography (1930-1965) (Metuchen, New Jersey: The
Scarecrow Press, Inc., 1967). This work is supplemented
by Professor Hayashi's Annual Steinbeck Bibliography (1971):
A Checklist of Steinbeck Criticism after 1968 (Muncie, In-
diana: John Steinbeck Society of America, 1971) and by an-
nual bibliographies in PMLA and American Literature. See
also Hayashi's A New Steinbeck Bibliography, 1929-1971.
(Metuchen, N.J.: Scarecrow Press, 1973).

Initial Reviews in Periodicals (listed in Hayashi's John
Steinbeck: A Concise Bibliography [1930-1965]):

Benet, William Rose. Saturday Review of Literature,
   12 (June 1, 1935), 12.
Chamberlain, John. Current History, 42 (July 1935), 7.
Colby, Harriet. New York Herald Tribune Books,
   June 2, 1935. p. 4.
Mangione, Jerre. New Republic, 83 (July 13, 1935),
   285.
Marsh, Fred T. New York Times, June 2, 1935. p. 6.
Neville, Helen. Nation, 140 (June 19, 1935), 720.
Chicago Daily Tribune, June 1, 1935. p. 14.
New York Herald Tribune Books, June 2, 1935. p.
   4.
Saturday Review (London), 140 (November 23, 1935),
   501.
Spectator, 155 (December 6, 1935), 960.
Time, 39 (May 18, 1942), 84.
Times (London) Literary Supplement, December 21,
   1935. p. 877.

Selected Criticism

Alexander, Stanley. "The Conflict of Form in Tortilla
Flat." American Literature, 40 (March 1968), 58-66.
Excellent argument that a combination of mock-heroic
and pastoral devices create a serious conflict in the
satiric form of Tortilla Flat.

Baker, Carlos. "Steinbeck of California." Delphian Quarterly. 23 (Spring 1940). Early attack on Tortilla Flat's
seeming lack of structure.

Beach, Joseph Warren. American Fiction 1920-1940. New
York: Macmillan, 1942. Comments on Tortilla Flat reprinted in Tedlock, E. W., Jr. and Wicker, C. V.,
eds., "Introduction," Steinbeck and His Critics. Albuquerque: University of New Mexico Press, 1957. Hereafter cited as SHC. Beach's comments on Tortilla Flat
(pp. 317-22) are a brief and accurate early perception of
conflicts of sympathy and satiric intent.

Carpenter, Frederick I. "John Steinbeck: American Dreamer." Southwest Review, 26 (July 1941). Reprinted in
SHC, pp. 68-79. An early mention of the inadequacies
of Danny's fraternity as a society. Also in SHC pp. 74-
75.

Champney, Freeman. "John Steinbeck, Californian," Antioch Review, 7 (Fall 1947). Reprinted in SHC, pp. 135-
51. Reads Tortilla Flat as a celebration of primitivism.

Fairley, Barker. "John Steinbeck and the Coming Literature." Sewanee Review. 50 (April-June 1942), 151-57.
An early questioning of whether Tortilla Flat actually does
represent Steinbeck's social sympathies.

Fontenrose, Joseph. John Steinbeck: An Introduction and
Interpretation. New York: Holt, Rinehart, and Winston,
1963. Discussion of the Arthurian theme as illuminating
middle ages and dignifying paisanos. Interesting comments on Tortilla Flat's paisanos as an organismic and
ecological social unit.

French, Warren. John Steinbeck. New York: Twayne Publishers, 1961. The best early reading of Tortilla Flat as
satire. Not much discussion of satiric form.

Gannett, Lewis. "Introduction," The Portable Steinbeck.
New York: The Viking Press, 1943. First publication
of Steinbeck's letter claiming the Arthurian framework
for Tortilla Flat.

Geismar, Maxwell. Writers in Crisis: The American Novel
between Two World Wars. Boston: Houghton Mifflin
Company, 1942. Perceptive early comment that Tortilla
Flat doesn't give a realistic portrayal of the significant
human values of paisano life.

Gibbs, Lincoln R. "John Steinbeck: Moralist." Antioch
Review. 2 (Summer 1942). Reprinted in SHC, pp. 92-
103. Concerned with the philosophy of the paisanos.
Says it lacks range.

Hyman, Stanley Edgar. "Some Notes on John Steinbeck."
Antioch Review, 2 (Summer 1942). Reprinted in SHC,
pp. 152-66. Says Tortilla Flat carries "natural man" to
extreme.

Justus, James H. "The Transient World of Tortilla Flat."
Western Review, 7 (1969), 55-60. Sees the paisano
fraternity as a dream society threatened by the establishment, by self-questioning, and by the rhetorical
presence of the narrator. A footnote to Lisca's discussion and a weak anticipation of Alexander's.

Kinney, Arthur F. "The Arthurian Cycle in Tortilla Flat."
Modern Fiction Studies, 11 (Spring 1965), 11-20. Reprinted in Davis, Robert Murray, ed., Steinbeck: A
Collection of Critical Essays. Englewood Cliffs, N.J.:
Prentice-Hall, 1972. A basic argument for the Arthurian
theme as an informing structural and thematic principle
in Tortilla Flat.

Levant, Howard. "Tortilla Flat: The Shape of John Steinbeck's Career." PMLA, 85 (October 1970), 1087-95.
Argues against the Arthurian frame as a meaningful principle of structure and theme.

Lisca, Peter. The Wide World of John Steinbeck. New
Brunswick, N.J.: Rutgers University Press, 1958. Lisca's introduction and his chapter on Tortilla Flat give a
good survey of critical response. He denigrates the Arthurian reading and analyzes the "strong but different
philosophic-moral system" of Tortilla Flat's paisanos as
it is revealed in plot and style.

Marks, Lester J. Thematic Design in the Novels of John
Steinbeck. The Hague, Paris: Mouton, 1969. A very
brief comparison of Tortilla Flat to other early works.

Moore, Harry Thornton. The Novels of John Steinbeck: A
First Critical Study. Chicago: Normandie House, 1939.
An early criticism of Tortilla Flat commenting on its
supposed lack of structure.

Ross, Woodburn. "John Steinbeck: Earth and Stars. " University of Missouri Studies in Honor of A. H. R. Fairchild. ed. Charles T. Proudy. Columbia: University
of Missouri Press, 1946. Reprinted in SHC, pp. 167-
82.

Steinbeck, John. "Foreword. " Tortilla Flat. Modern Library edition. New York: Random House, 1937. Contains Steinbeck's famous disclaimer of having presented
the paisanos as curious or quaint.

_____. "My Short Novels. " Wings. October 1953.
Reprinted in SHC, pp. 38-40. Describes publication
background of Tortilla Flat.

Tedlock, E. W. , Jr. and Wicker, C. V. , eds. "Introduction. "
Steinbeck and His Critics. Albuquerque: University of
New Mexico Press, 1957. Good survey of Steinbeck
criticism to 1957.

Wilson, Edmund. "The Californians: Storm and Steinbeck. "
New Republic, 103 (December 9, 1940), 784-87. Early
comment on "primitivism. " An interesting notice of
qualities of artifice in characterization in Tortilla Flat.

Chapter 14

STEINBECK'S THE WINTER OF OUR DISCONTENT

By Reloy Garcia

I. THE BACKGROUND

In preparing his The Winter of Our Discontent, John
Steinbeck accumulated a number of debts. The novel contains several minor borrowings and echoes to Wordsworth,
to Coleridge, and to Shakespeare's Romeo and Juliet, which,
while fitting into the overall scheme, really attest to Steinbeck's diverse reading rather than to systematic borrowing.
The novel has two major influences: first, the New Testament, particularly Matthew (whom Ethan Allen Hawley calls
"pretty wonderful and--scary," see Matthew: Chapters 26-
28), Mark (see especially Chapters 14-16), Luke (see especially Chapters 22-24), and--to a lesser extent--John (see
Chapters 17-19). Often Hawley will paraphrase or quote
Christ, the most notable example being Christ's "Eli, Eli,
lama sabach thani?." ("My God, my God, why hast thou for-
saken me?") The second major influence is T. S. Eliot's
The Wasteland, an influence Donna Gerstenberger has already
traced (see Selected Bibliography). From these two sources
Steinbeck borrows quotes, characters, themes, and imagery.

Lesser but still important influences are Shakespeare's
Richard III, from whose opening lines Steinbeck picked the
title for his novel, and the life of Ethan Allen (1739-1789),
who serves as a model of how Ethan Allen Hawley should be
but is not. Just as Shakespeare's hero-villain, Richard, de-
generates in the conflict with his brother, from a cold
Machiavellian plotter to an emotional sinner who derives
pleasure from pain and evil, so too does Ethan degenerate
in conflict with his "brother," Danny Taylor, over the "kingdom" of Taylor's Meadow. Yet Ethan does not rise nearly
so high nor fall so far as Richard; nor does he rescue from
defeat a Pyrrhic victory. Ethan is never large enough to be

244

thoroughly corrupted or impressively evil. In addition, Steinbeck names his protagonist for Ethan Allen, a rambunctious "green mountaineer" patriot of mixed motives who risked everything for principles. It was he who captured Ticonderoga from the British and who subsequently, as a militia general, worked for independent status for Vermont, playing off the British against his own countrymen. In Chapter III of The Winter of Our Discontent, Steinbeck makes a loose knot between the real Ethan Allen and his own, while never tying the knot. The controlling principle in Steinbeck's use of both Richard and Ethan Allen is to show how the heroic has become the mock-heroic.

The foregoing major and secondary influences shape the novel's immediate source, an earlier short story entitled "How Mr. Hogan Robbed a Bank" (Atlantic Monthly, March, 1956), a fact Joseph Fontenrose and Warren French point out. The original short story seems a disturbingly small frame for heroes and heroic action and we can only speculate why Steinbeck retained the bank robbery motif. Here bank robberies are mentioned at least twice prior to Ethan's own aborted plan. Fontenrose sees the retention of the robbery incident as a structural flaw. My own opinion is that it constitutes a nice ironic hit. For what need is there to rob openly and risk imprisonment when one can steal legally and be a city father?

Although Steinbeck had lived in New York in 1925, it was not until 1943 that he began his extended residence there, and not until 1945 that he bought a home there. The book germinated in the released spirit of the post-War period, an age gone sour through graft, payola, scandals, and seemingly general corruption. The Winter of Our Discontent, which won the left-handed blessing of the Book of the Month Club in 1961, is the record of the country's malaise, of the country's unfulfilled dreams and unmet obligations, and of what happens to principles, to dreams, and to ideals in the care of the moneylenders.

II. PLOT SYNOPSIS

Ethan Allen Hawley, "just under forty, " Mason, Harvard graduate, ex-Army officer, lives in New Baytown, Long Island, New York, with his wife, Mary, and two children, Ethan Allen, Jr. , 14 and Ellen, 13. The descendant of once-rich and proud Puritans and whaling-captain

privateers, he is now a lowly clerk in a store he once owned
and lost through mismanagement to a Sicilian immigrant, Al-
fio Marullo. The bulk of the family fortune, however, was
lost by his father in unwise investments in obsolete muni-
tions. As the story opens on Good Friday of 1960, the intense pressures to regain the family's lost fortune and standing are directed at him from both within and outside his immediate family.

     Ethan and Mary awaken and discuss the day's activ-
ities, he by setting them against the backdrop of Christ's
crucifixion with his joking but double-layered comments.
Mary mentions that Margie Young-Hunt, the town whore and
descendant of witches, will read the family fortune from a
wicked deck of cards, the Tarot pack. On his way to work
Ethan carries on a conversation with the town banker's red
setter, and shortly after discusses an old bank robbery with
Joey Morphy, the bachelor teller at the First National Bank.
As he sweeps the pavement, Mr. Baker, the town banker,
attempts to induce him to invest Mary's inheritance from her
dead brother's will ($6,500), but he refuses to do so. Mr.
Baker appeals to the adventuring spirit of his forebears, to
their lost influence, and to his pride. They discuss a lost
ship, the Belle-Adair, as it turns out burned by Baker's ancestors for insurance money. Margie enters later and
tempts him with her body, but he refuses this offer also.
Marullo enters briefly and gives him a lesson on how to
make money through the shrewd manipulation of money, a
theory Ethan rejects as unfeeling. Mr. Biggers, a seller
for B. B. D. and D., offers Ethan a bribe if Ethan will buy
from his company exclusively, leaving a new billfold and a
new twenty dollar bill. Joey returns and congratulates him
on his good fortune.

     Upon his return home, he is told that his children
are entering a national "I Love America" essay contest, and
that Margie has prophesied wealth and influence for Ethan.
Unable to sleep, he goes to the Old Harbor to his "Place,"
a 4 x 4 x 5 cave-like retreat to which he repairs prior to
important decisions and events. There he begins to question
his moral scheme and wonders if morality is not relative in
a Darwinian world. On his way to work Saturday, he discusses a bank robbery at Floodhampton with Stoney Smith,
the day constable. He asks Smith to look in on his boyhood
companion and "brother," Danny Taylor, who was expelled
from the Naval Academy and who is now the town drunk.
Margie enters the store and he sees her with new and

lecherous eyes. Throughout the day he is greeted by the
observation that he is "a new man," and that he somehow
looks different. Baker invites the Hawley family over on
Sunday at four to discuss business. And Biggers returns to
have his money--but not his wallet--returned with the blunt
statement that "the bids aren't all in." At the Hawley house
later, Margie begins to read his fortune but is interrupted
by a recurrent vision of a snake shedding its skin.

On Sunday morning Marullo, having learned of the rejected bribe, brings Ethan an offering of candy Easter eggs.
During a noon nap, Ethan dreams that Danny is melting
while he is helpless to retain his friend's shape. At the
Baker home that afternoon, Ethan learns that Baker and other prominent village fathers plan to buy strategic parts of
New Baytown and to turn out the conservative Town Council
and Town Manager once they have consolidated their pur-
chases. They lack only an airport, Baker confesses, and
the only area suitable for it is Taylor Meadow, which is
owned by Danny Taylor, the town drunk and boyhood companion of Ethan Hawley.

Knowing that Danny will misuse money to satisfy his
drinking habits, Ethan visits him under the false pretense
that he wishes to pay for Danny's treatment. Danny sees
through his plan and is willing to accept $1,000 only if he
receives the money in cash and returns no I.O.U. Correctly
gauging that Danny's physical decline is not a good indicator
of his moral health, Ethan incurs a moral debt by promising
to bring the money to Danny's shack. In a strange monologue, Ethan then discusses the family talisman, a translu-
cent stone, and relates a suggestive, Freudian incident in
which his sleep-walking daughter caresses the stone until
she is "like a fulfilled woman."

On Monday morning Morphy confides to Ethan his suspicion that Marullo entered the country illegally. Ethan subsequently times himself in a plan to rob the bank across the
alley. When Marullo enters, Ethan tests Morphy's theory
by suggesting that Marullo make a trip to Sicily. He dodges
the suggestion, then offers Ethan a partnership in the store.
Marullo leaves but returns and excitedly advises Ethan to
accept Biggers' bribe. That evening, Ethan leaves the
promised $1,000 at Danny's shack.

Later, Ethan finds Danny's will against the store door,
together with a note saying, "This is what you want." Then

Ethan anonymously reports Marullo's illegal entry to Immigration officials, one of whom comes to New Baytown later, asking questions about Marullo. As the momentum of the story increases, Baker reveals to Ethan that State officials are investigating corruption among town officials. Later, local officials are subpoenaed by the Grand Jury. On July 2, just as Ethan is to effect his robbery plan, a Department of Justice official brings word that Marullo, who has been arrested, wishes to give his store to Ethan. Ironically, Ethan learns later that Morphy sensed that a robbery was imminent. On the following day Ethan learns that his son has won honorable mention in the "I Love America" contest. Again Ethan dreams of Danny, this time that he is leaving by airplane. Baker comes to the store with the suggestion that Ethan run for Town Manager, but Ethan will not commit himself. He does commit himself to a deal with Mr. Biggers, and shortly afterwards cashes in on his $1,000 investment: Danny has committed suicide. At three that afternoon he confronts a shocked Baker with Danny's will and demands 51% of their partnership, a demand Baker accedes to.

       That night Ethan meets Margie and goes to her home for a drink and whatever other pleasures the night affords. They discuss his metamorphosis and he leaves, disturbed at how much she knows of him. On his way home a representative from the "I Love America" contest greets him with the unsettling news that his son's essay is a montage whose parts were stolen from Henry Clay, Daniel Webster, Jefferson, and others, a fact reported by an anonymous writer. Ethan enters, to find his daughter--the anonymous informer-- beaten by Ethan Jr., who disclaims guilt at the blatant plagiarism, claiming that "everyone does it ... right up to the top. " Thoroughly destroyed, Ethan sneaks razor blades and leaves for his cave retreat. Water-soaked at the "Place," he reflects that his "light is out, " and reaches for the razor blade to cut his wrists, only to discover that he has carried off the family talisman. He then rejects or, at least, postpones suicide, and fights the water, resolving to return the talisman to his daughter so that her light will not go out.

III.   CRITICAL EXPLICATION

       As is often the case with Steinbeck's work, The Winter of Our Discontent has a mixed parentage and a hybrid personality whose social themes operate simultaneously on various complementary levels: the present in New Baytown,

L. I. , New York; 18th Century America; and the last hours
of Christ. Indeed, the Temptation, Betrayal, and Crucifixion give the novel both its pattern and its gallery of characters. It is nothing new for Steinbeck to release modern
characters set in the molds of Biblical prototypes into the
modern wilderness. That is what he did most notably in
The Grapes of Wrath and East of Eden. What is most significant about The Winter of Our Discontent is the loss of
objectivity with which he examined human will and capacity
for good and evil before, and the new and embittered malaise
which informs this novel. For the book is Steinbeck's Vanity
Fair or, even more accurately, his "wasteland," complete
with quester, tempters, prophetess, and even Eliot's wild
deck of cards, the Tarot pack, a fact Donna Gerstenberger
has noted and examined insightfully. [1] The novel casts Steinbeck in his role as social critic, bringing into his sights
whoever worships the "Great God Currency. "[2] He indicts
natives of whatever country, wherever materialism advances
and evil is overlooked or rewarded.

          To effect this morality play in a small primer for
misguided patriots, Steinbeck returns to his favorite font,
the Bible, confining his interests largely to the New Testament while echoing the Old. There he finds models for his
characters, reasoning that "if the laws of thinking are the
laws of things, then morals are relative too, and manner
and sin--that's relative too in a relative universe" (65). In
effect, he asks, "what is truth?" and determines that there
is none. And when Biggers returns to determine how much
he will have to pay to bribe Ethan into selling him the store
account, Ethan says, "I will not sell my master short" (73).
The "metamorphosis, " as Ethan himself calls it, can not be
checked once he has determined that morals are relative,
like the dollar in a free market. It is ironical, then, when
Hawley jests that he has designed an Easter hat, "a simple,
off-the-face crown of thorns in gold with real ruby droplets
on the forehead" (112), and proclaims, like a Judas priest,
that "Christ is risen. All's right with the world" (111).
Thus, Ethan's entry into the cave and subsequent moral decline is the novel's pivot. Joseph Fontenrose perceptively
concludes that "plainly this is another example of myth inversion. It is the betrayer Judas who experiences the passion and resurrection; and he betrays Pontius Pilate....
The gospel story is thus satirically inverted in order to suit
it to the rituals of the true American religion of today, as
Steinbeck sees it, a religion whose churches are business
house and bank. "[3]

What is most surprising about this interesting though
largely unsuccessful modern rendering of Christ's betrayal
is that it is virtually over before the novel is under way.
By the end of the third chapter, the metamorphosis is complete; in Christ, Judas, and Pilate. In an interesting though
unsuccessful experiment in characterization, he makes of his
Ethan Allen Hawley a Christ figure who undergoes a peculiar
metamorphosis or "resurrection" through the Good Friday
weekend, to evolve into Judas, the betrayer. Like Christ,
Hawley first withstands successive temptation of pride, an
appeal made by Mr. Baker, his banker; the flesh, in the
body of Margie Young-Hunt, the novel's prophetess and town
whore; and what might loosely be called the material world,
whose agent is Mr. Biggers, the seller for B. B. D. and D.
Co. , who offers Ethan a bribe. The ethics of the material
world are later given effective voice in the person of Hawley's employer, Mr. Marullo, who declares the Great God
Currency's single dogma: "Business is money. Money is
not friendly. . . . Money is not nice. Money got no friends
but more money" (27). Just as he rejected the previous
three temptations, Ethan repudiates the business ethics of
Mammon. However, once he is alone loosening morals
jingle in his pocket and he moves away from his orthodox
code with surprising speed, embracing in a weekend what a
life had refused. Just prior to his descent into his "cave"
or "Place, " he echoes the words of Christ on the Cross:
"lama sabach thani" (32), but the place is a hellish retreat
where his intellect betrays him by giving him the tools to
rationalize away his imminent evil. After his emergence,
he addresses his flock--the canned fish and other grocery
staples--in un-Christian terms, Ethan is a "new man" with
a changed moral framework code directly the antithesis of
that of a lifetime. From here to the end of the book, the
exceptionally effective eighth chapter aside, the book drifts
for a painfully long time. It is of limited interest to see
Steinbeck's Christ-turned-Judas manipulate others to gain a
tainted fortune. As a consequence of Steinbeck's inability to
fire his work with interest, the book seems longer than it
ought to be, a bloated short story rather than a full-fledged
novel.

      This misjudgment of the work's proper nature is par-
ticularly disappointing because the story has a good deal going for it. Its superficiality belies the various Biblical levels
it operates on. For not only is Hawley a Christ and Judas
figure, but a Prodigal Son and Cain figure, who declares that
"I am my brother's keeper and I have not saved him" (48),

but who qualifies it when pressed publicly: 'I feel I should
be my brother Danny's keeper" (121); yet, he is devising a
plan to betray his spiritual brother even as he says this.
The betrayer motif is the novel's central metaphor, thread-
ing together the betrayal of Christ, of Danny, of Marullo,
of the New Baytown's corrupt city fathers, and even of Ethan
Jr. Steinbeck, unfortunately, is unable to bring this fertile
Biblical subsoil to fruition, or to involve the reader's interest meaningfully, chiefly because the reader has no active
role in unwinding the novel; the work is all done for him, the
conclusions and moral judgments obvious and pre-determined.
Thus The Winter of Our Discontent never becomes a living
indictment, staining the reader's hands. And Ethan, despite
his degeneration, goes from one flat condition (unadulterated
goodness) to another (complete evil), never going through the
internal conflict necessary to infuse him with life and interest. He surrenders too easily, too quickly, for too little.
Ethan says that "a story must have some points of contact
with the reader to make him feel at home in it. Only then
can he accept wonders" (80). This story, while offering obvious points of contact to its readers, does not send a
charge through them. Consequently, we do not accept the
novel's mock-Biblical wonders simply because they are not
wondrous.

Steinbeck's main intention in casting heroic shadows
on a contemporary stage--those of Christ, Shakespeare's
Richard III, and Ethan Allen--is to show us how both the
stage and the actors have diminished in scope and will. The
earth-eclipsing sacrifice of Christ is distorted and parodied
by Ethan's aborted suicide; and looking over his shoulder at
the patriots who risked everything, Ethan can say, "there
were giants on the earth in those days" (81), but the sweep-
ing and boisterous movements of the patriot who lends the
protagonist his name but not his personality are gone. Even
the awful majesty of the evil deeds of Shakespeare's villain,
whose words give the novel its title, are here diluted. In
Steinbeck's view, ours is the era of the mean and dirty little
deed done in silence and with impunity if one is clever.
Ethan thus is more Prufrock than Richard. Musing over the
pettiness of the malefactors around him, he judges that
"their crimes are little crimes and their success is small
success. If the town government and the business complex
of New Baytown were ever deeply investigated it would be
found that a hundred legal and a thousand moral rules were
broken, but they were small violations or petty larceny.
They abolished part of the Decalogue and kept the rest" (104).

What demeans them in his eyes is not so much that they do
evil, but that they are petty. While he commits evil acts
on a larger scale, his hand does not grow to fit the sword;
he remains a little man afraid of the consequences of his
acts, an ineffective example of what happens to men committed to money and material things; they lose themselves in
direct ratio to what they acquire. As Hawley says, "when
a condition or a problem becomes too great, humans have
the protection of not thinking about it. But it goes inward
and minces up with a lot of other things already there and
what comes out is discontent and uneasiness, guilt and a
compulsion to get something--anything--before it is all gone"
(174-175). This novel is a sermon, then, about that discontent and how it festers, but, as Granville Hicks correctly
suggests, "the book is neither convincing as a piece of fiction nor persuasive as a sermon."[4]

There is nothing wrong in a fictionist's use of the
theme of greed and its destructive effects, provided that the
theme works in tandem with the other elements of fiction;
it is this lack which points out the novel's real weaknesses:
faulty handling of point of view; poorly drawn characters; a
flat and ineffective background; an intrusive author; a super-
ficially treated complex of themes. Benjamin DeMott charges
that Steinbeck's "central situation ... never really becomes
a situation because it interests its creator merely as an excuse for chatter about how to be really good."[5] And Warren
French perceptively notes that the distinctive quality of the
parent short story, "How Mr. Hogan Robbed a Bank," is
that "Steinbeck at last achieves the complete objectivity that
his comments about employing a 'non-teleological viewpoint'
indicate that he sought.... His aims are artistic, not social...."[6] In this expanded treatise on the death of American values, however, Steinbeck puts the art after the hearse;
the theme rides the esthetics off into the plains of mediocrity, while Steinbeck the sage displaces the novelist.

While The Winter of Our Discontent is important for
what it reveals of Steinbeck's social vision, his views are
neither new nor penetrating, and the characters who embody
them are never so fully or carefully developed as to serve
as general models either of evil or of good perverted.
French says that the novel is weak primarily because of
"Steinbeck's failure to create sharply defined characters,"[7]
while Granville Hicks feels that "what is wrong with the novel
is simply that it isn't plausible."[8] The truth is that there
are many things wrong with the novel, and perhaps both the

implausibility and the sketchily drawn characters are due to
Steinbeck's subjugation of art to a public goal, to his proxi-
mity to the work.   He is too cautious lest the reader miss
his obvious social criticism.   Consequently, he dilutes his
work for easier consumption, and repeatedly breaks the integrity of the work with editorial laments on the moral condition of America and the world.   The old specter, docile
simplicity, does the work from the beginning.   Only in chapter eight, with its suggestive Freudian overtones, does Steinbeck imply more than he says.   Apart from this chapter,
there is little that has not been better treated by other
American authors.

Probably the only new thing (for Steinbeck) of moderate interest, is Steinbeck's peculiar handling of point of view.
The novel is divided into two major parts, the first containing ten chapters, the second twelve.   The first two chapters
in each part are treated in third person omniscient, the rest
in first person central.   Joseph Conrad works a similar experiment in Lord Jim, whose opening chapters are third person omniscient, the bulk of the work being handled in first
person peripheral. [9]   But in Conrad the transition from one
point of view to the other is deceptively smooth; in Steinbeck's lesser novel the transition bumps against the reader's
sensibility.   Furthermore, as French points out, the "mixed
construction leads both to some tedious repetition and destruction of any consistent identification between Hawley and
the reader. "[10]   Hawley, significantly, never really directly
addresses the reader to strike that identifying chord which
utilizes the chief advantages of first person central point of
view: immediacy, vividness, and self-revelation.   The dis-
embodied Hawley speaks, to whomever, in a kind of vacuum
never filled by the presence of a breathing and feeling narrator.   My own suspicion is that Steinbeck is experimenting
with the interior monologue.   If so, the experiment does not
work.

A last minor but chronic and bothersome shortcoming
in the novel is the protagonist's inclination to refer to his
wife in childlike and silly terms: "little mouse of mouse-
ness, " "Mary Manyflowers, " "pigeon-flake, " "my holy quail, "
"Chloe, " "Helen, " "Cuddles, " "Columbine, " and "my ablative
absolute, " among many others.   We ask, as Mary does,
"why do you call me silly names?   You hardly use my
name" (114).   But the answer is a cliché: "To avoid being
repetitious and tiresome, but in my heart your name rings
like a bell" (114).   Both the nicknames and the response

make for a glucosity of sentiment that would make a diabetic
cringe.

Taken together, the shortcomings listed above amount
to a crippling indictment of the novel. The Winter of Our
Discontent, in all probability, is more properly a short story
than a novel. The effect here is to stretch sparse materials
beyond their limits. Yet, the novel is revealing for what it
tells us both of Steinbeck's dimmed literary vision in the
1960s and for a heightened moral sense which would eventually lead him in a quest for a better America, if not for
better fiction.

Notes

1. See Donna Gerstenberger, "Steinbeck's American Waste-
    land," MFS, 11 (April, 1965), 59-65.

2. John Steinbeck, The Winter of Our Discontent (New York:
    The Viking Press, 1961), p. 150. Hereafter, refer-
    ences to the novel will be incorporated parenthetically
    into the text.

3. John Steinbeck: an Introduction and Interpretation (New
    York: Holt, Rinehart and Winston, Inc., 1963), p.
    135.

4. in Saturday Review, 44 (June 24, 1961), 11.

5. in Hudson Review, 14 (Winter, 1961-62), 622.

6. "Steinbeck's Winter Tale," MFS, 11 (Spring, 1965), 66.

7. Ibid., p. 74.

8. Hicks, Saturday Review, p. 11.

9. This novel, incidentally, also grew from a short story,
    which accounts for its mixed point of view.

10. French, p. 74.

PART IV.   APPARATUS FOR RESEARCH PAPERS

A. Ten Questions for Discussion

1. How does Steinbeck adapt the betrayal, crucifixion and resurrection of Christ to suit his own needs in The Winter of Our Discontent?
2. What other Biblical characters does Steinbeck use besides Christ, Judas, and Pilate?   How does he employ them?
3. Is there a pattern in Ethan's sermons to his "congregation"?   Are there Biblical parallels for them?   Is the Sermon on the Mount one of them?
4. What parallels do you note between this novel and Eliot's The Wasteland?   What tempters and/or prophets or seers do you note?   How does Joey Morphy fit in here?
5. What use does Steinbeck make of dreams in the novel? Explicate the examples you find.
6. What use does Steinbeck make of animals and/or vegetation in this novel?
7. Steinbeck is noted for his vivid handling of context, of "the spirit of place. "   What is noteworthy about his handling of scene or context here?
8. Warren French suggests that there are marked parallels between Ethan Allen Hawley and Salinger's Holden Caulfield.   Support or refute French's thesis.
9. Is Steinbeck experimenting with the interior monologue here?   If so, how does it differ from that of Woolf, Joyce, or Faulkner?   What other technical experiments is Steinbeck working with?
10. Evaluate the novel.   What are its strengths?   Its weaknesses?   Do you agree with the thesis that the novel is a "bloated" short story?   What do you think of the various evaluations of the book cited above?

B.   Suggested Topics for Research Papers

1. The Easter Imagery in Steinbeck's The Winter of Our Discontent.
2. Steinbeck's Use of Richard III in The Winter of Our Discontent.
3. The Sermons in Steinbeck's The Winter of Our Discontent.
4. The Prodigal Son Motif in Steinbeck's The Winter of Our Discontent.
5. The Abel-Cain Motif in Steinbeck's The Winter of Our Discontent.

6. Steinbeck's Animal Tropes in The Winter of Our Discontent.
7. The Women in Steinbeck's The Winter of Our Discontent.
8. The Nymphet Archetype in Steinbeck's The Winter of Our Discontent.
9. The Great Mother Archetype in Steinbeck's The Winter of Our Discontent.
10. The Malignant Female in Steinbeck's The Winter of Our Discontent.
11. The Interior Monologue in Steinbeck's The Winter of Our Discontent.
12. The Light Imagery in Steinbeck's The Winter of Our Discontent.
13. Irony in Steinbeck's The Winter of Our Discontent.

C. Selected Bibliography

DeMott, Benjamin. Review in Hudson River, 14 (Winter, 1961-62), 622. [An unfavorable review of The Winter of Our Discontent, faulting its treatment of "scene" as "completely unrealized" and its dialogue as "embarrassingly out of touch." According to DeMott, the novel is generally weak.]

Fontenrose, Joseph. John Steinbeck: an Introduction and Interpretation. (American Authors and Critics Series.) New York: Holt, Rinehart and Winston, Inc., 1963. [Devotes pp. 132-137 to The Winter of Our Discontent. Professor Fontenrose gives a quick plot summary and builds a good framework for a reading of the novel as a "myth inversion." He agrees with Granville Hicks that Ethan Allen Hawley is not a credible character and that his transformation is improbable.]

French, Warren G. "Steinbeck's Winter Tale," Modern Fiction Studies, 11 (Spring, 1965), 66-74. [An interesting analysis of the novel's departures from its immediate source, "How Mr. Hogan Robbed a Bank." The second and less useful half of the article is a comparative study of Ethan Allen Hawley and Salinger's Holden Caulfield.]

Gerstenberger, Donna. "Steinbeck's American Wasteland," Modern Fiction Studies, 11 (Spring, 1965), 59-65. [An excellent but too-brief analysis of Steinbeck's use of T. S. Eliot's The Wasteland. Professor Gerstenberger provides an additional layer of interpretation with her study.]

The Winter of Our Discontent 257

Hayashi, Tetsumaro, ed. John Steinbeck: a Concise Bibliography. Metuchen, N.J.: The Scarecrow Press, Inc.,
1967, pp. 149-151. [An indispensable bibliography, list-
ing entries from 1930-1965, thirty-eight of which deal
with The Winter of Our Discontent. See also his A New
Steinbeck Bibliography 1929-1971 (Scarecrow Press,
1973).

Hicks, Granville. Review in Saturday Review, 44 (June 24,
1961), 11. [A brief but thorough drubbing of the novel
as a "superficial" work whose central weaknesses are
lightness, slickness, and, mostly, implausibility. I have
listed here only two reviews, which capture the discordant
tenor of the critical reception. Other reviews, mostly
negative, but less convinced of the novel's weaknesses
than Hicks' review, are Orville Prescott's in New York
Times (June 23, 1961), p. 27; Edward Weeks's in Atlantic, 208 (July, 1961), 122; Asher Byrnes' in New Republic, 145 (August 21, 1961), 24; Carlos Baker's in New
York Times Book Review, 7 (June 25, 1961), 3; and J.
N. Hartt's in Yale Review, 52 (Winter, 1962), 305-306.
None of these reviews, however, is of much help in a
scholarly interpretation and evaluation of the novel.]

Chapter 15

STEINBECK ON SCREEN

by Robert E. Morsberger

I. BACKGROUND AND CRITICISM

One test of the vitality of an artist's work is its being translated into other media and passing into popular culture as part of the heritage of his times. By this standard, John Steinbeck is one of the most vigorous and vital American writers. Not only have Tortilla Flat, Of Mice and Men, The Grapes of Wrath, The Red Pony, and Cannery Row become almost legendary in a sense that few other works of fiction have, but from Steinbeck's fiction have come a folk song, "Tom Joad"; a ballet, "Curley's Wife"; an opera, Of Mice and Men; two distinctive musical scores by Aaron Copland; illustrations by Orozco and Thomas Hart Benton; and a round dozen motion pictures plus several notable television productions. In addition, Steinbeck wrote two films, The Forgotten Village and Viva Zapata!, directly for the screen. Of the motion pictures, none are less than competent, and a remarkable number have become film classics, more than from the work of any other American writer.

Steinbeck's films fall into four categories: those he adapted from his fiction, those he wrote especially for the screen, those adapted by others from his fiction, and those based upon unpublished stories.

Steinbeck's first really popular work in all media was Of Mice and Men. With it he began the practice of writing simultaneously a novel and a play which he later repeated with The Moon Is Down, Burning Bright, and Sweet Thursday (which furnished the libretto for the Rodgers and Hammerstein musical, Pipe Dream). Of these, only Of Mice and Men was really successful, but it was one of the most memorable plays of the 1930s and won the New York Drama

258

Critics' Circle Award. It now seems a natural for the movies, but in the late 1930s Hollywood thought its language and
plot were too shocking to be screened. Nevertheless, director Lewis Milestone (celebrated for All Quiet on the Western
Front) and producer Hal Roach (hitherto noted for Laurel and
Hardy comedies) decided to gamble on making a low-budget
production of it for United Artists.

The cast had no big names. None of the stage players were retained; instead of Wallace Ford and Broderick
Crawford, George was played by Burgess Meredith, hitherto
a stage star whose only previous screen credit was as Mio
in Winterset,[1] and Lennie was Lon Chaney, Jr. in his first
starring role. Perhaps his hulking presence as a half-wit
did as much as the example of his father to later trap him
in the rut of monster movies, but he gave a sympathetic
performance of extreme sensitivity that one would not expect
from seeing him subsequently as the Frankenstein monster,
the mummy, or the wolf man. Betty Field replaced the
stage's Claire Luce as Curley's wife, who has no name in
the novel but is called Mae in the film. Curley was Bob
Steele, previously seen only in routine B-class Westerns.
As Crooks, Leigh Whipper had one of the most eloquent and
dignified roles the screen had so far provided for a black
actor. Charles Bickford was a stalwart Slim and Roman
Bohnen a sentimental old Candy.

The film was shot on the Agoura Ranch of William
Randolph Hearst, which was rented for a mere $25 a day.
Completed in 42 days for under $300,000, Of Mice and Men
was "the most economical Grade A movie to come out of
Hollywood in a decade."[2] The musical score was by Aaron
Copland, his first of several movies from books that have
become part of Americana (the others being Our Town, The
Red Pony, and The Heiress), and into it he wove themes
derived from or related to American folk music.

The screenplay by Eugene Solow, approved by Steinbeck, is faithful to the sources but supplements the play
with details taken from the book. Solow deleted some of
Steinbeck's then censorable language, but the virile vernacu-
lar still came through. The great advantage of the film was
its ability to show the farm life, with its combined loneliness
and beauty, and to present the migrants' love of the land
more meaningfully than stage sets could do. Showing the
fields and hills of California, the entire farm and the actual
farm work, the hands' messroom and bunkhouse, the town

cafe, the film succeeded admirably in communicating a sense
of time and place which is not only essential to Steinbeck's
story but preserves for audiences a visual record of the
1930s that is a counterpart to Gregg Toland's photography
for The Grapes of Wrath, which despite its brilliance,
showed very little of actual farm life. Charles Higham and
Joel Greenberg praise the film's "background of economic
misery coupled with rural lyricism, a combination that
brings out some of Milestone's finest qualities: a beautiful
feeling for the farm, the land and its workers ... and an
instinctive sympathy for the pathos, loneliness, and tawdry
pleasures of the itinerant farm hands."[3] Otis Ferguson,
reviewing the film for The New Republic, faulted the book
for seeming to have been written with the stage scenes in
mind and found the movie more fluid, "in many visual qualities more actual and vivid."

     The movie opens with the then novel device of begin-
ning the action before giving the title and credits. We first
see George and Lennie fleeing an armed posse and escaping
by hopping on a passing freight train. We then read the title and credits on the side of passing boxcars. Thus the
theme of fear and flight is immediately established, and the
opening scene balances the ending. Next comes the evening
camping by the bank of the Salinas River. Apparently to
keep women in the audience from being terrified by a mouse,
the film replaces Lennie's dead mouse with a bird, thus losing half the point of the title. Instead of moving immediately
to the bunkhouse, as the play does, the movie shows us
around the farm. To demonstrate his strength, Lennie lifts
a grain wagon with Slim sitting on it and George hanging on
the wheel, a somewhat contrived implausibility perhaps borrowed from Les Miserables, but which also has a folk quality as a feat of strength. As Curley, Bob Steele is small
and vicious, but he wears black leather gloves on both hands,
thus coming across as a dirty boxer rather than an insecure
husband who wears one vaseline-filled glove on his left hand
to keep it soft for his bride. Accordingly, the impact is
blunted when Lennie crushes that hand.

     Nevertheless, the movie Of Mice and Men is a closer
and more complete version of the book than any other film
of a major Steinbeck novel. Brilliant though The Grapes of
Wrath is on screen, it is still more a condensation and synopsis, evading some of the more explicit social and political
details of the book. Of Mice and Men is on a smaller scale,
but it benefits by a tight unity and by a stronger story line,

one that has almost taken on archetypical folk elements in
its embodiment of American loneliness, self-destructive innocence, and the dream of a place of one's own, elements
that are more timeless and universal than the outrages in-
flicted on the Okies. People are still dreaming the same
dreams as George and Lennie and are still being hurt by
them. The scene where Lennie and Curley's wife are talking at cross purposes, without hearing each other, about
two conflicting dreams--one of his own place on the land and
the other of escaping from the land to the excitement of the
city and becoming a movie star--was perhaps the most moving in the film. Lennie's subsequent murder of Mae is less
brutally handled in the film than on stage. Someone working
on the film wanted another person to kill Curley's wife and
have Lennie get the blame. Critics found that throughout the
film, George was more sympathetic, Lennie less feeble-
minded, and Curley's wife more appealing and soulful, but
without being untrue to Steinbeck. "Hollywood for once displays deep respect for a serious writer," wrote Frank Hoellering in The Nation. [4] The New York Times reviewer appreciated "the feeling of seeing another third, or thirtieth of
the nation, not merely a troupe of play-actors living in a
world of make-believe. "[5]

Though the film was an unqualified critical success,
it did poorly at the box office. Though it has become a
critical cliché to accuse Steinbeck of sentimentalism, in
1940, Of Mice and Men was too "grim and uncompromising, "
without enough escapist fare. Advertising was therefore
shifted to emphasize sex, by featuring sensual poses of Betty Field with the captions, "Unwanted, she fought for the
one thing that is every woman's birthright" and "A thrilling
drama of careless love. "[6]

This campaign failed, but the picture finally took its
place among those in demand at classic film festivals.
Though less monumental a film than The Grapes of Wrath,
Of Mice and Men is possibly the most wholly satisfying movie made from Steinbeck's novels. [7]

Early 1940 was a banner season for Steinbeck films.
Almost concurrently with Of Mice and Men came the release
of The Grapes of Wrath, the most controversial of Steinbeck
books and films and his one movie to be acclaimed as an un-
questioned classic. George Bluestone has written a detailed
and thorough comparison of the movie and the book as a
chapter of Novels Into Film, [8] and Warren French has written

an entire book on the history of the movie version, so there
is no need for this ground to be retraced here. The screenplay has been published, [9] so students can make their own
analysis and comparison to the novel.

Considering the furor raised over the book, which
was denounced as obscene and subversive and was burned
by the authorities in several communities, it is remarkable
that the film was made at all, at least with reasonable fidel-
ity to the book. [10] Nevertheless, a novel that won the Pulitzer Prize and was heading the best-seller lists promised
some profits. Yet skeptics predicted that the film could not
be made with any integrity. Militant conservatives in California as a whole and Hollywood in particular denounced the
entire project as an unAmerican lie and threatened bans and
boycotts. On the other hand, when Darryl F. Zanuck bought
the screen rights for 20th Century-Fox in April, 1939, Communists accused him of doing so to keep the book off the
screen, and liberals suggested that Zanuck would either
shelve it to protect the banking and agricultural interests or
would water it down into sentimental soap opera.

Zanuck himself was not crusading. He saw The
Grapes of Wrath (like How Green Was My Valley, which he
made a year later) not as a social document so much as a
family picture but about a family surviving stress. [11] John
Ford, who directed the film, said, "Listen, I'm apolitical
and so is Darryl. Darryl just said, 'I think there's a good
story in it.'"[12] Nevertheless, Zanuck's career is notable
for a number of socially-conscious films, from I Am a Fugitive from a Chain Gang (1932) to Gentleman's Agreement
(1947) and The Snake Pit (1948), and Ford was celebrated
for his dynamic direction of The Informer (1935).

Zanuck paid Steinbeck $75,000 for the screen rights,
after which the author technically had no say about the adaptation. But Zanuck wanted Steinbeck to be involved and consulted with him before having Nunnally Johnson write the
screenplay. Recalling that Steinbeck was "highly suspicious, "
Zanuck says he told the novelist, "We intend to follow the
exact book. But there are certain things we can't show.
We can't show the baby sucking the woman's breast. These
things can never be passed by the Hays office."[13] Apparently a confused Zanuck had in mind Rose of Sharon's offering her breast to the starving old man, for he added, 'I
never have been satisfied with the last scene, when Joad
leaves. I have the feeling I'd like to hear from the old man

and lady. " "I don't know about that, " Steinbeck replied. [14]

In fact Johnson deleted all the novel's sequences after
the episode at the government camp except for the episode
at the Hooper ranch and the death of Casy, which is lifted
bodily and placed before the government camp. Thus, as
Bluestone points out, the film has a more upbeat ending,
without departing from Steinbeck's material. For the most
part, Johnson used Steinbeck's own dialogue; but he skillfully
shuffled passages around, sometimes altering the sequences
and context. Originally the screenplay ended with Tom's
saying farewell to his mother, to become a protest activist,
but Zanuck ultimately had his way in bringing back Ma Joad.
He wrote in a final scene showing the Joads driving away
from the government camp but heading with renewed confidence to look for work. Zanuck himself wrote Ma's concluding speech and is pleased with the fact that some critics
thought it came directly from the 'book. In fact, it para-
phrased two lines from the end of Chapter 20: "They ain't
gonna wipe us out. Why, we're the people--we go on. "[15]
Zanuck's ending has the following dialogue:

> PA: ...we shore takin' a beatin'.
>
> MA: (chuckling) I know. Maybe that makes us
> tough. Rich fellas come up an' they die, an' their
> kids ain't no good, an' they die out. But we keep
> a-comin'. We're the people that live. Can't no-
> body wipe us out. Can't nobody lick us. We'll
> go on forever, Pa. We're the people. [16]

Thus, as Lester Asheim and George Bluestone point
out, "the affirmative ending implies that action is not required since the victims of the situation will automatically
emerge triumphant. "[17] Bluestone further notes how the
screenplay throughout blunts Steinbeck's detailed attacks on
specific oppressors by generalizing the oppression and ex-
empting from blame all legal authorities and business exploiters, leaving only the Hooper ranch managers, irregular
hired deputy-guards, and unidentified vigilantes as villains.

Even so, the film is an infuriating chronicle of man's
inhumanity to man. Zanuck maintained strict security, or-
dering Nunnally Johnson, "I want complete secrecy in reference to The Grapes of Wrath script. Instead of having the
first script mimeographed, as is our usual custom, I want
you to make only three copies--one for yourself and two for

me.   A number of more or less unfriendly newspapermen
are waiting to grab our first script to actually find out what
we have done with this great book. "18   Zanuck anticipated
sufficient opposition that he produced the film under the
counterfeit title Highway 66.   Production went so rapidly
that the New York premiere was held on January 24, 1940,
a mere nine months after the film rights were purchased.

In general, critics were wildly enthusiastic, though
Martin Quigley, the editor of Motion Picture Herald, editor-
ialized in January, 1940 against the film's content and suggested that its facts were false, and the then conservative
Time spoke of "the exaggerations, propaganda and phony
pathos of John Steinbeck's best-selling novel.... Pinkos
who did not bat an eye when the Soviet Government exter-
minated 3,000,000 peasants by famine, will go for a good
cry over the hardships of the Okies. "19   In fact, Zanuck,
before making the movie, had private investigators check
Steinbeck's accuracy.   They found that if anything the author
had understated the appalling conditions of the migrant farm
workers.

The cast was superlative.   Only Henry Fonda was a
star, but he was then noted for his subtle underplaying of
rustic types, and as Tom Joad he gave the most persuasive
performance of his career. 20   The movie was not a star
vehicle but stressed the interaction of the group, who looked
like an authentic family down on their luck but determined
to survive.   As Ma Joad, Jane Darwell won the Academy
Award for best supporting actress.   Fonda was nominated
for best actor but was inexplicably beaten by James Stewart's slicker and far less memorable performance in The
Philadelphia Story.   Likewise, the movie lost the Academy
Award as best picture of the year to Hitchcock's glossy
thriller, Rebecca.   Hollywood was still rewarding more conventional boxoffice hits, and The Grapes of Wrath was too
scruffy for Award ceremonies (though John Ford won the
best director award).   Some years later, it was re-released
with Ford's mediocre Tobacco Road as a double-feature of
poor whites.

Director John Ford later became noted primarily for
making John Wayne Westerns, which seem hardly in keeping
with Steinbeck's social protest unless one sees The Grapes
of Wrath only as a wagons-West romance.   George Bluestone
states that Ford "never lists The Grapes as one of his favorite films" and quotes him as saying, "I never read the

book. "21 But when Peter Bogdanovich asked Ford why he
was attracted to filming the novel, he replied, "I just liked
it, that's all. I'd read the book--it was a good story--and
Darryl Zanuck had a good script on it. The whole thing ap-
pealed to me--being about simple people--and the story was
similar to the famine in Ireland, when they threw the people
off the land and left them wandering the roads to starve.
That may have had something to do with it--part of my Irish
tradition--but I liked the idea of this family going out and
trying to find their way in the world. "22

       The direction by John Ford, music by Alfred Newman
(minimizing orchestral moments and consisting primarily of
"Red River Valley" and other themes in the folk idiom played
on a single accordion by Dan Borzage), and photography by
Gregg Toland (who also filmed Citizen Kane) received universal praise for their stark realism, comparable to that of
Pare Lorentz's great proletarian documentary films of the
1930s. The only complaint was that the children at the
migrant camps did not look hungry enough. (Compare them
to the news photographs in Steinbeck's Their Blood Is
Strong.) Otherwise, the film's greatest asset is its cinema-
tography, its visual record of the Depression--the look of
the dustbowl, the jalopies chugging West, the weedpatch
camps, and the dispossessed families. The film is a movie
equivalent of such books of Depression photographs as You
Have Seen Their Faces and Let Us Now Praise Famous
Men. As such, it is an indispensable supplement to the
novel.

       The Grapes of Wrath was a considerable commercial
success, but Steinbeck avoided going after the big money of
Hollywood. Instead, for his next project he undertook to
write a screenplay for an uncommercial semi-documentary
film about science vs. superstition in a small Mexican
mountain village. He told Herbert Kline, "Zanuck is offering me five thousand a week to write a Hollywood movie,
but I like your offer better, Herb--to write with no pay on
a film I really want to do in Mexico...."23 Critics had
praised the documentary quality of The Grapes of Wrath and
Of Mice and Men; now Steinbeck would provide the real thing.

       To make his movie, Steinbeck teamed up with direc-
tor Herbert Kline and cinematographer Alexander Hackensmid
(now Hammid), who together had filmed the anti-Fascist
documentaries, Crisis and Lights Out in Europe. The original plan was for a documentary about Fascist attempts in

Mexico to overthrow the liberal government of President Cardenas--a sort of Mexican equivalent to Hemingway's The Spanish Earth--with scenes of insurrectionary violence contrasted with ordinary people trying to improve their way of life. Steinbeck mailed Kline a draft for such a story; but by the time he arrived in Mexico, Kline and his assistants, working on the peaceful side of the documentary, had unearthed a great deal of material about the efforts of rural doctors to eradicate disease and superstition among village children. This so intrigued Steinbeck that he made it rather than impending civil war the subject of his script, though he did plan for a while to end with his enlightened protagonists joining the anti-Fascist battle. [24]

After roughing out a new story about the conflict between superstition and medical science, Steinbeck and his associates spent months in Mexico investigating specific details of village life and interviewing doctors of the Mexican Rural Medical Service who had been frustrated by the Indians' fatalism and the hostility of curanderas or herbalist witch doctors. From this research, Steinbeck fashioned his final screenplay. He explained that he had written "a very elastic story," which was actually a question, the answers to which he got when "the crew moved into the village, made friends, talked, and listened."[25] The script is not a conventional scenario with dialogue, for the filmmakers planned to use illiterate Indians who knew no English and in some cases spoke only Aztec. Accordingly, Steinbeck's screenplay is entirely narrated, while the native cast perform the events being described.

At first, it was difficult to obtain a willing cast. Naturally suspicious of outsiders and of non-Indians, the villagers thought that the cameras were surveying instruments and that the filmmakers were going to steal their land. Wealthy landowners resented the peasants' being paid fair wages and campaigned to drive the filmmakers out, stoning their cars and defaming their motives; but the local priest and a peasant who had the sense to realize that the wages were real persuaded the villagers to cooperate. But since Kline could not find one family that corresponded to Steinbeck's characters, he tried to cast members from various families, only to find that the literal-minded peasants thought that this involved adultery and immorality. Finally, Kline recruited principal performers from other less primitive villages where the Indians had some exposure to city ways and brought them in to make friends with the peasants of the forgotten village, who then agreed to enact the rest of the roles. Most fortunately, the local curandadera agreed to play herself and offered advice on village folklore. [26]

The completed film shows both Steinbeck's sympathy for the ignorant villagers and his commitment to improving their way of life through science. His protagonist, a village boy named Juan Diego, is driven away after he brings in a rural medical team to fight a cholera epidemic by disinfecting poisoned wells and providing innoculations. The superstitious Indians would rather have their children die and go to heaven than be innoculated, but Juan Diego carries his afflicted sister to the doctors and has her treated. At the end, he goes to the city to study medicine and eventually returns to bring enlightenment to his people.

As a study of superstitious peasant life in Mexico, The Forgotten Village can be related to The Pearl; but it has far more authenticity, for though the villagers were enacting Steinbeck's story, it was their story as well; and the documentary details of village life were filmed as they happened. In addition, Steinbeck's experience with reactionary landowners, his introduction to progressive President Cardenas, and his original plan for a film about civil war between Fascists and liberals helped lay the groundwork for Viva Zapata! a decade later.

The Forgotten Village, brilliantly photographed and eloquently narrated by Burgess Meredith (from Of Mice and Men), received superlative reviews but was never widely distributed because the major studios then controlled the theatres through block booking. It played only in the circuit of small independent art theatres. In 1947, it won first prize as the Best Feature Documentary at the Brussels World Film Festival, and it is on the Brandon list of "Ten Best" American documentaries. (A 16 mm. print is available for distribution from Tom Brandon in New York.) But Steinbeck's and Kline's favorite review came from a Mexican villager who said some years later, "Jefe, the children do not die here anymore."

The next Steinbeck film moved from peasants to paisanos. Tortilla Flat would seem a difficult book to adapt to the screen on at least two counts. On the one hand, it is virtually plotless and consists of a series of rambling episodes connected only loosely if at all. On the second hand, its amiable amorality would be unlikely to pass the Hays

Office's censorship. Steinbeck's paisanos utterly reject the
American success dream; the antithesis of Benjamin Franklin, the heroes of Horatio Alger, and the Protestant work
ethic still extolled by Richard Nixon, the paisanos spend
their time boozing and wenching, happy if they have just
enough money for a gallon of wine.

In 1938, Jack Kirkland, who dramatized the immense-
ly successful Tobacco Road, adapted Tortilla Flat for the
stage, but his efforts were a failure. Paramount bought the
screen rights for the ridiculously low figure of $4000, of
which Steinbeck's agent got ten percent. At the time, Steinbeck thought his share was a fortune. Apparently so did
Paramount, for several years later it fired its editor for
spending studio money on so hopeless a project. The former
editor then repurchased the film rights and sold them to
MGM for $90,000. Steinbeck meanwhile had second thoughts
and tried without success to buy back the book for $10,000
to keep it from being filmed. [27] He wrote to his friend Beth
Ingels the prediction that MGM's version would have no resemblance to his novel. [28] Certainly it seemed an unlikely
project for the studio that produced the Andy Hardy and
Lassie series.

The screenplay by John Lee Mahin and Benjamin Glazer does take considerable liberty with the book, yet salvages
more than one might expect. In search of a plot, the
scenarists extracted the episode of Danny's temporary romance with Sweets Ramirez and made it the backbone of the
film. In the novel, Danny is a paisano veteran of World
War I who returns home to find that he has inherited two
houses from his grandfather. After a series of picaresque
adventures, his new standing as a well-to-do bachelor (by
the impoverished standards of Tortilla Flat) causes Dolores
(Sweets) Ramirez to dream "of being his lady." This does
not mean his wife; she and Danny are both cheerfully promis-
cuous. Sweets is hardly a virginal ingenue: "She was not
pretty, this lean-faced paisana, but there was in her figure
a certain voluptuousness of movement ... ordinarily her
voice was shrill, her face hard and sharp as a hatchet, her
figure lumpy and her intentions selfish. "[29] She seduces
Danny for a chapter, at the end of which his friends free
him from her. The movie turns this less than idyllic episode into an uplifting romance, with Hedy Lamarr (hardly
hatchet-faced and lumpy) as Sweets and John Garfield as a
clean-cut Danny. Pilon, Pablo, and Danny's other friends
then plot to keep him from marrying Sweets. The novel ends

with Danny's death after a spectacular orgy; in the film, he
is hurt in an accident, and Pilon then becomes "heavily religious. " Danny gets a job (unthinkable in the novel) to prepare for marriage, and the film ends with his nuptials to
Sweets. With Pilon reformed and Danny a responsible husband, even Louis B. Mayer was satisfied. So were most of
the critics, though Bosley Crowther made a few digs at the
rejection of a workaday world.

The screenplay made no attempt to retain the archaic
pronouns and verbs ("Thou hast brandy? ") by which Steinbeck
tried to convey the flavor of Spanish as Hemingway later did
in For Whom the Bell Tolls. Instead, the performers relied
on pseudo-Spanish accented English, though if they were actually speaking Spanish they would have no discernible accent.
The accents themselves were a confused mixture. Spencer
Tracy played Pilon with the same accent he had used as
Manuel the Portuguese fisherman in Captains Courageous. He
gave a likeable performance but was not very convincing as
a paisano. John Garfield played Danny with his usual tough-
guy New York speech. Akim Tamiroff had his customary
thick Slavic accent as Pablo, Hedy Lamarr spoke with a
lingering Hungarian flavor, and Frank Morgan as the Pirate
had hardly any accent at all.

Nevertheless, it was Morgan who stole the show, by
unanimous critical acclaim. The episode, in which the Pirate
gives a gold candle to St. Francis, is followed to church by
his dogs, who break into the service, and then takes his
dogs to the forest to tell them of the saint, who appears to
the dogs in a vision, was retained intact and proved to be
the most charming episode in the film.

As for the conversion of Pilon, Philip T. Hartung
found the film sentimental and condescending on religious
matters, Manny Farber objected to an inserted religiosity,
and Bosley Crowther complained that "a certain exaggerated
piety has crept into the latter part of this film. "[30] Otherwise, the movie was well received. Reviewers liked the
performances and the direction by Victor Fleming, whose
earlier films include Captains Courageous, The Wizard of
Oz, and Gone with the Wind. Time found the film "human
and appealing"; The New Yorker considered it charming;
Newsweek admired its atmosphere and character and thought
the screenplay provided more continuity than the book while
retaining "a reasonable facsimile of the Steinbeck flavor";
and Commonweal called it "an intelligent, charming film" in

which the script "retains the warmth and style of the original." Finally, Bosley Crowther praised its "solid humor and compassion" and called it "a winning motion picture and a deterrent to respectable enterprise."

When The Moon Is Down was published in 1942, James Thurber reviewed it for The New Republic and faulted it for sentimentality and naiveté in its portrayal of the Nazi occupiers of Norway as lonely, homesick men who would be destroyed by the superior morale of the unconquerable people. Following Thurber's lead, other critics and readers denounced Steinbeck as being "soft" on Nazism; our official propaganda was that the Wehrmacht consisted only of monsters, and Steinbeck had dared suggest that some German troopers were human beings. Even so, it should have been evident that the book is anything but pro-Nazi; its thesis is that a free people will resist oppression at any price, and by the end of the narrative the Norwegians have risen to drive out their conquerors. Far from abetting the enemy, Steinbeck wrote the book partly as the result of a conference with Colonel William J. Donovan of OSS on means of supporting resistance movements in European nations occupied by the Axis powers. 31

Even though some superpatriots labeled Steinbeck a Fascist (three years before, they had labeled him a Communist), the novel sold nearly 1,000,000 copies in its first year. 32 The dramatic version, written at the same time, fared less well; it ran only nine weeks in New York. Even so, 20th Century-Fox paid an unprecedented $300,000 for the film rights. 33 Clearly, Steinbeck's stock had gone up since he received $4000 for Tortilla Flat and $75,000 for The Grapes of Wrath. The book was the most expensive aspect of the movie production. To economize thereafter, Fox used no big-name actors and simply redressed the sets for the Welsh mining village of John Ford's How Green Was My Valley and used them for Norway.

Nunnally Johnson, who had done such a notable job with The Grapes of Wrath, wrote the scenario and also produced the film. When Johnson asked Steinbeck for suggestions, the latter replied, "Tamper with it." In fact, Johnson was faithful to the original in plot and dialogue, using much of Steinbeck's language verbatim. His main contribution was to open up the action and to dramatize episodes that are only offstage in the novel and play. The movie shows the initial Nazi invasion, the storm troopers massacring a handful of

Norwegian soldiers, the details of German brutality and growing Norwegian fury. (As in The Grapes of Wrath and later
in Viva Zapata!, it is the spontaneous anger of the oppressed
that turns resentment into resistance.) Thus Time's reviewer found the Nazis much harsher in the film and the story
consequently more effective as it used "the sharp language
of action rather than introspective comment" to "describe
the villagers' growing hatred and resistance, the Nazis'
growing fear."[34] Steinbeck himself, congratulating Johnson
for the adaptation after he saw the film, acknowledged,
"There is no question that pictures are a better medium for
this story than the stage ever was. It was impossible to
bring the whole countryside and the feeling of it onto the
stage, with the result that the audience saw only one side of
the picture."[35]

     Accordingly, The Moon Is Down is a particularly ap-
propriate work to analyze for the differences in media.
Steinbeck conceived of it simultaneously as a novel and a
play; as a result, the novel seems too contrived, limited to
sets and scenes that can be translated to the stage with no
difficulty. Both versions are in print and can be compared
in detail. Though the screenplay has not been published, it
might be a rewarding exercise to consider the problems and
opportunities of adaptation. Often critics complain that movies spoil a stage play by violating its unities and inserting a
meaningless variety of locales; but in the case of The Moon
Is Down, the limits of the stage seem to have handicapped
the novel, while the film overcame these obstacles, winning
more critical acclaim than the other versions.

     With controversy over the book still fresh, reviewers
were primed to see whether the film made the Nazis in any
way sympathetic. Bosley Crowther was gratified to find that
Nunnally Johnson "has carefully corrected the most censur-
able features of the work" by making Colonel Lanser "a
cold and ruthless tyrant ... he has wrung out such traces of
defeatism as were apparent in the book and has sharpened
with vivid incidents the horror of being enslaved."[36] (Actually the book's resistance thesis is a rejection of defeatism.)
According to Crowther, Sir Cedric Hardwicke turned Lanser
into a cold, contemptuous intellectual. Newsweek's reviewer
praised the "cold, impersonal intelligence" that Hardwicke
gave Lanser and stated that he much preferred the casting
of Hardwicke and Henry Travers in the film to that of Otto
Kruger and Ralph Morgan on stage as Lanser and Mayor
Orden.[37] Yet the scenario is faithful to Steinbeck's

characterization of the Nazi commander; calling Hardwicke's
performance "magnificent," Philip T. Hartung describes the
film's Lanser as "a wise, experienced officer who learned
in the last war not only how a conquered people behaves but
also the futility of expecting a complete vanquishment."
Above all, the film retained Steinbeck's psychology; and while
Time's reviewer found this questionable and "an extraordinar-
ily naive view of the facts of Nazi life,"[38] Hermine Rich
Isaacs wrote in Theatre Arts that Johnson's adaptation was
"faithful to the author's almost revolutionary concept of the
Nazis as credible human beings, invested with intelligence as
well as sheer brute strength and subject to the fallibility of
mortals. They have a three-dimensional quality that stands
out in bold relief against the usual run of Nazi villain, Hollywood style....   In Lanser's sense of the futility of the
Nazi brutalities is the most convincing promise of their
eventual nemesis."[39]

        Two other films on the Norwegian resistance move-
ment were released at the same time as The Moon Is Down;
Columbia's The Commandos Strike at Dawn, with Paul Muni,
and Warners' The Edge of Darkness, starring Errol Flynn
and Walter Huston, directed by Lewis Milestone. All three
had a favorable reception, but critics were unanimous in
preferring the low budget The Moon Is Down, saying that even
the lack of star performers was an asset because the unfamiliar faces aided the film's realism. Irving Pichel's direction received universal acclaim. Above all, The Moon Is
Down stood out from the usual war films of violent adventure
as "essentially a conflict of ideas."[40] Bosley Crowther found
it too Socratic and dispassionately intellectual yet concluded
that it is the "most persuasive philosophical indictment of the
'new order' that the screen is ever likely to contain."[41] If
it had more words than action, Hermine Isaacs found its
words great; "the speeches that rang out most gloriously
from the pages of the novel sound a clarion call once more
upon the screen, ... eloquent reminders that in talking pictures there is a seat up near the throne for talk that is
worth hearing."[42] Apparently, in the movies The Moon Is
Down found the proper medium for its message.

        Steinbeck's next World War II film revived the contro-
versy over The Moon Is Down. Alfred Hitchcock seems an
unlikely director for Steinbeck; but in 1944, 20th Century-
Fox released a movie billed as "Alfred Hitchcock's Production of Lifeboat by John Steinbeck." The actual scenario is
by Jo Swerling, who had written a number of Gary Cooper

films for Samuel Goldwyn, such as Pride of the Yankees.
Since Steinbeck's original story is unpublished, it is impossible to determine which details were contributed by Steinbeck, Swerling, and Hitchcock. Hitchcock's own comments
do not clarify the matter much; he recalls, "I had assigned
John Steinbeck to the screenplay, but his treatment was incomplete and so I brought in MacKinlay Kantor, who worked
on it for two weeks. I didn't care for what he had written
at all ... and hired another writer, Jo Swerling, who had
worked on several films for Frank Capra. When the screenplay was completed and I was ready to shoot, I discovered
that the narrative was rather shapeless. So I went over it
again, trying to give a dramatic form to each of the sequences. "43

The dialogue and some of the characterizations are
not recognizably Steinbeck's, but the structure and philosophy
of the film resemble some of his other work. Essentially,
Lifeboat is an allegory of the war, with the democratic nations drifting aimlessly at sea. As in The Wayward Bus,
Steinbeck isolates a representative group of characters and
then lets them interact. In this case, we have the survivors
of a freighter, sunk by a German U-boat, plus the comman-
dant of the U-boat itself, which was also destroyed in the
encounter, adrift together in the ship's launch. Except for
the ending, when an Allied destroyer sinks a German supply
ship, all the action is confined claustrophobically to the lifeboat, which provides Steinbeck with a microcosm and Hitchcock with the opportunity for some ingenious directing.

The characters consist of Connie Porter (Tallulah
Bankhead), a wealthy and arrogant reporter; Kovac the oiler
(John Hodiak), an embittered member of the proletariat whom
Connie calls a fellow traveler; Rittenhouse (Henry Hull), a
conservative millionaire; Gus (William Bendix), a seaman
with an injured leg; Joe or Charcoal (Canada Lee), a Negro
steward; a British radio operator (Hume Cronyn); an American Red Cross nurse; an English woman with her dead baby;
and the Nazi (Walter Slezak).

The controversy came over the characterization of the
representatives of democracy vs. the Nazi. The former are
for the most part confused and ineffectual, whereas the Nazi
shows such supreme resourcefulness that he almost becomes
their captain. He keeps the boat from capsizing, takes over
navigation, amputates Gus's gangrenous leg, rows when the
others are too weak, keeps their morale up with his wit and

unfailing good spirits, and shows such self-confidence that
the other survivors often look to him for leadership. As a
result, the old charges that Steinbeck was soft on Nazis or
even pro-Nazi were resurrected. Before, he was accused
of making the Nazis too weak; now he was charged with making them too strong. Hostile critics objected that the Nazi
is the most admirable character in the film, which promotes
the myth of the Aryan superman; and Dorothy Thompson
gave Lifeboat "ten days to get out of town. "[44] What she
proposed to do after that deadline, she did not say, and in
fact the movie had a long and successful run in New York.

      Steinbeck, of course, was not pro-Nazi, nor was
Hitchcock. In fact, the Nazi is treacherous from the start,
and his good humor is invariably sinister. He steers the
boat towards a German supply ship; and when Gus, whose
life he had saved by the amputation, discovers this ruse, he
throws Gus overboard to drown. Learning of his treachery,
the others turn on the Nazi in savage fury and beat him to
death. This virtual lynching recalls Steinbeck's story "The
Vigilante" and scenes of mob violence from In Dubious Battle.
Aside from it, the democratic survivors are not only presented sympathetically, but they grow in humanity. Mrs.
Porter comes off her high horse and has a romance with
Kovac; the millionaire learns to respect the oiler and to do
his share of seamanship; the radio operator and the nurse
fall in love. Yet though they learn a bit of teamwork
("There's a hunger in men to work together, " wrote Steinbeck
in In Dubious Battle), they are often quarrelsome and confused. In terms of Steinbeck's allegory, Hitchcock explained
that the film intended to show that "while the democracies
were completely disorganized, all of the Germans were
clearly headed in the same direction. So here was a statement telling the democracies to put their differences aside
temporarily and to gather their forces to concentrate on the
common enemy, whose strength was precisely derived from
a spirit of unity and of determination. "[45] According to
Manny Farber, "The film's design is to show how this
Nazi ..., by taking advantage of the others' humanity, sense
of fair play, divided aims and general physical and mental
debility, gains control, " but "This intended parallel of the
way the Nazis came into power ... is never essentially convincing. "[46]

      Critical reception was quite divided. Time's review-
er, calling Lifeboat "remarkably intelligent" and "one of the
most ambitious films in years, " thought that it paralleled

e. e. cummings'

> King Christ this world is all aleak;
> and life preservers there are none ...

and that it was "an adroit allegory of world shipwreck."[47]
Newsweek and the New York Times found it exciting and
provocative. Other critics complained that there was not
enough grim realism of men against the sea. James Agee
judged that "As allegory, the film is nicely knit, extensively
shaded and detailed, and often fascinating. But the allegory
itself is always too carefully slide-ruled, and the basic idea
is artificial."[48] Except for insufficient shipwrecked realism,
Hitchcock's direction was a tour-de-force; and Tallulah Bankhead (in her first film in 11 years) and William Bendix gave
the best screen performances of their careers.

Lifeboat is significant for Steinbeck studies in its use
of allegory (recalling The Grapes of Wrath, The Wayward
Bus, East of Eden) and in its treatment of recurring Steinbeck themes: the nature of leadership, group man, the ani-
mality of man hypnotized by mass action, and the stripping
away of civilized surfaces to reveal the essential person.
Unfortunately, the finished product that Swerling and Hitchcock provided is more slick than substantial, more a nautical
Stagecoach than a serious study of survival, war, Nazism,
communism, capitalism, or anything else. James Agee
claims it could have been "a great and terrifying film,"[49]
but it is mainly an ingenious entertainment.

Steinbeck's third and last World War II movie takes
place on the home front. A Medal for Benny is based upon
an unpublished story by Steinbeck and Jack Wagner. The
screenplay that Frank Butler made from it has been published, however, as one of ten Best Film Plays, 1945,
edited by John Gassner and Dudley Nichols. It is recognizable Steinbeck material, cut from the same cloth as Tortilla
Flat. Its protagonists are ne'er-do-well paisanos from a
small California town, but the time is now 1942, and the nation is at war. Benny, the title character, is never seen
in the film, for he has been run out of town as an undesirable character after a brawl with the police. Nevertheless,
like Danny and Pilon in Tortilla Flat, Benny is muy hombre
with an overdose of charisma. Just as Danny becomes a
god at the end of the novel, Benny has become a legend for
his roistering, prowess, pranks, and amours. Despite his
absence, his presence is felt throughout the film. However,

it becomes increasingly clear that Benny is (as Time's reviewer put it) "a five-star heel. "

He has left behind a sweetheart, Lolita Sierra (Dorothy Lamour), who has been faithful to him more from a
sense of duty than of affection. She is meanwhile wooed by
an amiable scamp, Joe Morales (Arturo De Cordova), who
considers himself twice as good a man as Benny any day.
Lolita is clearly drawn to Joe but feels it her patriotic duty
to remain Benny's girl because he is now in the Army. Joe
perseveres in a comic courtship, a mixture of combat and
romance, until he breaks down Lolita's barriers and wins the
love that she reluctantly felt for him all along. Their happiness is interrupted by the news that Benny has been killed
in action and is to be awarded posthumously the Congressional Medal of Honor for his heroism in killing 100 Japanese. Unaware of Lolita's real feelings, the community ex-
pects her to undergo an emotional suttee; even the radio
broadcasts that the memory of Benny will be enshrined forever in Lolita's heart.

Meanwhile, the mayor and chamber of commerce have
gone wild with the publicity that Benny's belated fame has
given the town. They try to use Lolita and Benny's shiftless
father Charley (J. Carrol Naish) as part of their scheme to
exploit the awarding of the medal for all the profit it is
worth. Here, the screenplay gets in some sharp satire on
wartime profiteering and on the chamber of commerce mentality. At first the city officials don't realize that Benny
Martin is really named Martini and that he is a Chicano from
the wrong side of town. When they do, they then move Charley Martini from his shack (he thinks they are going to evict
him for nonpayment of rent) into a new house, just long
enough to make a good impression when a general and other
celebrities come to award the Congressional Medal. But
when Charley realizes what is going on, he walks out in disgust and returns home, so that the medal is awarded among
the cackling chickens, unwashed children, and disheveled surroundings of the barrio. For most of the film, Charley has
been a comic character, but he now takes on dignity as he
maintains that a hero can come from any kind of background
and not only the middle class.

At the end, Joe Morales joins the Army and leaves
for the war, but it is now made public that Lolita is his girl
and will be waiting when he returns.

A Medal for Benny is not a great film, but it was
rated as one of the ten best of the year. Irving Pichel, who
directed The Moon Is Down, did another fine job with Benny;
and Dorothy Lamour and J. Carrol Naish received the best
notices of their careers. Naish was nominated for the
Academy Award as best supporting actor. Philip T. Hartung
called the film a "lovely little job,"[50] and Bosley Crowther
wrote that "Particular credit is here given to Mr. Steinbeck
because the spirit of the work is so richly consistent with
the spirit of all his 'paisano' yarns."[51] In fact, A Medal
for Benny comes closer than the movie version of Tortilla
Flat to the real flavor of that novel.

Appearing first as a magazine story, The Pearl was
published in book form to coincide with the release of the
movie version. Steinbeck's tale of a poor Mexican fisherman
who finds a fabulous pearl of great price only to learn that
it brings corruption to his community, disaster to his family, and death to his son, attempts with considerable success
to convey the quality of a legend and of a medieval exemplar
set among simple folk in modern times. It is unlikely material for Hollywood. In fact the movie version that RKO
released in 1948 was actually a Mexican production, filmed
in Mexico with Mexican performers acting in English, under
the direction of Emilio Fernandez. As the first Mexican
movie to be widely shown in the United States, it is something of a landmark. As a film on its own terms, it has
considerable interest.

The screenplay is a collaboration by Steinbeck, director Emilio Fernandez, and Jack Wagner, who was co-author
of the original story of A Medal for Benny. It follows Steinbeck's novella in basic plot but alters some significant elements. Charles R. Metzger has made a detailed comparison
of the film and the book.[52] To summarize, Metzger notes
that the priest and Kino's older brother Juan Tomás are left
out, the great work knife or machete with which Kino defends
himself is omitted, and an elaborate fiesta plus a drinking
sequence are inserted. The flight is prolonged and is shifted
from the high mountains to a mangrove swamp and finally to
foothills behind the seacoast, perhaps because of more available locations. Metzger concludes that these alternations
weaken Steinbeck's symbolism and dilute his themes. In addition, he complains that the protagonists are too attractive,
well-dressed, and movie-starish for a peasant fisherman and
his wife, that the villagers in general are dressed in well-
laundered peasant uniforms rather than realistic rags, and

that the fiesta is too professionally choreographed. The
Pearl lacks the grubby realism of The Forgotten Village.
Professor Metzger's critique should be read in full for a
perceptive analysis of both book and film. Despite his reservations, he finds that the film salvages much of Steinbeck's
message of corruption, survival and hope.

Heading the cast as the only box-office name was
Pedro Armendariz, who had portrayed the relentless lieuten-
ant in The Fugitive, John Ford's version of Graham Greene's
The Power and the Glory; his later Hollywood films include
John Wayne's Three Godfathers and The Conqueror (with
Wayne as Genghis Khan). His Kino has a virile presence
but is perhaps too prone to a simple-minded stare.

The great virtue of The Pearl is its exceptionally fine
photography, opening with shots of mountains, the curve of
shoreline, sea and surf, and beautifully composed frames of
robed women and white-clad men; proceeding to good underwater scenes of pearl-diving, and culminating in a battle on
the beach. Much of the book translated beautifully into visual images. John McCarten praised the photography of the
Pacific coast of Mexico and thought the players were ar-
ranged like Orozco murals.

However, Time's reviewer found the photography too
romantic, the dialogue pseudo-Biblical, and the conflict between good and evil too simple. [53] Robert Hatch objected to
false primitivism, pretentiousness, and performances "at a
level just above the aborigine." He felt that The Pearl
lacked the feel of legend and that its language was "a lab-
ored pidgin that bears no relation to colloquial, not to mention domestic, speech in any language."[54] This is debatable;
the Mexicans accepted both the story and its language. Bosley Crowther, more impressed, called The Pearl "a stern,
bitter, brutal and fatalistic dramatization of a tragic folk
tale, bleak in its ultimate conclusions about the enslavement
of underprivileged man. And although it is richly rewarding,
pictorially and dramatically ... it is likely to leave the emotions exhausted and depressed."[55]

The Pearl can be related to The Forgotten Village and
to Viva Zapata!, Steinbeck's other films of Mexico: to the
former in its portrayal of Mexican peasant life and of superstition; to the latter in its condemnation of the unjustly
wealthy and of man's inhumanity to man. The final sequences
also recall the story "Flight." At first, the film seems

Marxist, like The Treasure of the Sierra Madre, but it is
more medieval, like "The Pardoner's Tale" with its theology
of retribution. Of course, Steinbeck was not a Marxist but
sometimes a primitivist, yet it is noteworthy that Marxist
ideology is often set against a primitive Catholic country.

In the 1940s, Hollywood had considerable success with
movies pairing a child with an animal--My Friend Flicka,
National Velvet, the Lassie series, and most recently The
Yearling. It therefore seemed natural to follow these hits
with a movie of The Red Pony. However, The Red Pony is
handicapped by the lack of a strong narrative line; it consists
of four loosely related short stories, only two of which involve a pony. The episodes focus on the boy Jody Tiflin
and his painful growth into an awareness of suffering, death,
the problems of adulthood, and the conflict between generations. Despite some lyric passages of farm life and un-
spoiled nature, the stories are essentially grim, with a relentless biological and psychological realism that is far from
conventional Hollywood romance. It would take considerable
skill to turn The Red Pony into a box-office success.

Nevertheless, Republic studios decided to try. Now
defunct, Republic had been a B-class studio noted mainly for
second-rate Westerns, though it occasionally stretched its
low budgets to try and turn out a prestige film, usually starring John Wayne. The Red Pony was to be its prestige film
for 1949. Steinbeck himself wrote the screenplay, the only
time he had a sole hand in adapting one of his works. To
do so, he combined "The Gift," "The Leader of the People,"
and part of "The Promise," with a happier ending. The result was a leisurely, casual, and rambling story that some
critics and audiences found tedious. Probably because the
boy in The Yearling, filmed just three years before, is also
named Jody, Steinbeck changed Jody Tiflin's name to Tom.
For no accountable reason, he changed the parents' names
from Carl and Ruth Tiflin to Fred and Alice.

The production reunited the team of director Lewis
Milestone and composer Aaron Copland, who had worked together on Of Mice and Men. Myrna Loy, somewhat too sophisticated, played the mother; a dour Shepperd Strudwick,
the father; and a somewhat hammy Louis Calhern, the grandfather. Reviewers gave the best notices to Robert Mitchum
as Billy Buck; Mitchum looked too young, lean, and sleepy-
eyed for Steinbeck's grizzled and thickset stablehand, but he
was properly laconic and relaxed in the role. As the boy,
Peter Miles got mixed reviews.

The movie as a whole made no great mark. It had
good location filming in color but lacked excitement except
for one scene of violent horror when the boy fights and kills
a vulture perched on his dead pony. Bosley Crowther found
the picture moody and depressing. [56] Robert Hatch considered it maudlin, and Time found the book's harsh realities
muted. [57] But Philip T. Hartung praised the portrait of family relationships and thought the story of Peter's growing
maturity "fascinatingly told," and Newsweek admired both
Steinbeck's screenplay and the film's "honest tenderness."[58]
In the long run, the movie has been pretty well forgotten;
its most durable contribution is a fine score by Aaron Copland that compares favorably with his Rodeo and Billy the
Kid as a vigorous musical rendition of Western Americana;
it is frequently heard as a self-contained concert piece.

A new movie of The Red Pony has now been made for
television, starring Henry Fonda and Maureen O'Hara; it was
broadcast in the spring of 1973.

Steinbeck seemed to have particularly good relations
with 20th Century-Fox; five of his films were made at that
studio. Therefore, when Fox decided to follow the success
of several British film anthologies of stories by Somerset
Maugham (Quartet, Trio, Encore) by giving a similar treatment to O. Henry, it asked Steinbeck to stand in for the late
author and introduce his work. Released in 1952, O. Henry's Full House consisted of five stories, each made by a
different director: "The Cop and the Anthem," "The Last
Leaf," "The Clarion Call," "The Gift of the Magi," and "The
Ransom of Red Chief." In his only screen performance,
Steinbeck opened the film by talking about O. Henry and his
work, then took down a volume of stories and began reading
from "The Cop and the Anthem," which the performers
(Charles Laughton and Marilyn Monroe) then took over. The
subsequent stories were linked by Steinbeck's transitional
narration.

The film was only a moderate success, and Steinbeck
himself received generally bad notices. According to Newsweek, "John Steinbeck acts as a shaggy, wry-necked master
of ceremonies";[59] and Bosley Crowther found it "a little unfortunate that John Steinbeck, with a painfully gravel-coated
voice, has been asked to stand in for the dead author and
introduce the tales."[60] The Christian Century noted Steinbeck's "ineffective commentary," and Library Journal claimed
his diction was "terrible."[61] Possibly Steinbeck was not to

blame; for according to The Nation, Steinbeck had "an unctu-
ous bass voice dubbed in by Ward Bond."[62] No other source
mentions any dubbing. At any rate, in his debut as perform-
er, Steinbeck was no Charles Dickens or Mark Twain.

In the same year, Fox released the only film for
which Steinbeck wrote a complete original screenplay with
conventionally spoken dialogue. Steinbeck's initial plan for
the Mexican documentary that became The Forgotten Village
was a study of insurrection and of civil war between reactionary and progressive forces. Now in Viva Zapata! he
turned back to the Mexican revolution to give this theme a
full historical treatment. I have elsewhere analyzed Zapata!
at length[63] and shall give only a brief account of it here.
Deriving his material only slightly from Edgcumb Pinchon's
Zapata, the Unconquerable, Steinbeck presented in the screenplay his final statement about the nature of leadership, land
reform, and revolution. Thus while Viva Zapata! is a significant and exciting film in its own right, it can be provoca-
tively cross-related to In Dubious Battle, Their Blood Is
Strong, The Grapes of Wrath, The Forgotten Village, The
Moon Is Down, and The Pearl.

In the film, Zapata does not seek leadership and indeed tries at times to avoid it. But as he encounters a
series of outrages perpetrated under the dictator Porfirio
Diaz, he cannot help becoming actively involved in opposition
that is at first spontaneous but quickly takes on the form of
revolution. Zapata is not a dialectician nor a conscious revolutionary but the spokesman for a peasantry that can toler-
ate no more oppression. Because of his eloquence in speech
and effectiveness in action, he has leadership thrust upon
him and finds himself in command of a revolutionary army.
After Diaz is defeated and replaced by the well-meaning but
ineffectual liberal Madero, Zapata hopes to return home; but
Madero is murdered by counterrevolutionary forces under
General Huerta, and Zapata finds himself embattled once
more against the new tyrant. The revolution is repeatedly
betrayed by cynical or fanatical politicians exploiting the
people for their own ambition or ideology. Even Zapata
finds that power inevitably corrupts. After the defeat of
Huerta, he has a chance to be President; but when he almost initiates a purge against new dissidents, he suddenly
realizes with a shock that he has started upon the path of
dictatorship, and in revulsion he relinquishes power and returns to the people. Like Mayor Orden in The Moon Is
Down, Zapata insists that the people do not need a strong

man to lead them, that there's no genuine leader but themselves: "A strong man makes a weak people. Strong people don't need a strong man."

    The professional revolutionary devoted to power at all
costs is represented by Fernando, one of Zapata's support-
ers who eventually betrays him to his death by the forces of
Carranza and Obregon. Whereas Zapata is an unlettered
man of the people whose wife begins teaching him to read
on their wedding night, Fernando is a detached intellectual,
a loveless, fanatical ideologue who insists that there must be
more killing and that any opposition to a revolutionary regime
must be ruthlessly purged. The contrast between Fernando
and Zapata parallels the distinction in Albert Camus's The
Rebel between the rebel as a creative nonconformist dedicated to freedom for everyone and the revolutionary as an
enslaving liberator for whom ideas are more important than
individuals and who justifies terror and tyranny in the name
of utopia. Fernando is like Mac in In Dubious Battle, who
manipulates the strikers not for their sake (he hopes many
of them will be killed) but for the sake of an ultimate Communist victory, whereas Zapata is closer to Tom Joad.

    Viva Zapata! was dynamically directed on location by
Elia Kazan. As Zapata, Marlon Brando received an Academy
Award nomination for best actor of 1952, and Anthony Quinn
won the best supporting actor award as Zapata's roistering
brother Euphemio. Critical opinion was divided; some reviewers faulted the film for clichés, but most praised it as
a subtle and eloquent study of revolution and the nature of
power.

    In 1955, Steinbeck and Elia Kazan teamed up again,
this time for a movie version of East of Eden. The screenplay is by playwright Paul Osborn, whose work included
Mornings at Seven and adaptations for the stage of A Bell
for Adano and Point of No Return. Finding Steinbeck's
sprawling novel too unwieldy for a normal length film, Osborn used only the final section, the conflict between teenage
Cal and Aron Trask for the affection of their father Adam
and of Aron's girl Abra. The film opens at approximately
Chapter 37 in Part Four of the novel. Even so, Osborn
omits many details from Steinbeck's remaining 170 pages;
Lee, the Chinese philosopher servant, is missing, and the
plotting at Kate's brothel is deleted. Instead, Osborn adds
a good many episodes involving the three young people, flesh-
ing out the film to two and a half hours' running time.

In some ways, Osborn strengthens the final section of
the novel. Steinbeck's Cal, though a Cain figure, is not
really very diabolical; we are told of his vaguely wicked
ways, but he basically comes through as a well-meaning and
clean-cut lad. Though he is said to suffer from a sense of
rejection, he generally has his father's affection as well as
the loyalty of Lee and the friendship of Abra. Abra, he insists, is his brother's girl, and Cal makes no attempt to
take her from Aron, though he does end up with her. In the
film, Cal is much more moody and violent, an embittered
young man whose actions are often self-destructive, and who
attempts from the first to steal Abra from his insipid brother. Osborn makes the relationship of Cal to Abra and Aron
a bit like that of Heathcliff to Cathy and Linton in Wuthering
Heights. Abra, though played by the delicate Julie Harris,
is a tantalizing flirt in the film rather than the noble, vi-
brant young girl in the novel. As played by James Dean,
the film's Cal is an intense if somewhat inarticulate romantic
who has a number of passionate scenes with Abra. Aron,
played by Richard Davalos, is comparatively colorless, but
he is not planning to become a celibate priest. In the novel
Abra finally turns from Aron because of his program of celi-
bacy and his impossibly high-minded standards of goodness.
In the film, Abra is swept away by the more aggressive and
magnetic character of Cal.

Osborn's script never explains the degenerate background of Kate, the boys' evil mother, nor does she commit
suicide after encountering Aron; she merely appears as the
black-shrouded madam of a brothel. (Even so, Jo Van Fleet
won the Academy Award as the best supporting actress in the
role.) On the other hand, Osborn makes the father (Raymond Massey) into a coldly aloof patriarch, much less kindly
and sympathetic than Steinbeck's Adam Trask. By a brilliant
stroke, Osborn moves Adam's financial ruin with refrigerated
lettuce from the beginning to near the end of the final sequence, so that it is more climactic and makes Cal's efforts
to salvage his father's fortune more dramatic. In the novel,
Cal borrows from Lee the $5000 he invests in beans; in the
film, he borrows it from his mother. Cal's bean-farming
is off-stage in the book, but the film evokes a lot of lyric
and emotional intensity from Cal's eager husbandry, so that
when he gives the rejected gift to his father, the disappointment is much harsher and more traumatic. In the novel,
the occasion of Cal's gift is his brother's homecoming from
college; but in the movie Aron does not go away, and the
gift is a birthday present to the father. Aron's present in

the film is the announcement of his engagement to Abra (thus doubly frustrating Cal). In the book, Aron gives no present at all. Thus Osborn develops an emotional climax far more shattering than Steinbeck's. When his gift is rejected in the novel, Cal runs out of the room choking wordlessly; in the film, James Dean delivers an eloquently tortured speech about rejected love that makes a scene of memorable power.

This is what made the movie into a cult film with the young. Despite mixed reviews, East of Eden became a touchstone for rebellious and frustrated young people in the 1950s and started the legend of James Dean. Elia Kazan had wanted Brando as Cal; but when the star was unavailable, Kazan recruited a young unknown, James Dean, whose only previous work had been some supporting roles on stage. Dean's nervous, mumbling, Actors Studio method irritated many reviewers, who called him a shambling imitation of Brando, but he projected his own sympathetic image as a very vulnerable, sensitive, misunderstood youth with whom many young viewers profoundly identified. A second Dean film, Rebel without a Cause, capitalized on this image. Before his third film, Giant, was released, Dean was killed in the wreck of his sports car, in September, 1955.

At this point, a brief legend took over. Many of Dean's bereaved fans refused to believe that he was dead; others developed a morbid necrophilia over him that surpassed the hysteria over the death of Valentino. A year after Dean's death, the studios still received over 7000 fan letters a month addressed to him. Entire issues of fan magazines were devoted to him. Exploiters vended model heads of Dean in stone, bronze, and plastic Miracleflesh, while spiritualists put heartbroken fans in touch with Dean's spirit. To his admirers, Dean symbolized temperamental, rejected, misunderstood youth; one fan wrote that "To us teenagers, Dean was a symbol of the fight to make a niche for yourselves in the world of adults."64 Boys admired his rebelliousness, and girls wanted to comfort him like a stray pet. The adulation of Dean became so emblematic that John Dos Passos included a capsule biography of him in Midcentury, where his petulant rebelliousness and the sloppy emotionalism of his fans is contrasted to the stoic discipline of General Dean in Korea. Thus the movie of Steinbeck's book indirectly generated a key chapter of Dos Passos' novel.

On its own terms, the film records the Steinbeck country around Salinas in splendid color photography. The

main theme from Victor Young's musical score became a
popular jukebox tune for several years.   Fumbling or not,
Dean's performance was profoundly moving.   Gerald D. Mc-
Donald called East of Eden "one of the best films of this or
any other year; a film which gives deeply disturbing insight
into what psychologists call the feeling of rejection."[65]   In
its dramatization of the generation gap, the movie may have
had more impact than Steinbeck's novel.

The last Hollywood film to be made from a Steinbeck
book is The Wayward Bus, released in 1957.   The year before, 20th Century-Fox had a hit with Bus Stop, featuring
Marilyn Monroe in her first respectable dramatic role.   Perhaps Fox could repeat the success with another bumpy bus
ride, this time starring Jayne Mansfield.   The role of Camille in Steinbeck's novel might do for Miss Mansfield what
Bus Stop had done for Miss Monroe.

William Saroyan did a first script for The Wayward
Bus, keeping closely to the book, but for some reason his
scenario was rejected and replaced by a rather cliché-ridden
one by Ivan Moffat, that streamlined Steinbeck's story and
removed some subtleties from his characters.   The novel's
bus driver, Juan Chicoy, is "perhaps fifty years old";[66] in
the film, he is a twentyish romantic lead played by Rick
Jason.   The novel's Ernest Horton is a little man with a
"tight, hairy moustache"; the film has him played by tall
Dan Dailey with a clean-shaven wide grin.   Steinbeck's mid-
dle-aged Alice Chicoy "was wide-hipped and sag-chested and
she walked well back on her heels.   She was not in the least
jealous of the calendar girls and the Coca-Cola girls.   She
had never seen anyone like them...."[67] In the film she is
played by sexy pin-up Joan Collins.   The Pritchards are
pretty faithful to the book.   But Bosley Crowther complained
that "The script, done by Ivan Moffat, is a snarl of paltry
and patchy plots in which the characters switch horses, psychologically, almost as often as they pile on and off the
bus."[68]   Time called the film a "wild ride down a California
cutoff from Tobacco Road."[69]

Steinbeck's story was oversimplified in the film, which
spent more time on the spectacle of floods, landslides, and
bridges being washed away than on complexities of character.
His religious symbolism was completely jettisoned, and his
ambiguous open ending was tidied up by the film's having a
repentent Alice Chicoy meet her husband at the end of the
line and Ernest Horton propose marriage to Camille,

promising her a stove that plays "Tenderly" when the steak
is done. Steinbeck's Camille is an intelligent girl with a
gift for sharp dialogue and the ability to see through people.
Jayne Mansfield's Camille is more the stereotyped dumb
blonde.

Within the limitations of the script, the cast did well;
and critics and audiences found the film sufficiently lively
and entertaining. However, when Philip T. Hartung of Commonweal said in his review that Steinbeck's novel "overloaded
his assembled group with problems and clichés, "[70] Paula
Haigh replied that Hartung had not adequately noted differences between the film and the book. She pointed out that
his indiscriminately charging the novel with the same alleged
faults as the adaptation is misleading and does not give Steinbeck a fair hearing. Her insistence that a film critic should
not pass judgment on a movie's literary source unless he also examines it on its own terms, with a full awareness of
differences in story, character, media, and narrative technique shows the approach that should be applied to any adaptation from one artistic medium to another.

A final film from Steinbeck's fiction is unknown to the
public at large. In the 1960s, novelist and bull-fight expert
Barnaby Conrad (Matador) got Steinbeck's permission to
adapt and film "Flight, " a short story from The Long Valley.
Conrad did his own scenario and production, on a minimum
budget raised from contributors he persuaded to invest in the
project, along with a considerable investment of his own (in
his words, "every cent in the world that I owned then and
now! "). [71] Using unknown local performers, Conrad filmed
the story in the mountains east of Monterey. The results
are uneven. The director was Louis Bispo, then about 28
years old, who had had television experience but had never
made a film. Conrad says, "I think he did well considering
I would write the screenplay in the morning for the scenes
we were going to shoot that afternoon! " Some of the photography is murky, and it is sometimes apparent that the production is an amateur one. On the other hand, its lack of
studio slickness provides a compensating believability. There
is an excellent musical score by guitarist Laurindo Almeida.

Conrad's main mistake was to stretch the short story
out into a feature-length film that could be shown as a main
attraction in theatres instead of making a short picture like
the prize-winning "An Occurrence at Owl Creek Bridge. " He
himself states, "The whole trouble with the picture is that it

should have been a short film--about the length of The Red
Balloon, 45 minutes. When we sunk so much of other people's money in it we had a responsibility to try to get it
back for them. Everyone assured us greenhorns that a film
under 80 minutes wouldn't make any money.... " So Conrad
expanded the story to an 83-minute feature. To do so, he
spun out the events leading to the killing at fumbling and
tedious length. Once the pursuit began, the film picked up
considerably, but the tension of Pepé's desperate flight was
interrupted by an interpolated episode of an eccentric old
man and his daughter in a mountain cabin. This sequence
was interesting in itself but digressed from Steinbeck's
straight narrative line. Steinbeck himself said, "That guy
that plays the old man deserves an Oscar. " He was Ed
Smith, only 40 years old; but instead of winning an award,
he was "beaten to death in Santa Rita Prison a few years
ago after being picked up on some vague charge. "

        Conrad also added scenes and dialogue for the pursu-
ers. The story, however, confines itself to Pepé once the
flight begins. The tension is heightened by the fact that he
does not know who the pursuers are or how close they are
behind him; he never sees the men who track and kill him.
The movie therefore loses the economy and unity of Steinbeck's story. Its virtues are an almost documentary quality
as though we are not watching fiction but an actual event
take place.

        Conrad's investment did not pay off. The film has
rarely been shown, though it was the official American entry
at the Edinburgh Film Festival. It got excellent reviews
there and in London but was panned at San Francisco. In
February, 1971, it was featured at San Jose State University's
Steinbeck film festival. It deserves a wider circulation.
Steinbeck liked the film and suggested that Conrad add a
narration written and spoken by him, and such a sequence
was filmed in Monterey and added to open the movie. In the
fall of 1972, Conrad decided to cut the picture the way he
wanted it, regardless of feature distribution. It now runs
45 minutes and is considerably better, according to Conrad,
who writes that he is tempted to cut 18 more minutes, "(the
entire blind girl-old man business, which I dreamed up simply because how long can you ask an audience to watch a kid
run up and down a mountain?)--to get it down not only short-
er but truer to Steinbeck's story.... " Currently, there is
no distributor for the film, which is available only from
Barnaby Conrad himself, at 8132 Puesta Del Sol, Carpinteria,

California 93013.

      Steinbeck's contribution to motion pictures is signifi-
cant both for his own work and for the history of films.
For a long time, literary critics tended to look down upon
most movies as a subliterary genre, and some complained
of Steinbeck's fiction that it seemed to be written with the
movies in mind. More positively, one can assert that some
of his passages of descriptive narration reveal the sharp,
objective detail of the camera eye. Now that motion pictures are being recognized as a vital art form and that popular culture is being granted some legitimacy, Steinbeck's
best films as well as his fiction can be seen as having entered into the American heritage.

Notes

1.   James Cagney, Spencer Tracy, and John Garfield had
       all wanted the role.

2.   Life, 8 (January 8, 1940), 42.

3.   Charles Higham and Joel Greenberg, Hollywood in the
       Forties (New York: Paperback Library, 1970), p.
       78.

4.   Frank Hoellering, "Review of Of Mice and Men," Na-
       tion, 150 (January 20, 1940), 80.

5.   H. T. S., "Review of Of Mice and Men," New York
       Times, February 27, 1940, p. 9:2.

6.   William K. Everson, The Films of Hal Roach (Green-
       wich, Connecticut: Museum of Modern Art, New
       York, 1971), pp. 75, 77.

7.   A 1968 television film of Of Mice and Men, starring
       George Segal and Nicol Williamson as George and
       Lennie had interesting but somewhat self-conscious
       performances and lacked the authenticity of the
       original.

8.   George Bluestone, Novels into Film (Baltimore: Johns
       Hopkins Press, 1957; Berkeley and Los Angeles:
       University of California Press, 1966).

9. John Gassner and Dudley Nichols, eds., Twenty Best
    Film Plays (New York: Crown, 1943).

10. In the 1930s, movie versions of An American Tragedy,
    Babbitt, Miss Lonelyhearts, and Sanctuary were
    quite emasculated in their translation to the screen,
    and even in the late 1950s The Sound and the Fury
    and a remake of Sanctuary were distorted almost
    beyond recognition.

11. Mel Gussow, Don't Say Yes Until I Finish Talking: A
    Biography of Darryl F. Zanuck (Garden City, N.Y.:
    Doubleday, 1971), p. 95.

12. Ibid., p. 90.

13. Gussow, pp. 90-91.

14. Ibid., p. 91.

15. Steinbeck, The Grapes of Wrath (New York: Viking,
    1939), p. 383.

16. Twenty Best Film Plays, p. 377.

17. Bluestone, p. 167.

18. Gussow, p. 90.

19. Time, 35 (February 12, 1940), 70.

20. Fonda became associated with Steinbeck projects. In
    the 1960s, the author requested Fonda as narrator
    for Walt DeFaria's television productions of Travels
    with Charley and America and Americans, and Fonda
    spoke the eulogy at Steinbeck's funeral.

21. Bluestone, p. 169.

22. Peter Bogdanovich, John Ford (Berkeley: University of
    California Press, 1968), p. 76.

23. Herbert Kline, "On John Steinbeck," Steinbeck Quarter-
    ly, 4, (Summer, 1971), 82-3.

24. Ibid., pp. 82, 84, 86.

25. Steinbeck, The Forgotten Village (New York: Viking, 1941), p. 5.

26. Herbert Kline, "The Forgotten Village, An Account of Film Making in Mexico," Theatre Arts, 25 (May, 1941), 337-41.

27. Time, 39 (May 18, 1942), 84.

28. John H. Bunzel, "Welcoming Address: Steinbeck Country," Steinbeck Quarterly, 4 (Summer, 1971), 72.

29. Steinbeck, Tortilla Flat (New York: Modern Library, 1937), pp. 153-4.

30. Philip T. Hartung, "Review of Tortilla Flat," Commonweal, 36 (June 12, 1942), 182; Manny Farber, "Review of Tortilla Flat," New Republic, 106 (June 1, 1942), 766; Bosley Crowther, "Review of Tortilla Flat," New York Times, May 27, 1942, p. 27:1.

31. Lewis Gannett, "John Steinbeck's Way of Writing," Steinbeck and His Critics, ed. E. W. Tedlock, Jr. and C. V. Wicker (Albuquerque: University of New Mexico Press, 1957), p. 35.

32. Time, 41 (April 5, 1943), 54.

33. Ibid., 39 (May 18, 1942), 84.

34. Ibid., 41 (April 5, 1943), 54.

35. "Brighter Moon," Newsweek, 21 (April 5, 1943), 86.

36. Bosley Crowther, "Review of The Moon Is Down," New York Times, March 27, 1943, p. 8:6.

37. "Brighter Moon," p. 86.

38. Time, 41 (April 5, 1943), 54.

39. Hermine Rich Isaacs, "The Films in Review," Theatre Arts, 27 (May, 1943), 289-90.

40. Ibid., p. 289.

41. Crowther, "Review of The Moon Is Down," p. 8.

42. Isaacs, p. 289.

43. François Truffaut, Hitchcock, with the collaboration of Helen G. Scott (New York: Simon and Schuster, 1967), p. 113.

44. David Lardner, "The Current Cinema," New Yorker, 19 (February 4, 1944), 65.

45. Truffaut, p. 113.

46. Manny Farber, "Among the Missing: Hitchcock," New Republic, 110 (January 24, 1944), 116.

47. Time, 43 (January 31, 1944), 94.

48. James Agee, "Films," Nation, 158 (January 22, 1944), 108.

49. Ibid.

50. Philip T. Hartung, "Review of A Medal for Benny," Commonweal, 42 (May 18, 1945), 119.

51. Bosley Crowther, "Review of A Medal for Benny," New York Times, May 24, 1945, p. 15:2.

52. Charles R. Metzger, "The Film Version of Steinbeck's The Pearl," Steinbeck Quarterly, 4 (Summer, 1971), 88-92.

53. Time, 51 (March 1, 1948), 84.

54. Robert Hatch, "Review of The Pearl," New Republic, 118 (March 1, 1948), 25.

55. Bosley Crowther, "Review of The Pearl," New York Times, February 18, 1948, p. 36:4.

56. Bosley Crowther, "Review of The Red Pony," New York Times, March 9, 1949, p. 33:2.

57. Robert Hatch, "Review of The Red Pony," New Republic, 120 (March 21, 1949), 30; Time, 53 (March 28, 1949), 96.

58. Philip T. Hartung, "Review of The Red Pony,"

Commonweal, 49 (April 1, 1949), 611; Newsweek, 33 (March 21, 1949), 89.

59. Newsweek, 40 (October 6, 1952), 111.

60. Bosley Crowther, "Review of O. Henry's Full House," New York Times, October 17, 1952, p. 33:1.

61. Christian Century, 69 (November 26, 1952), 1391; Library Journal, 77 (November 15, 1952), 1981.

62. Nation, 175 (November 22, 1952), 475.

63. Robert E. Morsberger, "Steinbeck's Zapata: Rebel Versus Revolutionary," Steinbeck: The Man and His Work, ed. Richard Astro and Tetsumaro Hayashi (Corvallis: Oregon State University Press, 1971), pp. 43-63.

64. Margaret Moran, "Letter to the Editors," Life, 41 (October 15, 1956), 19.

65. Gerald D. McDonald, "Review of East of Eden," Library Journal, 80 (March 1, 1955), 555.

66. Steinbeck, The Wayward Bus (New York: Viking, 1947), p. 6.

67. Ibid., pp. 5-6.

68. Bosley Crowther, "Review of The Wayward Bus," New York Times, June 6, 1957, p. 35:2.

69. Time, 69 (June 17, 1957), 99.

70. Philip T. Hartung, "Review of The Wayward Bus," Commonweal, 66 (June 21, 1957), 66.

71. Letter from Barnaby Conrad to Robert E. Morsberger, May 7, 1973. All subsequent quotes are from this letter.

II.   TEN QUESTIONS FOR DISCUSSION

1. How do criteria differ for judging film and fiction?
2. What are the problems in adapting various Steinbeck

Steinbeck on Screen 293

works to the screen?

3. How do the movie versions of Steinbeck's fiction differ from the sources? What has been cut, added, or altered?
4. Are differences between film and book justifiable?
5. What are the assets of movie versions of Steinbeck's fiction?
6. What are the limitations and liabilities?
7. How do works that Steinbeck wrote for the screen relate to and illuminate his other works?
8. How do Steinbeck's novels compare in stage and screen versions?
9. How do films translate descriptive passages into visual images?
10. How much does the casting of a film version affect the reader's image of a book's characters? Does Tom Joad look like Henry Fonda? What if the casting is inappropriate?

III. STEINBECK FILMS

Here is a complete list of films written by John Steinbeck for the screen or adapted by Steinbeck and others from his fiction. It also includes one film narrated by Steinbeck. The films are listed in chronological order, with the major credits.

Of Mice and Men
Screenplay by Eugene Solow, adapted from the John Steinbeck play. Directed and produced by Lewis Milestone. Musical score by Aaron Copland. A Hal Roach presentation. United Artists, 1940.

George ... Burgess Meredith	Candy ... Roman Bohnen
Lennie ... Lon Chaney, Jr.	Whit ... Noah Beery, Jr.
Mae ... Betty Field	Jackson ... Oscar O'Shea
Slim ... Charles Bickford	Carlson ... Granville Bates
Curley ... Bob Steele	Crooks ... Leigh Whipper

The Grapes of Wrath
Screenplay by Nunnally Johnson. Musical score by Alfred Newman. Directed by John Ford. Photography by Gregg Toland. Produced by Darryl F. Zanuck. 20th Century-Fox, 1940.

Tom Joad ... Henry Fonda   Al ... O. Z. Whitehead
Ma Joad ... Jane Darwell   Muley ... John Qualen
Casy ... John Carradine   Noah ... Frank Sully
Grampa ... Charley Grapewin   Uncle John ... Frank Darien
Rosasharn ... Dorris Bowdon   Winfield ... Darryl Hickman
Pa Joad ... Russell Simpson   Ruth Joad ... Shirley Mills

The Forgotten Village
        Story and screenplay by John Steinbeck. Music by
Hanns Eisler. Photography by Alexander Hackensmid. Narrated by Burgess Meredith. Produced and directed by Herbert Kline. An Arthur Mayer--Joseph Burstyn release,
1941.

Tortilla Flat
        Screenplay by John Lee Mahin and Benjamin Glazer.
Directed by Victor Fleming. Produced by Sam Zimbalist.
MGM, 1942.

Pilon ... Spencer Tracy   The Pirate ... Frank
                                                 Morgan
Danny ... John Garfield   Pablo ... Akim Tamiroff
Dolores (Sweets) Ramirez ... Hedy Lamarr

The Moon Is Down
        Screenplay by Nunnally Johnson. Directed by Irving
Pichel. Produced by Nunnally Johnson. 20th Century-Fox,
1943.

Colonel Lanser ... Sir Cedric   Madame Orden ... Margaret
                Hardwicke   Wycherly
Mayor Orden ... Henry Travers   Lt. Tonder ... Peter Van
                                                 Eyck
Dr. Winter ... Lee J. Cobb   Peder ... Irving Pichel
Molly Morden ... Dorris   George Corell ... E. J.
                Bowdon   Ballantine

Lifeboat
        Screenplay by Jo Swerling from a story by John Stein-
beck. Directed by Alfred Hitchcock. Produced by Kenneth
Macgowan. 20th Century-Fox, 1944.

Connie Porter ... Tallulah   Rittenhouse ... Henry Hull
                Bankhead

Gus ... William Bendix   Kovac ... John Hodiak
The German ... Walter Slezak   Stanley Garrett ... Hume
                                                    Cronyn
Alice Mackenzie ... Mary   Joe ... Canada Lee
                    Anderson

A Medal for Benny

Screenplay by Frank Butler from a story by John
Steinbeck and Jack Wagner. Directed by Irving Pichel.
Produced by Paul Jones. Paramount, 1945.

Lolita Sierra ... Dorothy   Charley Martini ... J.
                 Lamour   Carrol Naish
Joe Morales ... Arturo De   Raphael Catalina ... Mikhail
               Cordova   Rasummy

The Pearl

Screenplay by John Steinbeck, Emilio Fernandez, and
Jack Wagner. Directed by Emilio Fernandez. Produced by
Oscar Danugers. RKO, 1948.

Kino ... Pedro Armendariz
Juana ... Maria Elena Marques

The Red Pony

Screenplay by John Steinbeck. Music by Aaron Copland. Directed and produced by Lewis Milestone. Republic,
1949.

Alice Tiflin ... Myrna Loy   Tom [Jody] ... Peter Miles
Billy Buck ... Robert Mitchum   Teacher ... Margaret
                                              Hamilton
Grandfather ... Louis Calhern   Beau ... Beau Bridges
Fred Tiflin ... Shepperd Strudwick

A new version of The Red Pony, starring Henry Fonda and
Maureen O'Hara, was televised by NBC on March 18, 1973.

Viva Zapata!

Screenplay by John Steinbeck. Directed by Elia Kazan. Produced by Darryl F. Zanuck. 20th Century-Fox,
1952.

Emiliano Zapata ... Marlon   Pancho Villa ... Alan Reed
                    Brando
Josefa ... Jean Peters   Madero ... Harold Gordon
Eufemio ... Anthony Quinn   Pablo ... Lou Gilbert
Fernando ... Joseph Wiseman   Senora Espejo ... Mildred
                                                    Dunnock
Don Nacio ... Arnold Moss   Huerta ... Frank Silvera
Soldadera ... Margo

O. Henry's Full House, based on five stories: "The Cop and
the Anthem, " "The Clarion Call, " "The Last Leaf, " "The
Gift of the Magi, " "The Ransom of Red Chief. " Narrated
by John Steinbeck.   20th Century-Fox, 1952.

East of Eden
        Screenplay by Paul Osborn.   Music by Victor Young.
Directed by Elia Kazan.   Warners, 1955.

Abra ... Julie Harris   Sam ... Burl Ives
Cal Trask ... James Dean   Will ... Albert Dekker
Adam Trask ... Raymond   Ann ... Lois Smith
              Massey
Aron Trask ... Richard Davalos   Kate ... Jo Van Fleet

The Wayward Bus
        Screenplay by Ivan Moffat.   Directed by Victor Vicas.
Produced by Charles Brackett.   20th Century-Fox, 1957.

Johnny Chicoy ... Rick Jason   Mildred Pritchard ...
                                            Dolores Michaels
Alice Chicoy ... Joan Collins   Prichard ... Larry Keating
Camille ... Jayne Mansfield   Morse ... Robert Bray
Ernest Horton ... Dan Dailey   Mrs. Pritchard ... Kathryn
Norma ... Betty Lou Keim   Givney

Flight
        Screenplay by Barnaby Conrad.   Music written and
played by Laurindo Almeida.   Directed by Louis Bispo.
Produced by Barnaby Conrad.

IV. SELECTED BIBLIOGRAPHY

Bluestone, George. Novels into Film. Baltimore: Johns
    Hopkins Press, 1957; Berkeley and Los Angeles: Univer-
    sity of California Press, 1966. Includes a detailed study
    of the film version of The Grapes of Wrath.

Bogdanovich, Peter. John Ford. Berkeley: University of
    California Press, 1968. Contains a discussion with the
    director about the film of The Grapes of Wrath.

Bunzel, John H. "Welcoming Address" to Steinbeck Country:
    a Conference and Film Festival, Steinbeck Quarterly, 4
    (Summer, 1971), 69-73. Discusses Steinbeck films in
    general and quotes Steinbeck letters about the filming of
    his work.

Conrad, Barnaby. Fun While It Lasted. New York: Ran-
    dom House, 1969. Contains an account of filming Flight.

Everson, William K. The Films of Hal Roach. Greenwich,
    Connecticut: Museum of Modern Art, New York, 1971.
    Discusses the filming of Of Mice and Men.

French, Warren. Filmguide to The Grapes of Wrath.
    Bloomington: Indiana University Press, 1973.

Gassner, John and Dudley Nichols, eds. Best Film Plays,
    1945. New York: Crown, 1947. Contains Frank Butler's
    screenplay of A Medal for Benny.

_____. Twenty Best Film Plays. New York: Crown,
    1943. Contains Nunnally Johnson's screenplay of The
    Grapes of Wrath.

Gussow, Mel. Don't Say Yes Until I Finish Talking: A
    Biography of Darryl F. Zanuck. Garden City, New York:
    Doubleday, 1971. Discusses the 20th Century-Fox produc-
    tion of The Grapes of Wrath.

Kline, Herbert. "'The Forgotten Village, An Account of
    Film Making in Mexico,'" Theatre Arts, 25 (May, 1941),
    336-43.

_____. "On John Steinbeck," Steinbeck Quarterly, 4 (Sum-
    mer, 1971), 80-88. Recollections of filming The Forgot-
    ten Village, by the director.

Metzger, Charles R. "The Film Version of Steinbeck's The
Pearl," Steinbeck Quarterly, 4 (Summer, 1971), 88-92.

Morsberger, Robert E. "Steinbeck's Zapata: Rebel Versus
Revolutionary," Steinbeck: The Man and His Work, ed.
Richard Astro and Tetsumaro Hayashi. Corvallis: Oregon State University Press, 1971, pp. 43-63. A detailed
analysis of Viva Zapata! and its relationship to Steinbeck's
other work.

Steinbeck, John. The Forgotten Village. New York: Viking, 1941. The published text of the screenplay.

Truffaut, François. Hitchcock, with the Collaboration of
Helen C. Scott. New York: Simon and Schuster, 1967.
Includes a discussion of Lifeboat.

CONTRIBUTORS

ASTRO, RICHARD: Associate Professor of English, Oregon State University; Chairman, Editorial Board of the Steinbeck Quarterly (1972-73); co-editor with Tetsumaro Hayashi of Steinbeck: The Man and His Work (1971); Director of the Steinbeck Conference at Oregon State University, 1970; author of From Chaos to Cosmos: Edward F. Ricketts and the Fiction of John Steinbeck (1963).

BENTON, ROBERT M.: Associate Professor of English, Central Washington State College; published in such journals as American Literature, Early American Literature and Steinbeck Quarterly as well as in a book, Steinbeck: The Man and His Work.

COURT, FRANKLIN E.: Assistant Professor of English, Northern Illinois University; published in such journals as English Literature in Transition, Modern Fiction Studies and Steinbeck Quarterly.

COX, MARTHA HEASLEY: Director of the Steinbeck Research Center and Professor of English, California State University at San Jose, California; Director of the Steinbeck Conference and Film Festival, California State University at San Jose, 1971; Visiting Associate Editor of the Steinbeck Quarterly (Summer 1971); author of numerous books and articles.

DEMOTT, ROBERT: Assistant Professor of English, Ohio University; member of the Editorial Board of the Steinbeck Quarterly; published on Steinbeck, Thoreau, Ezra Pound, Robinson Jeffers, and others.

FRENCH, WARREN: Chairman and Professor of English, Indiana University-Purdue University at Indianapolis; President of the John Steinbeck Society of America; Senior Editorial Advisor of the Steinbeck Quarterly; author/editor of numerous books including John Steinbeck (1971), A Companion to The Grapes of Wrath (1963), and A Film Guide to The Grapes of Wrath (1973).

299

GARCIA, RELOY: Professor of English, Creighton University; Chairman of the Editorial Board of the Steinbeck Quarterly (1973-74); author/editor of numerous books and a monograph entitled Steinbeck and D. H. Lawrence: Fictive Voices and the Ethical Imperative (1972); published in such journals as D. H. Lawrence Review and Steinbeck Quarterly.

HAYASHI, TETSUMARO: Associate Professor of English, Ball State University; founder and Director of the John Steinbeck Society; founder and Editor-in-Chief of the Steinbeck Quarterly and General Editor of the Steinbeck Monograph Series; Honorary Life Academician of the Communications Guild (Great Britain); Honorary Judge of the Steinbeck Essay Contest to be held in Great Britain, 1974; author/editor of nine books including John Steinbeck: A Concise Bibliography (1967), Steinbeck: The Man and His Work with Richard Astro, and Steinbeck's Literary Dimension (1973), and such monographs as John Steinbeck: A Guide to the Doctoral Dissertations (1971), and The Special Steinbeck Collection of the Ball State University Library with Donald L. Siefker (1972); International Rotary Junior Fellow, 1954-55; Folger Senior Fellow, Summer, 1972; Director of the Steinbeck Society Meeting at the MLA in Chicago, 1973.

LISCA, PETER: Professor of English, University of Florida; Senior Editorial Advisor of the Steinbeck Quarterly; author/editor of several books including The Wide World of John Steinbeck (1958) and The Grapes of Wrath: Text and Criticism (1972); author of 40 articles on Steinbeck, Hemingway, Fitzgerald, Faulkner, Chaucer, Hopkins, and Tourneur; Fulbright Professor at the University of Warsaw, Poland, 1973-74.

METZGER, CHARLES R.: Professor of English, University of Southern California; author/editor of two monographs and a book; Editorial Consultant for the Emerson Society Quarterly.

MORSBERGER, ROBERT E.: Professor of English, California State Polytechnic University; author/editor of numerous books and articles; a frequent contributor to the Steinbeck Quarterly.

PEREZ, BETTY LOUISE YATES: Instructor of English, University of Florida; published an article on "House and Home; Thematic Symbols in The Grapes of Wrath" in The Grapes of Wrath: Text and Criticism (1972); teaching also at Santa Fe Junior College of Gainesville.

PETERSON, RICHARD F.: Assistant Professor of English, Southern Illinois University; published in such journals as Ball State University Forum, Steinbeck Quarterly, contributed to a book, Steinbeck's Literary Dimension.

SIEFKER, DONALD L. (Indexer): Assistant Professor of Library Service and Head of the Division of Information Sources and Reference, Ball State University Library; Executive Editor of the Steinbeck Quarterly; indexer of the Steinbeck Quarterly and Steinbeck's Literary Dimension; associate compiler of The Special Steinbeck Collection of the Ball State University Library with Tetsumaro Hayashi (1972).

SIMPSON, ARTHUR L., JR.: Associate Professor of English, University of Wyoming; published in such journals as Explicator, Modern Philology, Philological Quarterly, and Steinbeck Quarterly.

SLATER, JOHN FREDERICK: Assistant Professor of English, University of Wyoming.

INDEX

by Donald L. Siefker

Absalom, Absalom! (Faulkner), 101, 104
The Adventures of Huckleberry Finn (Twain), 164, 224, 234
Agee, James, 265, 275
Albee, Edward, 166
Alexander, Stanley, 234, 241
"Alfred Hitchcock's Production of Lifeboat by John Stein-
  beck," 272
Alger, Horatio, 268
Alice's Adventure in Wonderland (Carroll), 3
All Quiet on the Western Front (Remarque), 259
Allee, Warder Clyde, 169, 183, 184
Almeida, Laurindo, 286
The American Adam (Lewis), 150
The American Dream (Albee), 166
American Fiction 1920-1940 (Beach), 241
American Literary Naturalism: A Divided Stream (Walcutt),
  65
Anderson, Sherwood, 88, 89, 90, 104
Animal Aggregations (Allee), 183
Annual Steinbeck Bibliography (Hayashi), 240
Armendariz, Pedro, 278
"The Artist as Magician" (French), xiii-xvi
Asheim, Lester, 263
Astro, Richard, vii, 36, 124, 168-86, 191, 298, 299
Atlantic Monthly, 245
Autobiography (Franklin), 16

Bailey, Edna W., 183
Baker, Carlos, 241, 257
Bankhead, Tallulah, 273, 275
Bartel, Roland, 124
Beach, Joseph Warren, 241
"The Bear" (Faulkner), 74
A Bell for Adano (F)*, 282

*(F) = Film title

Bendix, William, 273, 275
Benton, Robert M., 69-86, 299
Benton, Thomas Hart, 258
Berry, Anthony J., 170, 174
Best Film Plays, 1945 (Gassner), 297
Between Pacific Tides (Edward Ricketts & Jack Calvin), 27,
   169, 175
Bickford, Charles, 259
Billy Budd (Melville), 142
Billy the Kid (F), 280
Bispo, Louis, 286
Bluestone, George, 261, 263, 264, 297
Bogdanovich, Peter, 265, 297
Bohnen, Roman, 259
Bond, Ward, 281
Boren, Lyle, 31
Borzage, Dan, 265
Bound East for Cardiff (O'Neill), 166
The Boys in the Back Room (Wilson), xiv, 70
Brando, Marlon, 282, 284
Brandon, Tom, 267
Brontë, E., 283
Bunzel, John H., 297
Burns, Robert, 143, 144
Bus Stop (F), 285
Butler, Frank, 275, 297
Byrnes, Asher, 257

Caldwell, Erskine, 265
Calhern, Louis, 279
Calvin, Jack, 27, 169, 175
Campbell, Joseph, 191, 213
Camus, Albert, 282
Capote, Truman, 146
Capra, Frank, 273
Captains Courageous (F), 269
Cardinal (Velaquez), 95
Carpenter, Frederick I., 241
Carroll, Lewis, 3
A Casebook on "The Grapes of Wrath" (Donohue), 29
Champney, Freeman, 241
Chaney, Lon, Jr., 259
Chavez, Cesar, 44, 55
Chekhov, Anton Pavlovich, 70
Christian Century, 280
Citizen Kane (F), 265
Collins, Joan, 285

304

The Commandos Strike at Dawn (F), 272
Commonweal, 31, 269, 286
A Companion to "The Grapes of Wrath" (French), viii, 29
Congressional Record, 31
The Conqueror (F), 278
Conrad, Barnaby, 74, 286, 287, 297
Conrad, Joseph, 253, 286
Convivio, 35
Cooper, Gary, 272
Cooper, James Fenimore, 140, 141
Copland, Aaron, 258, 259, 279, 280
Court, Franklin E., 155-67, 299
Covici, Pascal, 70, 75, 174, 179
Cox, Martha Heasley, 107-28, 299
Crawford, Broderick, 155, 259
Crisis (F), 265
Cronyn, Hume, 273
Crowther, Bosley, 269, 270, 271, 272, 277, 278, 280, 285
Cummings, Edward Estlin, 275

Dailey, Dan, 285
Dante Alighieri, 35, 36, 38
Darwell, Jane, 264
Davalos, Richard, 283
Davis, Elmer, 69
Davis, Robert Murray, 242
Dean, James, 283, 284
De Cordova, Arturo, 276
The Deerslayer (Cooper), 140
DeMott, Benjamin, 252, 256
DeMott, Robert, viii, xi, 187-213, 299
Desire Under the Elms (O'Neill), 142
Dickens, Charles, 281
Ditsky, John, xi
The Divine Comedy (Dante), 35
Don Juan in Hell (Shaw), 39
Doñohue, Agnes McNeill, 29
Donovan, Colonel William J., 270
Don't Say Yes Until I Finish Talking: A Biography of Darryl
    F. Zanuck (Gussow), 297
Dos Passos, John, 284
Dubliners (Joyce), 88

The Edge of Darkness (F), 272
Eliade, Mircea, 195
Eliot, T. S., 138, 244, 249, 255, 256

Emerson, Ralph Waldo, 13, 38, 140
Encore (Maugham), 280
Everson, William K., 297

Fairley, Barker, 241
"The Fall of the House of Usher," (Poe), 104
Farber, Manny, 269, 274
Faulkner, William, 69, 74, 88, 101, 104, 141, 142, 166, 255
Ferguson, Otis, 260
Fernandez, Emilio, 277
Fiedler, Leslie, 138, 139, 150
Field, Betty, 259, 261
Filmguide to "The Grapes of Wrath" (French), 297
The Films of Hal Roach (Everson), 297
Fitzgerald, Francis Scott Key, 101
Fleming, Victor, 269
Flynn, Errol, 272
Fonda, Henry, 264, 280
Fontenrose, Joseph, 55, 60, 124, 125, 173, 177, 188, 212, 241, 245, 249, 256
For Whom the Bell Tolls (Hemingway), 269
Ford, John, 31, 262, 264, 265, 270, 278
Ford, Wallace, 155, 259
Franklin, Benjamin, 12, 16, 268
Frazer, J. G., 10
French, Warren, viii, xiii-xvi, 29-46, 61, 125, 150, 212, 217, 222, 223, 224, 229, 241, 245, 252, 253, 255, 256, 261, 297, 299
Frohock, Wilbur Merrill, 48, 49, 55
From Ritual to Romance (Weston), 10
The Fugitive (F), 278
Fun While It Lasted (Conrad), 297

Gannett, Lewis, 131, 223, 242
Garcia, Reloy, vii, 244-57, 300
Garfield, John, 268, 269
Gassner, John, 297
Geismar, Maxwell, 48, 50, 225, 242
Gentleman's Agreement (Hobson), 262
Gerstenberger, Donna, 244, 249, 256
Giant (F), 284
Gibbs, Lincoln R., 242
Gide, André, 70
Glazer, Benjamin, 268
Go Down, Moses (Faulkner), 88

The Golden Bough (Frazer), 10
Goldwyn, Samuel, 273
Gone With the Wind (F), 269
"The Grapes of Wrath": Text and Criticism (Lisca), viii, 29
The Great Gatsby (Fitzgerald), 101
Greenberg, Joel, 260
Greene, Graham, 278
The Greening of America (Reich), 44
Gussow, Mel, 297

Hackensmid, Alexander, 265
Haigh, Paula, 286
The Hairy Ape (O'Neill), 142
Hammerstein, Oscar, 258
Hardwicke, Sir Cedric, 271, 272
Harris, Julie, 283
Harris, Sam H., 155
Hartt, Julian N., 50, 257
Hartung, Philip T., 269, 272, 277, 280, 286
Hatch, Robert, 278, 280
Hawthorne, Nathaniel, 104
Hayashi, Tetsumaro, vii, viii, x, 240, 257, 300. See also
    Astro, Richard.
Hearst, William Randolph, 259
Hemingway, Ernest, 73, 266, 269
The Hero with a Thousand Faces (Campbell), 213
Hicks, Granville, 252, 256, 257
Higham, Charles, 260
Hitchcock (Truffaut), 298
Hitchcock, Alfred, 264, 272, 273, 274, 275
Hobson, Laura, 2
Hodiak, John, 273
Hoellering, Frank, 261
The House of the Seven Gables (Hawthorne), 104
How Green Was My Valley (Llewellyn), 262, 270
Howe, Julia Ward, 31
Hugo, Victor, 260
Hull, Henry, 273
Huston, Walter, 272
Hyman, Stanley Edgar, 242

I Am a Fugitive from a Chain Gang (F), 262
In Cold Blood (Capote), 146
The Informer (F), 262
Ingels, Beth, 268
Ingram, Forrest L., 30

Irving, Washington, 7
Isaacs, Hermine Rich, 272

James, Henry, 104
Jason, Rick, 285
Jefferson, Thomas, 12
John Ford (Boguanovich), 297
John Steinbeck (French), viii, 43, 212, 241
John Steinbeck (O'Connor), 74
John Steinbeck: A Concise Bibliography (1930-1965) (Haya-
shi), 240, 257
John Steinbeck: An Introduction and Interpretation (Fonten-
rose), 212, 241, 256
John Steinbeck and Edward F. Ricketts (Astro), viii
The John Steinbeck Society of America, viii
Johnson, Nunnally, 262, 263, 270, 271, 272, 297
"The Jolly Corner," (James), 104
Joyce, James, 88, 255
Jung, C. G., 10, 189, 190, 192, 213
Justus, James H., 242

Kantor, MacKinlay, 273
Kaufman, George S., 155
Kazan, Elia, 282, 284
Kernan, Alvin B., 240
Kerouac, Jack, 147
Kesey, Ken, 166
Kinney, Arthur F., 242
Kipling, Rudyard, 70
Kirkland, Jack, 268
Kline, Herbert, 265, 266, 267, 297
Kruger, Otto, 271

Lamarr, Hedy, 268, 269
Lamour, Dorothy, 276, 277
Laughton, Charles, 280
Lawrence, David Herbert, 70, 140, 141
Lee, Canada, 273
LeMaster, J. R., 191, 199, 212
Let Us Now Praise Famous Men (Agee), 265
Levant, Howard, 64, 242
Levine, Stuart, xiv
Lewis, Richard Warrinton Baldwin, 150
Library Journal, 280
Lieber, Todd, 212

Lights Out in Europe (F), 265
Lisca, Peter, vii, viii, 1-4, 19, 29, 30, 32, 42, 55, 69,
    77, 79, 102, 123, 126, 144, 145, 151, 188, 212, 215,
    216, 222, 227, 242, 300
Llewellyn, Richard, 262, 270
The Long Voyage Home (O'Neill), 166
Lord Jim (Conrad), 253
Lorentz, Pare, 265
Love and Death in the American Novel (Fiedler), 138, 150
Loy, Myrna, 279
Luce, Claire, 259

Macbeth (Shakespeare), 120
McCarten, John, 278
McDonald, Gerald D., 285
McIntosh & Otis, 93
Mack, Maynard, 232, 234
Madinabeitia, Manuel, 182
The Magic Mountain (Mann), 39
Mahin, John Lee, 268
Malory, Thomas, 36, 216, 239
Man and His Symbols (Jung), 213
Mann, Thomas, 39
Mansfield, Jayne, 285, 286
Marks, Lester, 188, 213, 243
Massey, Raymond, 283
Matador (Conrad), 286
Matlack, Mrs. W. H., 32
Maugham, Somerset, 280
Mayer, Louis B., 269
Melville, Herman, 7, 142, 189
Memoirs (Anderson), 89
Meredith, Burgess, 259, 267
Metzger, Charles R., 19-28, 277, 278, 298, 300
Midcentury (Dos Passos), 284
Miles, Peter, 279
Milestone, Lewis, 259, 260, 272, 279
Milton, John, 59, 60, 66
Les Misérables (Hugo), 260
Mitchum, Robert, 279
Mizener, Arthur, xiv
Moby Dick (Melville), 142
Modern Satire (Kernan), 240
A Modest Proposal (Swift), 233
Moffat, Ivan, 285
Monroe, Marilyn, 280, 285
The Moon of the Caribbees (O'Neill), 166

Moore, Harry T., 123, 124, 125, 137, 191, 243
Morgan, Frank, 269
Morgan, Ralph, 271
Mornings at Seven (F), 282
Morseberger, Robert E., 258-98, 300
Morte d'Arthur (Malory), 36, 216, 239
Motion Picture Herald, 264
Movie Stars in Steinbeck Films, 293-96
Muni, Paul, 272
Murray, Henry, 213
My Friend Flicka (F), 279
Mysticism and Religion (Russell), 183
Myth and Literature (Vickery), 213
Myth and Mythmaking (Murray), 213
"The Mythology of American Life: America and Americans"
(Peterson), 5-18

Naish, J. Carrol, 276, 277
Nation, 281
National Velvet (F), 279
Needham, Wilbur, 187-89
Neumann, Erich, 206
New Republic, 270
A New Steinbeck Bibliography: 1929-1971 (Hayashi), 240,
257
New York Times, 275
New Yorker, 269
Newhall, Scott, 173
Newman, Alfred, 265
Newsweek, 269, 271, 275, 280
Nichols, Dudley. See Gassner, John.
Nixon, Richard, 268
North American Review, 69
The Novel of Violence in America (Frohock), 48
Novels Into Fiction (Bluestone), 261, 297
The Novels of John Steinbeck: A First Critical Study
(Moore), 243

O. Henry. See Porter, William Sydney.
O. Henry's Full House (F), 280
O'Connor, Richard, 74
"Of Mice and Men (Play)" (Court), 155-67
O'Hara, Maureen, 280
One Flew Over the Cuckoo's Nest (Kesey), 166
O'Neill, Eugene, 142, 143, 166
Orozco, Jose Clement, 258

Osborn, Paul, 282, 283, 284
Otis, Elizabeth R., x
Ott, Evelyn, 191

Paine, Thomas, 12
Paradise Lost (Milton), 59, 60, 66
"Passage to India," (Whitman), 39
Perez, Betty L., 47-68, 300
The Performing Self (Poirier), 139
Peterson, Richard F., 5-18, 87-106, 301
The Philadelphia Story (F), 264
Pichel, Irving, 272, 277
Pinchon, Edgcumb, 281
The Pioneers (Cooper), 140
Pipe Dream (Rodgers & Hammerstein), 258
Poe, Edgar Allan, 94, 104
Point of No Return (F), 282
Poirier, Richard, 139
Pope, Alexander, 234
The Portable Jung (ed. Campbell), 213
Porter, William Sydney, 280
The Power and the Glory (Greene), 278
Prescott, Orville, 257
Pride of the Yankees (F), 273
Psychology and Alchemy (Jung), 192

Quartet (Maugham), 280
Quigley, Martin, 264
Quinn, Anthony, 282

The Rape of the Lock (Pope), 234
Rascoe, Burton, 139
The Readers' Guide to Periodical Literature, 44
Rebecca (F), 264
The Rebel (Camus), 282
Rebel Without a Cause (F), 284
The Red Balloon (F), 287
Reich, Charles A., 44
Remarque, E. M., 259
Richard III (Shakespeare), 244
Ricketts, Edward Flanders, viii, 19, 27, 36, 37, 38, 57, 58,
    74, 107, 168-86, 191
Ritter, William Emerson, 168, 178, 183, 184
Roach, Hal, 259
Rodeo (F), 280

311

Rodgers, Richard, 258
Romeo and Juliet (Shakespeare), 244
Roosevelt, Eleanor, 32
Ross, Woodburn, 243
Russell, Bertrand, 183

St. Thomas Aquinas, 35, 36, 37, 38
Salinger, Jerome David, 44, 255, 256
Saroyan, William, 285
Saturday Evening Post, 69
The Saturday Review of Literature, 69
Scott, Helen C. See Truffaut, Francois.
Scribner's, 69
Seattle Post-Intelligencer, 77
Seixas, Antonia, 151
Shakespeare, William, 120, 142, 149, 244
Shaw, George Bernard, 39
Siefker, Donald L. , 301
Simpson, Arthur L. Jr. , 214-43, 301
Sinclair, Upton, 31
Slater, John F. , 129-54, 301
Slezak, Walter, 273
Smith, Ed. , 287
Social Work Today, 31
Solow, Eugene, 259
The Sound and the Fury (Faulkner), 141, 166
The Snake Pit (Ward), 262
The Spanish Earth (Hemingway), 266
Steele, Bob, 259, 260
Steinbeck, Carol, 170, 181
Steinbeck, John
  America and Americans, 1, 5-18
  "Breakfast" (LV), 75, 76, 84
  Burning Bright, 2, 3, 142, 150, 184, 258
  Cannery Row, 2, 19-28, 36, 74, 75, 184, 258
  "The Chrysanthemums" (LV), 71
  Cup of Gold, 15, 130, 211, 214
  East of Eden, 2, 3, 15, 211, 249, 275, 282, 284, 285
  "Flight" (LV), 69, 73, 74, 84, 126, 177, 239, 278, 286,
    297
  The Forgotten Village, 3, 113, 150, 176, 183, 258, 267,
    278, 281, 297, 298
  "The Gift" (LV), 80, 81, 279
  The Grapes of Wrath, xiii, xv, 1, 2, 3, 29-46, 47, 49,
    65, 69, 75, 76, 129, 130, 143, 148, 155, 169, 176,
    178, 183, 184, 214, 249, 258, 260, 261, 262, 263,
    264, 265, 270, 271, 275, 281, 297

"The Great Mountains" (LV), 81
"The Harness" (LV), 1, 76, 77
"How Mr. Hogan Robbed a Bank, " 245, 252, 256
In Dubious Battle, 2, 3, 20, 36, 43, 47-68, 69, 76, 129,
    131, 143, 144, 148, 169, 177, 178, 184, 214, 274,
    281, 282
"Johnny Bear" (LV), 77, 78, 84
"The Leader of the People" (LV), 44, 69, 82, 177, 279
Lifeboat, 272, 273, 274, 275, 298
The Log from the Sea of Cortez, 74, 107, 108, 168, 170-
    75, 177-80, 182-86
The Long Valley, 69-86, 286
A Medal for Benny, 275, 277, 297
The Moon Is Down, 1, 2, 150, 166, 258, 270, 271, 272,
    277, 281
"The Murder" (LV), 69, 78
"My Short Novels, " 243
Of Mice and Men, 1, 2, 3, 30, 47, 77, 98, 129-54, 169,
    177, 214, 258, 259, 260, 265, 267, 279, 297
Of Mice and Men (Play), 155-67
Once There Was a War, 2
The Pastures of Heaven, xvi, 2, 3, 30, 78, 87-106, 141,
    150, 214, 215, 239
The Pearl, xiii, 3, 107-28, 150, 239, 267, 277, 278,
    281, 298
"The Pearl of the World, " 108
"The Promise" (LV), 81, 279
"The Raid" (LV), 61, 66, 69, 76, 77
The Red Pony (LV), xiii, 1, 2, 69, 70, 79, 82, 84, 258,
    279, 280
"Saint Katy the Virgin" (LV), 79, 84
Sea of Cortez (with Edward F. Ricketts), 2, 3, 5, 57,
    58, 65, 144, 151, 168-86
The Short Reign of Pippin IV, 2, 3
"The Snake" (LV), 74
Sweet Thursday, 1, 2, 26, 258
Their Blood Is Strong, 30, 265, 281
To a God Unknown, xvi, 2, 101, 102, 140, 142, 143,
    150, 187-214
Tortilla Flat, 2, 3, 47, 104, 129, 146, 150, 169, 211,
    214-43, 258, 267, 268, 270, 275, 277
Travels with Charley in Search of America, 1, 2, 3, 5,
    6, 17, 183
"The Vigilante" (LV), 77, 274
Viva Zapata!, 258, 267, 271, 278, 281, 282, 298
The Wayward Bus, 273, 275, 285
"The White Quail" (LV), 69, 72, 84
The Winter of Our Discontent, 2, 244-57

Steinbeck: A Collection of Critical Essays (Davis), 242
Steinbeck and D. H. Lawrence (Garcia), viii
Steinbeck and His Critics (Tedlock and Wicker), 69, 241, 243
Steinbeck Film List, 293-96
Steinbeck Monograph Series, vii
"Steinbeck On Screen," (Morseberger), 258-98
Steinbeck Quarterly, vii, viii
Steinbeck Society of America; see John Steinbeck Society of
    America.
Steinbeck: The Man and His Work (Astro and Hayashi), viii,
    298
"Steinbeck's Cannery Row" (Metzger), 19-28
"Steinbeck's The Grapes of Wrath" (French), 29-46
"Steinbeck's In Dubious Battle" (Perez), 47-68
"Steinbeck's The Long Valley" (Benton), 69-86
"Steinbeck's Of Mice and Men (Novel)," (Slater), 129-54
"Steinbeck's The Pearl" (Cox), 107-28
"Steinbeck's Sea of Cortez" (Astro), 168-86
"Steinbeck's To a God Unknown" (DeMott), 187-213
"Steinbeck's Tortilla Flat" (Simpson), 214-43
"Steinbeck's The Winter of Our Discontent" (Garcia), 244-57
Stevenson, Robert Louis, 95, 96
Stewart, James, 264
Stowe, Harriet Beecher, 29
Street, Webster F., 170, 191
Strudwick, Shepperd, 279
Studies in Classic American Literature (Lawrence), 140
Swerling, Jo, 272, 273, 275
Swift, Jonathan, 233

Tamiroff, Akim, 269
Taylor, C. V., 168
"Teaching Steinbeck" (Lisca), 1-4
"Teddy" (Salinger), 44
Tedlock, E. W., Jr., 69, 241, 243
Theatre Arts, 272
Thematic Design in the Novels of John Steinbeck (Marks),
    213, 243
Theory of Literature (Wellek), 45
Thompson, Dorothy, 274
Thoreau, Henry David, 13, 149
Three Godfathers (F), 278
Thurber, James, 270
Time, 264, 269, 271, 272, 274, 276, 278, 280, 285
Tobacco Road (F), 264, 268
Toland, Gregg, 260, 265
Tracy, Spencer, 269

Travers, Henry, 271
The Treasure of the Sierra Madre (F), 279
Trio (Maugham), 280
Truffaut, Francois, 298
"The Turning Point: The Pastures of Heaven" (Peterson),
    87-106
Twain, Mark, 164, 224, 234, 281
Twenty Best Film Plays (Gassner), 297

Uncle Tom's Cabin (Stowe), 29

VanFleet, Jo, 283
Velasquez, 95
Vickery, John, 213
Viking Portable Steinbeck (Covici), 75

Wadlington, Warwick, 45
Wagner, Jack, 275, 277
Walcutt, Charles Child, 65
Walden (Thoreau), 149
Ward, Mary Jane, 262
Warren, Austin, 45
The Waste Land (Eliot), 244, 255, 256
Watt, F. W., 125
Wayne, John, 264, 278, 279
Wellek, Rene, 45
Weston, Jessie, 10
Whipper, Leigh, 259
Whitman, Walt, 39, 140
Wicker, C. V. see Tedlock, E. W., Jr.
The Wide World of John Steinbeck (Lisca), viii, 19, 30, 77,
    79, 102, 144, 212, 242
Wilson, Edmund, xiv, 70, 150, 232, 243
Winesburg, Ohio (Anderson), 88, 89, 90, 104
The Wizard of Oz (F), 269
Woman's Home Companion, 108
Woolf, Virginia, 255
Writers in Crisis (Geismar), 48, 242
Wuthering Heights (Brontë), 283

The Yearling (F), 279
You Have Seen Their Faces (Caldwell), 265
Young, Victor, 285

Zanuck, Darryl F., 262, 263, 264, 265, 297
Zapata, the Unconquerable (Pinchon), 281
Zola, Emile, 94